The Illinois Family Law Paralegal

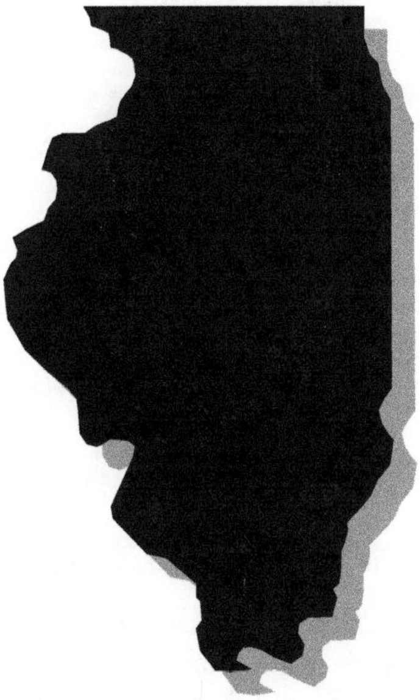

Elizabeth McGuan, J.D.

CAROLINA ACADEMIC PRESS
Durham, North Carolina

Library of Congress Cataloging-in-Publication Data

Names: McGuan, Elizabeth, author.
Title: The Illinois family law paralegal / Elizabeth McGuan.
Description: Durham, North Carolina : Carolina Academic Press, 2024. |
Includes bibliographical references and index.
Identifiers: LCCN 2023058887 | ISBN 9781531022822 (paperback) |
ISBN 9781531022839 (ebook)
Subjects: LCSH: Domestic relations--Illinois. | Domestic relations--Moral and ethical aspects--Illinois. | Legal assistants--Illinois--Handbooks, manuals, etc.
Classification: LCC KFI1294 .M34 2024 | DDC 346.77301/5--dc23/eng/20240117
LC record available at https://lccn.loc.gov/2023058887

Carolina Academic Press
700 Kent Street
Durham, North Carolina 27701
(919) 489-7486
www.cap-press.com

Printed in the United States of America

Summary of Contents

Contents

Acknowledgments

With deep appreciation to Judge Robert Douglas, Associate Judge for the 18th Judicial Circuit, DuPage County and former Adjunct Faculty Member at the College of DuPage Paralegal Studies Program; attorney Elizabeth Krueger, who has been practicing family law for more than 40 years; and my father, Steve Stasinos, who has been teaching for nearly 70 years, for their review of the text. I am indebted to Todd Holes, paralegal and college tutor, for his outstanding review of the citation format. There is no one whose citation skills I respect more. And special thanks to Ayesha Mohammed, now a third-year law student, for her research assistance as a paralegal student in the spring of 2021.

I am grateful to you all.

Notes

People form families in many ways: as single parents, as adoptive parents, and with same-sex and opposite-sex partners. In recognition of this fact, I have attempted to use gender-neutral language. However, there are times when, for clarity, singular nouns require a single pronoun. In order to both avoid ambiguity and be gender-neutral, I have adopted Rule 101(d) from the Circuit Court of the 18th Judicial Circuit, which provides:

> *Gender*. When used in the Rules of the Circuit Court of the 18th Judicial Circuit, words or phrases that import the masculine or feminine genders shall be construed to include all genders, unless such construction would be inconsistent with the manifest intention of the context.

As applied, "a respondent must file his answer" may be construed as "a respondent must file her answer." And "Wife and Husband" may be construed as "Wife and Wife" and "Husband and Husband."

Equally important, families are formed by people of all ethnicities and cultures, which they may express in their children's names. To avoid the appearance of favoring or discriminating against any particular ethnicity or culture, when I needed a name in an example, I referred to the Social Security Administration's list of most commonly reported baby names in 2000.

This book celebrates all families, however and by whomever they are formed.

The Illinois Family Law Paralegal

One

Ethics in the Family Law Office

Overview

At the same time they are undergoing the breakdown of a relationship, family law clients are engaged in high-stakes litigation, which could result in the loss of a home, a secure retirement, or the right to make decisions for their children. Accordingly, family law clients must have complete confidence that their legal team is operating competently and with unquestioned loyalty on their behalf. Because ethical dilemmas can arise at any stage of family law litigation, paralegals must be familiar with the ethical rules and able to apply them at all times.

Ethics in the Family Law Office

Ethics embody the principles of conduct to be followed by professionals and paraprofessionals.[1] Attorneys in Illinois must comply with the Illinois Rules of Professional Conduct, as put forth by the Attorney Registration and Disciplinary Commission of the Supreme Court of Illinois. Attorneys are licensed by the Commission and can be disciplined if they violate the rules.

Although they are not licensed, paralegals must comply with ethical rules as well. Their conduct is guided by the Illinois Paralegal Association's Illinois Code of Paralegal Ethics, which is intended to "assist the paralegal to understand jurisdictional standards of ethical responsibility and to enhance the quality of the delivery of legal services."[2] The Code is provided in Appendix A at the end of this text. It is also available online.[3]

Ethical Duties Applying to All Legal Professionals

Competency

All legal professionals have an ethical duty to provide competent representation to their clients.[4]

Valid Law

Competent legal representation requires the application of valid, or current, law. Because the law changes over time, as statutes are amended or found unconstitutional and cases are reversed by appellate courts or overruled by later cases, paralegals must ensure that the legal authority on which they rely is still valid.

EXAMPLE Savanah, a paralegal, is asked to draft a pretrial memorandum using one used in a prior client's case as a model. She assumes the caselaw is still current and does not perform a cite check. She has not complied with the ethical duty of competency. The caselaw may no longer be valid.

Similarly, most firms maintain libraries of commonly used forms. The forms may be stored in a file cabinet as paper copies but are more likely stored on a computer as fillable PDFs. Because courts update the forms periodically and will reject an out-of-date form, paralegals need to confirm they are using the most up-to-date form available.

Attention to Detail

Competent representation requires careful attention to detail. This involves proofreading documents carefully to ensure they are legally correct. A mistake in a contract, such as a marital settlement agreement, could lead to litigation to determine the parties' intent. In addition to being legally correct, documents submitted to courts must conform to formatting requirements, such as paper size and page limits. Be sure to check local court rules: an inaccurately formatted document may be rejected by the court.

EXAMPLE Paralegal does not check a client's financial affidavit before tendering it to opposing counsel. The income provided on the client's tax return is double the income listed on the financial affidavit. Because the financial affidavit is signed under the penalty of perjury, Paralegal has potentially subjected the client to serious consequences. At best, the law firm can overcome the burden against their client and amend the record. Still, errors are embarrassing and can cause clients, and even the court, to lose trust in the firm's ability to manage their cases.

Tracking Deadlines

Tracking dates, such as statutes of limitation or filing deadlines, is critical in the practice of law. Missing a statute of limitations will cause your client to lose the opportunity to pursue a claim. Missing a filing deadline will delay and possibly damage your client's case.

Most firms use multiple systems for tracking dates, including an electronic docketing system. Because many firm management software programs exist, it's important to be proficient in the one used by the firm.

EXAMPLE An order reads, "Respondent has 28 days to respond, Petitioner has 14 days to reply, and the matter is set for hearing on May 30, 2024, at 9:00 a.m." Paralegal enters the due dates, including setting "ticklers," or reminders, seven days in advance of the due dates. Paralegal has complied with the duty of competency.

Training

Finally, legal professionals must have been trained to perform the tasks they are assigned. If a paralegal is unsure how to complete a task, it is important to ask for guidance.

EXAMPLE Supervising Attorney directs Paralegal to draft a motion to dismiss, using the statute as a guide. Paralegal discovers the statute contains two different motions to dismiss. Rather than guess which motion is to be used, Paralegal asks Supervising Attorney.

Paralegals can maintain competency by enrolling in continuing education opportunities. Some opportunities include:

- Workshops offered by the Illinois Paralegal Association;
- Classes offered by paralegal studies programs; and
- Tutorials provided by software vendors.

Confidential Information

All legal professionals have a duty to keep information relating to the client's representation confidential.[5] To represent their clients, attorneys must be fully informed about the clients' situations. And for clients to reveal the deeply personal information their attorneys need, the clients must know it will be held in confidence.

The duty to guard confidential information outlasts the representation of the client. After a client's matter has been completed, and even after the client's death, the information obtained during representation remains confidential.

At times, a client may bring a third party to a meeting with the legal team. In that case, the client should be advised that the third party does not have an ethical duty to keep the information confidential.

> **EXAMPLE** Client's mother accompanies Client to appointments to offer emotional support. The attorney ascertains that Client understands he is waiving his confidentiality with respect to his mother. The law office, however, is still bound.

Under prior rules, attorneys could communicate information that was already a matter of public record. However, under current rules, attorneys cannot disclose anything they learned in the course of representation.

> **EXAMPLE** Law Office represents Wife on a petition for overdue child support from Husband, who is running for local office. A reporter calls Law Office to verify the allegations. Even though the reporter found the name and phone number of Law Office on the petition filed with the circuit court, Law Office should not reply regarding the motion or even acknowledge representing Wife.

Outside the Office

Violations of the rule protecting client information are most likely to occur outside of the office, in a social context. For example, legal professionals may want to discuss their day with their partners. While some information may be shared in a theoretical way, great care must be taken not to disclose anything that would permit their partners to identify the client.

> **EXAMPLE** Paralegal and her husband attend a PTA meeting at their neighborhood elementary school. In the hall, Paralegal sees a man who is a client in the family law firm where she works. Paralegal does not tell her husband about the man's divorce or even disclose that the man is a client.

Inside the Office

Care must be taken to protect client information within the office as well. During the workday, legal professionals may leave files open on their desks, where they would be visible to a visitor. To prevent inadvertent disclosure, before a visitor arrives, be sure files are closed and computer screens are not visible. Similarly, while a paralegal may exchange a greeting with a client in the waiting room, private matters should be discussed in an office where they cannot be overheard.

> **EXAMPLE** Paralegal has scheduled a meeting with a client in her office to complete some discovery requests. In preparation for the meeting, Paralegal returns the files she was working on to the storage room, leaving only the client's file on her desk.

Finally, great care must be taken in communicating client information. When information was communicated through letters, there was limited risk of inadvertent disclosure. The process was slow: the recipient's name had to be typed on an envelope and attachments had to be photocopied. Now that so much information is communicated through email, the risk of inadvertent disclosure is much higher. Most firms have policies in place to avoid accidental disclosure of client information. At a minimum, good practice includes checking the names of the recipients carefully before sending an email, especially when "replying all." To prevent mistakes, some firms disable the auto-fill feature or require emails to be sent through their firm management software.

Exceptions to the Rule of Confidentiality

The Illinois Code of Paralegal Ethics provides exceptions to the duty of confidentiality in very limited circumstances, such as with the client's informed, written consent or to comply with a court order. If the client sues the attorney (say, for malpractice) the attorney is not bound by the duty. And, while a client's *past* acts are covered by the duty of confidentiality, an exception to the duty is provided to prevent the client from committing an act that could result in *future* death or serious bodily harm. Because of the consequences of the decision, the paralegal should seek direction from the supervising attorney before acting.

Conflict of Interest

Finally, all legal professionals must demonstrate undivided loyalty to their clients.[6] Consequently, they cannot represent two clients whose interests are directly adverse to each other, such as the husband and wife in a divorce case, or the buyer and seller in a real estate transaction.

With Current Clients

> **EXAMPLE** Wife retains Firm for a divorce. The next day, Husband calls for a consult. Because Wife is a current client, Firm cannot meet with Husband.

On occasion, a wife and husband may come to consultation appointment together, asking if the firm can represent them both because "everything is worked out." Even if it were true (which likely it is not), because their interests are adverse to each other, the firm cannot represent them both.

With Former Clients

As with the duty to guard confidential information, the duty of loyalty endures after the client's case is over. Law firms maintain lists of former clients, and before taking a new client, they confirm the potential new client is not adverse to a former client.

Some family law attorneys work as mediators or guardians *ad litem*, and the parties' names in those cases must be included on the list. Even though the attorneys have not represented a party, their work has made them adverse to both parties in the future.

EXAMPLE Attorney served as guardian *ad litem* when A and B got divorced. Paralegal was involved with the matter. B has post-decree issues and wants to hire Attorney. Attorney and Paralegal are adverse to the client. B may have to retain a different firm.

Changing Firms

Even though law firms maintain records of former clients, it is good practice for paralegals to maintain personal records as well. This is especially true for freelance paralegals who represent clients at multiple firms. Personal records are also helpful if a paralegal changes firms. If paralegals work on a client's case at one firm and then take a position at another, they may find themselves representing the client on the other side of the case. The conflict would not show up on either firm's record.

EXAMPLE While employed at Law Firm A, Paralegal represented Husband in the formation of his business and acquired information about his financial position. After a few years, Paralegal leaves Law Firm A and takes a job at Law Firm B. At Law Firm B, paralegal discovers that Husband and Wife are getting a divorce, and Law Firm B represents Wife. Paralegal is in conflict with Husband and should immediately inform the supervising attorney in Law Firm B.

The Unauthorized Practice of Law

While the duties of providing competent representation, guarding client confidentiality, and avoiding a conflict of interest apply to all legal professionals, paralegals have an additional duty: they must not engage in the unauthorized practice of law.[7]

The practice of law is limited to attorneys who have been licensed by the Attorney Registration and Disciplinary Commission. The unauthorized practice of law is forbidden in Illinois and can result in ethical, civil, and criminal penalties.[8] To avoid the unauthorized practice of law, paralegals must be mindful of two main points.

Supervision by an Attorney

First, while paralegals are capable of performing meaningful tasks in a law office, their work must always be supervised by an attorney. Paralegals cannot provide legal services directly to the public.

> **EXAMPLE** After working for a family law firm for several years, Paralegal has experience drafting petitions for the dissolution of marriage. On Saturdays, she meets clients in a church basement to draft petitions. Although Paralegal views this work as a public service and does not charge clients for it, it is still the unauthorized practice of law.

The Practice of Law

Second, even when operating under the supervision of an attorney, there are some tasks paralegals cannot perform. Only attorneys can represent clients in court, give legal advice, and establish the attorney-client relationship.

Represent Clients in Court

While paralegals go to courthouses for many reasons, such as to assist the attorney, conduct legal research, and file court documents, only an attorney can step in front of a judge on a client's behalf. Similarly, only attorneys can sign pleadings or motions filed with the court.

The prohibition on representing clients in courts does not apply to administrative agencies. For example, the Social Security Administration allows paralegals to represent clients at administrative hearings. In addition, accredited representatives can represent clients before the Executive Office of Immigration Review (the immigration courts and Board of Immigration Appeals). Because rules vary by agency, it's important to check each agency's specific requirements.

Give Legal Advice

Paralegals may be the main point of contact between the anxious client and the busy attorney. Consequently, paralegals must confirm that their clients understand they are not attorneys and are not giving legal advice. Paralegals should indicate their titles when speaking on the telephone. Additionally, their title should be included in their email signature block.

It can be challenging to draw a line between stating the law and giving legal advice. Legal advice is the *application* of the law to the client's specific facts.

> **EXAMPLE** A potential client asks if he can keep the car his parents gave him when he gets divorced. The paralegal knows that because gifts are non-marital property, they are not subject to division by the court. However, if the paralegal applies the law to the client's facts, and says he can keep the car, the paralegal has given legal advice.

To avoid the appearance of giving advice, paralegals should not even state the law. Instead, they should indicate their status as a paralegal and say they will consult with an attorney, who will call back with the answer.

Establish the Attorney-Client Relationship

Finally, the paralegal cannot establish a relationship between the firm and the client. While paralegals answer the telephone and often make the initial contact with the client, only the attorney can decide whether to take the client's case. The decision will be made based on an analysis of the type of law involved, the amount of time the matter will take, and the firm's other responsibilities.

Even without a signed retainer agreement, lawyers have been found to represent clients if the client thinks the firm represents them. Consequently, it is critical to avoid committing the firm unintentionally.

> **EXAMPLE** In an initial telephone call, Paralegal says, "Yes, we handle that kind of case." Client assumes Firm is representing him and does not go to the next court date. Judge finds Client in default. Because Client thought he was being represented, Firm has violated its ethical duty and may also be liable for professional malpractice.

Establishing a relationship includes setting the legal fees. A potential client may ask a paralegal what the cost is for a "no contest" divorce or the total cost for a divorce. Because answering this question requires legal analysis, such as gauging how complex the issues are, setting legal fees is also reserved for attorneys.

Chapter Summary

Ethics embody the principles of conduct to be followed by professionals and paraprofessionals. All legal professionals must comply with the ethical duties of competency and confidentiality. In addition, they must avoid conflicts of interest with current and former clients. While complying with these duties, paralegals must also guard against the unauthorized practice of law. While paralegals can perform meaningful work, they must always be supervised by an attorney. In addition, paralegals cannot represent a client in court, give legal advice, or establish an attorney-client relationship, which includes setting legal fees.

Key Terms

Ethics

Competency

Confidential Information

Conflict of Interest

The Unauthorized Practice of Law

Discussion Questions

1. Attorneys in Illinois are required to complete 30 hours of continuing legal education every two years. Six of the hours must be in the area of professional responsibility, or ethics, including at least one hour in the area of diversity and inclusion and one in the area of mental health and substance abuse. Should paralegals have a continuing education requirement as well? Why or why not? If so, in what areas?
2. Conflicts of interest most often arise between adverse clients. But could paralegals have such strong personal views they were adverse to a client? Could a paralegal that was a member of PETA (People for the Ethical Treatment of Animals) work on the legal team representing a criminal defendant accused of animal cruelty?
3. How should a paralegal respond if a potential client asks, "Tell me, do I have a case?"

4. Some law firms provide a script for paralegals who answer the phone to ensure they are not giving legal advice. Would you like that? Why or why not?
5. Under what circumstances can an attorney be responsible for a paralegal's violation of an ethical duty? Refer to Illinois Rule of Professional Conduct 5.3, Supervision of Non-Lawyer Assistants.
6. How would you respond if an attorney asked you to notarize a client's signature on a blank contract and then mail it to the client for signature, keeping in mind both your ethical duties and your need for continued employment? Are there options that permit you to comply with ethical duties and complete the task assigned?
7. Some states have started licensing paralegals, allowing them to perform legal services directly to the public. If so, what agency should license them in Illinois? Should licensed paralegals be subject to discipline for violating ethical rules?
8. The "justice gap" has been defined as "the difference between the civil legal needs of low-income Americans and the resources available to meet those needs." https://justicegap.lsc.gov/. The Supreme Court noted that "permitting separate billing of … paralegal hours at market rates might 'reduc[e] the spiraling cost of civil rights litigation' by encouraging attorneys to delegate to these individuals tasks which they would otherwise perform themselves at higher cost." *Missouri v. Jenkins by Agyei*, 491 U.S. 274, 297 (1989). Would licensing paralegals address the "justice gap" in the United States?
9. The need for low-cost legal services is greatest in certain subject areas, including domestic relations. In fact, DuPage County has a designated "*pro se* courtroom" for domestic relations litigants who represent themselves. Would licensing paralegals permit more parties to be represented? Would it promote the efficient administration of justice, or ensure more equitable outcomes?

Endnotes

1. Ill. Code P'legal Ethics pmbl.
2. *Id.*
3. https://ipaonline.clubexpress.com/content.aspx?page_id=22&club_id=812874&module_id=186400 (last visited June 29, 2023).
4. Ill. Code P'legal Ethics r. 2.
5. Ill. Code P'legal Ethics r. 6.
6. Ill. Code P'legal Ethics r. 5.
7. Ill. Code P'legal Ethics r. 1(b).
8. 705 ILCS 205/1 (West, Westlaw Classic through P.A. 103-2 of the 2023 Reg. Sess.).

Two

Marriage

Overview

The right to marry is protected by the United States Constitution. The Supreme Court of the United States has struck down state laws that restrict that right, such as those prohibiting interracial[1] and same-sex marriages.[2] Yet, the right is not absolute. The state can restrict the right to marry in order to advance a compelling state interest. As you read, consider what restrictions by the state are permitted and what interests those restrictions advance.

Marriage

The Definition of Marriage

Marriage is the legal recognition of the union of two people. Without losing their status as separate individuals, through their marriage, they have gained the status of one married couple. In Illinois, marriage is governed by the Illinois Marriage and Dissolution of Marriage Act (IMDMA).[3]

Legal Changes Marriage Makes

Marriage promotes social stability. As one court stated, "Civil marriage enhances the welfare of the community. It anchors society by encouraging stable relations over transient ones." To encourage marriage, the state provides benefits to married couples.[4] Some of the benefits are listed below:

- The ability to file income taxes jointly with the Internal Revenue Service and the Illinois Department of Revenue;
- The ability to inherit through state intestacy statutes, which determine the disposition of a person's property if they die without a will;[5]
- The ability to claim Social Security benefits based on a spouse's wages;
- Entitlement to benefits under a spouse's 401(k) plan through the Employee Retirement Income Security Act of 1974 (ERISA);

- The right to obtain medical coverage offered by a spouse's employer or through the Patient Protection and Affordable Care Act;[6]
- The ability to sue for wrongful death of a spouse and other claims; and
- The ability to petition for immigration benefits for family members.

EXAMPLE Jacob and Matthew live in the same house but are unmarried. They must file taxes as individuals. They cannot file taxes jointly, taking advantage of the lower tax rate.

EXAMPLE In contrast, Emily and Olivia are married when Emily is killed in a car accident. Olivia can file a wrongful death claim.

Restrictions on Marriage

Restrictions the State Can Not Impose

Interracial Marriage: The Liberty Interest

The right to choose a spouse is a liberty interest protected by the United States Constitution's Due Process clause.[7] In *Loving v. Virginia*, in 1967, the Supreme Court struck down a Virginia law that prohibited interracial marriage.[8] In later cases, the Court struck down laws that prohibited prisoners[9] and men who were behind on child support payments[10] from marrying.

Same-Sex Marriage: Equal Protection of the Law

The equal protection clause prevents the state from discriminating against similarly situated persons;[11] however, for many years, opposite-sex couples could enter marriages while same-sex couples could not.

In an effort to provide legal recognition of same-sex couples, some states enacted civil union or domestic partnership laws. While civil unions provided legal recognition of the union at the state level, they were not recognized at the federal level. On June 1, 2011, the Illinois Civil Union Act went into effect.[12] The Act permitted civil unions between same- or opposite-sex couples.

On November 5, 2013, Illinois joined a number of other states which permitted same-sex marriage by enacting the Religious Freedom and Marriage Fairness Act.[13] The Act replaced the words "a marriage between a man and a woman" is valid with "a marriage between two individuals" is valid. It also provided that "all laws of this State applicable to marriage, whether they derive from statute, administrative or court rule, policy, common law, or any other source of civil or criminal law, would apply equally to marriages of same-sex and different-sex couples and their children."[14] Further, the Act allowed couples to convert their civil unions to marriages by getting a license and paying a fee (and for the first year, or until May 31, 2015, the fee was waived).

As soon as the Act was signed by the governor, Vernita Gray and her female partner sought a marriage license from the Cook County Clerk. Gray was terminally ill and unlikely to live until the Act went into effect on June 1, 2014.[15] When the clerk would not issue the license without a court order, Gray filed suit in federal court. The court found no compelling reason for delaying the license when the state had already indicated its approval of same-sex marriage and granted the order. Gray and her partner were married on November 27, 2013.

In 2015, one year after Illinois enacted the Religious Freedom and Marriage Fairness Act, the ability to enter same-sex marriages became the law in all 50 states. In *Obergefell v. Hodges*, the Supreme Court of the United States held that state laws that prohibited same-sex marriages were unconstitutional.[16]

Restrictions the State Can Impose

Bigamy

Bigamy is the act of entering a second marriage while a first marriage is in effect. All states, including Illinois, prohibit bigamous marriages. In addition to being a bar to marriage, bigamy is a crime.[17]

> **EXAMPLE** Husband is married to Wife when he meets Girlfriend. Husband is prohibited from marrying Girlfriend.

Incest

Incest is the act of marrying a close relative. All states, including Illinois, prohibit incestuous marriages; however, they define them differently. The Illinois statute prohibits:

> (2) A marriage between an ancestor and a descendant or between siblings, whether the relationship is by the half or the whole blood or by adoption;
>
> (3) A marriage between an uncle and a niece, between an uncle and a nephew, between an aunt and a nephew, or between an aunt and a niece, whether the relationship is by the half or the whole blood;
>
> (4) A marriage between cousins of the first degree; however, a marriage between first cousins is not prohibited if:
>
> > (i) Both parties are 50 years of age or older; or

(ii) Either party, at the time of application for a marriage license, presents a certificate signed by a licensed physician stating they are permanently and irreversibly sterile.[18]

EXAMPLE Madison and Joshua were born to the same biological parents. They cannot marry.

While the IMDMA prohibits the marriage of relatives related by blood (by consanguinity), it also prohibits marriages of those related by relationship (by affinity), such as adopted siblings.

EXAMPLE Presume Madison's biological parents adopted Joshua when he was six days old. Now in their twenties, Madison and Joshua want to get married. Although they are not related by blood, their marriage is prohibited.

Underage Marriage

The IMDMA places age restrictions on marriage. Parties must have attained the age of 18 years at the time the marriage license is effective.[19]

EXAMPLE Boyfriend and Girlfriend are both 18 years old. They can obtain a marriage license.

If one or both of the parties is under 18, they can marry if they are at least 16 years of age and have either the consent of both parents (or legal guardians) or judicial approval.

EXAMPLE Boyfriend is 18, but Girlfriend is 17. They cannot marry unless either Girlfriend's parents consent or a judge gives approval.

Out-of-State Marriage to Circumvent Illinois' Laws

Finally, if a person who lives in Illinois and intends to continue to live in Illinois goes to another state and contracts a marriage that is prohibited in Illinois, the marriage is null and void.[20]

> **EXAMPLE** Daniel and Hannah live in Illinois. They are first cousins in their twenties who want to marry. Because their marriage is prohibited in Illinois, they travel to Alabama, where first cousins can marry, and return to Illinois. Their marriage is not valid in Illinois.

Formalities Required

Persons with the legal ability to enter a marriage must comply with certain formalities. To be valid, their marriage must be licensed, solemnized, and registered.[21]

The License

The parties must first obtain a license from the county clerk in the county in which they plan to marry.[22] They must prove they are of age and not currently married.

> **EXAMPLE** Parties bring birth certificates to prove their age. This is Husband-to-Be's second marriage. He brings a copy of the Judgment for Dissolution of his first marriage as well.

After confirming the parties are of age and not currently married, the clerk issues the license. By statute, the license becomes effective one day after the date of issuance and expires 60 days after it becomes effective.[23]

> **EXAMPLE** Abigail and Ethan make a spur-of-the-moment decision to get married. They obtain a license from the county clerk's office at noon. At one o'clock they cross the street to the courthouse and join the line of couples waiting to be married by a judge. Their license is not yet in effect.

Solemnization (the Ceremony)

Once the parties have obtained a license, they must solemnize, or celebrate their marriage. The marriage ceremony can be performed by religious clergy or in accordance with any Indian Nation, Tribe, or Native Group. If the couple prefers a civil wedding, the ceremony can be performed by a judge or a retired judge.[24]

Sometimes a couple prefers to have a friend or family member celebrate their marriage. To serve as a celebrant (also known as an "officiant") the friend or family member must be ordained. A number of organizations provide ordination online, many of which are "interfaith" or "nondenominational." To ensure the organization is reputable, the Illinois Secretary of State's office provides a list of nonprofit religious organizations in good standing. However, a marriage is not invalidated if the person solemnizing it was not legally qualified.

EXAMPLE Abigail and Ethan wait until the following day and ask Jake, a friend who was recently ordained through an online organization, to marry them. After the ceremony, they discover that Jake was not ordained; he had made a fake certificate of ordination on his computer. Their marriage is still valid.

Registration

Two witnesses sign the marriage license, which the officiant, or the parties themselves, mail to the county clerk that issued it for registration.[25]

EXAMPLE Abigail's sister and Ethan's brother sign the marriage license. Abigail and Ethan mail it to the county clerk, who registers their marriage. They have complied with all formalities required for a valid marriage.

Common Law Marriage

Common Law Marriage Defined

A common law marriage is one in which a couple has not complied with the formalities required for a valid marriage but lives together and holds themselves out to the public as married. While eight states legally recognize common law marriages,[26] Illinois does not. Common law marriages contracted in Illinois after June 30, 1905, are invalid.[27] However, Illinois will recognize a common law marriage if a couple enters it in a state that recognizes it and then moves to Illinois.

EXAMPLE Logan and Samantha enter a common law marriage in Rhode Island. After living there for ten years, they move to Illinois with their children. Illinois will recognize their marriage.

Living Together without Marriage

Sometimes couples in Illinois live together without complying with the formalities of marriage. During their time together, they cannot take advantage of the benefits the state offers to married couples, such as filing taxes jointly.

Further, if their relationship breaks down, they cannot use the provisions of the IMDMA that permit equitable distribution of the property married couples acquired together. Unlike the state of California, which awarded "palimony" ("alimony" to a "pal" as opposed to a former spouse) at the end of a long relationship,[28] the state of Illinois does not recognize property claims made by unmarried parties.[29]

The Illinois Supreme Court articulated this position in the case of *Hewitt v. Hewitt*.[30] In *Hewitt*, the plaintiff and respondent lived together for fifteen years in an "unmarried, family-like relationship."[31] During that time they had three children together. When the relationship broke down, the plaintiff filed an action against the respondent to recover an equal share of the property they had accumulated. The Court held that the petitioner's claims were "unenforceable for the reason that they contravene[d] the public policy, implicit in the statutory scheme of the Illinois Marriage and Dissolution of Marriage Act, disfavoring the grant of mutually enforceable property rights to knowingly unmarried cohabitants."[32]

EXAMPLE Ashley moves into Jeremy's apartment during their senior year in college. When they discover they are expecting a child, they move from the apartment into a house. Jeremy purchases the house in his name, and Ashley and Jeremy work and make house payments. Ten years later, the parties' relationship breaks down. Because the parties are not married, the court will not recognize the house as marital property. The house belongs to Jeremy.

However, the children born to unmarried parents are the legally recognized children of the parties.[33] The parties resolve issues about the children, such as child support and allocation of parental responsibilities, using the Illinois Parentage Act of 2015.[34]

EXAMPLE Ashley and Jeremy are the legal parents of their child. The court recognizes each parent's rights to time with, and responsibility for, their child.

Chapter Summary

While couples may choose to marry for personal, social, or religious reasons, marriage, the legal recognition of the union of two people, is a state-regulated event. Because marriage is a right protected by the Constitution, the state can only impose restrictions on that right when they advance a state interest. States can prohibit the marriage of those who are already married, are related, or are underage. However, courts have struck down prohibitions on other restrictions, such as same-sex and interracial marriage.

States have the authority to require certain formalities. To be valid in Illinois, a marriage must be licensed, solemnized, and registered. A "common law marriage" is one in which couples live together and hold themselves out as married but do not comply with the formalities required for a valid marriage. While common law marriage is recognized in some states, it has not been recognized in Illinois since 1905. Couples who live together in Illinois do not receive the legal benefits of marriage during the relationship. In addition, should the relationship end, they cannot use the IMDMA to ensure equitable distribution of their property.

Key Terms

Marriage

Bigamy

Incest

Underage Marriage

Solemnization

Celebrant

Common Law Marriage

Discussion Questions

1. Until 2016, Illinois permitted one fiancé(e) to sue the other for breaking their engagement under the Breach of Promise Act. What was the policy behind this cause of action? What is the legislative policy for repealing it? Do you agree? *See* Alienation of Affections Abolition, 740 ILCS 15/10.1 (2016).
2. What if a fiancé(e) breaks an engagement after the other has incurred non-refundable expenses on the wedding, such as a deposit on a hall? Should they have a right to sue for recovery of the expenses?

3. Who keeps the engagement ring in a broken engagement? Does it matter whether the man or the woman broke off the engagement? Should it matter? Would it be different if one party had given the other a car in contemplation of their marriage, instead of a diamond ring? *See Harris v. Davis*, 139 Ill. App. 3d 1046, 487 N.E.2d 1204 (5th Dist. 1986).

4. Utah reduced its bigamy statute from a felony to a misdemeanor because it prevented abused wives in plural marriages from seeking help. What do you think of the policy? Are there other ways to help victims in plural marriages escape abuse?

5. Public health considerations motivate the prohibition of marriages between relatives related by blood (consanguinity). What policy consideration might be behind the prohibition on marriages of relatives related by relationship (affinity)? It has been said that marriages promote social stability. How would a marriage between an uncle and niece, or adopted siblings, affect family relationships?

6. A Dutch court barred a man from making sperm donations after he was discovered to be the father of over 500 children, in order to bar possible incestuous marriages between his children.[35] What should the state do about marriages between parties who didn't know they were related? Declare them null and void? How can the state prevent cases of "accidental incest?" Should the state require DNA testing before issuing marriage licenses? Make it optional?

7. The dissent in *Obergefell* argues that for millennia marriage was defined as the relationship between one man and one woman. If the majority changed the definition of marriage, what prevented it from being changed again to include three parties? "It is striking how much of the majority's reasoning would apply with equal force to the claim of a fundamental right to plural marriage." *Obergefell v. Hodges*, 576 U.S. 644, 704 (2015).

8. Sometimes couples live together for a period of time before they get married. Because the length of the marriage is a factor in allocating property, should a court consider the time spent living together? Why or why not? Consider a case in which the court did not consider the 13 years the couple had lived together when allocating property. The court considered only their marriage of less than one year. *See In re Marriage of Allen*, 2016 IL App (1st) 151620, 62 N.E.3d 312.

9. How can a couple that lives together protect their property interests? Before same-sex marriage was available, same-sex couples looked for legal ways to ensure an inheritance for partners, such as adoption. Are there other ways as well?

10. How about joint ownership of property? Or contract law? As noted in *Hewitt* and the line of cases that follow its holding, "unmarried individuals may make express or implied contracts with one another." *Blumenthal v. Brewer*, 2016 IL 118781, ¶ 87, 69 N.E.3d 834, 860.

Forms

1. Marriage License, online application at:

   https//www.dupagecounty.gov/CountyClerk/1822/

Endnotes

1. Loving v. Virginia, 388 U.S.1 (1967).
2. Obergefell v. Hodges, 576 U.S. 644 (2015).
3. 750 ILCS 5/101(West, Westlaw Classic through P.A. 103-21 of the 2023 Reg. Sess.).
4. Goodridge v. Dep't of Pub. Health, 440 Mass. 309, 798 N.E.2d 941 (2003).
5. 755 ILCS 5/2-1 (West, Westlaw Classic through P.A. 103-21 of the 2023 Reg. Sess.).
6. 42 U.S.C.A. § 18001.
7. U.S. CONST. AMEND. XIV.
8. Loving v. Virginia, 388 U.S.1 (1967).
9. Turner v. Safley, 482 U.S. 78 (1987).
10. Zablocki v. Redhail, 434 U.S. 374 (1978).
11. "The constitutional guarantee of equal protection requires that similarly situated individuals be treated similarly." People v. Baker, 2020 IL App (2d) 181048, ¶ 10, 173 N.E.3d 244, 247.
12. 750 ILCS 75 (West, Westlaw Classic through P.A. 103-21 of the 2023 Reg. Sess.).
13. 750 ILCS 80/10 (West, Westlaw Classic through P.A. 103-21 of the 2023 Reg. Sess.).
14. *Id.*
15. Gray v. Orr, 4 F. Supp. 3d 984 (N.D. Ill. 2013).
16. Obergefell, 576 U.S. 644 (2015).
17. 720 ILCS 5/11-45(a) (West, Westlaw Classic through P.A. 103-21 of the 2023 Reg. Sess.).
18. 750 ILCS 5/212(a) 2-4ii.
19. *Id.* § 203(1).
20. *Id.* § 216.
21. *Id.* § 201.
22. *Id.* § 203.
23. *Id.* § 207.
24. 750 ILCS 5/209(a).
25. Witness signatures are not necessary. A marriage is still valid even if there are no witnesses.
26. https://www.ncsl.org/human-services/common-law-marriage-by-state (last visited June 29, 2023). Colorado, Iowa, Kansas, Montana, New Hampshire, South Carolina, Texas, and Utah.

27. 750 ILCS 5/214.
28. Marvin v. Marvin, 18 Cal. 3d 660 (1976).
29. Hewitt v. Hewitt, 77 Ill. 2d 49, 394 N.E.2d 1204 (1979)
30. *Id.*, 394 N.E.2d 1204
31. *Id.* at 52, 349 N.E.2d at 1205
32. *Id.* at 65, 394 N.E.2d at 1211.
33. 750 ILCS 5/212(c).
34. 750 ILCS 46 (West, Westlaw Classic through P.A. 103-21 of the 2023 Reg. Sess.).
35. https://www.nbcnews.com/news/world/sperm-donor-500-children-banned-court-netherlands-the-hague-parents-rcna82022

Three

Divorce, Declaration of Marital Invalidity, and Legal Separation

Overview

In the previous chapter, we learned about forming a marriage. In this chapter, we'll learn about ending one. Illinois law provides two ways to end a marriage: a dissolution (or "divorce"), which ends it prospectively, and a declaration of marital invalidity (or "annulment"), which ends it retroactively. In addition, a legal separation provides a way for married couples to separate their finances while keeping their marriage intact. As you read, consider why the General Assembly offers three different options and when a specific option might be appropriate.

Dissolution of Marriage

In a dissolution action, the court dissolves the legal bond formed by a marriage. In addition, the court allocates responsibility for any children born during the marriage and distributes property acquired during the marriage.

Filing Requirements

Residency

In order to file a petition for divorce in Illinois, "one of the parties must have been a resident of Illinois at the time the matter was commenced and must have been a resident for 90 days prior to the commencement of the proceeding."[1] If a party is in the military and stationed in Illinois for 90 days, the party satisfies the residency requirement as well.

> **EXAMPLE** Husband and Wife have lived in Illinois since they were born, including their entire married life. Illinois has jurisdiction over their divorce.

> **EXAMPLE** In contrast, Husband and Wife were married in Ohio and lived there for five years. Wife moved to Chicago, signed a lease on an apartment, and filed for divorce 30 days later. Because she was not a resident when the action commenced, she will have to maintain Illinois as her permanent home for at least 90 days before the court can enter a judgment of dissolution.

Home State

There is an additional residency requirement concerning children. Because family laws differ by state, a parent planning a divorce might unilaterally move with a child to a state where he thinks he will get a better outcome. To prevent this, in 1997 the National Conference of Commissioners adopted the Uniform Child-Custody Jurisdiction and Enforcement Act ("UCCJEA").[2] All 50 states (with the exception of Massachusetts) have adopted it. Pursuant to the UCCJEA, an initial custody determination must be brought in the child's home state, defined "as the state in which a child lived with a parent for at least six consecutive months immediately before the commencement of a child custody proceeding."[3] In the case of a child less than six months of age, the term means the state in which the child lived from birth with a parent.

> **EXAMPLE** Mother and Father have lived in Ohio since Child's birth nine years earlier. Mother takes Child to Illinois. Ninety days later, Mother files a petition for dissolution. Although Mother resides in Illinois, Ohio is still Child's home state. Should Father file a petition for dissolution in Ohio, the Ohio court would have jurisdiction over Child. Had Mother waited six months before filing, Illinois would have been Child's home state.

Determination of the child's home state is critical because the UCCJEA gives the initial courts continuing jurisdiction over the case.[4]

> **EXAMPLE** Mother, Father, and Child live in Illinois when the initial custody determination is made. Two years later, Father moves to Ohio and files an action to modify custody, thinking he will get a better outcome than he did in Illinois. Illinois courts have continuing jurisdiction over the case.

Married

The parties must be married to get a divorce. Illinois can grant the divorce of a couple who were married in another state, or even in another country. In addition, Illinois can grant the divorce of a couple in a common law marriage, as long as it was entered in a state where it is valid.

> **EXAMPLE** Husband and Wife fulfilled all the requirements for a valid common law marriage in their home state of Alabama. When they move to Illinois, they can use Illinois courts to get divorced.

Grounds

A final requirement is having grounds, or a basis, for the divorce. Until 1984, Illinois divorce law required the petitioner to prove that the respondent was at fault in some way, without cause or provocation by the petitioner. The fault grounds included adultery, extreme and repeated physical and mental cruelty, abandonment for at least a year, and a felony conviction.

In 1984, Illinois added a "no-fault" ground to the IMDMA,[5] and on January 1, 2016, fault-based grounds were abolished. Currently, the only ground available for a dissolution is "irreconcilable differences have caused the irretrievable breakdown of the marriage and the court determines that efforts at reconciliation have failed or that future attempts at reconciliation would be impracticable and not in the best interests of the family."[6]

If the parties agree there are irreconcilable differences, there is no waiting period before the court can enter judgment.

> **EXAMPLE** While they are still living together, Wife files for divorce, alleging irreconcilable differences. Husband agrees. There is no waiting period before the court can enter a judgment of dissolution.

If the respondent does not agree, however, irreconcilable differences are presumed by six months' marital separation. Under Illinois caselaw, spouses using separate bedrooms in the same house are considered to be living separate and apart.[7]

EXAMPLE Although she would like to move to an apartment, Wife can't afford it. She moves into the guest bedroom. Six months later, even if Husband doesn't agree, she will have irrefutably proven the grounds of irreconcilable differences.

The Authority of the Court in a Dissolution Action

Terminate Marriage

First, the court can terminate the marriage. A judgment for dissolution essentially severs the bond that joined the couple at their wedding.

Provide for Children

Second, the court can provide for the children born to, or adopted by, the parties during the marriage, through allocations of decision-making responsibility, parenting time, and child support. (See Chapter 6, Children, and Chapter 7, Child Support.)

Distribute Property

Finally, the court can distribute the property acquired during the marriage and make provisions for spousal maintenance. (See Chapter 9, Property, and Chapter 8, Spousal Maintenance.)

Declaration of Invalidity of a Marriage (Annulment)

The IMDMA provides the law related to a judgment of declaration of invalidity of marriage, or, as it is more commonly called, an annulment.[8] While a judgment for divorce ends a marriage from the date of judgment forwards, a judgment for declaration of marital invalidity works backward, erasing the marriage.[9]

Grounds

As with a dissolution action, the party seeking an annulment must be a resident of the state of Illinois and married. If there are children, Illinois must be their home state. In contrast with a dissolution action, fault-based grounds are required for an action of declaration of marital invalidity.[10] The grounds include:

Lacked Mental Capacity

"A party lacked capacity to consent to the marriage at the time the marriage was solemnized, either because of mental incapacity or infirmity or because of the influence of alcohol, drugs, or other incapacitating substances."[11] This action must be brought within 90 days of the marriage.

> **EXAMPLE** A couple travel to Las Vegas for the weekend. After drinking heavily one evening, they stumble into a wedding chapel and get married. Either party can file for a declaration of marital invalidity on the grounds they lacked capacity to consent because they were under the influence of alcohol.

Fraud

"A party was induced to enter into a marriage by force or duress or by fraud involving the essentials of marriage."[12] Courts have construed the essentials of the marriage as the capacity for sexual relations. As a consequence, courts have not found fraud when the respondent made false representations as to fortune, character, or social standing. This action must also be brought within 90 days of the marriage.

> **EXAMPLE** During their courtship, David displays a lavish lifestyle, taking Sophia to expensive restaurants where he orders vintage wines. He proposes on the beach in Malibu with a two-carat diamond. After the honeymoon, Sophia discovers his Mercedes is only leased, the travel expenses (and the engagement ring) are on a credit card, and his international consulting firm has no clients. She would like to file for an annulment, claiming fraud. Because David's actions do not go to the essentials of the marriage, she likely does not have grounds (although she can file for divorce).[13]

Lacked Capacity to Consummate

"A party lacks the physical capacity to consummate the marriage by sexual intercourse and at the time the marriage was solemnized the other party did not know of the incapacity."[14] This action must be brought within one year after the petitioner discovered the condition.

> **EXAMPLE** On their wedding night, Party A discovers that because of a childhood injury, Party B is unable to consummate the marriage. Party A can file for an annulment within a year of their wedding night.

Underage

"A party was aged 16 or 17 years and did not have the consent of his parents or guardian or judicial approval."[15] This action must be brought before the underage party turned 18.

EXAMPLE Emma is 16 and Gary is 22 when they marry. Emma did not have parental consent or court approval. Emma can file for a declaration of invalidity before she turns 18. Gary cannot file a petition for a declaration of marital invalidity at any time.

Prohibited

A final ground for annulment is that the marriage is prohibited, either because it is incestuous or bigamous. Actions based on these grounds may be brought by either party or the state's attorney, at any time, not to exceed three years following the death of the first party to die.

EXAMPLE Isabella and Brandon marry in 2008 when Brandon is already married to Lauren. When Isabella finds out, she can file a declaration for marital invalidity. Because bigamy is a crime, the state's attorney can bring an action against Brandon as well.

EXAMPLE Similarly, even though they are brother and sister, Sarah and Ryan marry. Either of them could bring a petition for a declaration of invalidity of marriage. Because incest is a crime, the state's attorney can bring an action against them both as well.

Void or Voidable

Voidable

Some marriages are voidable, meaning the obstacle to a valid marriage can be removed. In the case of a lack of capacity, fraud, inability to consummate the marriage, or underage marriage, the marriage is voidable. The petitioner can stay in the marriage if they choose.

EXAMPLE In the case of the couple who got married in Las Vegas, the marriage is voidable. After they sober up, the obstacle of lack of capacity is removed. The parties may decide to stay together.

Void

In contrast, other marriages are void, meaning the impediment cannot be removed. In an incestuous marriage, such as Sarah and Ryan's, the impediment of their being brother and sister cannot be removed.

A bigamous marriage, like an incestuous marriage, is prohibited; however, the impediment in a bigamous marriage can be removed. In the case of Isabella and Brandon, if Brandon divorces Lauren (his first wife), Isabella and Brandon will be considered lawfully married as of the date of the divorce.[16]

The Status of Children

In the past, children born to unmarried parents did not have the same legal rights as children born to married parents, such as being able to inherit through their father.[17] However, those laws no longer exist. In Illinois, all children are lawful, whether their parents were married or not. Consequently, a declaration of marital invalidity does not affect the legal status of the children born during the marriage. Children born or adopted of a marriage declared invalid remain the lawful children of the parties.[18]

EXAMPLE Emma is 16 and Gary is 22 when they marry. Emma is also eight months pregnant. After giving birth to a baby girl the parties name Chloe, Emma moves home, and her parents encourage her to have the marriage annulled. If the annulment is granted, the marriage is considered to never have existed. However, Chloe is still the lawful baby of the parties. The annulment does not make her illegitimate. Emma and Gary can resolve parenting issues for Chloe, such as parenting time and child support, using the law for unmarried parents. (See Chapter 11, Parentage.)

Property and the Putative Spouse

Ordinarily, the annulment dates back to the date of the marriage, thereby erasing it completely. When that happens, the law considers the parties to have been in a common law marriage. As a common law marriage, the court does not have jurisdiction to make provisions related to the property or award maintenance.

But what happens to the person who marries a person who is already married, under the assumption the person they intended to marry was single? Fortunately, that person's property rights are protected. Illinois law provides that any person, having gone through a marriage ceremony and cohabited with another in the good faith belief that they were married to that person, is a putative spouse.[19] A putative spouse acquires the rights conferred upon a legal spouse, including the right to an award of property and spousal maintenance.

If there are both a legal spouse and a putative spouse, the court has the authority to apportion property, maintenance, and support rights among the claimants as appropriate in the circumstances and in the interests of justice.[20]

EXAMPLE In the earlier example, Isabella is a putative spouse. When she learns Brandon was already married to Lauren, Isabella can file for a declaration of marital invalidity. The court can apportion the property and award maintenance between all three of them, Isabella, Brandon, and Lauren.

Legal Separation

Some people seek financial and physical separation from their spouse; however, they do not want to get divorced. Perhaps their religion or moral values prohibit divorce. Alternatively, they may need to be married to remain eligible for health insurance or to receive social security or pension payments. A legal separation allows the court to enter judgment marking the end of the parties' financial union while maintaining the marriage itself.[21]

EXAMPLE Husband and Wife practice a religion that does not permit divorce. However, Husband's gambling has caused the couple financial stress, which has led to relational stress. Wife moves in with her sister and files a petition for legal separation.

After a judgment of legal separation, the parties are not free to remarry. Should one or both of them want to marry at a later time, they would need to file a petition for dissolution.

Filing Requirements

As with an action for dissolution, to file for a legal separation, one of the parties must have lived in Illinois, and the parties must be married. If there are children, it must be their home state. While the parties must be living separate and apart, no grounds are required.

Authority of Court in a Legal Separation

What the Court Has Authority to Do

The court has the authority to provide injunctive relief, that is, to order the parties to do or refrain from doing certain things while the action is pending. (See Chapter 5, Temporary Motions and the Financial Affidavit.) At the conclusion of the case, the court has the authority to award spousal maintenance, order child support, and allocate parental responsibilities.

What the Court Does Not Have Authority to Do

In an action for a legal separation, the court does not have the authority to value or allocate property.

> **EXAMPLE** Husband and Wife choose to enter a legal separation. Wife wants Husband to take responsibility for the Visa card debt of $18,000. Because Wife used the card to purchase designer shoes and handbags, Husband does not agree. The court cannot order Husband to take responsibility for the debt.

However, the court will approve an agreement the parties make, called a separation agreement, unless it is unconscionable.[22] Courts have defined an unconscionable agreement as one which is "improvident, totally one-sided or oppressive."[23] ("Unconscionability" is also discussed in Chapter 9, Property.)

> **EXAMPLE** Wife agrees to take 50% of the debt, and Husband grudgingly agrees. After verifying the parties' respective financial positions and determining the agreement is not unconscionable, the judge approves the agreement.

Chart Summarizing the Three Options

	Dissolution of Marriage	Declaration of Marital Invalidity	Legal Separation
Code Section	750 ILCS 5/401	750 ILCS 5/301	750 ILCS 5/402
Judgment Entered	Judgment of Dissolution of Marriage	Judgment of Declaration of Marital Invalidity	Judgment of Legal Separation
Grounds Required	No-fault grounds	Fault-based grounds	No grounds required
Decree Action	Works prospectively from date of judgment forward	Works retroactively from date of judgment backward	Works prospectively from date of judgment forward
Length of Marriage	From date of marriage to date of divorce	Were never married	Are still married
Court's Authority to Divide Property	Court has authority to divide property	Only if putative spouse	Court cannot divide. Parties' agreement must not be unconscionable
Spousal Maintenance Available?	Yes	Only if putative spouse	Yes
Child Support Available?	Yes—through 750 ILCS 5/505(a).	Illinois Parentage Act of 2015	Yes—through 750 ILCS 5/505(a).
Allocation of Parental Responsibilities?	Yes—through 750 ILCS 5/601.2(b)(1).	Illinois Parentage Act of 2015	Yes—through 750 ILCS 5/601.2(b)(1).

Chapter Summary

Illinois law provides two ways to terminate a marriage. First, an action for dissolution of marriage allows the court to terminate the marital relationship, allocate responsibility for any children born during the marriage, and distribute property acquired during the marriage. Second, an action for declaration of marital invalidity allows the court to terminate a marriage because of a defect that existed at the time of the marriage.

A judgment of marital invalidity works retroactively to the date of marriage, in essence erasing the marriage. Where obstacles to a valid marriage, such as incapacity, can be cured, the marriage is voidable. However, where obstacles to a valid marriage, such as incest, cannot be cured, the marriage is void.

Finally, through an action for legal separation, couples can end their financial union while remaining married. In an action for a legal separation, the court can order spousal maintenance and can determine child-related issues. And while the court does not have jurisdiction to value or award property acquired during the marriage, it will enter a settlement agreement by the parties unless it is unconscionable.

Key Terms

Dissolution of Marriage

Residency

Home State

Grounds

Irreconcilable Differences

Declaration of Marital Invalidity ("Annulment")

Bigamy

Incest

Void

Voidable

Putative Spouse

Legal Separation

Unconscionable

Discussion Questions

1. Until 1984, the General Assembly required fault grounds, in recognition of an expressed public policy to preserve marriages. In 1984, it permitted no-fault grounds. What do you suppose contributed to that change in policy?
2. The state can restrict a marriage if it advances a compelling state interest. Do you agree that the state's interest in preserving marriages is "no longer served when it is not also shared by the parties themselves"? *In re Marriage of Smoller*, 218 Ill. App. 3d 340, 344–45, 578 N.E.2d 256, 259 (1st Dist. 1991).

3. Has a parent who moves a child to another state for a better custody determination kidnapped the child? Would it make a difference if the move was before or after a custody judgment had been entered? *See* 750 ILCS 36/317, which discusses the respondent's obligation to repay costs spent by law enforcement in locating a missing child.
4. Courts limit the fraud ground concerning the "essentials of the marriage" to mean "capacity for sexual relations." Why does the court impose this limitation when there is already a ground for "inability to consummate"? Further, for many couples, a shared religion, a desire for children, and similar views about education, character, and politics are essential elements of a marriage. *See* https://www.newsweek.com/new-dating-app-trump-supporters-seeks-make-america-date-again-1171136 (last visited June 29, 2023).
5. In January 2004, Britney Spears filed an annulment action against Jason Alexander after a 55-hour marriage. Would her allegations have satisfied the grounds required by the Illinois Marriage and Dissolution of Marriage Act for an annulment? If voluntary intoxication permits the annulment of a marriage, should it be a way to void other contracts as well?
6. It has been said that by treating a marriage as though it never occurred, an annulment is a legal fiction. After a judgment for declaration, courts make decisions about the children born during the marriage but not about the property acquired. Should it treat them the same way? Why or why not?
7. What might make a property settlement agreement unconscionable? Why should the court refuse to enter an agreement the parties themselves agree to?
8. The Illinois Marriage and Dissolution of Marriage Act formerly allowed a civil action called "alienation of affection," which allowed married people to sue their spouse's paramour. Some states still allow this action (sometimes called "homewrecker actions"). *See* https//www.cnn.com/2019/10/02/us/alienation-of-affection-laws-north-carolina-lawsuit-trnd/index.html (last visited June 29, 2023).
9. Should Illinois have repealed the action? Why or why not?

Endnotes

1. 750 ILCS 5/401(a) (West, Westlaw Classic through P.A. 103-21 of the 2023 Reg. Sess.).
2. 750 ILCS 36 (West, Westlaw Classic through P.A. 103-21 of the 2023 Reg. Sess.).
3. *Id.* § 102(7).
4. *Id.* § 202(a).
5. S.H.A. ch. 40, ¶ 401(a)(2).
6. 750 ILCS 5/401(a).
7. In re Marriage of Dowd, 214 Ill. App. 3d 156, 573 N.E.2d312 (2d Dist. 1991).

8. 750 ILCS 5/301.
9. *Id.* § 304.
10. *Id.* § 301.
11. *Id.* § 301(1).
12. *Id.*
13. In re Marriage of Naguit, 104 Ill. App. 3d 709,433 N.E.2d 296 (5th Dist. 1982).
14. 750 ILCS 5/301(2).
15. *Id.* § 301(3).
16. In re Estate of Banks, 258 Ill. App. 3d 379, 629 N.E.2d 1223 (5th Dist. 1994).
17. Ill. Rev.Stat ch 3 § 2-2 (1976-77).
18. 750 ILCS 5/303.
19. *Id.* § 305.
20. *Id.*
21. 750 ILCS 5/402(a).
22. *Id.* § 402(b)(2).
23. In re Marriage of Gurin, 212 Ill. App. 3d 806, 816, 571 N.E.2d 857, 864 (1st Dist. 1991) (citing In re Marriage of Carlson, 101 Ill. App. 3d 924, 428 N.E.2d 1005 (1st Dist. 1981).

Four

Jurisdiction, Service, and Initial Pleadings

Overview

In the previous chapter, we discussed the three options available to married couples when their relationship breaks down. These options, or the rights of action available within a specific area of law, are known as "substantive law." In this chapter, we discuss the process used to move a case through the court system from start to finish, known as "procedural law." The rules that govern this process, contained in the Illinois Code of Civil Procedure and Illinois Supreme Court Rules, apply to civil litigation of all types. As you read, consider whether the procedural rules permit efficient, equitable resolution of family law actions.

Initiating a Dissolution Action

The initial pleading in all proceedings under the Illinois Marriage and Dissolution of Marriage Act is called a "petition."[1] These include proceedings for dissolution of marriage, dissolution of a civil union, declaration of marital invalidity, and legal separation. Otherwise, the titles of pleadings follow the Code of Civil Procedure.[2] The party initiating the action is called the "petitioner," and the party being sued is called the "respondent."

EXAMPLE Noah retains an attorney to file a divorce from Brianna. Noah is the petitioner, and Brianna is the respondent.

Ordinarily, one party files the petition. However, in limited situations the IMDMA permits parties to file a joint petition.[3] To use this joint, simplified dissolution procedure, the parties must agree that:

- Neither party needs spousal maintenance;
- They have no children;
- Their marriage lasted less than eight years;
- They have no retirement benefits (unless the combined value is less than $10,000);
- They have no real property; and
- The fair market value of their personal property is less than $50,000.

> **EXAMPLE** Husband and Wife have been married for three years. They work minimum-wage jobs, have no children, and live in an apartment. They can file a joint petition for dissolution using the simplified dissolution process.

The Petition and Supporting Documents

The Petition for Dissolution

A petition for dissolution of marriage or legal separation must state the following:

(1) The age, occupation, and residence of each party and his length of residence in this State;

(2) The date of the marriage and the place at which it was registered;

(2.5) Whether a petition for dissolution of marriage is pending in any other county or state;

(3) That the jurisdictional requirements of subsection (a) of 5/401 have been met and that irreconcilable differences have caused the irretrievable breakdown of the marriage;

(4) The names, ages, and addresses of all living children of the marriage and whether a spouse is pregnant;

(5) Any arrangements as to support, allocation of parental responsibility of the children and maintenance of a spouse; and

(6) The relief sought.[4]

The petition alleges the requirements for dissolution we saw in the previous chapter: residency in the state, marriage, and grounds. Additionally, it alleges whether the parties have children who would be subject to the UCCJEA.

When drafting the petition, each paragraph is numbered consecutively and contains a separate allegation.[5] Also, in order to protect their personal information, minor children are referred to by their initials, not their full names, and only the year of their birth is provided, not the date or month.[6]

> **EXAMPLE** The petition alleges that "during the marriage, three children were born to the parties, namely G.A.J, born in 2010, R.R.J., born in 2012, and G.E.J., born in 2014. No other children were born to or adopted by the parties and the petitioner is not now pregnant."

The petition must be verified by the client pursuant to 735 ILCS 5/1-109 of the Code of Civil Procedure, which provides that:

> Any pleading, affidavit, or other document certified in accordance with this Section may be used in the same manner and with the same force and effect as though subscribed and sworn to under oath, and there is no further requirement that . . . it be sworn before an authorized person.

Given the consequences of filing a petition with a false statement, violating this rule is a Class 3 felony. And finally, the petition must be signed by the attorney pursuant to Illinois Supreme Court Rule 137, which provides:

> The signature of an attorney or party constitutes a certificate by him that he has read the pleading, motion, or other document; that to the best of his knowledge, information, and belief formed after reasonable inquiry it is well grounded in fact and is warranted by existing law or a good-faith argument for the extension, modification, or reversal of existing law, and that it is not interposed for any improper purpose, such as to harass or to cause unnecessary delay or needless increase in the cost of litigation . . .

There are consequences for violating Illinois Supreme Court Rule 137, as there are with filing a petition with a false statement. The court can impose an appropriate sanction upon the attorney, a represented party, or both, which may include an order to pay to the other party the amount of reasonable expenses incurred because of the filing of the pleading, motion, or other document, including a reasonable attorney fee.

> **EXAMPLE** Attorney is pressed for time and uses ChatGPT to draft a client's petition for dissolution. Attorney does not verify that the cases cited by ChatGPT are still good law. As it turns out, the cases do not even exist. ChatGPT made them up. Attorney could face sanctions for signing a document that is not warranted by existing law, in violation of Supreme Court Rule 137.

Domestic Relations Summons

A summons is a form used to notify the respondent of the action against them and to give the court jurisdiction over them. In contrast to the summons used in other civil matters, a domestic relations summons includes a notice that an automatic stay is in effect that restrains the parties from concealing a child or abusing, harassing, or intimidating each other.[7]

County-Specific Forms

Some circuit courts require forms in addition to the petition and the summons. For example, Kane and Cook County Circuit Courts require a cover sheet, and Lake County Circuit Court requires a Certificate of Attorney form. Circuit court websites indicate the specific forms required.

Filing with the Appropriate Court

State Court

As marriage is not a power enumerated to the federal government in the United States Constitution, it is reserved to the states.[8] In Illinois, petitions for marriage-based actions start in the lowest level courts, the circuit courts.[9]

Venue

Venue, or location, refers to the specific circuit court within the state of Illinois in which an action is filed. In civil actions, venue is appropriate in the county where the petitioner or respondent resides. However, the Illinois Marriage and Dissolution of Marriage Act expands venue to any county within the state.[10]

> **EXAMPLE** Parties were married in McHenry County. When they broke up, Husband moved to Sangamon County. Wife hired an attorney whose office was in DuPage County. Wife's attorney makes a motion for leave to have the matter heard in DuPage County.

E-file

All civil cases in circuit courts have had to be filed electronically since January 1, 2018 (July 1, 2018, in Cook County).[11] Law offices use an e-filing service provider to connect to the state's single, centralized electronic filing manager (EFM) called eFil-eIL. Several e-filing service providers are available, such as Odyssey File and Serve and i2file. Information on the service providers can be found at http//efile.illinois-courts.gov/service-providers.htm.

Filing Fee

All counties charge a fee for filing a petition of dissolution. As of the publication of this text, for example, the filing fee in DuPage County is $343. The filing fee is paid at the time of filing.[12]

In order to ensure equal access to justice, Illinois provides a waiver of court fees for those who are unable to afford them. The waiver, found in the Code of Civil Procedure, is available for parties receiving means-based governmental public benefit programs or whose incomes are 125% or less of the current poverty level.[13] If a party makes an application for court fees, it is filed with the petition. A judge decides whether to grant it in full or in part or deny it.

Law Office Follow-Up

Once they receive notice that the court clerk has accepted the petition, law firms download a file-stamped copy and docket the date and courtroom of the first status date. Mindful of their responsibility to keep the client informed, at this time firms also provide a copy to the client.

Jurisdiction over the Respondent: Minimum Contacts

Jurisdiction refers to the authority of the court to hear a case. When a petitioner files a petition, they submit themselves to the court's authority. Obtaining jurisdiction, or authority, over the respondent is a two-step process. First, the respondent must have had such connection with the jurisdiction it is reasonable for him to anticipate being called into account there.[14] This level of connection, called "minimum contacts," satisfies the respondent's due process rights.

Resident of Illinois

Residents of Illinois can anticipate being sued in an Illinois court. Therefore, residency satisfies the respondent's due process rights.

The Long-Arm Statute

Even if not a resident of Illinois, the respondent can anticipate being sued in Illinois if he performed certain actions there. These actions, as provided in the "long-arm statute," permit the Illinois courts to reach beyond the border of the state to secure jurisdiction over the respondent. Actions related to family law include:

> (5) With respect to actions of dissolution of marriage, declaration of invalidity of marriage and legal separation, the maintenance in this State of a matrimonial domicile at the time this cause of action arose or the commission in this State of any act giving rise to the cause of action;
>
> (6) With respect to actions brought under the Illinois Parentage Act of 1984, as now or hereafter amended, or under the Illinois Parentage Act of 2015 on and after the effective date of that Act, the performance of an act of sexual intercourse within this State during the possible period of conception;
>
> (8) The performance of sexual intercourse within this State which is claimed to have resulted in the conception of a child who resides in this State;
>
> (9) The failure to support a child, spouse or former spouse who has continued to reside in this State since the person either formerly resided with them in this State or directed them to reside in this State. [15]

EXAMPLE Henry is on vacation in Illinois from California when he begins an intense, although short-lived, relationship with Abigail. Two weeks after Henry returns to California, Abigail discovers she is pregnant. Under Section (6), the Illinois courts have jurisdiction over Henry.

Service on the Respondent: The Notice Requirement

Once it is determined that the Illinois courts can exercise jurisdiction over the respondent because of his contact with the state, the next step is to notify him of the action. Again, the notice of an action against him is required to satisfy his due process rights.

Personal Jurisdiction

In order for the court to obtain personal jurisdiction, called *in personam* jurisdiction, over the respondent, the respondent must be personally served with the petition and summons by one of the methods provided by the Code of Civil Procedure.[16]

Law firms use different methods to obtain personal service, depending on the parties' situation.

Waiver of Service

To reduce expense, or to spare the respondent the experience of being served, some firms begin by giving the respondent the option to waive service.[17] The petitioner's attorney mails the petition and summons to the respondent. The respondent has 30 days to respond (60 if the respondent lives outside the United States). The respondent who signs and returns a waiver of service within that time is deemed to have been personally served.

EXAMPLE In order to minimize the costs of service, Petitioner's attorney mails a copy of the summons, petition, and a waiver of service to Respondent. Respondent promptly signs and returns the waiver. The court has jurisdiction over Respondent.

EXAMPLE In contrast, Respondent ignores the documents, playing video games and pretending his wife hasn't left. After thirty days pass, Petitioner's attorney must attempt another form of service.

Personal Service

With personal service, contact is made directly with the respondent. In Cook County, the sheriff must attempt service first.[18] If the sheriff is unable to serve the respondent, the petitioner can move to have a special process server appointed, generally a private investigator. In other counties, either a sheriff or private investigator may attempt service. Service must be made personally on the respondent, or it may be left at his house with an individual over 13 years of age.[19]

EXAMPLE Petitioner's attorney tenders the summons and petition to the sheriff's office and pays the appropriate service fee. The sheriff goes to Respondent's house and rings the doorbell. A teenager opens the door. After confirming that he lives in the house and is over 13, the sheriff hands him the documents. Respondent has been personally served.

Special Method

If no one answers the door, the petitioner may make a motion for permission to serve by special method, such as physically taping the petition and summons to the front door.[20] As this is an exception to personal service, the petitioner must show the court the efforts made to serve the respondent through standard methods.

> **EXAMPLE** A private investigator attempted service at Respondent's home on six separate occasions in the first 30 days without success. Each time the investigator saw cars in the driveway and lights on in the house. Once, hearing music playing, the investigator walked to the back of the house and discovered a picnic table with four cold drinks but no one in sight. Petitioner's attorney files a motion for special method.

A summons is only valid for 30 days. By the time a petitioner has made sufficient efforts to succeed on a motion for service by special method, it has likely expired. In that case, an alias summons must be obtained.

> **EXAMPLE** Satisfied that Petitioner has made sufficient efforts to serve Respondent, the court grants Petitioner's motion for service by special process server. The process server tapes the petition and alias summons to Respondent's front door and follows up with certified mail. Respondent has been personally served.

The Absent Spouse

There are times the respondent cannot be located. They may have moved out of the state, or even the country. Is the petitioner trapped in the marriage forever? Fortunately, the answer is no. Without personal service, the court does not have *in personam* jurisdiction over the respondent. However, the state retains jurisdiction over the marriage. Under its *in rem* jurisdiction, or jurisdiction "against the thing," the court can terminate the marriage.

Motion

The petitioner must make a motion for permission to serve by publication in a newspaper.[21] The motion must include an affidavit showing all attempts made to find the respondent.

EXAMPLE Petitioner and her husband were married for three years and had one child when Petitioner's husband was removed from the country by immigration officials. After a few years, Petitioner enters a relationship with Boyfriend and is now pregnant with his child. Petitioner would like to get divorced so she can marry before she gives birth. Petitioner's affidavit includes the facts that she has had no contact with Respondent since he was removed. Although she has not changed her phone number, he has not called. His phone number is out of service. His entire family is in Mexico, except for a cousin who lives in Chicago, who swears he does not know where he lives. The two former coworkers she could locate have not heard from him. He is not on Facebook or other social media. The judge grants the motion for service by publication.

Publication

Once the judge grants the motion for service by publication, the petitioner must publish notice of the case in a newspaper for three weeks. The notice must contain the title of the court, the title of the case, the names of the parties, and the docket number.

Authority of Court

With service by publication, the court has *in rem* jurisdiction and can terminate the marriage. In addition, the court can decide issues related to the children of the parties. (See Chapter 6, Children.)

However, because the Constitution prohibits the deprivation of property without due process of law, without *in personam* jurisdiction achieved through personal service, the court cannot award property or spousal maintenance.[22]

EXAMPLE In the example above, the court grants Petitioner a judgment of dissolution under its *in rem* jurisdiction obtained through publication. Based on the best interests of the child, the court awards parental responsibilities to Petitioner. However, without *in personam* jurisdiction obtained through personal service, the court cannot award Petitioner the furniture, car, or bank accounts acquired during the marriage.

If an absent spouse reappears and is personally served, the court can allocate the marital property. Should an absent parent return and request time with their children, they could ask the court to modify decisions on child-related issues. (See Chapter 12, Post-Decree Litigation.)

Proof of Service

The petitioner must file proof of service with the court. If the respondent waived service, the waiver is filed. If the respondent was personally served, the affidavit of service is filed, and, finally, if the respondent was served by publication, the proof of publication is filed.

Respondent's Response with the Court

Once the respondent has been served with the summons and petition, they have 30 days to respond, not counting the day of service.[23]

Respondent Does Not Respond

If the respondent does not want to be involved in the action, they do not have to be. If an athletic event is scheduled and a team does not attend, they forfeit the game. In the same way, if an action is filed and the respondent does not appear, the respondent can be defaulted.[24] The petition for dissolution goes to judgment without his involvement.

> **EXAMPLE** Respondent has been personally served with the petition and summons. She and her husband have been married for less than one year. They are both well-compensated professionals. The petition only asks for a judgment of dissolution. It does not ask for an award of spousal maintenance or an allocation of property. Respondent decides there's nothing worth fighting for and does not respond. Petitioner's attorney files a motion for default and the matter is set for prove-up. (See Chapter 10, Discovery, Pretrial, and Trial.)

Respondent Does Respond

Appearance

If the respondent wants to be involved, the respondent or his attorney prepares an appearance. The appearance is e-filed, and the respondent's attorney either pays the filing fee or requests a fee waiver. As of this publication, the fee for an appearance is $218 in DuPage County. The appearance and a notice of filing are mailed or emailed to the petitioner's attorney.[25]

Answer

While the respondent may request a bill of particulars,[26] or file a motion to dismiss the petition,[27] ordinarily, the respondent's pleading in response to the petition is an answer.[28] In their answer, the respondent responds to the allegations of fact made in the petition, either admitting, denying, or stating they lack the information necessary to answer the allegation.

> **EXAMPLE** In paragraph one, the Petition alleges Petitioner is 43 years of age, employed, and resides in Palatine, Cook County, Illinois. Because Respondent does not dispute the allegations, Respondent's answer is to admit.

The court accepts as true any allegations the respondent admits to, meaning the petitioner does not have to prove them at trial. Therefore, care must be taken in preparing an answer. While a petitioner should only allege one fact per paragraph, they might have alleged two. An admission to the paragraph would apply to both allegations.

> **EXAMPLE** The petition reads in paragraph three, "Respondent is 48 years of age, works at Hampton Motor Corporation, and earns $750,000 per year." In this case, Respondent is 48 years of age, works at Hampton Motor Corporation, but only earns $100,000 per year. In his answer, Respondent would admit being 48 years of age and working at Hampton Motor Corporation, but would deny the remaining allegations in the paragraph.

Counter-Petition for Dissolution

Any time before judgment is entered the petitioner may change their mind and withdraw the petition. When that happens, if the respondent wants to get divorced, the respondent has to start the process over by filing their own petition for dissolution.

To avoid this situation, many respondents file a counter-petition for dissolution against the petitioner along with their answer.[29] Then if a petitioner withdraws the petition, the case can be resolved on the respondent's counter-petition.

> **EXAMPLE** Petitioner files for divorce from Respondent and Respondent files a counter-petition. After a year of extensive litigation, the judge indicates at a pre-trial conference that Petitioner is unlikely to receive spousal maintenance from Respondent. Petitioner decides they are better off married, and withdraws the petition. The case can proceed on Respondent's counter-petition.

The counter-petition must be filed in the time allotted for the answer, that is, within 30 days.[30] If the respondent wants to file later in the case, they will have to ask the court's permission. Pursuant to Illinois Supreme Court Rule 183, "the court, for good cause shown, on motion after notice to the opposing party, may extend the time for filing any pleading ... which is required by the rules to be done within a limited period."[31]

EXAMPLE Presume that Respondent did not file a counter-petition. In that case, after a year of extensive litigation, if Petitioner withdraws the petition, Respondent must file a motion for leave to file a counter-petition. The burden will be on Respondent to show good reasons for not filing within the time limit.

The fee for the counter-petition is $125. Like the answer, it can be mailed or emailed to opposing counsel. Personal service is not required; the court already has jurisdiction over the petitioner.

Chapter Summary

Once family law litigants have chosen an action to pursue, their matter moves through the court system from the first filing to final judgment according to rules contained in the Illinois Code of Civil Procedure and Illinois Supreme Court Rules.

The petitioner initiates an action by filing a petition. For the court to have jurisdiction over the respondent, the respondent must have such contact with Illinois to anticipate being sued there. Residency in the state or committing any of the acts in the "long-arm statute" provides sufficient contact. Then, notice of the action must be given to the respondent. Personal service gives the court *in personam* jurisdiction over the respondent. The Code provides various methods to obtain personal service, including waiver, hand delivery, and posting. If the respondent cannot be personally served, they may be served by publication, which gives the court *in rem* jurisdiction. With *in rem* jurisdiction the court has authority to terminate the marriage; however, it does not have authority to divide the property.

Once the respondent has been notified of the action against them, they can decide whether to be involved or not. If the respondent does not respond, the petitioner can move for a default judgment. If the respondent chooses to be involved, they must file an appearance within 30 days of the service of summons. In the initial pleading, called an "answer," the respondent admits or denies the allegations contained in the petition. Along with an answer, many respondents file a counter-petition for dissolution of marriage.

Key Terms

Petition

Verification

Summons

Dissolution Stay

Venue

Jurisdiction

Minimum Contacts

Long-Arm Statute

In personam jurisdiction

In rem jurisdiction

Default Judgment

Appearance

Answer

Counter-Petition for Dissolution

Discussion Questions

1. Why did the General Assembly offer the joint simplified option for the dissolution of marriage? When might it be useful?
2. Recognizing the number of litigants who are self-represented, the Illinois Supreme Court issued standard forms. Are the forms accessible to someone without a legal education?
3. The statutory requirements for a fee waiver are provided at 735 ILCS 5/5-105. Should parties who satisfy the statutory requirements be denied a waiver because they hired an attorney to represent them?
4. Does the mutual restraining language on a domestic relations summons provide enough protection for the parties and their minor children? Would a violent respondent take it seriously?
5. Some states allow service on the respondent through social media, such as Facebook. Would this satisfy *in personam* jurisdiction? What would the petitioner use to provide proof of service with the court?
6. Personal service may be made on an individual over 13 years of age at the respondent's home. What if the petitioner answers the door? Does service on the petitioner satisfy service on the respondent?

7. Without *in personam* jurisdiction, the court cannot award property, yet the court can determine parental responsibilities. Aren't children a more important interest than property?
8. How should the court respond when a respondent is living in a foreign country and a local newspaper publication cannot be expected to notify him? Is it fair for the action against him to proceed when he cannot possibly know about it? On the other hand, is it fair to keep the petitioner trapped in the marriage?
9. What can a petitioner do to demonstrate they have tried to find the respondent, as required in support of a motion for service by publication?

Forms

1. Petition for Dissolution of Marriage

   https://ilcourtsaudio.blob.core.windows.net/antilles-resources/resources/f266290e-4d68-40fa-bc34-5d92233cc0c4/DWC%20Petition%20for%20Dissolution%20Marriage%20Civil%20Union.pdf
2. Joint Simplified Petition

   https://18thjudicial.org/18thJudicial/download/3257
3. Joint Simplified Affidavit, DuPage

   https://18thjudicial.org/18thJudicial/download/3258
4. Domestic Relations Summons

   https://ilcourtsaudio.blob.core.windows.net/antilles-resources/resources/2b052cc8-5066-4ffb-a678-e17edd400ef6/DIV%20Summons.pdf
5. County Specific forms, as provided by local court rules.

   https://cic.countyofkane.org/eForms/P1-CI-001-E.pdf
6. Fee Waiver

   https://ilcourtsaudio.blob.core.windows.net/antilles-resources/resources/52beec8c-25fc-4d0f-bc56-82a93b68d395/FW-CIV%20Application.pdf
7. Order for Fee Waiver

   https://ilcourtsaudio.blob.core.windows.net/antilles-resources/resources/aeb7187c-60d8-4245-b05c-7610a6745e56/FW-CIV%20Order.pdf
8. Appearance

   https://ilcourtsaudio.blob.core.windows.net/antilles-resources/resources/ea73b648-a088-4ca8-81cd-b8bc00c7da37/DIV%20Divorce%20Entry%20of%20Appearance%20Military%20Notice.pdf

9. Answer

   https://ilcourtsaudio.blob.core.windows.net/antilles-resources/resources/1fcceee2-ffe2-4c90-b428-fc696cce4d57/ANS%20Response%20to%20Complaint%20Petition.pdf

Endnotes

1. 750 ILCS 5/105(c) (West, Westlaw Classic through P.A. 103-21 of the 2023 Reg. Sess.).
2. *Id.*
3. *Id.* § 452.
4. *Id.* § 403(a) (1-6).
5. 735 ILCS 5/2-603(b) (West, Westlaw Classic through P.A. 103-21 of the 2023 Reg. Sess.).
6. Ill. Sup. Ct. R. 138.
7. 750 ILCS 5/501.1(a).
8. U.S. Const. amend X.
9. Ill. Const. art. VI, § 9.
10. 750 ILCS 5/104.
11. Ill. Sup. Ct. Order M.R. 18368.
12. https//www.dupageco.org/CourtClerk/3080/ Fee Book
13. 735 ILCS 5/5-105.
14. Int'l Shoe Co. v. Washington, 326 U.S. 310 (1945).
15. 735 ILCS 5/2-209(a).
16. 735 ILCS 5.
17. *Id.* § 2-213.
18. *Id.* § 2-202 (a).
19. *Id.* § 2-203(a).
20. *Id.* § 2-203.1.
21. *Id.* § 2-206(a).
22. Estin v. Estin, 334 U.S. 541 (1948).
23. Ill. Sup. Ct. R. 181.
24. 735 ILCS 5/2-1301(d).
25. Ill. Sup. Ct. R. 11.
26. 735 ILCS 5/2-607(a).
27. *Id.* § 2-615(a) and *Id.* § 2-619(a).
28. *Id.* § 2-602.
29. *Id.* § 2-608(a).
30. *Id.* § 2-608(b).
31. Ill. Sup. Ct. R. 183. *See also* 735 ILCS 5/2-1007.

1. PETITION FOR DISSOLUTION OF MARRIAGE

This form is approved by the Illinois Supreme Court and is required to be accepted in all Illinois Circuit Courts.

STATE OF ILLINOIS, CIRCUIT COURT ____ COUNTY	PETITION FOR DISSOLUTION OF MARRIAGE / CIVIL UNION (DIVORCE WITH CHILDREN)	*For Court Use Only*
Instructions ▾		
Directly above, enter the county where you will file this case.		
Enter your name as Petitioner.	**Petitioner** *(First, middle, last name)*	
Enter the name of your spouse as Respondent.	v.	
The Circuit Clerk will add a Case Number.	**Respondent** *(First, middle, last name)*	**Case Number**

1. **I am Petitioner in this case.**

In 2a, if you check "Yes," enter the date you started living in Illinois.

In 2b, if you check "Yes," enter the date Respondent started living in Illinois.

2. **I am providing the following information about where I live and where Respondent *(my spouse)* lives:**
   a. I live in Illinois
   ☐ Yes, since: ________________ *Date* ☐ No
   b. Respondent lives in Illinois
   ☐ Yes, since: ________________ *Date* ☐ No ☐ Do not know

In 3a, enter your age.

In 3b, check all boxes that apply to you. If you are employed, enter your job title and the name of your employer.

In 3c, if you want to go back to a former name, check "Yes" and enter that name.

3. **I am providing the following information about myself:**
   a. Age: ________
   b. I am employed *(check all that apply)*:
   ☐ Yes ☐ No ☐ I receive Social Security benefits
   I am employed as: ________________ *Job Title*
   I am employed by: ________________ *Employer Name*
   c. I would like to go back to a maiden or a former married name:
   ☐ Yes ☐ No
   Former name: ________________ *First* *Middle* *Last*

In 4a, enter Respondent's age.

In 4b, check the box that applies. Enter Respondent's current complete address if known.

In 4c, enter Respondent's current phone number.

4. **I am providing the following information about Respondent *(my spouse)*:**
   a. Age: ________
   b. I know Respondent's current address: ☐ Yes ☐ No
   Address: ________________ *Street, Apt #* *City* *State* *ZIP*
   c. Phone Number: ________________

In **4d**, check all boxes that apply to Respondent. If Respondent is employed, enter their job title and the name of their employer.
In **4e**, check the box that applies. If Respondent is on active duty with the military, you cannot use this form unless Respondent files an appearance.

d. Respondent is employed:
☐ Yes ☐ No ☐ Do not know
☐ Respondent receives Social Security benefits
Respondent is employed as: ______________________
Job Title
Respondent is employed by: ______________________
Employer Name

e. Respondent is currently on active duty as a member of the Armed Forces of the United States of America:
☐ Yes ☐ No ☐ Do not know

In **5**, check whether it is a marriage or civil union.
In **5a**, enter the date you were married/ united.
In **5b**, enter the county, state, and country where the marriage/ civil union happened.
In **5c**, check "Yes" if this is the first time you or Respondent have filed for divorce from each other.
In **5d**, enter the date you separated.
In **6a,** first check "Yes" if you are pregnant. Then say if the child is Respondent's.
In **6b,** first check "Yes" if Respondent is pregnant. Then say if the child is yours.

5. I am providing the following Information about the ☐ Marriage ☐ Civil Union:

a. We were married/united on: ______________
Date

b. We were married/united in: ______________________
County *State* *Country*

c. This is the first time that either Respondent or I have filed for dissolution of marriage or civil union in Illinois or any other state:
☐ Yes ☐ No

d. We have been separated since: ______________
Date

e. Irreconcilable differences have caused the irretrievable breakdown of the marriage or civil union.

6. I am providing the following information about children:

a. I am pregnant.
☐ Yes ☐ No
Respondent is the parent of the unborn child:
☐ Yes ☐ No ☐ Do not know

b. Respondent is pregnant.
☐ Yes ☐ No ☐ Do not know
I am the parent of the unborn child:
☐ Yes ☐ No ☐ Do not know

In **6c**, check "None" if you have no children with Respondent, who are under the age of 18. Otherwise, list the name and date of birth of each child in the box.

c. The minor children *(under the age of 18)* born to or adopted together by me and Respondent before or during our marriage/civil union are:
☐ None *(if you check this box, do not complete Sections 6 (d-g) or Section 7)*

	Name	Date of Birth
1.		
2.		
3.		
☐	I have listed additional minor children on the attached *Additional Minor Children* form.	

Enter the Case Number given by the Circuit Clerk: ____________________

In **6d**, check the box that applies to the children listed in **6c**.

If one or more of the children live with someone else, enter the first and last name of the non-parent, and the names of the children who live with the non-parent.

d. The minor children currently live:

☐ Primarily with me.

☐ Primarily with Respondent.

☐ With both of us.

☐ Not with either parent, but with someone else:

	Name of Non-Parent	Names of Children Living with the Non-Parent
1.		
2.		
3.		

Other places the minor children have lived in the last 5 years:

	City	State
1.		
2.		
3.		

In the past 5 years the children have lived with someone else and not with either parent:

☐ Yes ☐ No

	Name of Non-Parent	City	State
1.			
2.			
3.			

In **6e**, check "Yes" if the children listed in 6c have lived in Illinois for at least 6 months.

e. The minor children listed in Section 6c have lived in Illinois for the last 6 months:

☐ Yes ☐ No

In **6f**, check "None" if you have no children with Respondent who are 18 or older. Otherwise, list the name and age of each child 18 or older.

f. The adult children *(age 18 or older)* born to or adopted together by me and the Respondent before or during our marriage/civil union are:

☐ None

	Name	Age	Disabled	In School
1.			☐ Yes ☐ No	☐ Yes ☐ No
2.			☐ Yes ☐ No	☐ Yes ☐ No
3.			☐ Yes ☐ No	☐ Yes ☐ No
☐ I have listed additional adult children on the attached *Additional Adult Children* form.				

In **6g**, check "None" if the only children you had during the marriage/civil union are listed in **6c** and **6f**.

If you or Respondent separately had or adopted other children during the marriage/civil union, list their names and birthdates here.

Check the box to say whether the child belongs to you or Respondent.

g. The **other** children born to or adopted by either me or Respondent, but not both of us, during this marriage/civil union are:

☐ None

	Name	Date of Birth	Born to or Adopted by
1.			☐ Petitioner ☐ Respondent
2.			☐ Petitioner ☐ Respondent
3.			☐ Petitioner ☐ Respondent
☐ I have listed additional children on the attached *Additional Other Children* form.			

Enter the Case Number given by the Circuit Clerk: ______________________________

In **7a**, check the box that applies to the children listed in **6c**. Check "Yes" only if there is a court order giving someone else rights to the children or if there is a current court case in which someone else is asking for rights to the children.	**7. I am providing the following information about the care of the children:** a. There is another person, that is not Respondent or me, who claims to have an allocation of parental responsibility or parenting time *(custody/visitation rights)*: ☐ Yes ☐ No Information about the person claiming allocation of parental responsibility or parenting time: Name ______________________________ *First* *Last* Address: ______________________________ *Street, Apt #* *City* *State* *ZIP*
In **7b**, check the box that applies to the children listed in **6c**. If there is or was another court case, enter the county and state where it is or was and whether the case is still going on. If the case is still going on, enter the next court date.	b. I know of other court cases about the allocation of parental responsibility or parenting time: ☐ Yes ☐ No Information about the other court cases: Case Name: ______________________________ *Petitioner v. Respondent* Case Location: ______________________________ *County* *State* Case Number: ______________________________ This case is still ongoing: ☐ Yes ☐ No The next court date is: ____________________ *Date*
In **7c**, check the first box if you are attaching the *Parenting Plan* form. Check the second box if you will file it within 120 days of the date you file this *Petition*.	c. Allocation of parental responsibility: ☐ I have attached my *Parenting Plan* form to this *Petition* ☐ I will file my *Parenting Plan* form within 120 days of the date I file this *Petition*
In **8a**, check "Yes" if you or Respondent have unpaid debts from after the date of the marriage/civil union. Check "No" only if you are sure there are no unpaid debts.	**8. I am providing the following information about all of the debts that Respondent and I have after the date we got married/united *(both individually and as a couple)*:** a. Respondent and I have debts from the time of the marriage/civil union that are still owed *(either together or individually)*: ☐ Yes ☐ No
In **8b**, check "Yes" only if you and Respondent have agreed on who will pay which debts.	b. Respondent and I have already divided the debts from the time of the marriage/civil union that are still owed: ☐ Yes ☐ No
In **9a**, check "Yes" if either of you got any personal property after the date of the marriage/civil union. Check "No" only if you are sure there is no personal property.	**9. I am providing the following information about all of the personal property including bank accounts that Respondent and I own *(both individually and as a couple)*:** a. Respondent and I own personal property and/or bank accounts obtained during the marriage/civil union. ☐ Yes ☐ No b. Respondent and I have already divided the personal property and/or bank accounts obtained during the marriage/civil union. ☐ Yes ☐ No
In **9b**, check "Yes" only if you and Respondent have already divided all the personal property.	

Enter the Case Number given by the Circuit Clerk: ____________________

In **10a**, check "Yes" if together you and Respondent own a home, have a mortgage, or have a contract for deed.
In **10b**, check "Yes" if you own a home, have a mortgage, or have a contract for deed.
In **10c**, check "Yes" if Respondent owns a home, has a mortgage, or has a contract for deed.
In **11a,** check the box that applies to you.
In **11b,** check the box that applies to Respondent.
In **12**, check "Yes" if you have any claims that you are owed for money damages or injuries, whether you have filed the case or not.
In **13a**, check "Yes" if you can support yourself. Check "No" if you need support from Respondent.
In **13b**, check "Yes" if Respondent can support himself/herself.

10 I am providing the following information about real estate:

a. Respondent and I own or are buying real estate together:

☐ Yes ☐ No

b. I own or am buying real estate separately:

☐ Yes ☐ No

c. Respondent owns or is buying real estate separately:

☐ Yes ☐ No ☐ Do not know

11 I am providing the following information about pension/retirement accounts:

a. I have pension or retirement accounts *(including IRAs)*:

☐ Yes ☐ No

b. Respondent has pension or retirement accounts *(including IRAs)*:

☐ Yes ☐ No ☐ Do not know

12. I have a claim for money for injuries or damages that I have suffered *(worker's compensation, personal injury, accident, etc.)*:

☐ Yes ☐ No

13. I am providing the following information about maintenance *(also known as alimony)*:

a. I am able to support myself without maintenance:

☐ Yes ☐ No

b. Respondent is able to support himself/herself without maintenance:

☐ Yes ☐ No ☐ Do not know

I ASK THE COURT TO ORDER:

A. A *Judgment of Dissolution of Marriage/Civil Union (Divorce With Children)* for me and my spouse.

B. That the *Parenting Plan* for the minor children that I file be approved.

In **C**, check "Yes" if you want child support to be ordered.
In **D**, check "Yes" if you want support for an adult disabled child or for college expenses for an adult child.

C. Child support for the care or education of the minor children:

☐ Yes ☐ No

D. Support for the care or education of the adult children:

☐ Yes ☐ No

E. That I get to keep all of my non-marital/non-civil union property.

F. That Respondent gets to keep all of their non-marital/non-civil union property.

G A fair division of the marital/civil union property.

H. A fair division of the debts obtained during the marriage/civil union.

In **I**, check "Me" if you want to get maintenance from Respondent. Check "Respondent" if you want to pay maintenance to Respondent. Check "Neither" if you do not want to get or pay maintenance.	**I.** That maintenance be awarded to: ☐ Me ☐ Respondent ☐ Neither
In **J**, check "Yes" if you want to go back to using a former name.	**J.** That after the divorce I be allowed to return to using my former name: ☐ Yes ☐ No ☐ Not applicable
Under the Code of Civil Procedure, 735 ILCS 5/1-109, making a statement on this form that you know to be false is perjury, a Class 3 Felony.	**I certify that everything in the *Petition For Dissolution Of Marriage / Civil Union (Divorce with Children)* is true and correct. I understand that making a false statement on this form is perjury and has penalties provided by law under 735 ILCS 5/1-109.**
If you are completing this form on a computer, sign your name by typing it. If you are completing it by hand, sign and print your name.	/s/ ______________________ *Your Signature* ______________________ *Print Your Name* ______________________ *Telephone* ______________________ *Attorney # (if any)*
Enter your complete address, telephone number, and email address if you have one. If you need to keep your addresses secret from your spouse because of domestic violence, you may use another address. Those addresses must be ones at which you can receive mail about the case.	______________________ *Street Address* ______________________ *City, State, ZIP* ______________________ *Email*

GETTING COURT DOCUMENTS BY EMAIL: You should use an email account that you do not share with anyone else and that you check every day. If you do not check your email every day, you may miss important information, notice of court dates, or documents from other parties.

Print Form Save Form Reset Form

2. JOINT SIMPLIFIED PETITION

STATE OF ILLINOIS **UNITED STATES OF AMERICA** **COUNTY OF DU PAGE**
IN THE CIRCUIT COURT OF THE EIGHTEENTH JUDICIAL CIRCUIT

IN RE ☐ THE MARRIAGE OF
☐ CIVIL UNION OF

____
CO-PETITIONER NO. 1

vs

____
CO-PETITIONER NO. 2

____
CASE NUMBER

JOINT PETITION FOR SIMPLIFIED DISSOLUTION OF MARRIAGE/CIVIL UNION

File Stamp Here

Now come Co-Petitioners, without counsel and hereby petition this Honorable Court for a dissolution of marriage/civil union between them.

In support of this Petition for Dissolution of Marriage/Civil Union, the parties state as follows:

1. The co-petitioner No. 1 is presently ________ years of age, and is presently employed as a ____________________
   Co-Petitioner No. 1 resides at. ____

   Co-Petitioner No. 1 ☐ has ☐ has not resided in the State of Illinois for at least ninety (90) days immediately preceding the filing of the Petition for Dissolution of Marriage/Civil Union.

2. The co-petitioner No. 2 is presently ________ years of age, and is presently employed as a ____________________
   Co-Petitioner No. 2 resides at. ____

   Co-Petitioner No. 2 ☐ has ☐ has not resided in the State of Illinois for at least ninety (90) days immediately preceding the filing of the Petition for Dissolution of Marriage/Civil Union.

3. The parties have been married or in civil union for less than eight (8) years prior to the filing of this petition. They were married/civil union on ____________________ (month, day, year). The marriage/civil union was registered in

   ____________________ (county) ____________________ (state).

4. No children were born to the parties, nor were any children adopted during their relationship.
   (Type or print co-petitioner's No. 1 name) ________________________________, to her knowledge is not pregnant.

5. The parties have lived separate and apart for a continuous period in excess of six (6) months and irreconcilable differences have cause the irretrievable breakdown of their marriage/civil union. Efforts at reconciliation have failed and future attempts at reconciliation would be impractical and not in the best interest of the parties. The parties have signed an affidavit waiving the requirements for a continuous period living separate and apart in excess of two (2) years.
   The parties have lived separate and apart since (month, day, year) ________________________________.

6. Neither party is dependent on the other party for support (also known as alimony or maintenance), or each party is willing to waive the right to support. Both parties understand that consulting with attorneys may help determine eligibility for support. The parties waive any rights to maintenance.

7. Neither party has any interest in real property (real estate).

8. The parties have disclosed to each other all assets and their tax returns for all years of the marriage/civil union.

9. Neither party has a gross annualized income in excess of $20,000.

   Co-Petitioner's No. 2 gross annual income from all sources is $ ____________________.

   Co-Petitioner's No. 1 gross annual income from all sources is $ ____________________.

   The total annual income of the parties is less than $35,000.

10 The total fair market value of all joint property, after deducting all encumbrances, is less than $10,000, and the parties have executed a written agreement dividing all assets in excess of $100 in value and allocating responsibility for debts and liabilities between the parties. A copy of the written agreement, signed by both parties is filed with this petition.

11. (Optional) (type or print former/maiden name) ______________________________ former/maiden name/names was (type or print former/maiden name). ______________________________

Wherefore, the parties pray as follows:

A. That the parties be awarded a Judgment of Dissolution of Marriage/Civil Union dissolving the bonds of marriage/civil union existing between them.

B. That the written agreement of the parties dividing joint assets, debts and liabilities, a copy of which is filed with this petition, be incorporated into the final order and judgment of this Court granting the petition for dissolution of marriage/civil union.

C. (Optional) (type or print wife's name) ______________________________ be restored to the former/maiden name (type or print former/maiden name) ______________________________.

D. That this Court grant the parties such other and further relief as may be just.

______________________________	______________________________
Co-Petitioner's No. 1 Signature	Co-Petitioner's No. 2 Signature
Name: ______________________	Name: ______________________
Address: ______________________	Address: ______________________
City/State/Zip: ______________________	City/State/Zip: ______________________
Telephone Number: ______________________	Telephone Number: ______________________

VERIFICATION

STATE OF ILLINOIS)
) SS
COUNTY OF DU PAGE)

I, ____, being first duly sworn upon oath, depose and say that I have read the foregoing Joint Petition, understand the contents thereof, and believe the same to be true and correct to the best of my knowledge.

____
Co-Petitioner No. 1 Signature

Sworn and Subscribed before me

____
Date

____
Notary Public

I, ____, being first duly sworn upon oath, depose and say that I have read the foregoing Joint Petition, understand the contents thereof, and believe the same to be true and correct to the best of my knowledge.

____
Co-Petitioner No. 2 Signature

Sworn and Subscribed before me

____
Date

____
Notary Public

3. JOINT SIMPLIFIED AFFIDAVIT, DUPAGE

JOINT AFFIDAVIT (SIMPLIFIED DISSOLUTION OF MARRIAGE/CIVIL UNION) 3258 (Rev 12/20)

STATE OF ILLINOIS **UNITED STATES OF AMERICA** **COUNTY OF DU PAGE**
IN THE CIRCUIT COURT OF THE EIGHTEENTH JUDICIAL CIRCUIT

IN RE ☐ THE MARRIAGE OF
☐ CIVIL UNION OF

____
CO-PETITIONER NO. 1
vs

____
CO-PETITIONER NO. 2

____
CASE NUMBER

File Stamp Here

JOINT AFFIDAVIT REGARDING SEPARATION OF THE PARTIES DIVISION OF PROPERTY AND WAIVER OF BIFURCATED HEARING

Co-Petitioners, being first sworn on their oaths, depose and state as follows:

1. That irreconcilable differences have caused the irretrievable breakdown of their marriage/civil union.

2. That all efforts at reconciliation of the differences between the parties have heretofore failed and future attempts at reconciliation would be impractical and not in the best interest of the parties

3. That the parties have lived separate and apart for a continuous period of more than six (6) months prior to the date of this affidavit, having separated on or about (month, day, year) ______________________ and have remained living separate for all times thereafter.

4. (a) That each of the parties hereto expressly waive the requirement that the continuous period of living separate and apart be in excess of two (2) years in order for the Court to enter a Dissolution of Marriage/Civil Union based upon irreconcilable differences which have cause the irretrievable breakdown of their marriage: and

   (b) Each of the parties further stipulates that the requirement shall be reduced to a period of only in excess of six (6) months rather than in excess of two (2) years as provided by Section 401(a)(2) of the Illinois Marriage and Dissolution of Marriage Act.

5. That the joint property belonging to the parties has been divided according to the terms of the written agreement of the parties filed with the Petition for Dissolution of Marriage/Civil Union in this cause, and that the parties have executed all documents required to carry out the agreement.

6. That the parties waive any right either may have to a bifurcated hearing of this cause.

7. That each of the parties represents that the signing of this Affidavit is their individual sole, voluntary act.

______________________	______________________
Co-Petitioner No. 1 (print name)	Co-Petitioner No. 2 (print name)
______________________	______________________
Co-Petitioner No.1 Signature	Co-Petitioner No. 2 Signature

VERIFICATION

STATE OF ILLINOIS)

) SS

COUNTY OF DU PAGE)

I, ____ , being first duly sworn upon oath, depose and say that I have read the foregoing Joint Affidavit, understand the contents thereof, and believe the same to be true and correct to the best of my knowledge.

____

Co-Petitioner No.1 Signature

Signed and sworn to before me

____

Date

____

Notary Public

STATE OF ILLINOIS)

) SS

COUNTY OF DU PAGE)

I, ____ , being first duly sworn upon oath, depose and say that I have read the foregoing Joint Affidavit, understand the contents thereof, and believe the same to be true and correct to the best of my knowledge.

____

Co-Petitioner No. 2 Signature

Signed and sworn to before me

____

Date

____

Notary Public

4. DOMESTIC RELATIONS SUMMONS

This form is approved by the Illinois Supreme Court and must be accepted in all Illinois Courts.
Forms are free at ilcourts.info/forms.

STATE OF ILLINOIS, CIRCUIT COURT __________ COUNTY	**SUMMONS** **PETITION FOR DISSOLUTION OF MARRIAGE/CIVIL UNION**	*For Court Use Only*
Instructions ▾		
Enter above the county name where the case was filed.	____________________ **Petitioner** *(First, middle, last name)*	
Enter your name as Petitioner.	v.	
Enter the name of your spouse/partner as Respondent.	____________________ **Respondent** *(First, middle, last name)*	____________ **Case Number**
Enter the Case Number given by the Circuit Clerk.	☐ **Alias Summons** *(Check this box if this is not the 1st Summons issued for this Respondent.)*	

IMPORTANT: You have been sued.

- Read all documents attached to this *Summons*.
- You MUST file an official document with the court within the time stated on this *Summons* called an *Appearance* and a document called an *Answer/Response*. If you do not file an *Appearance* and *Answer/Response* on time, the judge may decide the case without hearing from you. This is called "default." As a result, you could lose the case.
- All documents referred to in this Summons can be found at ilcourts.info/forms. Other documents may be available from your local Circuit Court Clerk's office or website.
- After you fill out the necessary documents, you need to electronically file (e-file) them with the court. To e-file, you must create an account with an e-filing service provider. For more information, go to ilcourts.info/efiling. If you cannot e-file, you can get an exemption that allows you to file in-person or by mail.
- You may be charged filing fees, but if you cannot pay them, you can file an Application for Waiver of Court Fees.
- It is possible that the court will allow you to attend the first court date in this case in-person or remotely by video or phone. Contact the Circuit Court Clerk's office or visit the Court's website to find out whether this is possible and, if so, how to do this.
- Need help? Call or text Illinois Court Help at 833-411-1121 or go to ilcourthelp.gov for information about going to court, including how to fill out and file documents. You can also get free legal information and legal referrals at illinoislegalaid.org.
- ¿Necesita ayuda? Llame o envíe un mensaje de texto a Illinois Court Help al 833-411-1121, o visite ilcourthelp.gov para obtener información sobre los casos de la corte y cómo completar y presentar formularios.

In **1a**, enter the name and address of Respondent.

In **1b**, enter a second address for Respondent, if you have one.

In **1c**, check how you are sending your documents to Respondent.

1. Respondent's address and service information

a. Respondent's primary address/information for service:
Name *(First, Middle, Last)*: __________
Street Address, Unit #: __________
City, State, ZIP: __________
Telephone: __________ Email: __________

b. If you have more than one address where Respondent might be found, list that here:
Name *(First, Middle, Last)*: __________
Street Address, Unit #: __________
City, State, ZIP: __________
Telephone: __________ Email: __________

c. Method of service on Respondent
☐ Sheriff ☐ Sheriff outside Illinois __________ *County & State*
☐ Special process server ☐ Licensed private detective

Enter the Case Number given by the Circuit Clerk: ____________________

In **2**, Enter your name, address, phone number and email address, if you have one. If you do not want your spouse to know your address because of domestic violence, you may use another address. That address must be one at which you can receive mail about the case.

2. Contact information for the Petitioner:

Name *(First, Middle, Last)*: ____________________

Street Address, Unit #: ____________________

City, State, ZIP: ____________________

Telephone: ____________________ Email: ____________________

GETTING COURT DOCUMENTS BY EMAIL: You should use an email account that you do not share with anyone else and that you check every day. If you do not check your email every day, you may miss important information, notice of court dates, or documents from other parties.

Important information for the person getting this form:

You have been sued. Read all of the documents attached to this *Summons*.
To participate in the case, you must follow the instructions listed below. If you do not, the court may decide the case without hearing from you and you could lose the case. *Appearance* and *Answer/Response* forms can be found at: ilcourts.info/forms.

In **3a**, fill out the address of the court building where the Respondent may file or e-file their *Appearance* and *Answer/ Response*.

3. Instructions for person receiving this *Summons* (Respondent):

a. To respond to this *Summons*, you must file *Appearance* and *Answer/Response* forms with the court within 30 days after you have been served (*not counting the day of service*) by e-filing or at:

Address: ____________________

City, State, ZIP: ____________________

b. A DISSOLUTION ACTION STAY IS IN FULL FORCE AND EFFECT UPON SERVICE OF THIS SUMMONS. THE CONDITIONS OF THE STAY ARE SET FORTH ON THE BOTTOM OF THIS PAGE. ANY PERSON WHO FAILS TO OBEY THE DISSOLUTION ACTION STAY MAY BE SUBJECT TO PUNISHMENT FOR CONTEMPT.

In **3c**, fill out the clerk's phone number and website.
All of this information is available from the Circuit Clerk. Find their phone number at ilcourts.info/CircuitClerks.

c. You may be able to attend court by phone or video conference. This is called a "Remote Appearance."

Call the Circuit Clerk at: ____________________ or visit their website
Circuit Clerk's phone number

at: ____________________ to find out more about how to do this.
Website

STOP!
The Circuit Clerk will fill in this section.

Witness this Date: ____________________ *Seal of Court*

Clerk of the Court: ____________________

This *Summons* must be served within 30 days of the witness date.

STOP!
The officer or process server will fill in the Date of Service.

Date of Service: ____________________
(Date to be entered by an officer or process server on the copy of this Summons left with the Defendant or other person.)

CONDITIONS OF DISSOLUTION ACTION STAY
750 ILCS 5/501.1

(a) Upon service of a summons and petition or praecipe filed under the Illinois Marriage and Dissolution of Marriage Act or upon the filing of the respondent's appearance in the proceeding, whichever first occurs, a dissolution action stay shall be in effect against both parties, without bond or further notice, until a final judgement is entered, the proceeding is dismissed, or until further order of the court:

(1) restraining both parties from physically abusing, harassing, intimidating, striking, or interfering with the personal liberty of the other party or the minor children of either party; and

(2) restraining both parties from concealing a minor child of either party from the child's other parent. The restraint provided in this subsection (a) does not operate to make unavailable any of the remedies provided in the Illinois Domestic Violence Act of 1986.

(b) (Blank).

(c) (Blank).

(d) (Blank).

(e) In a proceeding filed under this Act, the summons shall provide notice of the entry of the automatic dissolution action stay in a form as required by applicable rules.

This form is approved by the Illinois Supreme Court and must be accepted in all Illinois Courts.
Forms are free at ilcourts.info/forms.

STATE OF ILLINOIS, CIRCUIT COUNTY __________ COUNTY	PROOF OF SERVICE OF SUMMONS AND PETITION FOR DISSOLUTION OF MARRIAGE/CIVIL UNION	*For Court Use Only*
Instructions		
Enter above the county name where the case was filed.		
Enter your name as Petitioner.	______________________ **Petitioner** *(First, middle, last name)*	
Enter the name of your spouse/partner as Respondent.	v.	
Enter the Case Number given by the Circuit Clerk.	______________________ **Respondent** *(First, middle, last name)* ☐ **Alias Summons** *(Check this box if this is not the 1st Summons issued for this Respondent.)*	______________________ **Case Number**

****Stop. Do not complete the form. The sheriff or special process server will fill in the form.****

My name ______________________ **and I state**
First, Middle, Last

☐ **that I served the *Summons* and *Petition for Dissolution of Marriage/Civil Union* on the Respondent**
______________________ **as follows:**
First, Middle, Last

☐ Personally on the Respondent:
☐ Male ☐ Female ☐ Non-Binary Approx. Age: ________ Race: ________
On this ____________ at this time: ________ ☐ a.m. ☐ p.m.
Address, Unit ______________________
City, State, ZIP: ______________________

☐ On someone else at the Respondent's home who is at least 13 years old and is a family member or lives there:
On this ____________ at this time: ________ ☐ a.m. ☐ p.m.
Address, Unit ______________________
City, State, ZIP: ______________________
And left it with: ______________________
First, Middle, Last
☐ Male ☐ Female ☐ Non-Binary Approx. Age: ________ Race: ________
and by sending a copy to Respondent in a postage-paid, sealed envelope to the above address on __________ , 20 ______ .

Enter the Case Number given by the Circuit Clerk: ____________________

☐ **I was not able to serve the *Summons* and Petition on Respondent:**

____ .
First, Middle, Last

I made the following attempts to serve the *Summons* and *Petition* on the Respondent:

1. On this date: ______________ at this time: ________ ☐ a.m. ☐ p.m.
   Address: ____________________
   City, State, ____________________
   Other information about service ____________________

2. On this date: ______________ at this time: ________ ☐ a.m. ☐ p.m.
   Address: ____________________
   City, State, ZIP: ____________________
   Other information about service attempt: ____________________

3. On this date: ______________ at this time: ________ ☐ a.m. ☐ p.m.
   Address: ____________________
   City, State, ZIP: ____________________
   Other information about service attempt: ____________________

DO NOT complete this section. The sheriff or private process server will complete it.

If you are a special process server, sheriff outside Illinois, or licensed private detective, your signature certifies that everything on the *Proof of Service of Summons and Petition for Dissolution of Marriage/Civil Union* is true and correct to the best of your knowledge. You understand that making a false statement on this form could be perjury.

Under the Code of Civil Procedure, 735 ILCS 5/1-109, making a statement on this form that you know to be false is perjury, a Class 3 Felony.

By:

____

Signature by: ☐ Sheriff
☐ Sheriff outside Illinois:

____
County and State
☐ Special process server
☐ Licensed private detective

____
Print Name

FEES

Service and Return: $ ________
Miles ________ $ ________
Total $ ________

If *Summons* is served by licensed private detective or private detective agency:
License Number: ____________________

Print Form Save Form Reset Form

16th JUDICIAL CIRCUIT
NEW CASE INFORMATION SHEET

Case No. ______________________

Plaintiff/Petitioner	Defendant/Respondent	File Stamp

All Parties must be listed on new case filing sheet, or on an attached sheet following the same format as below. (PLEASE TYPE OR PRINT)

1. Case Type __________ 2. Description: ______________________________
3. Claim Amount ______________ 4. Jury ________ (yes/no)
5. Return date/time (where return date summons is used): ______________________
6. Plaintiff Attorney's ARDC number: ______________________
   Attorney's Name: ______________________ (Last, First, MI)
7. **First named Plaintiff:** ______________________
   Address: ______________________
   City: ______________ State/Zip Code: ______________ Phone #: ______________
8. Additional Plaintiff/AKA/DBA/FKA/NKA/Other: ______________________
   Address: ______________________
   City: ______________ State/Zip Code: ______________ Phone #: ______________
9. Additional Plaintiff/AKA/DBA/FKA/NKA/Other: ______________________
   Address: ______________________
   City: ______________ State/Zip Code: ______________ Phone #: ______________

---

10. **First named Defendant:** ______________________
    Address: ______________________
    City: ______________ State/Zip Code: ______________ Phone #: ______________
11. Additional Defendant/AKA/DBA/FKA/NKA/Other: ______________________
    Address: ______________________
    City: ______________ State/Zip Code: ______________ Phone #: ______________
12. Additional Defendant/AKA/DBA/FKA/NKA/Other: ______________________
    Address: ______________________
    City: ______________ State/Zip Code: ______________ Phone #: ______________

P1-CI-001 (03/19)

6. APPLICATION FOR FEE WAIVER

This form is approved by the Illinois Supreme Court and is required to be accepted in all Illinois Circuit Courts.

STATE OF ILLINOIS, CIRCUIT COURT ____________ COUNTY	APPLICATION FOR WAIVER OF COURT FEES	*For Court Use Only*
Instructions ▾		
Directly above, enter the name of the county where the case was filed.		
Enter the name of the person who started the lawsuit as Plaintiff/Petitioner.	____________ **Plaintiff / Petitioner** *(First, middle, last name)*	
Enter the name of the person being charged as Defendant/ Respondent.	v. ____________	
Enter the Case Number given by the Circuit Clerk or leave this blank if you do not have one.	**Defendant /Respondent** *(First, middle, last name)*	____________ **Case Number**

NOTE:	If you are completing this form on behalf of a minor or an incompetent adult, provide that person's information on this form instead of your own information.

Instructions	
In **1a**, enter your full name	Pursuant to Illinois Supreme Court Rule 298 and 735 ILCS 5/5-105, I state:
In **1b**, only enter the year you were born. DO NOT enter your entire date of birth.	**1. I believe I cannot afford to pay the court fees, costs and charges in this case and I am providing the following information about myself:** a. Name: ____________ *First* *Middle* *Last* b. Year of Birth: ____________
In **1c**, enter your complete current address.	c. Street Address: ____________ City, State, ZIP: ____________
In **2a**, enter the number of people age 18 and older living in your house who you support. Support means that the people rely on you financially.	**2. I am providing the following information about people who live with me:** a. I support __________ adults *(not counting myself)* who live with me. b. I support __________ children under 18 who live with me.
In **2b**, enter the number of people under age 18 living in your house who you support.	**3. I am receiving 1 or more of the benefits listed below:** ☐ Yes ☐ No
In **3**, check "Yes" if you are currently receiving 1 or more of the benefits listed below. Be prepared to provide proof that you are currently receiving 1 of these benefits.	• Supplemental Security Income (SSI) (Not Social Security) • Aid to the Aged, Blind and Disabled (AABD) • Temporary Assistance to Needy Families (TANF) • SNAP (Food Stamps) • General Assistance (GA), Transitional Assistance, or State Children and Family Assistance
If you check "Yes" in **3**, skip **4** and sign the form. You do not have to complete **4**.	****If you answered "Yes" in section 3, you qualify for a fee waiver under 735 ILCS 5/5-105(a)(2)(i) and (b)(1). You can skip section 4 and sign the form.****

Enter the Case Number given by the Circuit Clerk: ______________________

> In **4a**, check "Yes" if you have applied for at least 1 of the benefits listed in section 3.
>
> In **4b**, check the box for each type of money you have received in the past month. Also enter the gross (before taxes) amount for each type.
>
> Under **Other** in **4b** and **4c**, include any money received from family or friends.
>
> In **4c**, check the box for each type of money you have received in the past 12 months. Also enter the gross (before taxes) amount for each type.

4. I checked "No" in section 3, so I am providing the following financial information:

a. I have a pending application for 1 or more of the benefits listed in section 3:
☐ Yes ☐ No

b. I received the following money in the past month. *(check all that apply)*
☐ My employment: $__________ ☐ Social Security (not SSI): $__________
☐ Child support: $__________ ☐ Unemployment: $__________
☐ Pension: $__________
☐ Money from other household members: $__________
☐ Other *(list type and amount)*: ______________________ $__________
☐ No income
Total of all money received in the past month: $__________

c. I received the following total amount of money in the past 12 months. *(check all that apply)*
☐ My employment: $__________ ☐ Social Security (not SSI): $__________
☐ Child support: $__________ ☐ Unemployment: $__________
☐ Pension: $__________
☐ Money from other household members: $__________
☐ Other *(list type and amount)*: ______________________ $__________
☐ No income
Total of all money received in the past 12 months: $__________

> In **4d**, check all of your debts and expenses for the past month and list the amount of money you pay each month for that expense.

d. My current monthly debts and expenses are listed below. *(check all that apply)*
☐ Rent: $__________ per month
☐ Home Mortgage: $__________ per month
☐ Other Mortgage: $__________ per month
☐ Utilities: $__________ per month
☐ Food: $__________ per month
☐ Medical: $__________ per month
☐ Car Loan: $__________ per month
☐ Childcare: $__________ per month
☐ Child Support: $__________ per month
☐ Other expenses not listed above *(list type and amount)*: ______________________
______________________ $__________
☐ Other debts not listed above *(list type and amount)*: ______________________
______________________ $__________
☐ I have no expenses

Total of all expenses: $__________ per month

> In **4e**, check all of the items owned by you and list the value of each item. If you own real estate, include the total you owe on any mortgage.
>
> Be prepared to provide documents showing your income, value of belongings (including real estate) and expense information when you file your forms.

e. I have the belongings listed below. *(check all that apply)*
☐ Bank accounts and cash totaling: $__________
☐ Home worth: $__________
The total I owe on my home mortgage is: $__________
☐ Other real estate, not including the house I live in, worth: $__________
The total I owe on my other mortgage is: $__________
☐ 1st vehicle worth: $__________ The 1st vehicle is paid off: ☐ Yes ☐ No
☐ 2nd vehicle worth: $__________ The 2nd vehicle is paid off: ☐ Yes ☐ No
☐ Other *(list items and value)*: ______________________ $__________
☐ None of the above

5 is optional. In **5**, list any reason why you or your family would face hardship if you have to pay the fees.

5. *(Optional)* My family or I would face substantial hardship if I have to pay the fees, costs, and charges because: _______________

____

____

____

____

Under Illinois Supreme Court Rule 137, your signature means that you have read the document, that to the best of your belief, it is true and correct and that you are not filing it for an improper purpose, such as to cause delay.

If you are completing this form on a computer, sign your name by typing it. If you are completing it by hand, sign and print your name.

If you are filling out this form for a minor or incompetent adult, sign and print your name and state your relationship to that person.

Enter your complete address, telephone number, and email address, if you have one.

/s/ _______________
Your Signature

____
Street Address

____
Print Your Name

____
City, State, ZIP

____
Relationship to Minor or Incompetent Adult (if applicable)

____
Telephone

____
Attorney # (if any)

____
Email

GETTING COURT DOCUMENTS BY EMAIL: You should use an email account that you do not share with anyone else and that you check every day. If you do not check your email every day, you may miss important information, notice of court dates, or documents from other parties.

7. ORDER FOR FEE WAIVER

This form is approved by the Illinois Supreme Court and is required to be accepted in all Illinois Circuit Courts.

STATE OF ILLINOIS, CIRCUIT COURT ______________ COUNTY	ORDER FOR WAIVER OF COURT FEES	*For Court Use Only*

Instructions ▼		
Directly above, enter the name of the county where the case was filed.		
Enter the name of the person who started the lawsuit as Plaintiff/Petitioner.	______________ **Plaintiff / Petitioner** *(First, middle, last name)*	
Enter the name of the person being sued as Defendant/Respondent	v.	
Enter the Case Number given by the Circuit Clerk or leave this blank if you do not have one.	______________ **Defendant / Respondent** *(First, middle, last name)*	______________ **Case Number**

Enter your full name as "Applicant."

Applicant Name: ______________________________
First *Middle* *Last*

DO NOT check any boxes or fill in any more blanks on this form. The judge will complete the rest of the form.

The Court having reviewed the *Application for Waiver of Court Fees* hereby finds:

1. ☐ The applicant **qualifies** for a **full (100%)** waiver of all fees, costs, and charges because:
   a. ☐ The applicant receives means-based government assistance under one or more of the following programs:
      - Supplemental Security Income (SSI) (Not Social Security)
      - Aid to the Aged, Blind and Disabled (AABD)
      - Temporary Assistance for Needy Families (TANF)
      - SNAP (Food Stamps)
      - General Assistance (GA), Transitional Assistance, or State Children and Family Assistance

      OR

   b. ☐ The applicant's personal income is **125%** or less of the current poverty level as established by the U.S. Dept. of Health & Human Services and the Applicant's non-exempt assets under 735 ILCS 5/12-901 and 735 ILCS 5/12-1001 are such that the applicant is unable to pay the fees, costs, or charges;
      OR

   c. ☐ Payments of fees, costs, and charges would result in substantial hardship to the applicant or his or her family.

2. ☐ The applicant **qualifies** for a **partial** *(75%, 50%, or 25%)* waiver of all fees, costs, and charges because the applicant's household income is:
   ☐ more than **125%** but not greater than **150%** (*75% waived*);
   ☐ more than **150%** but not greater than **175%** (*50% waived*);
   ☐ more than **175%** but not greater than **200%** (*25% waived*)
   of the current poverty level as established by the US Dept. of Health & Human Services and the Applicant's non-exempt assets under 735 ILCS 5/12-901 and 735 ILCS 5/12-1001 are such that the applicant is unable to pay the fees, costs, or charges.

3. ☐ There is a factual issue about the applicant's entitlement to a fee waiver. The nature of the factual issue is: ______________________________

Enter the Case Number given by the Circuit Clerk: ______________________

4. ☐ The applicant **does not qualify** for a fee waiver because *(must state specific reason)*:

____

____

IT IS HEREBY ORDERED:

A ☐ *Application for Waiver of Court Fees* is **GRANTED**, effective on the filing date of the *Application for Waiver of Court Fees.*

i. ☐ The applicant qualifies for a **full waiver**, and may participate in this case without payment of fees, costs, or charges.

ii. ☐ The applicant qualifies for a **partial fee waiver** as follows:

☐ **75%** of all fees, costs, and charges **are waived** (*and the applicant must pay 25% of all fees, costs, and charges*).

☐ **50%** of all fees, costs, and charges **are waived** (*and the applicant must pay 50% of all fees, costs, and charges*).

☐ **25%** of all fees, costs, and charges **are waived** (*and the applicant must pay 75% of all fees, costs, and charges*).

☐ The applicant must pay fees, costs, and charges currently due by: __________
Date

☐ Upon good cause shown, the applicant may make payments as follows *(describe deferral, installment plan, or other reasonable terms)*: __________

____

____

This order expires one year from the date of this order. The applicant may reapply before or after the expiration date. Fees, costs, and charges included in this waiver are: filing, service of process, publication, mediation, guardian ad litem, and any other fee listed in 735 ILCS 5/5-105(a)(2)(1).

B. ☐ *Application for Waiver of Court Fees* is **SET FOR HEARING** on

__________ at __________
Date *Time*

☐ in person at ______________________________________
Courthouse address *Courtroom*

☐ remotely by telephone at ______________________________
Call-in number for telephone remote appearance

☐ remotely by video conference at ______________________________
Video conference website

____.
Video conference log-in information (meeting ID, password, etc)

The applicant must bring the following **documents** to the hearing:

____

____

C. ☐ *Application for Waiver of Court Fees* is **DENIED**.
The applicant must pay all fees, costs, and charges currently due by: __________
Date

DO NOT complete this section. The judge will sign and date here.

ENTERED:

______________________________ ______________________________
Judge *Date*

Print Form Save Form Reset Form

8. APPEARANCE

This form is approved by the Illinois Supreme Court and is required to be accepted in all Illinois Circuit Courts.

STATE OF ILLINOIS, CIRCUIT COURT ______________ COUNTY	**ENTRY OF APPEARANCE** (PETITION FOR DISSOLUTION OF MARRIAGE/CIVIL UNION)	*For Court Use Only*
Instructions ▾		
Directly above, enter the county where this case was filed.		
Enter the name of the person who filed this case as Petitioner.	**Petitioner** *(First, middle, last name)* v.	
Enter the name of the Respondent.		
Enter the Case Number given by the Circuit Clerk.	**Respondent** *(First, middle, last name)*	**Case Number**

In **1**, enter your full name.	1. I, ______________________ (*First* *Middle* *Last*), am the Respondent and enter my appearance in this case.
	2. I want notice of any court dates in this case to be sent to me at the address below.
In **3**, check "Yes" if you are currently on active duty in the military or were released or terminated from active duty in the last 90 days or "No" if you are not.	3. I am currently on active duty in the U.S. military or I was released or terminated from active duty within the last 90 days: ☐ Yes* ☐ No
IMPORTANT:	If you are currently on active duty with the U.S. Military you have important rights that you may be giving up by signing this document. See 50 USC §§ 3931 to 3938a for more information or contact the Illinois Armed Forces Legal Aid Network at 855-452-3526 to speak to an attorney.
Under the Code of Civil Procedure, 735 ILCS 5/1-109, making a statement on this form that you know to be false is perjury, a Class 3 Felony.	**I certify that everything in the *Entry Of Appearance* is true and correct. I understand that making a false statement on this form is perjury and has penalties provided by law under 735 ILCS 5/1-109.** /s/ ______ *Your Signature* ______ *Street Address*
If you are completing this form on a computer, sign your name by typing it. If you are completing it by hand, sign and print your name.	______ *Print Your Name* ______ *City, State, ZIP*
Enter your complete address, telephone number, and email address if you have one.	______ *Email Address* ______ *Telephone* ______ *Attorney # (if any)*

GETTING COURT DOCUMENTS BY EMAIL: You should use an email account that you do not share with anyone else and that you check every day. If you do not check your email every day, you may miss important information, notice of court dates, or documents from other parties.

Print Form Save Form Reset Form

9. ANSWER

This form is approved by the Illinois Supreme Court and is required to be accepted in all Illinois Circuit Courts.

STATE OF ILLINOIS, CIRCUIT COURT _______ COUNTY	**ANSWER/RESPONSE TO COMPLAINT/PETITION**	*For Court Use Only*

Instructions ▾	
Directly above, enter the name of the county where the case was filed.	
Enter the name of the person or company that filed this case as Plaintiff/Petitioner.	**Plaintiff / Petitioner** *(First, middle, last name or Company)*
	v.
Enter your name as the Defendant/ Respondent.	
Enter the Case Number given by the Circuit Clerk.	**Defendant / Respondent** *(First, middle, last name)*

Case Number

In **1**, enter your full name.

In **2**, enter the number and letter of each paragraph and subparagraph in the Complaint/Petition.

- Check "Admit" if you agree all of the statements in the paragraph are true; or
- Check "Deny" if you disagree with any of the statements in the paragraph; or
- Check "Do Not Know" if you do not know if all of the statements in the paragraph are true or false. This means you do not have enough information to truthfully admit or deny the statements.

1. My name is: ____________________________________
First *Middle* *Last*

and I am the Defendant/Respondent.

2. My *Answer/Response to Complaint/Petition* is:

Paragraph Number	Subparagraph Letter *(if applicable)*			
________	________	☐ Admit	☐ Deny	☐ Do Not Know
________	________	☐ Admit	☐ Deny	☐ Do Not Know
________	________	☐ Admit	☐ Deny	☐ Do Not Know
________	________	☐ Admit	☐ Deny	☐ Do Not Know
________	________	☐ Admit	☐ Deny	☐ Do Not Know
________	________	☐ Admit	☐ Deny	☐ Do Not Know
________	________	☐ Admit	☐ Deny	☐ Do Not Know
________	________	☐ Admit	☐ Deny	☐ Do Not Know
________	________	☐ Admit	☐ Deny	☐ Do Not Know
________	________	☐ Admit	☐ Deny	☐ Do Not Know
________	________	☐ Admit	☐ Deny	☐ Do Not Know
________	________	☐ Admit	☐ Deny	☐ Do Not Know
________	________	☐ Admit	☐ Deny	☐ Do Not Know
________	________	☐ Admit	☐ Deny	☐ Do Not Know
________	________	☐ Admit	☐ Deny	☐ Do Not Know
________	________	☐ Admit	☐ Deny	☐ Do Not Know
________	________	☐ Admit	☐ Deny	☐ Do Not Know
________	________	☐ Admit	☐ Deny	☐ Do Not Know
________	________	☐ Admit	☐ Deny	☐ Do Not Know
________	________	☐ Admit	☐ Deny	☐ Do Not Know
________	________	☐ Admit	☐ Deny	☐ Do Not Know
________	________	☐ Admit	☐ Deny	☐ Do Not Know
________	________	☐ Admit	☐ Deny	☐ Do Not Know

Enter the Case Number given by the Circuit Clerk: ____________________

If you run out of space, list additional paragraphs on an *Additional Paragraphs for Answer/Response to Complaint/Petition* form, check the box, and file it with this form.

____________ ____________ ☐ Admit ☐ Deny ☐ Do Not Know

____________ ____________ ☐ Admit ☐ Deny ☐ Do Not Know

☐ I have listed additional statements on the *Additional Paragraphs for Answer/Response to Complaint/Petition* form.

735 ILCS 5/2-605(a) requires that if the Complaint/Petition is verified by oath that the *Answer/Response to Complaint/Petition* must also be verified.

If the Complaint/Petition is verified by oath, then I certify that my answers above are true and correct. I understand that making a false statement on this form is perjury and has penalties provided by law under 735 ILCS 5/1-109.

735 ILCS 5/2-610(b) requires that you swear to a lack of knowledge if you cannot admit or deny any of the statements in the Complaint/Petition.

Where I answer "Do Not Know" to paragraphs in section 2, above, I certify that I do not have enough information to admit or deny the statements in these paragraphs. I understand that making a false statement on this form is perjury and has penalties provided by law under 735 ILCS 5/1-109.

IL Supreme Court Rule 137 requires the *Answer/Response to Complaint/Petition* be signed.

If you are completing this form on a computer, sign your name by typing it. If you are completing it by hand, sign and print your name.

Enter your complete address, telephone number, and email address, if you have one.

/s/ *Your Signature*	*Street Address*
Your Name	*City, State, ZIP*
Telephone	*Email*
Attorney # (if any)	

GETTING COURT DOCUMENTS BY EMAIL: You should use an email account that you do not share with anyone else and that you check every day. If you do not check your email every day, you may miss important information, notice of court dates, or documents from other parties.

In **1a**, enter the name, mailing address, and email address of the party you are sending the document to. If they have a lawyer, you **must** enter the lawyer's information.

In **1b**, check the box to show how you are sending the document.

CAUTION: If you and the person you are sending the document to have an email address, you **must** use one of the first two options. Otherwise, you may use one of the other options.

PROOF OF DELIVERY

1. I am sending the *Answer/Response to Complaint/Petition*

a. To:

Name: ____________________________________

First *Middle* *Last*

Address: ____________________________________

Street, Apt # *City* *State* *ZIP*

Email address: ____________________

b. By:

☐ An approved electronic filing service provider (EFSP)

☐ Email *(not through an EFSP)*

Only use one of the methods below if you do not have an email address, or the person you are sending the document to does not have an email address.

Enter the Case Number given by the Circuit Clerk: _______________

☐ Personal hand delivery to:
- ☐ The party
- ☐ The party's family member who is 13 or older, at the party's residence
- ☐ The party's lawyer
- ☐ The party's lawyer's office

☐ Mail or third-party carrier

Instructions	Form
In **c**, fill in the date and time that you are sending the document.	c. On: _______________ (*Date*) at: _______________ (*Time*) ☐ a.m. ☐ p.m.
In **2**, if you are sending the document to more than 1 party or lawyer, fill in **a**, **b**, and **c**. Otherwise leave **2** blank.	**2.** I am sending the *Answer/Response to Complaint/Petition*
In **2a**, enter the name, mailing address, and email address of the party you are sending the document to. If they have a lawyer, you **must** enter the lawyer's information.	a. To: Name: _______________ *First* *Middle* *Last* Address: _______________ *Street, Apt #* *City* *State* *ZIP* Email _______________
In **2b**, check the box to show how you are sending the document. **CAUTION:** If you and the person you are sending the document to have an email address, you **must** use one of the first two options. Otherwise, you may use one of the other options.	b. By: ☐ An approved electronic filing service provider (EFSP) ☐ Email *(not through an EFSP)* *Only use one of the methods below if you do not have an email address, or the person you are sending the document to does not have an email address.* ☐ Personal hand delivery to: ☐ The party ☐ The party's family member who is 13 or older, at the party's residence ☐ The party's lawyer ☐ The party's lawyer's office ☐ Mail or third-party carrier
In **c**, fill in the date and time that you are sending the document.	c. On _______________ (*Date*) at: _______________ (*Time*) ☐ a.m. ☐ p.m.
If you are sending your document(s) to more than 2 parties or lawyers, check the box and file the *Additional Proof of Delivery* with	☐ I have completed an *Additional Proof of Delivery* form.
Under the Code of Civil Procedure, 735 ILCS 5/1-109, making a statement on this form that you know to be false is perjury, a Class 3 Felony.	**I certify that everything in the *Proof of Delivery* is true and correct. I understand that a false statement on this form is perjury and has penalties provided by law under 735 ILCS 5/1-109.**
If you are completing this form on a computer, sign your name by typing it. If you are completing it by hand, sign and print your name.	/s/ _______________ *Your Signature* — _______________ *Street Address* _______________ *Print Your Name* — _______________ *City, State, ZIP*
Enter your complete address, telephone number, and email address if you have one.	_______________ *Email* — _______________ *Telephone* **GETTING COURT DOCUMENTS BY EMAIL:** You should use an email account that you do not share with anyone else and that you check every day. If you do not check your email every day, you may miss important information, notice of court dates, or documents from other parties.

Print Form Save Form Reset Form

Five

Temporary Motions and the Financial Affidavit

Overview

It can take many months, or even years, for a divorce to move from initial pleadings to final judgment; however, some things cannot wait. For example, one parent may move out of the marital residence and stop providing financial support for the children. For issues that cannot wait, the Illinois Marriage and Dissolution of Marriage Act permits courts to grant temporary relief, which is decided on a summary, or expedited, basis. As you read, see if the need for quick resolution is balanced against the need for accurate fact-finding.

Financial Matters

Kinds of Financial Matters

Child Support

Either party may make a motion for temporary child support.[1]

> **EXAMPLE** Father moves out of the marital residence and stops depositing his paycheck into the family checking account. Mother can bring a motion for temporary child support.

Spousal Maintenance

Additionally, either party may make a motion for temporary spousal maintenance.[2]

> **EXAMPLE** By agreement, the parties arranged their life so Dylan could devote himself to his political career, which required long days and out-of-town travel. Anthony managed their homes and supported Dylan's career. Dylan moves out, leaving Anthony without an income. Anthony can bring a petition for spousal maintenance.

Interim Attorney's Fees

Sometimes one party has a lower income than the other party or has less access to marital bank accounts. When that happens, the party with the lower income may be less able to represent themself in the divorce process. To allow the party with the lower income to participate in the litigation, the Illinois Marriage and Dissolution of Marriage Act allows them to petition the court to order the other party to contribute to their attorney's fees and costs.[3]

> **EXAMPLE** During their marriage, Wife earned $35,000 per year. Husband earned $180,000 per year. When Husband filed for divorce, he opened a new checking account and deposited his paycheck into it. Then he retained the most prestigious law firm in the city. Wife's income barely covers the costs of her groceries and gasoline for her car. She attempts to represent herself, using forms from the local law library. Wife cannot represent herself on parity with Husband and can file a motion for interim attorney's fees.

In assessing an award for interim attorney's fees, the court considers a number of factors, including:

> (A) The income and property of each party, including alleged marital property within the sole control of one party and alleged non-marital property within access to a party;
>
> (B) The needs of each party;
>
> (C) The realistic earning capacity of each party;
>
> (D) Any impairment to present earning capacity of either party, including age and physical and emotional health;
>
> (E) The standard of living established during the marriage;
>
> (F) The degree of complexity of the issues, including allocation of parental responsibility, valuation or division (or both) of closely held businesses, and tax planning, as well as reasonable needs for expert investigations or expert witnesses, or both;

(G) Each party's access to relevant information;

(H) The amount of the payment or payments made or reasonably expected to be made to the attorney for the other party; and

(I) Any other factor that the court expressly finds to be just and equitable.[4]

> **EXAMPLE** In the example above, the court will consider factors (A)–(C).

The Financial Affidavit

Temporary orders for financial issues are decided in a summary or expedited manner based on a financial affidavit. To ensure consistency, the Illinois Marriage and Dissolution of Marriage Act requires that one form of a financial affidavit, as determined by the Supreme Court, be used statewide.[5]

The financial affidavit is a standardized, multi-page form in which the parties disclose their income, assets, and liabilities. Financial affidavit forms are available as fillable PDFs on the Illinois Supreme Court Approved Forms website. They are also available on computer programs, such as Family Law Software. Along with the financial affidavit, the parties provide supporting documents in the form of tax returns, pay stubs, and bank statements.[6]

All parties, even if they are not moving for temporary relief, are required to exchange financial affidavits within 30 days of the respondent's appearance.[7] If a party moves for temporary financial relief before the 30 days have passed, the financial affidavit is tendered to the other party along with the motion.[8]

> **EXAMPLE** In the child support example above, Husband and Wife exchange financial affidavits, three years' tax returns, and six months' pay stubs. In addition, they each include six months' statements from their checking accounts. The court can make an award of interim attorney's fees and costs on the basis of the financial affidavit (and supporting documentation) alone.

Sanctions

The court decides motions for temporary relief on the basis of the financial affidavit. Given the unfairness that would result from an inaccurate financial affidavit, making a false statement on one is perjury and carries penalties provided by law under the Illinois Code of Civil Procedure at 735 ILCS 5/109. Further, the IMDMA provides that if a party intentionally or recklessly files an inaccurate or misleading financial affidavit, the court "shall impose significant penalties and sanctions, including but not limited to costs and attorney's fees."[9]

Attention to Detail

While an attorney will do the final review, paralegals often work closely with clients to complete the financial affidavit and compile the supporting documentation. Consequently, paralegals must understand the financial affidavit and be aware of commonly misunderstood areas.

For example, the budget on the financial affidavit calls for amounts on a monthly basis. However, some items (such as homeowner's insurance) are billed annually, so the amount per month must be calculated. A similar calculation must be performed with respect to income. While some people are paid on a monthly basis, it is more likely they are paid on a weekly, biweekly, or semi-monthly basis. Lastly, it is essential to ensure the client's financial affidavit is consistent with the supporting documents.

EXAMPLE Wife states on her financial affidavit that she earns $3,000 per month; however, her paychecks indicate she earns $6,000 per month. As Wife is paid twice per month, she has likely copied the information from her paycheck directly into the financial affidavit instead of converting semi-monthly to monthly income.

Non-Financial Matters

The IMDMA also provides relief for non-financial situations that cannot wait until final judgment for resolution.

Exclusive Possession of the Marital Residence (Marital Eviction)

Once parties decide to end their marriage, continuing to live in the same residence can be stressful. Often one or both parties wish the other would leave. The court can grant exclusive possession of the marital residence to one spouse during the dissolution, but only if the spouse can prove the "physical or mental well-being of either spouse or his or her children is jeopardized by occupancy of the marital residence by both spouses."[10]

EXAMPLE After Wife files for dissolution, Husband sulks, eats junk food, and refuses to help with the children or yard work. While the situation is unpleasant, Wife can likely not prove Husband jeopardizes her or the children.

EXAMPLE In contrast, after Wife files for dissolution, Husband begins drinking heavily, displaying outbursts of temper, cursing and insulting her, and shouting at the children for no reason. One night, Husband throws an iron at Wife, narrowly missing her head. The next day, he comes home with a gun. Wife's attorney could file a petition for exclusive possession.

In the second example, Husband's acts likely meet the definition of abuse under the Illinois Domestic Violence Act. Wife could file a petition for an order of protection as well. (See Chapter 13, Domestic Violence.)

Companion Animal

Either party may petition or move for the temporary allocation of, and responsibility for, a companion animal jointly owned by the parties.[11] As used in this section, "companion animal" does not include a service animal.[12] In issuing an order under this subsection, the court shall consider the well-being of the companion animal. However, the General Assembly did not provide factors for the court to use in determining the well-being of the companion animal.

EXAMPLE The parties adopted a puppy shortly after they were married. Wife worked from home, and the puppy slept on her feet under her desk. When the parties separated several years later, Wife moved into an apartment that did not allow animals. When Husband blocked Wife's access to the dog, Wife moved for temporary allocation of the companion animal. The court awarded Wife time with the dog at a dog park every Saturday and Sunday afternoon from 1:00 p.m. to 3:00 p.m.

Other Appropriate Relief

Finally, the Illinois Marriage and Dissolution of Marriage Act allows for entry of a temporary restraining order ("TRO") or preliminary injunction ("PI") to preserve the *status quo*, that is, the last peaceful status, between the parties.[13] These temporary orders require a party to do or refrain from doing certain things until they can be decided permanently at trial.

By statute, injunctive orders may restrain a party from transferring or concealing property, except that used in the normal course of business or for necessities of life.[14] Additionally, they can restrain a party from striking or interfering with the personal liberty of another or removing a child from the jurisdiction.[15]

> **EXAMPLE** The parties have a bank account in both names containing $45,000. Abigail fears that when Hunter learns she filed a petition for dissolution of marriage he will withdraw and hide the money. There is no other money in the marital estate to compensate her if he does. Abigail's attorney moves for a temporary restraining order preventing either party from withdrawing the money until further order of the court.

To grant preliminary relief, the trial court must find that:

(1) The plaintiff possesses a certain and clearly ascertainable right that needs protection;

(2) The plaintiff will suffer irreparable harm without the protection of the injunction;

(3) There is no adequate remedy at law; and

(4) There is a substantial likelihood that the plaintiff will succeed on the merits of the case.[16]

> **EXAMPLE** Abigail's right to an equitable share of the $45,000 needs protection. If the money is withdrawn, there are no marital assets to compensate her for it. No legal remedy exists to stop Hunter from withdrawing money from an account in his name. Abigail will likely be awarded an equitable share of money in the account at trial. Accordingly, the court grants the order, which is in effect until entry of the judgment for dissolution.

Finally, for matters for which injunctive relief is inappropriate, the court allows motions for any other appropriate relief.

> **EXAMPLE** Husband and Wife have depleted the funds in their joint savings account paying their attorney's retainers. They have a CD worth $25,000; however, it is not due to mature for six months. Wife moves the court to permit the parties to redeem the CD so they can use the funds for living expenses.

Procedure: Motion Practice

The Motion

The motion for temporary relief is prepared, and the attorney signs it. If it is verified, the client signs it as well. A notice of motion is prepared to inform the opposing party of the date and time the motion will be presented to the court.

During the pandemic, most court business was conducted remotely. Some courts still allow remote participation. If so, the notice of motion should include language indicating how to access the remote court date.

Date for Presentment

Counties have different procedures for obtaining the date to present a motion. These procedures should be posted on the court website. In DuPage County, for example, except for the automatic status date, all domestic relations court dates and times are obtained from the trial judge or one of the court schedulers at the direction of the trial judge.

The date of presentment must be far enough in the future to ensure the other party has notice.[17] Pursuant to DuPage County local rules:

> The hearing on a motion shall proceed not less than five (5) court days after the effective date of service as defined by Supreme Court rule 12(c). If notice of motion is by personal service delivered by 4:00 p.m., hearing on the motion shall proceed not less than the second court day following personal service.

If an injury would occur before the regular presentment date, the motion may be filed and presented as an emergency.[18] An emergency motion must be accompanied by an affidavit stating the reason the requested relief is necessary on an emergency basis.

> **EXAMPLE** Presume Wife overhears Husband arranging to meet his girlfriend at O'Hare in two days. He tells her he has two one-way tickets to Rio de Janeiro. Wife sees that $2,750 has been charged on their Visa card to American Airlines. Wife's attorney prepares to present the motion as an emergency.

E-filing the Motion and Notice of Motion

There is no fee for filing a motion. Only the original petition and answer require a fee; subsequent filings do not.

Service

Service of the motion and notice of motion may be made by mail or email; personal service was only required for the petition and summons.

Tendering the Financial Affidavit

The financial affidavit and supporting documents are tendered to the other party; they are not filed with the court. As proof the financial affidavit was tendered, a certificate of compliance is filed with the court. Good practice includes listing the supporting documentation provided with the financial affidavit on the certificate of compliance.[19]

Courtesy Copies

A cover letter and courtesy copies of the motion and notice of motion are sent to the judge before the date for presentment. Because attorneys are prohibited from any "*ex parte*," or one-sided, communication with the judge, opposing counsel must be copied on the cover letter.[20]

Law Office Follow-Up

The date of presentment is docketed in the firm's docketing system, and as with all court-filed documents, copies are sent to the client.

Chapter Summary

It can take many months, or even years, for a divorce to move from initial pleadings to final judgment. Some issues cannot wait that long for resolution. The Illinois Marriage and Dissolution of Marriage Act provides options for relief during the dissolution process. These temporary orders last during the pendency of the litigation and do not prejudice either party to a full hearing on the issue.

The Illinois Marriage and Dissolution of Marriage Act allows for temporary orders related to financial matters, such as child support and spousal maintenance. In addition, to allow both parties to participate equally, the court can order interim attorney's fees. Because temporary matters need to be resolved quickly, financial matters are resolved on a summary, or expedited, basis, often using information found on the financial affidavit. Since it is the basis of the award, the financial affidavit must be completed accurately, and the court can order sanctions for incomplete or inaccurate forms.

In addition to financial matters, the Illinois Marriage and Dissolution Act provides for a grant of exclusive possession of the marital residence and allocation of the care and custody of a companion animal. Finally, the Illinois Marriage and Dissolution of Marriage Act leaves the door open for injunctive and other temporary relief for disputes that might arise during the litigation.

Key Terms

Temporary Relief

Summary

Expedited

Financial Affidavit

Sanction

Interim Fee

Marital Eviction

Companion Animal

Injunctive Relief

Status Quo

Discussion Questions

1. A full hearing is decided on the basis of witness testimony and documentary evidence. Is enough protection given to the party obligated to pay support at an expedited hearing, which is decided on the basis of a financial affidavit?
2. Sometimes one party does not have access to financial documents. Are there other ways to obtain information? How would you determine the fair market value of a residence? A vehicle? The Internal Revenue Service makes prior-year tax returns available. *See* https://www.irs.gov/individuals/get-transcript (last visited June 29, 2023).
3. Why is a hearing required for motions on marital eviction when it is not required for motions on financial matters? Can the evidence needed to sustain a motion for marital eviction be obtained from an affidavit?
4. The marital eviction statute requires the "physical or mental well-being of either spouse or his or her children is jeopardized by occupancy of the marital residence by both spouses." Is physical abuse required?
5. Tension is likely high between divorcing spouses. Can their arguing rise to the level required for marital eviction? *See In re Marriage of Engst*, 2014 IL App (4th) 1310788 N.E.3d 613.
6. Motions heard on an emergency basis must be accompanied by an affidavit stating the reason the requested relief is an emergency. What situations satisfy this requirement? Potential harm to a child? Is harm to property sufficient?

7. Before the amendment to the IMDMA, effective 2018, pets were considered property. However, the language "allocation of responsibility based on the well-being of a companion animal" is similar to the language "allocation of parental responsibility based on the best interest of the child." Consider *In re Marriage of Enders v. Baker*, 2015 IL App (1st) 142435, 48 N.E.3d 1277, which referenced a case from New York. "The New York Supreme Court declined to apply the 'best interests' of the dog standard because dogs do not rise to the same level of importance as children. The court applied a 'best for all concerned' standard, maintaining that 'household pets enjoy a status greater than mere chattel.'" Is this a more appropriate means of allocating responsibility for pets?
8. The General Assembly provided a list of 15 factors for the court to consider when determining the best interest of the child, but no factors for determining the well-being of a companion animal. What factors could a judge consider when determining the well-being of a companion animal?
9. Should financial support be ordered against the non-resident companion animal owner for pet food? What about veterinary expenses?
10. Does an allocation of responsibility include authority to make decisions such as spaying or neutering a companion animal? What if it is a valuable show animal? Further, does an allocation of responsibility change who *owns* the animal? The owner of a dog can be held liable for injuries it causes. For example, over 5,300 postal carriers were bitten by dogs in 2022. *See* https://about.usps.com/newsroom/national-releases/2023/0601-usps-releases-dog-bite-national-rankings.htm (last visited June 29, 2023).

Forms

1. Financial Affidavit

   https://ilcourtsaudio.blob.core.windows.net/antilles-resources/resources/2cb2c0ce-20f8-4eb5-9d23-05664d7f4404/FA%20Financial%20Affidavit.pdf
2. Proof of Delivery (windows.net) of Financial Affidavit

   https://ilcourtsaudio.blob.core.windows.net/antilles-resources/resources/3f0fe267-e8c6-46dc-9d69-517ce4df9e22/CC%20Proof%20of%20Delivery.pdf
3. Motion for Temporary Relief

   https://www.circuitclerkofwillcounty.com/DesktopModules/EasyDNNNews/DocumentDownload.ashx?portalid=0&moduleid=518&articleid=195&documentid=414

4. Interim Fee Award Order (windows.net)

   https://ilcourtsaudio.blob.core.windows.net/antilles-resources/resources/effc8569-5099-4022-b06c-01d490c69185/DAF%20Interim%20Fee%20Award%20Order.pdf

Endnotes

1. 750 ILCS 5/501(a)(1) (West, Westlaw Classic through P.A. 103-21 of the 2023 Reg. Sess.).
2. *Id.*
3. *Id.* § 501(c-1) (1). Also, per § 508(f), be sure to have included the Client's Rights and Responsibilities in the legal services agreement.
4. *Id.* § 501(c-1) (1) (A-I).
5. 750 ILCS 5/501.
6. *Id.*
7. 18th Judicial Cir. Ct. R. 15.05 (a)(1)(a).
8. *Id.* at 15.05(a)(1)(c).
9. 750 ILCS 5/501(a)(1).
10. *Id.* § 501(c-2).
11. *Id.* § 501(f).
12. *Id.* § 501(f).
13. In re Marriage of Joerger, 221 Ill. App. 3d 400, 581 N.E.2d 1219 (4th Dist. 1991).
14. 750 ILCS 5/501(a)(2)(i).
15. *Id.* § 501(a)(2)(ii) and (iii).
16. In re Marriage of Schmitt, 321 Ill. App. 3d 360, 371, 747 N.E.2d 524, 533 (2d Dist. 2001).
17. 18th Judicial Cir. Ct. R. 604(d).
18. 18th Judicial Cir. Ct. R. 6.08. Rules vary by county.
19. Ill. Sup. Ct. R. 201(m).
20. Ill. R. Prof'l Conduct R. 3.5.

1. FINANCIAL AFFIDAVIT

This form is approved by the Illinois Supreme Court and is required to be used in all Illinois Circuit Courts.

STATE OF ILLINOIS, CIRCUIT COURT ______________ COUNTY	FINANCIAL AFFIDAVIT (FAMILY & DIVORCE CASES) ☐ Pre-Judgment ☐ Post-Judgment	*For Court Use Only*
Instructions ▾		
Enter above the county name where the case was filed.		
Enter name of the Petitioner, the Respondent, and the case number as listed in the initial Petition or Complaint.	______________________________ **Petitioner** *(First, middle, last name)* v. ______________________________	
Enter the Case Number given by the Circuit Clerk.	**Respondent** *(First, middle, last name)*	______________ **Case Number**

IMPORTANT: (1) If you intentionally or recklessly enter inaccurate or misleading information on this form, you may face significant penalties and sanctions, including costs and attorney's fees; (2) If you need more room for a section, complete and attach the *Additional Information* form for that section. *Do not file this document and the enclosures with the Circuit Clerk unless a local rule or court order requires you to do so.* Ask the Circuit Clerk where to find these rules.

NOTE: Do not include in this affidavit any Social Security or individual taxpayer-identification numbers, driver's license numbers, financial account numbers, or debit or credit card numbers. If any of these items are included on documents you are going to attach to this affidavit, hide them by covering them with black ink or otherwise removing.

In **3a-d**, check the boxes of the documents you are attaching to this form as evidence of your income, assets, and debts. If you select **3d**, enter the names of the additional documents you are attaching.

In **4**, do not complete **4b** and **4c** if your contact information is protected pursuant to court order because of domestic violence or abuse.

1. I am the ☐ Petitioner ☐ Respondent in this case.

2. I swear or affirm the information in this *Financial Affidavit* and all attached statements are true and correct as of ____________ .
Date

3. I attached the most recent copies of the following documents *(Check all that apply. You must attach these documents if you have or can get them.)*

a. ☐ pay stubs or other proof of income
b. ☐ income tax returns *(including K-1, W-2, 1099, and all schedules.)*
c. ☐ bank statements
d. ☐ other documents in verifying your debts in 14 and your assets in 15:
____
____

4. Information about myself

a. Name ______________________________
First *Middle* *Last*
b. Phone Number ______________
c. Home Address ______________________________
Street Address, Apt.
____
City *State* *ZIP*
d. Date of Birth ____________

5. Information about other household members

I live with another adult who helps me pay my expenses. This person is not the Petitioner or Respondent in this case. ☐ Yes ☐ No

Enter the Case Number given by the Circuit Clerk: ______________________________

In **6**, check all that apply. Provide all information requested about your jobs, including all full-time, part-time, temporary, contract, or other work. Provide all the requested information about any business you own or operate and the business income.
If you have more than one job or business, fill out and attach the *Additional My Employment/ Business* forms.
In **6b**, enter your total gross income from this employer from January 1 of this year through the date you complete this form.
In **6c**, check the box that best describes your self-employment, and/or the box that describes the type of business you have. List the name and address of the business, and the gross receipts for last year and this year.

6. My Employment/Business

a. I am ☐ unemployed

b. I am ☐ employed by someone else

Employer name ______________________________

Employer address ______________________________
Street Address, Apt.

____
City *State* *ZIP*

Number of paychecks per year: ☐ 12 *(monthly)* ☐ 24 *(two times a month)* ☐ 26 *(every two weeks)* ☐ 52 *(weekly)* ☐ I am paid in cash

Gross income *(pay before taxes and deductions)* so far this year $__________ as of __________ .
Date

c. Self-Employment or Other Business Income:

☐ own a business as a sole proprietorship.
☐ as an independent contractor.
☐ as a member of a partnership.
☐ as a member of a limited liability company (LLC) not treated as a corporation.
☐ closely held corporation.
☐ other flow-through business entity.

Business name: ______________________________

Business address: ______________________________
Street Address, Apt.

____
City *State* *ZIP*

Gross business receipts for last year $__________ and so far this year $__________

Ordinary and necessary expenses required to carry on the business for this year $__________ and last year $__________

Do you receive any of the following from the business (*check all that apply*):

☐ Reimbursed meals
☐ Company car
☐ Free housing or housing allowance
☐ Other: ______________________________

(You must attach complete federal and state business tax returns for the most recent tax year.)

☐ I have attached one or more *Additional My Employment/Business* forms.

In **7a**, check only one. In **7a-e**, enter the information you submitted on last year's IRS tax return. If you did not file a tax return for last year, check **Did not file** in **7a**, leave **7b-d** blank, but still complete **7e**.	**7. My gross income and taxes from last year** a. Tax filing status ☐ Married *(Joint)* ☐ Married *(Separate)* ☐ Single ☐ Head of Household ☐ Did not file b. Number of dependent exemptions claimed ________ c. Total number of exemptions claimed ________ d. I claim on my federal tax return ☐ the standardized deduction ☐ itemized deductions e. Gross income *(before taxes and deductions)* last year $ ________

For help in calculating monthly amounts, see *How to Complete a Financial Affidavit (Family & Divorce Cases)*.

In **8, Regular employment earnings** mean the monthly gross income you receive on a regular basis from employment.

8. My monthly gross income from all sources

Regular employment/self-employment earnings from all jobs *(salary, wages, base pay, etc)*	$
Overtime	$
Commission	$
Tips	$
Bonus	$
Pension	$
Annuity	$
Interest income	$
Dividend income	$
Trust income	$
Social Security Retirement	$
Social Security Disability	$
Social Security Income (SSI) *(not included as income for child support purposes)*	$
Unemployment	$
Disability payment *(not Social Security)*	$
Workers' Compensation	$
TANF and SNAP *(not included as income for child support purposes)*	$
Military allowances	$
Investment income	$
Rental income	$
Partnership income	$
Distributions and draws	$
Royalty income	$
Maintenance received under an order entered in this case or another case that you must report as income on your tax return	$
Maintenance received under an order entered in this case or another case that you do not have to report as income on your tax return	$
Child support for children of this relationship *(if this support is paid by the other parent, it does not affect the support calculation)*	$
Social Security payment made to the children of this relationship based on your disability or retirement	$
Gifts of money	$
Other: ______________________	$
Total Gross Monthly Income	$ 0.00

If you have other income not listed in **8**, describe the source of the income in **Other** and enter the monthly amount.

In **Total Gross Monthly Income**, add the amounts in **8** together and enter the total.

In **9**, use information from your paystubs, tax records, and other sources to identify the deductions being taken from your income. List money deducted for health insurance below in Section **13**.

In **Total Monthly Deductions,** add the amounts from **9** together and enter the total.

9. My monthly payroll deductions

Federal tax	$
State tax	$
FICA *(or Social Security equivalent, for example, Self-employment) tax)*	$
Medicare tax	$
Mandatory retirement contributions *(by law or condition of employment, but only if no FICA or Social Security equivalent)*	$
Total Monthly Deductions	$ 0.00

In **10**, list any maintenance payments you are making. If you are not sure about whether your payments are tax-deductible, speak to your attorney or tax-preparer. Generally, maintenance payments court ordered after January 1, 2019 are not tax deductible.

10. Monthly maintenance payments

Maintenance being paid or payable to the other party by you under a court order in this case	$
Maintenance being paid under a court order to a former spouse by you, which is tax deductible to you	$
Maintenance being paid under a court order to a former spouse by you, which is not tax deductible to you	$
Total Maintenance Payments	$ 0.00

For **11,** attach a copy of the support order and proof that you are making the payments, e.g. cancelled checks, court records.

For help in calculating monthly amounts, see *How to Complete a Financial Affidavit.*

11. Monthly child Support payments

Child support being paid for the children of this relationship under a court order in this case or a different case	$
Child support being paid under a court order for children not shared with the other party and who are not part of this case	$
Child support being paid, but there is no court order, for children not shared with the other party and who are not part of this case and (1) that are presumed to be yours, (2) for whom there is a voluntary acknowledgment of paternity (VAP) signed by you and the other parent, **OR** (3) for whom there is a court order naming you as a parent, but there is no support order	$
Total Child Support Payments	$ 0.00

In **12a**, enter the amount your household spends on each item each month.

If you have other living expenses not listed in **12a**, describe the expense in **Other** and enter the monthly amount.

12. My monthly Living Expenses

a. Household Expenses

Mortgage or rent	$
Home equity *(HELOC)* and second mortgage	$
Real estate taxes	$
Homeowners or condo association dues and assessments	$
Homeowners or renters insurance	$
Gas	$
Electric	$
Telephone	$
Cable or satellite TV	$
Internet	$
Water and sewer	$
Garbage removal	$
Laundry and dry cleaning	$

In **Subtotal Monthly Household Expenses**, add the amounts in **12a** together and enter the total.	House cleaning service	$
	Necessary repairs and maintenance to my property	$
	Pet care	$
	Groceries, household supplies, and toiletries	$
	Other: ______________________	$
	Subtotal Monthly Household Expenses	$ 0.00

In **12b**, enter the amount you spend monthly on each type of transportation expense.	b. Transportation Expenses	
If you have other transportation expenses not listed in **12b**, describe the expense in **Other** and enter the monthly amount.	Car payment	$
	Repairs and maintenance	$
	Insurance, license, registration and city sticker	$
	Gasoline	$
	Taxi, ride-share, bus, and train	$
	Parking	$
	Other: ______________________	$
In **Subtotal Monthly Transportation Expenses**, add the amounts in **12b** together and enter the total.	**Subtotal Monthly Transportation Expenses**	$ 0.00

In **12c**, enter the amount you spend monthly **only for yourself** on each type of expense. Do not include expenses you are reimbursed for through insurance or your employer.	c. Personal Expenses	
	Medical *(out-of-pocket expenses)*	
	Doctor visits	$
	Therapy and counseling	$
	Dental and orthodontia	$
	Optical	$
	Medicine	$
	Life insurance	
	Life *(term)*	$
	Life *(whole or annuitty)*	$
	Clothing	$
	Grooming (*hair, nails, spa, etc.)*	$
	Gym & Club membership Dues	$
	Entertainment, dining out, and hobbies	$
If you have other personal expenses not listed in **12c**, describe the expense in **Other** and enter the monthly amount.	Newspapers, magazines, and subscriptions	$
	Gifts	$
	Donations *(political, religious, charity, etc.)*	$
	Vacations	$
	Mandatory or voluntary union, trade or professional association dues	$
	Professional fees *(accountants, tax preparers, attorneys)*	$
	Other: ______________________	$
In **Subtotal Monthly Personal Expenses**, add the amounts in **12c** together and enter the total.	**Subtotal Monthly Personal Expenses**	$ 0.00

In **12d**, enter the amount spent monthly for the minor and dependent children of this relationship only.	d. Minor and Dependent Children Expenses	
	Clothing	$
	Grooming *(hair, nails, spa, etc.)*	$
	Education	
	Tuition	$
	Books, fees, and supplies	$
	School lunch	$
	Transportation	$

	School-sponsored trips and special events	$
	Uniforms	$
	Before and after-school care	$
	Tutoring and summer school	$
In **Medical**, do not include expenses you are reimbursed for through insurance or your employer.	Medical *(out-of-pocket expenses)*	
	Doctor visits	$
	Therapy and counseling	$
	Dental and orthodontia	$
	Optical	$
	Medicine	$
	Allowance	$
	Childcare and sitters	$
If there are other child-related expenses not listed in **12d**, describe the expense in **Other** and enter the amount.	Extracurricular activities and sports *(including equipment, uniforms, etc.)*	$
	Summer and school-break camps	$
	Vacations *(children only)*	$
	Entertainment, dining out, and hobbies *(children only)*	$
	Gifts children give to others	$
In **Subtotal Monthly Minor and Dependent Children Expenses**, add the amounts in **12d** together and enter the total.	Other: ______________________	$
	Subtotal Monthly Minor and Dependent Children Expenses	$ 0.00
	Total Monthly Living Expenses *(add the subtotals from 12a-d above)*	$ 0.00

In **13**, enter information about the primary health insurance you have for yourself and your family.

If you have more than one **Health Insurance** carrier, then list other health insurance company in the *Additional Health Insurance* forms and attach it.

13. Health Insurance

I have health insurance: ☐ Yes ☐ No

The insurance company is: ______________________

The type of insurance is: ☐ Medical ☐ Dental ☐ Optical

Deductible: Per individual $__________ Per family $__________

It covers: ☐ Me ☐ My spouse/partner ☐ My dependents

Type of Policy: ☐ HMO ☐ PPO ☐ Other

Provided by: ☐ Employer ☐ Private Policy ☐ Other Group ☐ Medicaid/All Kids

Monthly cost is paid by: ☐ Me ☐ My spouse ☐ Other

Total number of people covered by this policy: ________

The amount I pay monthly for insurance for children of this relationship: $

The amount I pay monthly for deductibles, co-insurance, and co-payments for the children of this relationship: $

Total Monthly Health Insurance Cost $ 0.00

☐ I have attached one or more *Additional Health Insurance* forms.

In **14**, enter your debts including credit cards and past due bills. Do not include debt payments previously listed in **12** and **13** above, such as your mortgage or car payment.

14. My Debts *(do not list expenses included in section 12)*

	Creditor Name	Describe Nature of Debt *(parking tickets, household goods, attorney's fees, etc.)*	Amount Owed	Monthly Payment Being Made
1.			$	$
2.			$	$
3.			$	$
4.			$	$
5.			$	$
6.			$	$

If you have more than 4 creditors, list them on *Additional My Debts* forms and attach them.

In **Total Monthly Debt Payments**, add the Monthly Payment amounts from **14** together and enter the total. Include any debts listed on any *Additional My Debts* forms.

☐ I have attached one or more *Additional My Debts* forms.

Amount from *Additional My Debts (if any)* $

Total Monthly Debt Payments $ 0.00

Note: **Fair Market Value (FMV) is generally defined as a selling price for an item to which an unrelated buyer and seller can agree. For more information on FMV, read *How to Complete a Financial Affidavit (Family & Divorce Case)* available at https://www.illinoiscourts.gov/documents-and-forms/approved-forms/.**

In **15a**, enter your cash and cash equivalents. Do not list account numbers.

15. My Assets

a. Cash and Cash Equivalents *(list balance as of the date of this affidavit)*

Checking, Savings, Money Market, and Other Bank or Credit Union Accounts

	Name of Bank or Institution	Name on Account	Account Type	Balance
1.				$
2.				$
3.				$
4.				$

If you have more than 4 **Checking, Savings, Money Market or Other Bank or Credit Union Accounts**, list them in *Additional Cash and Cash Equivalents* forms and attach them.

☐ I have attached one or more *Additional Cash and Cash Equivalents* forms.

Certificates of Deposit *(list balance as of the date of this affidavit)*

	Name of Bank or Institution	Name on Account	Balance
1.			$
2.			$
3.			$

If you have more than 3 **Certificates of Deposit**, list them in *Additional Certificates of Deposit* forms and attach them.

☐ I have attached one or more *Additional Certificates of Deposit* forms.

Cash and Prepaid Debit Cards *(list balance as of the date of this affidavit)*

	Location of Cash/Card	Held By	Balance
1.			$
2.			$
3.			$

A **Prepaid Debit Card** is a card that can be used to make purchases much as you would use cash. Many prepaid cards carry the brand of a card network, like MasterCard, Visa, or American Express.

☐ I have attached one or more *Additional Cash and Prepaid Debit Card* forms.

If you have more than 3 **Cash or Prepaid Debit Cards** or locations for your cash, list them in *Additional Cash and Prepaid Debit Card* forms and attach them.

Enter the Case Number given by the Circuit Clerk: ______________________

In **15b**, enter information for your investments and securities.

If you have more than 3 Investment Accounts and Securities, list them in *Additional Investment Accounts and Securities* forms and attach them.

b. Investment Accounts and Securities *(list FMV or balance as of the date of this affidavit)*

Stocks, Bonds, Options, Employee Stock Ownership Plans

	Company Name	# Shares	Type	Owner	FMV
1.					$
2.					$
3.					$

☐ I have attached one or more *Additional Investment Accounts and Securities* forms.

If you have more than 3 **Investment/Brokerage Accounts, Mutual Funds, and Secured or Unsecured Notes**, list them in *Additional Investment/Brokerage Accounts, Mutual Funds, and Secured or Unsecured Notes* forms and attach them.

Investment/Brokerage Accounts, Mutual Funds, and Secured or Unsecured Notes *(list balance as of the date of this affidavit)*

	Description of Asset	Owner	Balance
1.			$
2.			$
3.			$

☐ I have attached one or more *Additional Investment/Brokerage Accounts, Mutual Funds, and Secured or Unsecured Notes* forms.

In **15c**, enter information for your real estate, including your home if you own it.

If you have more than 3 pieces of **Real Estate**, list them in *Additional Real Estate* forms and attach them.

c. Real Estate *(list FMV and balance due as of the date of this affidavit)*

	Address	Name on Title	FMV	Balance Due
1.			$	$
2.			$	$
3.			$	$

☐ I have attached one or more *Additional Real Estate* forms.

In **15c** and **15d**, in **Balance Due**, enter the total amount remaining on your loan.

In **15d**, enter information about your motor vehicles.

If you have more than 4 **Motor Vehicles**, list them in *Additional Motor Vehicles* forms and attach them.

d. Motor Vehicles *(cars, boats, trailers, motorcycles, aircrafts, etc.)* (*list FMV and balance due as of the date of this affidavit*)

	Year, Make, and Model	Name on Title	FMV	Balance Due
1.			$	$
2.			$	$
3.			$	$
4.			$	$

☐ I have attached one or more *Additional Motor Vehicles* forms.

In **15e**, enter information about your business interests. In **Type of Business**, enter whether the business is a corporation, S Corp, or LLC, etc.

If you have more than 3 **Business Interests**, list them in *Additional Business Interests* forms and attach them.

e. Business Interests *(list FMV as of the date of this affidavit)*

	Name of Business	Type of Business	% of Ownership	FMV
1.				$
2.				$
3.				$

☐ I have attached one or more *Additional Business Interests forms.*

In **15f**, enter information about each life insurance policy you have for yourself, the other party, or your children.

If you have more than 3 **Life Insurance Policies**, list them in *Additional Life Insurance Policies* forms and attach them.

f. Life Insurance Policies *(list cash balance as of the date of this affidavit)*

	Name of Insurance Company	Type of Policy	Death Benefit	Cash Value
1.			$	$
2.			$	$
3.			$	$

☐ I have attached one or more *Additional Life Insurance Policies* forms.

In **15g**, enter information about retirement benefits (vested and non-vested).

If you have more than 4 **Retirement Benefits and Deferred Compensation** plans, list them in *Additional Retirement Benefits and Deferred Compensation* forms and attach them.

g. Retirement Benefits and Deferred Compensation *(pension plan, annuity, IRA, 401(k), 403(b), SEP) (list FMV and or account balance as of the date of this affidavit)*

	Name of Plan	Type of Plan	FMV or Account Balance
1.			$
2.			$
3.			$
4.			$

☐ I have attached one or more *Additional Retirement Benefits and Deferred Compensation* forms.

In **15h**, enter information for valuable collectible items.

If you have more than 2 **Valuable Collectibles,** list them in *Additional Valuable Collectibles* forms and attach them.

h. Valuable Collectibles *(coins, stamps, art, antiques, etc.)*

	Description	FMV
1.		$
2.		$

☐ I have attached one or more *Additional Valuable Collectibles* forms.

In **15i**, enter information for other personal property with fair market value over $500.

If you have more than 2 items of **Personal Property Valued Over $500**, list them in *Additional Other Personal Property Valued over $500* forms and attach them.

i. Other Personal Property Valued Over $500

	Description	FMV
1.		$
2.		$

☐ I have attached one or more *Additional Other Personal Property Valued over $500* forms.

In **15j,** enter information for assets or property you transferred or sold in the last 2 years with FMV of at least $1,000. Do not include income items listed above in **8.**

If you have sold or transferred more than 2 **Assets or Properties Within the Last 2 Years With a FMV of at Least $1,000**, list them in *Additional Transfer or Sale of Assets or Property Within the Last 2 Years with a FMV of at least $1,000* forms and attach them.

j. Transfer or Sale of Assets or Property Within the Last 2 Years With a FMV of at Least $1,000

	Description	Transferred or Sold to	Date of Transfer	Amount
1.				$
2.				$

☐ I have attached one or more *Additional Transfer of Sale of Assets or Property Within the Last 2 Years With a FMV of at Least $1,000* forms.

Enter the Case Number given by the Circuit Clerk: ____________________

In **16**, enter information about lawsuits and claims you have filed or have been filed against you. If you did not recover anything, enter $0. If your case is still pending or has not yet been filed, enter unknown.

If you have more than 3 **Lawsuits and Claims**, list them in *Additional Lawsuits and Claims* forms and attach them.

16. Lawsuits and Claims *(workers' compensation, disability, etc.)*

	Case Number	Date Lawsuit or Claim Filed	Amount Recovered
1.			$
2.			$
3.			$

☐ I have attached one or more *Additional Lawsuits and Claims* forms.

In **17**, enter information about your federal and state tax returns for the last 2 years. Check **Refund** if you received money or a check, or **Amount Owed** if you owed additional taxes.

17. Income Tax Refunds or Amounts Owed for the Last 2 Years *(federal and state)*

	Tax year	Federal		State	
1.		☐ Refund	$	☐ Refund	$
		☐ Amount Owed	$	☐ Amount Owed	$
2.		☐ Refund	$	☐ Refund	$
		☐ Amount Owed	$	☐ Amount Owed	$

IMPORTANT: If you intentionally or recklessly enter inaccurate or misleading information on this form, you may face significant penalties and sanctions, including costs and attorney's fees.

Under the Code of Civil Procedure, 735 ILCS 5/1-109, making a statement on this form that you know to be false is perjury, a Class 3 Felony.

After you finish this form, sign and print your name and date it.

I certify that everything in the *Financial Affidavit* is true and correct. I understand that making a false statement on this form is perjury and has penalties provided by law under 735 ILCS 5/1-109.

Your Signature ____________________ *Your Name* ____________________

Date ____________________

Print Form Save Form Reset Form

2. PROOF OF DELIVERY OF FINANCIAL AFFIDAVIT

This form is approved by the Illinois Supreme Court and is required to be accepted in all Illinois Circuit Courts.

STATE OF ILLINOIS, CIRCUIT COURT COUNTY	PROOF OF DELIVERY	*For Court Use Only*

Instructions ▾	
Directly above, enter the name of the county where the case was filed.	
Enter the name of the person or company that filed this case as Plaintiff/Petitioner.	**Plaintiff / Petitioner** *(First, middle, last name or Company)*
Enter the name of the Defendants/ Respondents.	v.
Enter the Case Number given by the Circuit Clerk.	**Defendants / Respondents** *(First, middle, last name, or business name)* — **Case Number**

In **1**, enter the name of each court document you are sending.

In **1a**, enter the name, mailing address, and email address of the party you are sending the document to. If they have a lawyer, you **must** enter the lawyer's information.

In **1b**, check the box to show how you are sending the document.
CAUTION: If you and the person you are sending the document to have an email address, you **must** use one of the first two options. Otherwise, you may use one of the other options.

In **c**, fill in the date and time that you are sending the document.

1. I am sending the following court document: ______________________

a. To:
Name: ______________________
First *Middle* *Last*
Address: ______________________
Street, Apt # *City* *State* *ZIP*
Email address: ______________________

b. By:
☐ An approved electronic filing service provider (EFSP)
☐ Email *(not through an EFSP)*
Only use one of the methods below if you do not have an email address, or the person you are sending the document to does not have an email address.
☐ Personal hand delivery to:
 ☐ The party
 ☐ The party's family member who is 13 or older, at the party's residence
 ☐ The party's lawyer
 ☐ The party's lawyer's office
☐ Mail or third-party carrier

c. On: ______________ at: ______________ ☐ a.m. ☐ p.m.
Date *Time*

Enter the Case Number given by the Circuit Clerk: ______________________

Instructions	
In **2**, if you are sending the document to more than 1 party or lawyer, fill in **a**, **b**, and **c**. Otherwise leave **2** blank.	**2.** I am sending this document:
In **2a**, enter the name, mailing address, and email address of the party you are sending the document to. If they have a lawyer, you **must** enter the lawyer's information.	a. To: Name: ______________________ *First* *Middle* *Last* Address: ______________________ *Street, Apt #* *City* *State* *ZIP* Email address: ______________________
In **2b**, check the box to show how you are sending the document. **CAUTION:** If you and the person you are sending the document to have an email address, you **must** use one of the first two options. Otherwise, you may use one of the	b. By: ☐ An approved electronic filing service provider (EFSP) ☐ Email *(not through an EFSP)* *Only use one of the methods below if you do not have an email address, or the person you are sending the document to does not have an email address.* ☐ Personal hand delivery to: ☐ The party ☐ The party's family member who is 13 or older, at the party's residence ☐ The party's lawyer ☐ The party's lawyer's office ☐ Mail or third-party carrier
In **c**, fill in the date and time that you are sending the document.	c. On: ______________ at: ______________ ☐ a.m. ☐ p.m. *Date* *Time*
If you are sending your document to more than 2 parties or lawyers, check the box and file the *Additional Proof of Delivery* with this form.	☐ I have completed an *Additional Proof of Delivery* form.

Instructions	
Under the Code of Civil Procedure, 735 ILCS 5/1-109, making a statement on this form that you know to be false is perjury, a Class 3 Felony.	**I certify that everything in the *Proof of Delivery* is true and correct. I understand that a false statement on this form is perjury and has penalties provided by law under 735 ILCS 5/1-109.** /s/ ______________________ ______________________ *Your Signature* *Street Address*
If you are completing this form on a computer, sign your name by typing it. If you are completing it by hand, sign and print your name.	______________________ ______________________ *Print Your Name* *City, State, ZIP*
Enter your complete address, telephone number, and email address, if you have one.	______________________ ______________________ *Telephone* *Email* ______________________ *Attorney # (if any)*

GETTING COURT DOCUMENTS BY EMAIL: You should use an email account that you do not share with anyone else and that you check every day. If you do not check your email every day, you may miss important information, notice of court dates, or documents from other parties.

Print Form Save Form Reset Form

PRINT

CLEAR

IN THE CIRCUIT COURT OF THE TWELFTH JUDICIAL CIRCUIT
WILL COUNTY, ILLINOIS

____
Petitioner
vs

______________________________ CASE NO: ______________________________
Respondent

PETITION FOR TEMPORARY RELIEF

NOW COMES the Petitioner/Respondent, ______________________________, and for his/her
(Circle one)

Petition for Temporary Relief, states as follows:

1. Petitioner's Petition for Dissolution of Marriage/Civil Union is pending.
(Circle one)
2. There was born to or adopted by the parties the following children: [list the initials of the minors along with the year that they were born]
____
____.
3. Petitioner/Respondent is a fit and proper person to have the temporary care, custody, control, and
(Circle one)
education of the child(ren).
4. Petitioner/Respondent needs temporary child support, temporary maintenance, and/or temporary
(Circle one)
attorney's fees:
   (a) The parties have ________ minor children, currently residing with the Petitioner/Respondent,
   (Circle one)
   and the requesting party herein has insufficient funds to support the minor child(ren) [child support request – strike out if does not apply].
   (b) The Petitioner/Respondent does not have sufficient funds to support himself/herself during the
   (Circle one)
   pendency of this cause [maintenance requested – strike out if does not apply]
5. That the opposing party is able bodied, employed and well able to contribute to the support of the Petitioner/Respondent/ the minor child(ren) of the parties.
(Circle one)

WHEREFORE, the Petitioner/Respondent, ______________________________, prays that this
(Circle one)

Court enter an Order granting her/him the temporary custody of the child(ren) of the parties, temporary child support and temporary maintenance, and for any other and further relief as this Court in equity deems just and reasonable.

____
(Signature)

ANDREA LYNN CHASTEEN, CLERK OF THE CIRCUIT COURT OF WILL COUNTY

Original – Court Copy – Plaintiff Copy – Defendant

163 (12/16)

CERTIFICATE

Under penalties of perjury as provided by law pursuant to Section 1-109 of the Code of Civil Procedure, the undersigned certifies the statements set forth in this instrument are true and correct, except as to matters therein stated to be on information and belief, and as to such matters, the undersigned certifies as aforesaid that he/she verily believe the same to be true.

____
(Signature)

Attorney or Party, if not represented by an Attorney
Name ______________________________
ARDC # ______________________________
Firm Name ______________________________
Attorney for ______________________________
Address ______________________________
City & Zip ______________________________
Telephone ______________________________

ANDREA LYNN CHASTEEN, CLERK OF THE CIRCUIT COURT OF WILL COUNTY

4. INTERIM FEE AWARD ORDER

This form is approved by the Illinois Supreme Court and is required to be used in all Illinois Circuit Courts.

STATE OF ILLINOIS, CIRCUIT COURT COUNTY	INTERIM FEE AWARD ORDER ☐ Pre-Judgment ☐ Post-Judgment	*For Court Use Only*
____________________ **Petitioner** *(First, middle, last name)* v. ____________________ **Respondent** *(First, middle, last name)*		____________ **Case Number**

☐ A non-evidentiary hearing ☐ an evidentiary hearing was held on the Petition of ☐ Petitioner ☐ Respondent seeking an award of interim attorney's fees and costs pursuant to 750 ILCS 5/501(c-1); the court has jurisdiction over the parties and subject matter; the court reviewed the Petition, affidavit(s) and responsive pleading, if any, and considered all relevant factors; the court finds:

A. ☐ The party from whom attorney's fees and costs are sought has the financial ability to pay reasonable amounts, and the party seeking attorney's fees and costs lacks sufficient assets or income to pay reasonable amounts. ☐ Alternatively, both parties lack financial ability or access to assets or income for reasonable attorney's fees and costs.

B. This award of interim attorney's fees and costs to the petitioning party is reasonable and in an amount necessary to enable that party to participate adequately in the litigation.

C. This interim fee award is ☐ by agreement of the parties ☐ not by agreement of the parties.

IT IS HEREBY ORDERED:

1. An interim fee award of $________ is entered in favor of ☐ Petitioner ☐ Respondent, to be paid by ☐ Petitioner ☐ Respondent or, in cases of disgorgement, by ☐ ____________________ *(Attorney or Law Firm)* to the petitioning party's counsel for reasonable fees and costs within ________ days.
2. The assessment of any interim fee award is without prejudice to any final allocation and without prejudice as to any claim or right of either party or any counsel of record at the time of the award.
3. Unless otherwise ordered by the court, interim awards, and all other payments by each party to counsel and related payments to third parties, shall be deemed to have been advances from the parties' marital estate.
4. Any portion of any interim award constituting an overpayment shall be remitted back to the appropriate party(s) or, alternatively, to successor counsel, as the court determines and directs after notice.
5. Other: ____

____

ENTERED:

____
Judge

____
Date

Print Form Save Form Reset Form

Six

Children

Overview

When parents are married, they are presumed to exercise parental responsibilities together. After they separate, parental responsibilities must be allocated between them by the court. Which parent will make significant decisions, such as whether to authorize elective surgery? Where will the child spend holidays?

The Illinois General Assembly provides factors to guide courts in their allocation of parental responsibilities. In addition, it provides a step-by-step process for the court to follow. As you read through this chapter, consider the effect of the allocation process on adverse parties who cannot go their separate ways when the litigation is over but must continue to raise their children together.

Allocation of Parental Responsibility

Until 2016, the IMDMA used the term "custody" for decision-making authority, and "visitation" for the time the noncustodial parent spent with his child. In 2016, the terms were revised. Now, "allocation of parental responsibilities: decision-making" is used instead of "custody," and "allocation of parental responsibilities: parenting time" is used instead of "visitation." Because the word "custody" exists in statutes outside the IMDMA, one parent is designated the "custodial" parent with respect to other statutes.[1]

Allocation of Parental Responsibility: Decision-Making

Standing: Decision-Making

All parents have standing to bring a petition for the allocation of parental responsibilities: decision-making. Married parents bring them in an action for dissolution, declaration of invalidity (annulment), or legal separation. Unmarried parents may bring them in a parentage action. (See Chapter 11, Parentage.)

Recognizing the superior right of parents to raise their children,[2] the IMDMA extends standing beyond parents grudgingly, to step-parents, grandparents, and non-parents in possession of the child, under very narrow circumstances.[3]

EXAMPLE Grandmother (father's mother) watches Emma from 9:00 a.m. to 5:00 p.m. during the week when Father and Mother are at work. Grandmother does not have standing and cannot bring a petition for allocation.

EXAMPLE In contrast, Child's mother is dead and her father is in jail. Child is living with Grandmother, mother's mother. Grandmother has standing to bring a petition for allocation of parental responsibility.

Factors Used in Allocation: Decision-Making

Allocation of decision-making responsibility between the parents is based on the child's best interests. In determining the child's best interests, the court is guided by the following factors:

(1) The wishes of the child, taking into account the child's maturity and ability to express reasoned and independent preferences as to decision-making;

(2) The child's adjustment to the child's home, school, and community;

(3) The mental and physical health of all individuals involved;

(4) The ability of the parents to cooperate to make decisions, or the level of conflict between the parties that may affect their ability to share decision-making;

(5) The level of each parent's participation in past significant decision-making with respect to the child;

(6) Any prior agreement or course of conduct between the parents relating to decision-making with respect to the child;

(7) The wishes of the parents;

(8) The child's needs;

(9) The distance between the parents' residences, the cost and difficulty of transporting the child, each parent's and the child's daily schedules, and the ability of the parents to cooperate in the arrangement;

(10) Whether a restriction on decision-making is appropriate under Section 603.10;[4]

(11) The willingness and ability of each parent to facilitate and encourage a close and continuing relationship between the other parent and the child;

(12) The physical violence or threat of physical violence by the child's parent directed against the child;

(13) The occurrence of abuse against the child or other member of the child's household;

(14) Whether one of the parents is a sex offender, and if so, the exact nature of the offense and what, if any, treatment in which the parent has successfully participated; and

(15) Any other factor that the court expressly finds to be relevant.[5]

> **EXAMPLE** During the marriage, Father chose the children's school, hired tutors, chose the children's medical providers, and attended all of their doctor's appointments, while Mother focused on her hobbies, chiefly breeding and showing Airedale Terriers. Under Factor (6), the parties' course of conduct, it is likely in the children's best interest to allocate significant decision-making authority to Father.

It is a common misconception that after they reach a certain age children can decide where they want to live. While their wishes are taken into account, in Illinois children do not make the decision. There are several reasons for this. One is that it is considered emotionally harmful to ask children to choose between their parents. Another is that children mature at different rates.

> **EXAMPLE** James, age 16, prefers to live with Mother, because she allows him to skip school and play video games, while Father requires him to attend school. Under Factor (1), James' preference is not likely to influence the court's decision.

Significant Decisions

The IMDMA defines "significant decisions" as those related to education, health, religion, and extracurricular activities.[6]

Sole or Joint Decision-Making Authority

Decision-making authority can be awarded to both parents (called joint decision-making authority), or it can be awarded to one parent (called sole decision-making authority). A separate determination can be made for each of the four areas.[7]

EXAMPLE Although they did not function well as a couple, the parties have similar views on child-rearing and have worked together well as parents since the children were born. A court will likely award joint allocation in all four areas.

EXAMPLE In contrast, Mother is a teacher. Father is a nurse. They were both competitive swimmers at a Catholic college. For several years, their children have planned to swim for their parents' alma mater. The court may award Mother decision-making over education, Father over medical care, and joint decision-making over religion and extracurricular activities.

Regardless of the allocation of decision-making authority, all parents have access to their children's medical and educational records.[8] In the example in which Mother has sole decision-making authority over education and Father does over medical care, they both have access to all of the children's records, educational and medical.

Finally, a parent not granted allocation retains responsibility for making routine and emergency decisions affecting the child's health and safety during that parent's parenting time.

EXAMPLE Father is not allocated significant decision-making authority. During his parenting time, he can decide whether to serve scrambled eggs or cold cereal for breakfast without consulting Mother.

EXAMPLE In contrast, Mother is allocated significant decision-making authority, and has determined Child should receive all the vaccinations recommended by Child's pediatrician. Father does not want to have Child vaccinated. Father cannot make this decision.

Allocation of Parental Responsibility: Parenting Time

A parent who is not granted significant decision-making responsibilities is still entitled to reasonable parenting time with the child.[9]

Standing

Parenting Time

Only parents can bring a petition for parenting time.[10]

> **EXAMPLE** In a dissolution proceeding, Father is granted sole decision-making authority. Mother can bring a petition for parenting time.

Visitation

The IMDMA allows certain non-parents to bring a petition for time with a child, called visitation. These include "siblings (of the whole or half-blood), stepparents, grandparents and great-grandparents."[11]

Petitions for visitation may only be granted if there has been an unreasonable denial of visitation by a parent and the denial caused the child undue mental physical or emotional harm.[12] There is a rebuttable presumption that a fit parent's actions are not harmful. As a result, the non-parents must overcome the presumption by demonstrating that the parent's denial caused the child harm.

> **EXAMPLE** Single Mother denied Grandmother (Father's mother) visitation with Child. Grandmother files a Petition for Visitation, alleging lost opportunities with Child. She has not met her burden of proving the denial caused Child undue harm.

> **EXAMPLE** In contrast, Single Mother is seriously injured in a car accident and spends months in the hospital and a rehabilitation center. During that time, Grandmother was the primary caregiver for Child, who developed a deep attachment to her. After Single Mother is released, she denies Grandmother visitation, and Child goes into a deep depression. Now, Grandmother has likely overcome the presumption.

Factors Used in Allocation: Parenting Time

If the parties cannot agree on a parenting time schedule, parenting time is allocated based on the best interest of the child.[13] While many of the factors are the same as those used in an allocation of decision-making, some are different. Those related to decision-making, prior course of conduct, and the ability to work together are omitted. Unique to parenting time are the following:

> (3) The amount of time each parent spent performing caretaking functions with respect to the child in the 24 months preceding the filing of any petition for allocation of parental responsibilities or, if the child is under 2 years of age, since the child's birth;
>
> (4) Any prior agreement or course of conduct between the parents relating to caretaking functions with respect to the child; and
>
> (12) The willingness and ability of each parent to place the needs of the child ahead of his or her own needs.[14]

The General Assembly defined "caretaking functions" as "tasks that involve interaction with a child or that direct, arrange, and supervise the interaction with and care of a child provided by others."[15] The statute provides examples of caretaking functions, such as:

> (1) Satisfying a child's nutritional needs; managing a child's bedtime and wake-up routines; caring for a child when the child is sick or injured; being attentive to a child's personal hygiene needs, including washing, grooming, and dressing; playing with a child and ensuring the child attends scheduled extracurricular activities; protecting a child's physical safety; and providing transportation for a child;
>
> (2) Directing a child's various developmental needs, including the acquisition of motor and language skills, toilet training, self-confidence, and maturation;
>
> (3) Providing discipline, giving instruction in manners, assigning and supervising chores, and performing other tasks that attend to a child's needs for behavioral control and self-restraint;
>
> (4) Ensuring the child attends school, including remedial and special services appropriate to the child's needs and interests, communicating with teachers and counselors, and supervising homework;
>
> (5) Helping a child develop and maintain appropriate interpersonal relationships with peers, siblings, and other family members;
>
> (6) Ensuring the child attends medical appointments and is available for medical follow-up and meeting the medical needs of the child in the home;

(7) Providing moral and ethical guidance for a child; and

(8) Arranging alternative care for a child by a family member, babysitter, or other childcare provider or facility, including investigating such alternatives, communicating with providers, and supervising such care.[16]

EXAMPLE Mother works from 6:00 a.m. to 2:00 p.m. so she can be home when the children return from school at 2:30 p.m. Upon hearing her car in the driveway, Father grabs his keys and leaves the house. Mother provides the children's after-school snack, supervises homework, makes dinner, monitors showers, and reads bedtime stories. Mother has provided caretaking functions.

In allocating parenting time, the court shall not consider a parent's conduct that does not affect that parent's relationship with the child.[17]

EXAMPLE During his parenting time, Father abstains from alcohol. When Mother is enjoying parenting time, Father drinks to excess. The court will not consider his drinking *per se*. Should he lose his driver's license, affecting his ability to transport the children, his drinking would affect his relationship with the children and could be considered in an allocation of parenting time.

The Parenting Time Schedule

No Schedule Provided in Statute

The statute does not provide a standard parenting time schedule, because what is in the best interest of the child depends on a number of factors, such as the age of the child, the distance between the parents' houses, and the location of the child's school. For some families, an equal parenting time schedule works; children may spend one week with one parent, and the following week with the other. For others, a more traditional "every other weekend and Wednesday afternoon" schedule may better serve the children's interests.

Schedule Must Be Enforceable

The IMDMA requires either a schedule that designates in which parent's home the child will reside on given days or a formula for determining such a schedule in sufficient detail that it can be enforced.[18]

EXAMPLE A parenting time schedule provides "Father has parenting time on weekends when he feels like it and Mother does not have anything else going on." This schedule cannot be enforced and will not be entered by the court.

Parenting time is protected, with criminal and civil penalties, for abuse.[19]

EXAMPLE Mother has parenting time on Wednesday at 3:30 p.m. When she arrives at Father's house to pick up the children, he is not home and does not respond to her texts or phone calls. Mother calls the local police department. Police officers investigate and file a report. She can use it for a civil action for abuse of allocated parenting time. In addition, the State's Attorney may file a criminal petition for unlawful visitation or parenting time interference.

The Parenting Plan

Statutory Requirements

Once an allocation of parental responsibilities has been made, it is memorialized in a parenting plan. At a minimum, a parenting plan must contain the following:

(1) An allocation of significant decision-making responsibilities;

(2) Provisions for the child's living arrangements and for each parent's parenting time;

(3) A mediation provision regarding the terms of allocation of parental responsibilities (this provision is not required if one parent is allocated all significant decision-making responsibilities);

(4) Each parent's right of access to medical, dental, and psychological records (subject to the Mental Health and Developmental Disabilities Confidentiality Act), child care records, and school and extracurricular records, reports, and schedules, unless expressly denied by a court order or denied under a provision of the Domestic Violence Act;

(5) A designation of the parent who will be denominated as the parent with the majority of parenting time for those state and federal statutes that require designation of custody or custodian;

(6) The child's residential address for school enrollment purposes only;

(7) Each parent's residence address and phone number, and each parent's place of employment and employment address and phone number;

(8) Procedure to follow if a parent changes his or her residence;

(9) Provisions requiring each parent to notify the other of emergencies, health care, travel plans, or other significant child-related issues;

(10) Transportation arrangements between the parents;

(11) Provisions for communications, including electronic communications, with the child during the other parent's parenting time;

(12) Provisions for resolving issues arising from a parent's future relocation, if applicable;

(13) Provisions for future modifications of the parenting plan, if specified events occur;

(14) Provisions for the exercise of the right of first refusal, if so desired; and

(15) Any other provision that addresses the child's best interests or that will otherwise facilitate cooperation between the parents. [20]

EXAMPLE A parenting plan provides that Father will pick up the children at Mother's house when he begins parenting time, and Mother will pick up the children at Father's house when she begins parenting time. This language satisfies (10) above.

EXAMPLE A child is five years old and does not have a cell phone. The parenting plan provides that the parent not exercising parenting time may make one phone call to the parent's phone every evening with the child at 7:00 p.m. This language satisfies (11) above.

Additional Language

The statutory requirements for a parenting plan leave a number of parenting issues unaddressed. If they are not addressed, they can be disputed.

EXAMPLE Child is invited to a friend's birthday party during Father's parenting time. Mother says she notified Father of the party via text. Father denies it. An hour before the party starts, Child realizes he doesn't have a present. Father says Mother should have bought it. Mother tells Father to buy it. Father demands payment over Zelle. When Mother refuses, Father says Child can go without a present. Mother replies with unflattering language.

Consequently, most family law firms attempt to address as many parenting issues in the parenting plan as possible.

> **EXAMPLE** A parenting plan provides that if a child has been invited to a birthday party, the parent exercising parenting time when the party takes place is responsible for buying the present and transporting the child to and from the birthday party.

Another common provision is that the parties communicate through Our Family Wizard, Talking Parents, or another parenting app (https://www.ourfamilywizard.com). Now, if Mother notifies Father of the birthday party, there is a record. In addition, knowing the record can be viewed by the court helps parents stay focused on the child.

The Process

The IMDMA provides a step-by-step process to be followed in an allocation of parental responsibilities. Courts keep the process moving because all allocation of parental responsibility proceedings must be resolved within 18 months from the date of service of the petition.[21]

The Initial Conference

When a case is filed with the clerk of the court under the IMDMA, it is assigned to a judge and an initial status conference is set. At the initial status conference, which must be held within 90 days after service of the petition,[22] the judge will ascertain whether service has been made on the respondent. Additionally, the judge will likely address two parenting issues:

Parenting Education Requirement

First, the judge will confirm if the parents complied with the parenting education requirement of Illinois Supreme Court Rule 924.[23] If the parents have not, they will likely be ordered to do so by the next court date.

Proposed Parenting Plan

Second, the judge will ask if the parents have decided on an allocation of parental responsibilities and parenting time. Under the IMDMA, both parties must present a proposed plan within 120 days.[24]

EXAMPLE The parents have agreed to share decision-making. Because they both provided caretaking functions and live less than a mile from each other, they agree to exercise parenting time on alternate weeks. They are ready to sign the parenting plan.

EXAMPLE In contrast, once he learns he will still have access to the school and medical records, Father agrees Mother shall have sole allocation of decision-making, recognizing she has made decisions for the children their entire lives. However, he wants more parenting time than the one Saturday afternoon each month at the public library that Mother is offering.

Mediation

If the parties have been unable to arrive at a parenting plan resolving all issues within 120 days, generally by the second court date, absent good cause, the judge will likely order them to attend mediation on the remaining issues.[25]

Defined

Mediation is a process in which a third party neutral assists the parents in allocating parental responsibility together. The mediator has no opinion on the issues and no authority over the parties. Instead, the mediator attempts to foster joint problem-solving by reducing emotion and reframing issues so the parties focus on their children.

EXAMPLE When Mediator asks Mother why she is proposing one afternoon per month of parenting time at the public library, Mother expresses outrage that Father's new girlfriend is already living at his apartment. Father responds with anger, saying he will not be controlled. Mediator helps them look at the impact a new significant other has on the children. If the children get attached to a new significant other, and the relationship ends, how will the children feel?

Non-Binding

Because the parties are not bound by an agreement they make in mediation, they are free to consider many possible alternatives.

EXAMPLE The parents agree to talk to their children's therapist for guidance on how long either of them should wait before introducing a new partner. Father agrees that his girlfriend will not be present during his parenting time yet, and Mother agrees to extend parenting time to every other weekend.

The Investigation

If parents are unable to arrive at a parenting plan, (either alone or with the help of a mediator), the court will have to make parenting decisions for them. Since judges cannot leave the bench to investigate the children's best interest, and since they rarely interview a child in chambers,[26] judges generally appoint an attorney for the minor child to do the investigation.

Attorneys for Minor Children

Illinois law provides three different types of attorneys for minor children.[27] A guardian *ad litem* ("GAL") investigates facts and makes a recommendation. In contrast, a child's representative reviews facts and then advocates for the child. Finally, an attorney for the child provides independent legal counsel for the child. All the attorneys for minor children are guided by the Illinois Supreme Court rules, which provide the minimum duties and responsibilities with which they must comply.[28]

Guardian ad Litem

Although practice varies by county, the attorney for the minor children used most is the GAL. In order to be appointed, GALs must have completed training required by the Illinois Supreme Court in the following areas:

- Child development;
- Ethics in child custody or allocation of parental responsibilities cases;
- Relevant substantive state, federal, and case law in custody or allocation of parental responsibilities and visitation or parenting time matters; and
- Family dynamics, including substance abuse, domestic abuse, and mental health issues.[29]

Once appointed, the GALs gather information for the judge in a number of different ways. They may talk to the child and interview parents in their office, or observe parents interacting with the child in their homes. Additionally, they may talk to the children's teachers or babysitters, or other family members, such as grandparents or step-parents. With proper authorization, they can access a minor child's educational and medical records.

> **EXAMPLE** Parents met at a "rave." During their courtship, they spent considerable time using drugs and going to parties. During the investigation, they both accuse the other of using drugs, and the GAL requires drug testing for both parents. Mother's comes back clean, supporting her statement that she quit when she became pregnant. Father's comes back, showing recent, heavy cocaine use. This factor is significant in the GAL's report.

Professional Evaluation

Although GALs are well trained, at times additional advice is needed. The court, or either parent, may request the advice of a professional in determining the child's best interests.[30] These professionals, generally doctors of psychology, perform evaluations and make conclusions.

> **EXAMPLE** When the GAL is troubled by some of Mother's behaviors, the court seeks an evaluation of Mother by a doctor of psychology. After submitting Mother to multiple tests and evaluations, the doctor concludes that Mother has borderline personality disorder. Although the children are attached to Mother, their best interest may be served by awarding Father majority parenting time.

At the end of the investigation, the GAL will make a report, which may be oral or written, to the judge. Because GALs are not bound by the evidence rules excluding hearsay, or out-of-court statements, they can report facts that would otherwise be inadmissible.[31]

Rejection of Recommendation

If both parties agree with the GAL's report, they sign a parenting plan, which is entered by the court as a Parenting Allocation Judgment ("PAJ"). Once entered, the PAJ has the force of law and can be enforced. However, if one parent does not agree, the matter is set for trial. (See Chapter 10, Discovery, Pretrial, and Trial).

Chapter Summary

When parents are married, they are presumed to exercise parental responsibilities together. After parents separate, the court has to allocate the responsibilities between them, which they do based on the best interest of the child. The IMDMA provides factors to guide courts in determining the best interest of the child with respect to decision-making. The IMDMA limits significant decisions to four main areas: education, religion, medical care, and extracurricular activities.

Parents not awarded allocation for decision-making are still awarded parenting time with their child. Similar to a determination of decision-making, the court makes the parenting time allocation between the parents based on the child's best interests, applying different factors, especially caretaking functions. Parenting time schedules vary; however, they must be written in sufficient detail to be enforced. A parent's time with his child is taken very seriously and is protected civilly and criminally.

It is hoped that parents can resolve parenting issues and arrive at a parenting plan together. If they cannot, the court will decide for them, following a step-by-step process laid out in law. First, the parties will work with a mediator. If they are unsuccessful, an attorney for the child, often a guardian *ad litem*, will be appointed to investigate and make a report. If the parties agree with the GAL's report, the matter is resolved, but if they don't, the matter heads to trial.

Key Terms

Standing
Allocation of Parental Responsibilities: Decision-Making
Significant Decisions
Allocation of Parental Responsibilities: Parenting Time
Caretaking Functions
Parenting Allocation Judgment
Mediation
Guardian *ad Litem*

Discussion Questions

1. In 2016, the General Assembly replaced the terms "visitation" with "parenting time" and "custody" with "allocation of parental responsibilities." Do these terms better reflect society in 2023?
2. The General Assembly has considered bills that create a rebuttable presumption that 50/50 parenting time is in the child's best interests. How does this compare with the best interest of the child standard currently used to determine parenting time? *See* https://aaml.org/wp-content/uploads/Equally-Shared-Physical-Custody_112022.pdf (last visited June 29, 2023).

3. The General Assembly defined caretaking functions in detail. Why are caretaking functions important in a determination of parenting time?
4. Parenting time is a right that will be protected. It is not an obligation that will be enforced. Why is that?
5. Suppose a child expresses a desire to begin gender-affirming care, such as puberty blocking medication. Is that a medical decision, which could be made by a parent with sole decision-making authority? If so, should the other parent be consulted? If parents share decision-making and disagree, how does the court determine the child's best interest? Or is this a new area of responsibility the General Assembly has not considered?
6. In the introduction to the IMDMA, the General Assembly articulated that one of its goals concerning the allocation process was "to minimize or eliminate rancor and the detrimental effect of litigation in any proceeding involving children." Have they achieved this goal?
7. All parenting issues must be resolved within 18 months from the service of the petition to the entry of the final order. What policy does that address? Does having a deadline affect the legislature's goal of eliminating rancor? If so, in what way?
8. The longer litigation lasts, the more expensive it is for the parties. How might the cost of prolonged litigation affect children's lives post-litigation?
9. Mediation is a required step before the parties go to litigation, except for good cause shown. Should domestic violence be accepted as a good cause? Why or why not? What else might be accepted as good cause?
10. Pursuant to 410 ILCS 705/10, the Personal Use of Cannabis, the presence of cannabinoid components in a person's fluid may not form the basis for an adverse finding in a family court. While cannabis is legal, it is mood-altering. Alcohol is legal, but most PAJs prohibit parents from using alcohol during parenting time. Should a PAJ include similar provisions about cannabis? Why or why not? Breathalyzers can detect recent use of alcohol. Are tests available to detect the recent use of cannabis?
11. Many Illinois families are "mixed status," meaning the parents hold different immigration statuses. However, the immigration status of a parent is not an enumerated factor in the statute. Should it be? Courts have considered the matter. *See Hupp v. Rosales*, 2013 IL App (4th) 130433-U. (Not reported in N.E.2d) (2013 WL 5435698). Further, pursuant to the Illinois rule of evidence, immigration status may not be introduced in civil matters. *See* 735 ILCS 5/8-2901. Should there be an exception for family law?

Forms

1. Parenting Plan

   https://ilcourtsaudio.blob.core.windows.net/antilles-resources/resources/a601856a-12e7-44fe-9076-88a8e150c3a7/DWC%20Parenting%20Plan.pdf

2. Mediation Order

   https://cic.countyofkane.org/eForms/P1-MISC-033-E.pdf

3. Mediation Report

   https://cic.countyofkane.org/eForms/P1-MISC-056-E.pdf

Endnotes

1. 750 ILCS 5/606.10 (West, Westlaw Classic through P.A. 103-21 of the 2023 Reg. Sess.). Note: the parent with majority parenting time is presumed to have custody pursuant to the School Code.
2. Troxel v. Granville, 530 U.S. 57 (2000).
3. 750 ILCS 5/601.2(b)(3-5).
4. a parent engaged in any conduct that seriously endangered the child's mental, moral, or physical health or that significantly impaired the child's emotional development;
5. *Id.* § 602.5(c)(1-15).
6. *Id.* § 602.5(b)(1-4).
7. *Id.* § 602.5(b).
8. *Id.* § 602.11(a).
9. *Id.* § 602.8(a).
10. 750 ILCS 5/602.8(a).
11. *Id.* § 602.9(c).
12. *Id.* § 602 (b)(4).
13. *Id.* § 602.7(a).
14. *Id.* § 602.7(a)(3)(4)(12).
15. *Id.* § 600 (c).
16. 750 ILCS 5/600 (c).
17. *Id.* § 602.7(c).
18. *Id.* § 602.10(f)(2)(B).
19. 720 ILCS 5/10-5.5 Unlawful Visitation or Parenting Time Interference and 750 ILCS 5/607.5(a) Abuse of Allocated Parenting Time.
20. 750 ILCS 5/602.10(f).
21. Ill. Sup. Ct. R. 922.
22. Ill. Sup. Ct. R. 904.
23. Ill. Sup. Ct. R. 924.
24. 750 ILCS 5/602.10(a).
25. Ill. Sup. Ct. R. 905.
26. 750 ILCS 5/604.10(a).

27. *Id.* § 506(a)(1-3).
28. Ill. Sup. Ct. R. 907.
29. 18th Jud. Cir. Ct. R. 15.14(a)(1).
30. 750 ILCS 5/604.10(b).
31. In re Marriage of Wycoff, 266 Ill. App. 3d 408, 639 N.E.2d 897 (4th Dist. 1994).

1. PARENTING PLAN

This form is approved by the Illinois Supreme Court and is required to be accepted in all Illinois Circuit Courts.

STATE OF ILLINOIS, CIRCUIT COURT COUNTY	**PARENTING PLAN** *(check the correct box)* ☐ Petitioner's Parenting Plan ☐ Respondent's Parenting Plan ☐ Agreed Parenting Plan ☐ Court's Parenting Plan	*For Court Use Only*

Instructions ▾		
Directly above, enter the county where you filed this case.		
Enter the full name of Petitioner, Respondent, and the case number as listed on the *Petition for Dissolution of Marriage/Civil Union (Divorce with Children).*	**Petitioner** *(First, middle, last name)* v. **Respondent** *(First, middle, last name)*	**Case Number**
Check the box for whose *Parenting Plan* this is.		

1. Parent Information:

Do not complete **1a** if Petitioner's information is protected because of domestic violence or abuse.

a. Petitioner's contact information:

Name: ______________________________
First *Middle* *Last*

Address: ______________________________
Street Address, Apt.

____
City *State* *ZIP*

Phone number: ______________
Email: ______________
Petitioner is employed: ☐ Yes ☐ No
Employer name: ______________
Employer address: ______________
Street Address

____
City *State* *ZIP*

Employer phone number: ______________

Do not complete **1b** if Respondent's information is protected because of domestic violence or abuse.

b. Respondent's contact information:

Name: ______________________________
First *Middle* *Last*

Address: ______________________________
Street Address, Apt.

____
City *State* *ZIP*

Phone number: ______________
Email: ______________
Respondent is employed: ☐ Yes ☐ No
Employer name: ______________

If this is an agreement, enter initials on each page.

Petitioner's initials: ______
Respondent's initials: ______

Enter the Case Number given by the Circuit Clerk: ______________________________

Employer address: ____
Street Address

____
City *State* *ZIP*

> For **1c**, if you plan to move, review **Section 10 (Relocation of Minor Children)** to see if that Section applies to your move.

Employer phone number: ____________________

c. If a parent plans to move, they must give the other parent at least 60 days notice, or notice as soon as possible of (1) the intended move date; and (2) the new address unless the address is protected because of domestic violence or abuse.

> In **2**, list the name and birth date for the minor children of the parties. This plan is only for children who are younger than 18.

2. This *Parenting Plan* is for the Following Children Born to or Adopted by the Parties:

	Name	Date of Birth
1.		
2.		
3.		
☐ I have listed additional minor children on the attached *Additional Minor Children* form.		

3. Rights and Responsibilities of Both Parents:

Each parent must:

a. Make day-to-day decisions for the children when they have them, such as routine discipline, minor medical treatment, curfew, chores, and hygiene.

b. Give the other parent the name, address, and telephone number of any health care provider for the children.

c. Have access to the children's school records, child care information, extracurricular activity schedules, and medical, dental, and mental health records unless access is denied by the court.

d. Notify the other parent as soon as possible of emergencies, health care, travel plans, or other significant child-related issues.

4. Significant Decision Making *(check only one option for each category)*:

a. Education decisions *(includes choice of schools and tutors)* will be made by:
☐ Both parents ☐ Petitioner ☐ Respondent

b. Health decisions *(includes medical, dental, and psychological decisions)* will be made by:
☐ Both parents ☐ Petitioner ☐ Respondent

c. Religious decisions will be made by:
☐ Both parents ☐ Petitioner ☐ Respondent ☐ Reserved

d. Extracurricular/recreational activities decisions will be made by:
☐ Both parents ☐ Petitioner ☐ Respondent

5. Parenting Time Schedule

(Instructions for this section):

Use the schedule below to show which parent has the child (or children) during each hour block shown. Overnight begins at 9:00 PM and ends at 8:00 AM the next day.

If the schedule will be the same every week, only fill in one schedule. If there will be two schedules that alternate every other week, fill in two schedules. If there will be more than two weekly schedules, fill in more schedules on the *Additional Parenting Time* form and Insert them after the next page.

Petitioner's initials: _______

Respondent's initials: _______

Enter the Case Number given by the Circuit Clerk: ______________________

Fill in the parents' names or initials in the chart below to show which parent has the child (or children) each day at each time listed.

Enter the parents' names and initials on the lines below:

Parent Name: ____________________ Initials: ________________
Parent Name: ____________________ Initials: ________________

Write the date that you want the Week 1 parenting time schedule to start.

Enter the parents' names or initials in each box to show who will have the child at each time and day. **Do not** leave any boxes blank. If the child is scheduled to be somewhere else, for example, school or after school activities, you still must enter the name or initials of the parent responsible for the child at that time.

a. Week 1 Schedule: Week 1 begins on: ________________
Date

Start time	Sunday	Monday	Tuesday	Wednesday	Thursday	Friday	Saturday
8 AM							
9 AM							
10 AM							
11 AM							
Noon							
1 PM							
2 PM							
3 PM							
4 PM							
5 PM							
6 PM							
7 PM							
8 PM							
9 PM - Overnight							

b. Week 2 Schedule:

Start time	Sunday	Monday	Tuesday	Wednesday	Thursday	Friday	Saturday
8 AM							
9 AM							
10 AM							
11 AM							
Noon							
1 PM							
2 PM							
3 PM							
4 PM							
5 PM							
6 PM							
7 PM							
8 PM							
9 PM - Overnight							

Petitioner's initials: _______
Respondent's initials: _______

Enter the Case Number given by the Circuit Clerk: ______________________________

Make a schedule for parenting time during the holidays. First read both options 1 and 2 and pick either option 1 or 2. If you want holidays that are not listed, you can write the holidays you want to add on the blank line in 1 or in the "other" boxes in option 2. In option 2, enter the start and end time for each holiday and check which parent has the holiday in even years and which has it in odd years.

c. Holiday Schedule *(check only one):*

1. ☐ The holidays shall be divided between the parents as follows:
   - In even-numbered years, Petitioner shall have the minor children on Group A holidays and Respondent shall have the minor children on Group B holidays.
   - In odd-numbered years, Petitioner shall have the minor children on Group B holidays and Respondent shall have the minor children on Group A holidays.

Group A Holidays:
- Thanksgiving Day
- Christmas Eve
- New Year's Eve
- ______________________________
- ______________________________
- ______________________________

Group B Holidays:
- 4th of July
- Labor Day
- Christmas Day
- ______________________________
- ______________________________
- ______________________________

2. ☐ The holidays shall be divided between the parents as follows:

Holiday	Time *(include a.m./p.m.)*		Even Years	Odd Years
	Start Time	End Time		
New Year's Day			☐ Pet. ☐ Res.	☐ Pet. ☐ Res.
Mother's Day			☐ Pet. ☐ Res.	☐ Pet. ☐ Res.
Memorial Day			☐ Pet. ☐ Res.	☐ Pet. ☐ Res.
Father's Day			☐ Pet. ☐ Res.	☐ Pet. ☐ Res.
July 4th			☐ Pet. ☐ Res.	☐ Pet. ☐ Res.
Labor Day			☐ Pet. ☐ Res.	☐ Pet. ☐ Res.
Halloween			☐ Pet. ☐ Res.	☐ Pet. ☐ Res.
Thanksgiving Day			☐ Pet. ☐ Res.	☐ Pet. ☐ Res.
Christmas Eve			☐ Pet. ☐ Res.	☐ Pet. ☐ Res.
Christmas Day			☐ Pet. ☐ Res.	☐ Pet. ☐ Res.
New Year's Eve			☐ Pet. ☐ Res.	☐ Pet. ☐ Res.
Other:			☐ Pet. ☐ Res.	☐ Pet. ☐ Res.
Other:			☐ Pet. ☐ Res.	☐ Pet. ☐ Res.
Other:			☐ Pet. ☐ Res.	☐ Pet. ☐ Res.
Other:			☐ Pet. ☐ Res.	☐ Pet. ☐ Res.
Other:			☐ Pet. ☐ Res.	☐ Pet. ☐ Res.

In **5d**, choose 1, 2 or 3. If you choose 3, you must write in the schedule you want.

d. School Spring Break

1. ☐ No specific spring break schedule *(follow the regular parenting schedule)*
2. ☐ In even-numbered years, Petitioner shall have the entire spring break.
   In odd-numbered years, Respondent shall have the entire spring break.
3. ☐ Other: ____
   ____

In **5e**, choose 1, 2 or 3. If you choose 3, you must write in the schedule you want.

e. School Summer Break

1. ☐ No specific summer break schedule *(follow the regular parenting schedule)*
2. ☐ Each parent shall have ______________ weeks in the summer:
   - In even-numbered years, Petitioner shall have first choice of dates.
   - In odd-numbered years, Respondent shall have first choice of dates.
   - Each parent will notify the other in writing by May 1st each year of the weeks they wish to have summer parenting time.

Petitioner's initials: ______
Respondent's initials: ______

3. ☐ Other: ____

____

In **5f**, choose 1, 2 or 3. If you choose 3, you must write in the schedule you want.

f. School Winter Break
   1. ☐ No specific winter break schedule *(follow the regular parenting schedule)*
   2. ☐ Each parent shall have one-half of the winter break:
      - In even-numbered years, Petitioner shall have the first half and Respondent shall have the second half.
      - In odd-numbered years, Respondent shall have the first half and Petitioner shall have the second half.
   3. ☐ Other: ____

____

g. Conflict
   If there is conflict, the priority will be:
   1st Priority: Holiday
   2nd Priority: School Break
   3rd Priority: Regular Weekday/Weekend

For example, it is your weekend to have the children, but Saturday is July 4th and it is the other parent's turn to have July 4th. Because the Holiday schedule has 1st Priority, the other parent will get their time on July 4th even though it is your weekend.

If you need more room to determine parenting time, check the box and fill out the *Additional Parenting Time* form and file it with this *Parenting Plan*.

☐ I have listed additional parenting time information on the attached *Additional Parenting Time* form.

In **6**, read all the options and choose which option for transportation works best. If you choose "a", check which parent will provide the transportation.

6. Transportation of Children ***(check only one)*****:**
   a. ☐ Petitioner ☐ Respondent shall provide all transportation.
   b. ☐ Each parent shall pick up the children at the start of their parenting time.
   c. ☐ Each parent shall drop off the children at the end of their parenting time.

Choose option **7a** or **7b**. If you check **7b**, you must list the address where the drop off and pick up of the children will be.

7. Exchange of Children:
   a. ☐ Drop off and pick up of the children will be at Petitioner's and Respondent's homes unless both parties agree in advance to a different meeting place.
   b. ☐ Drop off and pick up of the children shall take place at: ______________________

____

In **8**, check **8a** if there will be no right of first refusal. Check **8b** if there will be a right of first refusal.

8. First Refusal for Childcare:
   a. ☐ There is no right of first refusal.
   b. ☐ Each parent must offer the other a first right of refusal as follows:
      - If a parent needs childcare for a period of 24 hours or more during their time with the children, they must give the other parent the option to care for the children before finding other childcare.
      - As soon as the need for childcare is known, the other parent must be immediately notified.
      - The parent offered the right to care for the children must accept the offer within 2 hours, otherwise the parent needing childcare may use another caregiver.
      - Transportation of the children is the same as for other parenting time.

Petitioner's initials: ______

Respondent's initials: ______

In **9,** state when the children can communicate with the other parent. In **9a**, you must choose one of the 3 options. If you check **Other**, you must list when the parent is able to communicate with the children.

9. Communication:

a. The parent who does not have the children in their care may have electronic communication with the children *(check only one)*:

☐ Anytime

☐ Every day between _________ ☐ a.m. ☐ p.m. to _________ ☐ a.m. ☐ p.m.

☐ Other: _______________

b. Electronic communication includes telephone, e-mail, text, video, etc.

c. Electronic communication between the children and the other parent must not be unreasonably monitored or interrupted.

Relocation is when a parent seeks to move with children for distances of over 25 or 50 miles (depending on county where they live).

10a explains that the parent who has majority or equal parenting and wants to move with children must obtain the permission of the other parent or the court.

10b sets out the information that must be in the notice and when the notice must be given.

10. Relocation of Minor Children:

a. If a parent with the majority of the parenting time or equal parenting time wishes to move with the children, they must have the agreement of the other parent or permission from the court when:

1. The children's primary residence is in Cook, DuPage, Kane, Lake, McHenry, or Will county and the move is within Illinois but more than 25 miles away from their current residence; OR
2. The children's primary residence is in any other county in Illinois and the move is within Illinois but more than 50 miles away from their current residence; OR
3. The move is outside of Illinois and more than 25 miles from the children's primary residence.

b. The parent asking to move with the children must provide written notice to the other parent. The notice must:

1. Be given at least 60 days before the move unless that is impossible. If impossible, the notice must be given at the earliest date possible; AND
2. State the date the parent plans to move; AND
3. State whether the move is permanent or for a specific time period; AND
4. State the new address, if known, unless the address is protected because of domestic violence or abuse.

10c1 explains what to do if the parents agree on the move and no change to the *Parenting Plan* is needed.

10c2 explains what to do when the parents agree to the move and need to make changes to the *Parenting Plan*.

c. Agreement

1. If the parents agree on the move and no change is needed to the parenting time schedule, both parties shall sign the notices provided about the move and file it with the court. No court appearance is needed.
2. If the other parent agrees with the move but changes need to be made to parenting time schedule, and the parents are in agreement about the changes to the parenting time schedule, the moving parent must:
   - Have the other parent sign the notice provided about the move;
   - File the signed notice with the court; AND
   - File an updated parenting plan with the court. The court does not need to approve the move but the court must approve the changes to the *Parenting Plan*.

10d explains what to do if the parents agree with the move but can't agree about the changes to the parenting time schedule.

d. Partial Agreement

If the other parent agrees with the move, but both parents cannot agree on changes to the *Parenting Plan*, the moving parent must:

- Have the other parent sign the notice provided about the move;
- File the signed notice with the court;

Petitioner's initials: _______

Respondent's initials: _______

- Follow the Resolving Disagreements process set out below to try to reach an agreement with the other parent about changes to the parenting time schedule; AND

If no agreement can be reached after completing the Resolving Disagreements process, file a petition to modify the parenting time schedule with the court.

10e explains what to do when the other parent does not agree with the move.

e. No Agreement

If the other parent does not agree with the move, the parent relocating must:

- Follow the Resolving Disagreements process set out below to try to reach an agreement with the other parent; AND
- If no agreement can be reached after completing the Resolving Disagreements process, file a petition with the court asking for permission to move.

Some state or federal laws require picking a custodian for the children. In **11a**, choose the parent with the majority of the parenting time. If there is equal parenting time, check the parent that will be receiving Federal and State benefits for the children, like SNAP or TANF.

In **11b**, choose the parent that has the majority of the parenting time with the children. If there is equal parenting time, check the parent whose address will be given to the school as the children's home address.

11. Designation of Children's Custody and Residence for Other Purposes:

a. Designation of Custodian for Other Statutes

☐ Petitioner ☐ Respondent is the parent who has the majority of the parenting time with the children. This designation shall not affect parents' rights and responsibilities under the *Parenting Plan.*

b. Children's Residential Address

☐ Petitioner's ☐ Respondent's home is the children's residential address for school enrollment purposes only.

12. Changing the *Parenting Plan:*

If a parent wants to change this *Parenting Plan*, they should talk and try to reach an agreement on their own.

Follow the steps in "a" if there is an agreement. Follow the steps in "b" if there is not.

a. Agreement

- Temporary changes may be made without filing a written agreement with the court.
- Permanent changes should be made by filing a new *Parenting Plan* with the court.

b. No agreement

- Follow the Resolving Disagreements process set out below to try to reach an agreement about changes to the *Parenting Plan.* If an agreement is reached, follow the steps in **13a**.
- If no agreement can be reached after completing the Resolving Disagreements process, file a petition with the court asking for changes to be made to this *Parenting Plan.*
- This *Parenting Plan* must be followed until the parents complete the Resolving Disagreements process and agree to a new plan or a new *Parenting Plan* is approved by the court.

Petitioner's initials: ______
Respondent's initials: ______

Enter the Case Number given by the Circuit Clerk: ______________________

Check **13a** or **b.** If you check **b**, check the reason mediation is not required.

13. Resolving Disagreements *(mediation)*:

If a parent wishes to change this *Parenting Plan* or feels the other parent is not following this *Parenting Plan*, the parents should talk and try to come to an agreement on their own.

If an agreement cannot be reached, parents must follow the steps below:

a. ☐ Mediation is required on all issues.

Parents must first try to come to an agreement through mediation.

- Both parents must cooperate in scheduling and participating in mediation.
- Both parents must split the cost of mediation equally unless otherwise ordered by the court.

If mediation is unsuccessful, a parent must file a petition to modify this *Parenting Plan* or a petition to enforce this *Parenting Plan* with the court.

Emergencies: In an emergency situation, a parent may file a petition with the court to get an immediate resolution without first going through mediation.

b. ☐ Mediation is not required because:

☐ One parent has all significant decision making responsibility.

☐ There is a history of domestic violence between the parties.

☐ Other reason: ____

____

A parent must file a petition to modify this *Parenting Plan* or a petition to enforce this *Parenting Plan* with the court.

Petitioner's initials: ______

Respondent's initials: ______

If this is your plan, sign it. If both parents agree, both parents must sign the plan.

______________________ ______________________

Petitioner *Respondent*

DO NOT complete this section. The judge will sign and date here.

APPROVED:

______________________ ______________________

Judge *Date*

Print Form Save Form Reset Form

2. MEDIATION ORDER

IN THE CIRCUIT COURT OF THE SIXTEENTH JUDICIAL CIRCUIT
KANE COUNTY, ILLINOIS

Case No. ______________________

Petitioner		Respondent	File Stamp
Petitioner's Attorney		Respondent's Attorney	
Judge	Court Reporter/GAL	Deputy Clerk	
A copy of this order ☐ should be sent ☐ has been sent ☐ Pet. Atty. ☐ Resp. Atty. ☐ Other ______________			

Petitioner present in Open Court ☐ Yes ☐ No Respondent present in Open Court ☐ Yes ☐ No

MEDIATION ORDER (MEDO)

This cause coming before the Court, on the motion of________________________________;
the Court having jurisdiction and pursuant to Rule 14.15 of the Sixteenth Judicial Circuit Court,

IT IS HEREBY ORDERED:

That the parties are referred to ____,
whose address is ____, and phone number
is ______________________, for mediation on the disputed issue(s) of:

☐ Allocation of Parental Responsibilities: ☐ Decision Making and/or ☐ Parenting Time
☐ Relocation
☐ Financial
☐ Other: ____

That within three (3) days of the entry of this Order, counsel for the ☐ Petitioner ☐ Respondent (or, if there is not counsel, ☐ the parties) shall send to the Mediator a copy of this Order, as well as copies of the parties' proposed parenting plan, if any.

That within three (3) days of the entry of this Order, the parties shall contact the Mediator and **shall each pay one half of the initial retainer in the amount of** $ __________. That the parties shall thereafter be equally responsible for the remaining balance due to the Mediator for additional time spent, unless otherwise ordered by the Court.

That only written discovery on issues not being mediated shall be allowed until the mediation is completed or terminated by the Court.

That the Mediator shall file his/her appearance as a mediator within three (3) days of receipt of this Order or notify the parties or their counsel that he/she is unable to accept the appointment. By filing an appearance, the Mediator represents that he/she is in compliance with the qualifications/requirements set forth in Rule 14.15 necessary to serve as a mediator.

That the Mediator's AOIC Report shall be submitted to the Court and to the parties' attorney prior to the status date.

That Memorandum of Agreements arising out of this Court Ordered Mediation shall only be submitted to the parties' attorney (or parties if no attorney).

This matter is set for status on ______________ at ______________ in Courtroom ________.

Entered: ______________

Judge: ___________________________________

PETITIONER	RESPONDENT
Name: ______________________________	Name: ______________________________
Relation to Child: ______________________	Relation to Child: ______________________
Address: ____________________________	Address: ____________________________
City/State/ZIP: ________________________	City/State/ZIP: ________________________
Telephone: ___________________________	Telephone: ___________________________
Email: ______________________________	Email: ______________________________

PETITIONER'S ATTORNEY	RESPONDENT'S ATTORNEY
Name: ______________________________	Name: ______________________________
Address: ____________________________	Address: ____________________________
City/State/ZIP: ________________________	City/State/ZIP: ________________________
Telephone: ___________________________	Telephone: ___________________________
Email: ______________________________	Email: ______________________________

3. MEDIATION REPORT

IN THE CIRCUIT COURT OF THE SIXTEENTH JUDICIAL CIRCUIT
KANE COUNTY, ILLINOIS

Case No. ____________________

Plaintiff(s)		Defendant(s)	File Stamp
Plaintiff(s) Atty.		Defendant(s) Atty.	
Judge	Court Reporter	Deputy Clerk	
A copy of this order ☐ should be sent ☐ has been sent ☐ Plaintiff Atty. ☐ Defense Atty. ☐ Other ____________			

MEDIATION REPORT
(Illinois Supreme Court Rule 99)

1. Mediation was: ☐ ordered by the court ☐ by Joint Parenting Agreement
2. Mediation: ☐ did ☐ did not take place.
3. The issues concerned were: ☐ pre-decree ☐ post-decree ☐ not appropriate for mediation
4. This ☐ was ☐ was not a low-income case.
5. The mediation in this case concerned the following issues: ☐ custody ☐ visitation ☐ removal ☐ financial issues
6. An agreement was reached as to the following:
   ☐ No issues
   ☐ These issues: ☐ custody ☐ visitation ☐ removal ☐ financial issues
   ☐ all issues (Attach a copy of the mediation agreement)
7. The mediator is ☐ a licensed attorney ☐ a mental health professional ☐ other ____________
8. The mediation of a total of ____________ hours at a rate of ____________ per hour.
   Total fees ____________ ☐ paid in full ☐ paid in part, ____________ owing.
9. Date of referral or court order ____________
10. Date of first mediation session ____________
11. Date of last mediation session ____________
12. Mediator's report is a ☐ interim report ☐ final report
13. Additional sessions are ☐ recommended ☐ not recommended
14. Next scheduled session: ____________

Date: ____________

Mediator's Printed Name ____________
Mediator's Signature ____________
Address ____________
City, State and Zip ____________
Phone ____________

P1-MISC-056 (04/09)

Seven

Child Support

Overview

In the previous chapter, we addressed the allocation of parental responsibilities concerning decision-making and parenting time. In this chapter, we address the allocation of financial responsibility. As you read, consider whether the IMDMA considers all of the child's physical, mental, and emotional health needs and whether it is flexible enough to accommodate the many forms families come in today.

Child Support

The Duty to Support

Illinois uses the income shares model for child support, which attempts to recreate the lifestyle the child would have enjoyed had the parents remained married.[1] This model is used in proceedings for dissolution of marriage, legal separation, declaration of invalidity of marriage, dissolution of a civil union, and establishing paternity.

The court may order either or both parents to pay child support. The parent who pays support is the "obligor."[2] The parent receiving support is the "obligee," or more often, the "recipient parent."

Emancipation Events

The obligation to support a child lasts until the child turns 18, or graduates from high school, whichever is later.[3]

EXAMPLE Child is 17 when he graduates from high school. Child support continues until he turns 18.

EXAMPLE In contrast, Child turns 19 in November of his senior year in high school. Child support continues until he graduates the following May.

The Child Support Calculation

Child support is based on the parents' net incomes, that is, their gross incomes minus certain allowable deductions.[4]

Broad Definition of Income

Income is defined as "income from all sources."[5] In addition to base salary, bonuses, overtime, commissions, and tips are included in income. Spousal maintenance is considered income to the recipient spouse. Income outside of salary, such as interest, dividends, and even gambling winnings, is also included.

EXAMPLE Father pays child support on his base salary. Father receives a bonus, based on his employer's performance, at the end of each calendar year. The bonus is included in Father's income for child support purposes.

The only sources of income not included are benefits or income received by the parent from means-tested public assistance programs, such as Temporary Assistance for Needy Families ("TANF" or "welfare"), Social Security, and Supplemental Nutrition Assistance Program ("SNAP" or "food stamps.") Benefits or income received by a parent for other children in the household are also excluded from income.[6]

EXAMPLE Mother is a foster parent and receives $512 per month from the State of Illinois for the foster child's maintenance. This amount is not included in Mother's income.

Allowable Deductions

Only certain expenses can be deducted from a parent's gross income. These include federal and state income taxes, Social Security (FICA) or other mandatory retirement contributions, Medicare, and those expenses required for employment, such as union dues and uniforms.[7] Spousal maintenance is an allowable deduction from income for the obligor.

EXAMPLE Father' gross paycheck is $4,000 per month. Federal income tax on that amount is $639 per month. The $639 is deducted from his income before child support is calculated.

> **EXAMPLE** In contrast, Father's gross paycheck is $4,000 per month. Father contributes $960 to his 401(k) plan each month. The $960 is not deductible from his income for child support purposes.

The Formula

A child support obligation is allocated to each parent, based on the percentage they contribute to the total combined income.[8] Some law firms use commercial computer programs, such as Family Law Software, to perform the calculation. For smaller firms or self-represented parties, the Illinois Department of Health and Family Services provides a calculator on its website that is available to the public at no cost.

Non-Custodial Parent Awarded Fewer Than 146 Overnights

Child support is determined according to the following calculation:

1. Combine the parents' net incomes;
2. Obtain the base child support obligation for the number of children they are supporting from the Illinois Child Support Schedule (https//www.illinois.gov/hfs/ChildSupport/Pages/default.aspx);
3. Calculate each parent's percentage share of the base child support obligation.

> **EXAMPLE**
>
> 1. Father earns $7,000 per month net income. Mother earns $3,000 per month. Their combined net income is $10,000.
>
> 2. Mother and Father have two children. The Illinois Child Support Schedule provides that the base child support obligation for two children is $2,173. This is the amount they would have spent on their children had they remained married.
>
> 3. Mother earns 30% of their combined net income, and is allocated 30% of the child support, or $519. Father earns 70% of their combined net income and is allocated 70% of the child support, or $1,521. Father, the obligor, pays child support of $1,521 to Mother, the obligee. Mother does not pay Father $519; she is presumed to spend that amount on the children each month.

Non-Custodial Parent Awarded More Than 146 Overnights

The calculation above assumed Father was awarded fewer than 146 overnights per year. If Father had been awarded 146 or more overnights, called "shared physical care," the calculation would change,[9] to reflect that with the additional time, the parties have more duplicated expenses.

> **EXAMPLE** If Father in the example above had been awarded over 146 overnights, the base child support obligation would increase to $2,415 per month, but Father's child support obligation would drop to $973 per month.

Deviation from Guideline

The child support formula determines guideline support.[10] However, the court may deviate from guideline support when appropriate. Any deviation from the guidelines must be accompanied by written findings by the court specifying the reasons for the deviation.[11] These reasons may include:

A. Extraordinary medical expenditures necessary to preserve the life or health of a party or a child of either or both of the parties;

B. Additional expenses incurred for a child subject to the child support order who has special medical, physical, or developmental needs; and

C. Any other factor the court determines should be applied upon a finding that the application of the child support guidelines would be inappropriate, after considering the best interest of the child.[12]

> **EXAMPLE** Mother was paralyzed in a skiing accident and is confined to a wheelchair. While Mother is employed, a large percentage of her income goes to the equipment she needs, such as a motorized wheelchair and accessible transportation. The court deviates from guidelines and reduces her child support obligation pursuant to section (A).

Special Cases

Multiple Families

If a parent is supporting a child (not shared with the other parent in the present proceeding), the parent can request an adjustment to child support.[13]

Adjustment with Court Order

The court shall deduct from the parent's net income the amount of child support actually paid by the parent pursuant to a support order unless the court makes a finding that it would cause economic hardship to the child.[14]

> **EXAMPLE** Father and Mother are in a divorce proceeding. They have one daughter together. Father has a son from a prior marriage, for whom he was court-ordered to pay child support of $600 per month. Father can deduct the $600 from his income before child support is calculated for his daughter. Father and Mother both have good jobs. The deduction does not cause hardship to their daughter.

Adjustment without Court Order

If there is no court order, the court can deduct either the amount of financial support actually paid by the parent for the child, or 75% of the support the parent should pay under the child support guidelines, whichever is less.[15] The child may be living in or outside of that parent's household.[16]

> **EXAMPLE** Father and Mother have one daughter. After they divorce, Mother marries a professional athlete and gives birth to a son. They own multiple homes and travel between them on a private jet. The court will deduct 75% of the support Mother should pay for her son under guidelines, even though she actually spends far more on him.

Please note: Mother's child support obligation is calculated using Mother's income alone; her new husband's income is not included.

Minimum Child Support Obligation

There is a rebuttable presumption that a minimum child support obligation of $40 per month, per child, will be entered for an obligor who has actual or imputed gross income at or less than 75% of the most recent United States Department of Health and Human Services Federal Poverty Guidelines for a family of one person, with a maximum total child support obligation for that obligor of $120 per month to be divided equally among all of the obligor's children.[17]

EXAMPLE During a divorce proceeding, Father's company downsizes, and he is laid off. Because he was hired shortly before the layoff, he is not eligible for unemployment benefits. His child support for one child is set at the minimum of $40 per week.

EXAMPLE Similarly, Mother dropped out of school at age 16. She earns minimum wage working at a fast food restaurant. Because her income is below 75% of the Federal Poverty Guidelines, her child support obligation for two children is set at $80 per week.

Voluntary Unemployment or Underemployment

If the parent's lack of employment is voluntary, however, income can be imputed to him. In order to impute income, "a court must find that one of the following factors applies: (1) the payor is voluntarily unemployed; (2) the payor is attempting to evade a support obligation; or (3) the payor has unreasonably failed to take advantage of an employment opportunity." If none of these factors are in evidence, the court may not impute income to the noncustodial parent.[18]

EXAMPLE Mother held a secure job as an accountant at a stable firm for 15 years. During the breakdown of the marriage, she quit the job to start a business baking pies in a jar. After 18 months, the business is reporting a net loss of $343. As Mother is voluntarily unemployed, Mother's income as an accountant can be imputed for child support purposes.

When income is imputed, child support is calculated based on a determination of potential income. "A determination of potential income shall be made by determining employment potential and probable earnings level based on the obligor's work history, occupational qualifications, and prevailing job opportunities."[19]

> **EXAMPLE** Mother was earning $95,000 per year as an accountant. She had received cost-of-living raises every year. These factors are used in determining her potential income.

Zero Child Support

The IMDMA provides five categories of parents who are exempt from a child support obligation: those "with no gross income, who receive only means-tested assistance, or who cannot work due to a medically proven disability, incarceration, or institutionalization."[20] For the purpose of this statute, means-tested assistance is that which is based on income, such as Temporary Assistance for Needy Families ("TANF" or "welfare"), SSI, and Supplemental Nutrition Assistance Program ("SNAP" or "food stamps").

> **EXAMPLE** Parent was incarcerated for a criminal offense. Parent is exempt from a child support obligation.

Securing the Child Support Obligation

Life Insurance on the Obligor

A child support obligation is not terminated by the death of the parent. Should a child support obligor die, the amount of support may be enforced against his estate.[21] However, not all parents will leave an estate. Good practice is to require life insurance with the proceeds payable to the recipient parent as trustee for the benefit of the minor children.

It is also good practice to require insurance on the life of the recipient parent. While the recipient parent does not pay child support to the obligor, if the recipient parent dies, the obligor would become the residential parent. His expenses will increase, especially for childcare, and as a single parent, he will be responsible for them on his own.

Assets Instead of Income

In cases where a potential obligor cannot or will not pay child support, the court can order an asset seized and held in trust.[22]

> **EXAMPLE** Father is in jail for sexual assault of a minor. Mother files a motion with the criminal court to intercept the bail money to secure his support obligation. At the end of the criminal trial, Mother receives the $20,000 bail money to be held in trust for Daughter.

> **EXAMPLE** Similarly, Mother receives a large settlement from Worker's Compensation. Father can petition the domestic relations court to seize a portion of the settlement to be held in trust for the children's benefit.

Child Support Coverage

Direct and Indirect Needs

Child support is intended to cover the reasonable and necessary physical, mental, and emotional health needs of the child.[23] It covers both the direct costs of the child (clothes, food, and housing) and indirect costs (such as laundry and transportation).

> **EXAMPLE** Father's child support contribution is $1,245 per month. It is unlikely Mother's expenses for food, clothing, and housing for Child, age four, will reach $1,245 per month. However, it is understood that Child's clothing needs to be laundered, and Child needs to be transported to activities and appointments. These indirect costs are included in child support.

Duty to Account

The parent receiving child support has no duty to account for how it was spent.

EXAMPLE Child lives with Mother during the week and with Father on alternating weekends. When Father comes to pick up Child on Friday night after the first snowstorm of the winter, Child is wearing boots held together by duct tape. Child support is meant to cover clothing. Unless Mother can be shown to be neglecting Child, which would permit a petition for modification of allocation of parental responsibilities, Father can either buy Child new boots or live with the duct tape.

Other Child-Related Expenses

Children have expenses in addition to the direct and indirect expenses child support is meant to cover, such as educational and medical expenses. Accordingly, the court has the authority to order child-related expenses in addition to the child support obligation.

Expenses for Education and Extracurricular Activities

The court may order either or both parents owing a duty of support to the child to contribute to the reasonable school expenses incurred by the child, such as registration fees, books, and supplies.[24]

EXAMPLE Mother pays for Child's public school registration fees and sends Father a copy of the receipt. The court would likely find this reasonable. When Mother sends Father a bill for $500 for school pictures, the court will likely not find this reasonable.

In addition, parents can be ordered to pay expenses for extracurricular activities which are intended to enhance the educational, athletic, social, or cultural development of the child.[25]

EXAMPLE Child was recognized as an outstanding soccer player from his first days in park district leagues at age four. Now age 12, Child competes on a traveling team. In addition to their basic child support obligation, the court orders parents to contribute to Child's expenses for traveling soccer.

Childcare for Employment

Childcare expenses, for the production of income, can be ordered by the court.[26]

> **EXAMPLE** Mother leaves the children with sitters every evening so she can go out with her friends. As Mother does not use the sitter for the production of income, Father is not obligated to contribute to the expense.

If ordered, childcare expenses are in proportion to the parent's child support obligation.[27]

> **EXAMPLE** In the example provided for the base child support calculation, Younger Child, age two months, is in daycare full-time. Older Child, age seven, is in before and after-school care. The combined cost for childcare is $1,900 per month. Mother pays 30% and father pays 70% of the $1,900.

Medical Expenses

Insurance

The IMDMA reflects the General Assembly's intent that children should be covered by health insurance. Accordingly, the court can order either or both parents to initiate health insurance coverage.[28] Premiums are allocated between the parents in proportion to their respective incomes. If neither parent has employer-sponsored insurance, the court can order the custodial parent to apply for public health coverage and the other parent to pay a reasonable amount of the cost of the coverage. [29]

All Kids provides comprehensive, affordable, health insurance for children, regardless of their immigration status or health condition. All Kids covers medical, dental, and optical needs. Currently, over 1.6 million Illinois children are enrolled in All Kids.[30]

> **EXAMPLE** Neither parent is employed at a job that offers health insurance to its employees. Father, the custodial parent, enrolls Child in Illinois All Kids. Based on his income, the premium is $87 per month. As Father contributes 60% and Mother contributes 40% to their base child support obligation, the $87 is allocated between Parents, with Father paying 60%, and Mother paying 40%.

Expenses in Excess of Insurance

In addition to requiring contribution to medical insurance premiums, the court makes provision for medical expenses parents incur on behalf of the child. While a portion of the basic child support obligation is intended to cover out-of-pocket medical expenses, such as Tylenol and Band-Aids, the court can order either or both to contribute to reasonable health needs not covered by insurance.

EXAMPLE Mother fills a prescription for child. The copay is an expense in excess of insurance. She also picks up some over-the-counter cough drops for the child. This expense is included in the base child support obligation.

Procedure

The Initial Order

The initial child support order may be obtained in one of two ways.

Court Action

Married parents typically bring a petition for child support as part of a proceeding for divorce or legal separation. Unmarried parents may bring a petition for child support through parentage action. (See Chapter 11, Parentage). After verifying the parent's income and confirming the child support calculation is correct, the judge issues a child support order.

Administrative Procedure

Child support orders can be obtained through an administrative procedure as well. Federal law requires each state to designate an agency responsible for issuing and enforcing child support orders.[31] In Illinois, the agency is the Division of Child Support Services, located within the Illinois Department of Healthcare and Family Services. All parents, married or unmarried, can request help setting an initial child support order through the Department. Administrative procedures for obtaining an initial order are discussed more fully in the chapter on parentage. (See Chapter 11, Parentage.)

Ensuring Compliance

Nonpayment of child support is a primary reason almost one-half million children in Illinois receive public assistance.[32] Consequently, a number of laws and legal procedures exist to ensure compliance with child support orders.

Income Withholding Order

Once the order has been entered, child support can be deducted from the obligor's income by his employer. The process begins when the attorney for the recipient spouse mails the child support order, along with an Income Withholding Order ("IWO"), to the obligor's employer. By federal law, a standard IWO can be used in all states. The obligor's employer sends the child support payment to the Illinois State Disbursement Unit ("ILSDU"), which is the payment processing center for Illinois child support payments. The ILSDU disburses the funds via check, direct deposit, or debit card to the receiving families. The employer then pays the obligor the remaining income.

If an obligor does not have an employer because he is unemployed or self-employed he can be ordered to pay the ILSDU directly.

EXAMPLE Father is paid in cash. If he pays Mother directly, disputes could arise. Father is ordered to send the child support payment to the ILSDU. The child support obligation is accounted for.

Petition for Rule to Show Cause

Once an order is entered, it has the force of law and can be enforced by the court. If one party does not comply with any order, including a child support order, the other party can bring an action in court for contempt, called a petition for rule to show cause. (See Chapter 12, Post-Decree Litigation.)

Statutory Enforcement Mechanisms

Enforcement mechanisms are also provided in several statutes. The IMDMA permits the court to restrict the obligor's driving license and to require the obligor to perform community service.[33] The Non-Support Punishment Act provides criminal penalties for failure to comply with child support, including fines and imprisonment.[34] Finally, the Uniform Interstate Family Support Act permits an order from one state to be enforced in another.[35]

Administrative Enforcement

The Division of Child Support Services within the Department of Healthcare and Family Services provides enforcement as well. Through their administrative powers, they can intercept tax refunds, suspend driver's licenses, revoke professional and occupational licenses, deny recreational licenses for hunting or fishing, and deny passports. In addition, they can place liens on real and personal property, including bank accounts, lawsuit claims, and worker's compensation claims.[36] When the agency uses the court for enforcement, it is represented by the state's attorney for the county in which the case is filed.

Chapter Summary

Recognizing all parents' responsibility to support a child financially, the Illinois General Assembly provides that courts may order parents owing a duty of support to a child to pay an amount reasonable and necessary for support. In determining the amount of support to pay, courts use the income shares method, which approximates the standard of living the child would have enjoyed had the marriage remained intact. Income for child support is defined broadly as income from all sources, and only limited deductions are allowed. The statute provides options for low-income or institutionalized parents, as well as for parents with multiple families.

Child support is intended to cover direct costs (such as food, clothing, and housing) and indirect costs (such as laundry and transportation.) Recognizing children have costs beyond those covered by child support, the IMDMA permits the court to order the payment of child-related expenses, such as school, extracurricular activities, childcare for employment, and medical care. Because of the importance of enforcing child support orders, court, and administrative enforcement procedures are available.

Key Terms

Income from all Sources

Income Shares

Emancipation

Shared Physical Care

Allowable Deduction

Deviation

Impute

Zero child support order

Minimum child support order

503(g) Trust

"obligor"

"obligee" or "recipient"

Income Withholding Order (IWO)

Illinois State Disbursement Unit (ILSDU)

Discussion Questions

1. Child support is based on both parents' combined income, in an attempt to recreate the lifestyle the child would have had if the family had remained intact. Is it realistic to try to recreate the lifestyle of an intact family after it has separated into two households? On the other hand, is it fair to reduce the children's standard of living because their parents divorce?
2. Can you imagine circumstances in which the parent with majority parenting time was ordered to pay child support? *See In re Marriage of Turk,* 2013 IL App (1st) 122486, 996 N.E.2d 62.
3. Parents who do not pay child support shift the cost of caring for their children to the taxpayers of Illinois. Are the measures used to enforce child support obligations appropriate?
4. Should gifts be considered income for child support purposes? Would it make a difference if they were received on a regular basis? Should an inheritance be considered income?
5. How should child support be calculated for an obligor whose income fluctuates? For example, a construction worker may work overtime in the summer but be unemployed in the winter.
6. Should the recipient parent have a duty to account for how child support is spent? How should a court distinguish between "bad parenting" and "neglect"?
7. Pursuant to 750 ILCS 5/505(I), the parent with the majority parenting time is entitled to claim the dependency exemption for the parties' minor child. While under current tax law, the exemption does not exist, tax credits can be considerable. What if one parent doesn't earn enough to use the entire credit? Should the court allow flexibility?
8. Suppose the parent with decision-making authority for extracurricular activities enrolls the child in a soccer camp in Italy that costs $10,000 per week (exclusive of airfare). Should the other parent be required to contribute? The IMDMA authorizes the court to order contribution to "reasonable" expenses.
9. If a parent marries a second time, the new spouse's income is not included in a child support obligation. What is the public policy behind this section of the IMDMA?
10. Suppose a parent uses alternative medicine, such as acupuncture, for the child. Should those costs be allocated to the other parent? In some studies, gluten-free casein-free (GFCF) diets have been shown to be successful in improving symptoms of autism. *See* https://www.ncbi.nlm.nih.gov/pmc/articles/PMC7651765/ (last visited June 29, 2023). Should the cost of wheat-free and milk-free products be considered medical expenses?

Forms

1. Illinois Standardized Forms - Approved - Order for Support (windows.net)
   https://ilcourtsaudio.blob.core.windows.net/antilles-resources/resources/e3440546-6e6b-4904-9cab-2b029894c518/DCS%20Order%20For%20Support.pdf
2. Income Withholding Order for Support (IWO)
   https://ilcourtsaudio.blob.core.windows.net/antilles-resources/resources/711e5993-468b-47d0-8b75-692162b356e1/IWO%20Income%20Withholding%20for%20Support%20Federal%202023.pdf

Endnotes

1. 750 ILCS 5/505(a)(1) (West, Westlaw Classic through P.A. 103-21 of the 2023 Reg. Sess.).
2. *Id.* § 505(a).
3. *Id.*
4. *Id.* § 505(1.5)(A). *See also Id.* § 505(a)(3)(B) standardized tax amount shall be used unless certain requirements are met.
5. *Id.* § 505(a)(3)(A).
6. *Id.* § 505(a)(3)(A).
7. 750 ILCS 5/505(a)(3)(D).
8. *Id.* § 505(a)(1)(A-F).
9. *Id.* § 505(a)(3.8).
10. *Id.* § 505(a)(3.3).
11. *Id.* § 505(a)(3.4).
12. *Id.* § 505(a)(3.4)(A-C).
13. 750 ILCS 5/505 (a)(3)(F)(I).
14. *Id.* § 505(a)(3)(F)(I)(i).
15. *Id.* § 505(a)(3)(F)(I)(ii).
16. *Id.* § 505(a)(3)(F)(I)(ii).
17. *Id.* § 505(a)(3.3a).
18. In re Marriage of Gosney, 394 Ill. App. 3d 1073, 1077, 916 N.E.2d 614, 618–19 (4th Dist. 2009).
19. 750 ILCS 5/505(a)(3.2).
20. *Id.* § 505(a)(3.3b).
21. *Id.* § 510(d).
22. *Id.* § 503(g).
23. *Id.* § 505(a).
24. *Id.* § 505(a)(3.6).
25. 750 ILCS 5/505(a)(3.6).
26. *Id.* § 505(3.7).
27. *Id.* § 505(3.7)(B).
28. *Id.* § 505(505 (a)(4)(A).
29. https//www.illinois.gov/hfs/MedicalPrograms/AllKids/Pages/about.aspx

30. *Id.*
31. Social Security Act. 42 U.S.C.A. Ch. 7, Subch. IV, Pt. D.
32. https://hfs.illinois.gov/childsupport/parents/programs.html.(Acessed June 29, 2023).
33. 750 ILCS 5/505(a-5).
34. 750 ILCS 16/101(West, Westlaw Classic through P.A. 103-21 of the 2023 Reg. Sess.).
35. 750 ILCS 22/101(West, Westlaw Classic through P.A. 103-21 of the 2023 Reg. Sess.).
36. Ill. Admin. Code tit. 89 § 160.70.

1. ORDER FOR SUPPORT

This form is approved by the Illinois Supreme Court and is required to be accepted in all Illinois Circuit Courts.

STATE OF ILLINOIS, CIRCUIT COURT COUNTY	**ORDER FOR SUPPORT** ☐ Initial ☐ Modification ☐ Enforcement	*For Court Use Only*
Instructions ▾		
Directly above, enter the county where you filed this case.	______________________ **Petitioner** *(First, middle, last name)*	
Enter the full name of Petitioner, Respondent, and the case number the Circuit Clerk gave this case.	v.	______________________ **IV-D Case Number**
Enter the IV-D case number if you know it.	______________________ **Respondent** *(First, middle, last name)*	______________________ **Case Number**

NOTE:	• DO NOT fill out the rest of this form unless the judge tell you complete it. • You **MUST BRING** the social security numbers of both Petitioner and Respondent to the court hearing.

THE COURT FINDS:

☐ 1. ☐ Petitioner ☐ Respondent must pay support.
The person paying support is called "Obligor" in this *Order*. The Obligor is: ______________________
The person receiving support is called "Obligee" in this *Order*. The Obligee is: ______________________

☐ 2. The children covered by this *Order* are: ______________________
____
____

☐ 3. The combined gross income ☐ does ☐ does not exceed the uppermost levels of the schedule of basic support obligations.

☐ 4. The net income of Obligor is $ ______________ per ___________ calculated by
☐ the standardized tax amount.
☐ the individualized tax amount.
☐ the agreement of the parties.

☐ 5. The net income of Obligee is: $ ______________ per ___________ calculated by
☐ the standardized tax amount.
☐ the individualized tax amount.
☐ the agreement of the parties.

☐ 6. The adjusted net income for Obligor is: $ ______________ per ___________ .

☐ 7. The adjusted net income for Obligee is: $ ______________ per ___________ .

☐ 8. The Basic Combined Support Obligation $ ______________ per ___________ .

☐ 9. Obligor's income is at or below 75% of the Federal Poverty Guidelines for a family of 1 person. Child support is capped at $40 per month per child up to a maximum of $120 per month.

☐ 10. Obligor receives only means tested assistance or cannot work due to a medically proven disability, incarceration or institutionalization.

☐ 11. Shared physical care: Each parent exercises 146 or more overnights per year. Basic Child Support Obligation is: $ ______________ per ______________ *(multiply amount in paragraph 8 x 1.5)*.

☐ 12. Split care: Each of the parents has physical care of at least one, but not all of the children.

☐ 13. The amount of child support arrearage is: $ __________ as of __________ *Date*
plus an interest amount of: $ __________

☐ 14. The amount of maintenance arrearage is: $ __________ as of __________ *Date*
plus an interest amount of: $ __________

☐ 15. The amount of retroactive child support is: $ __________ from __________ *Date* to __________ *Date*

☐ 16. The amount of retroactive maintenance is: $ __________ from __________ *Date* to __________ *Date*

☐ 17. The amount of child support cannot be stated only in a dollar amount because some or all of the net income of Obligor is uncertain as to source, time of payment, or amount.

IT IS ORDERED:

A. That Obligor will pay:

☐ 1. Maintenance ☐ Yes ☐ No

a. The current maintenance payment is: $ __________

b. The maintenance arrearage/retroactive payment is: $ __________

c. The total maintenance payment is: $ __________

d. Maintenance is to be paid:

☐ Once a week ☐ Once every other week

☐ Once a month ☐ Twice a month on: __________ *Date* and __________ *Date* .

e. Maintenance payments begin __________ *Date* .

f. This maintenance order ends on: __________ *Date* .

☐ 2. Child Support ☐ Yes ☐ No

a. The current child support payment is: $ __________

b. The child support arrearage/retroactive payment is: $ __________

c. The total child support payment is: $ __________

d. Child support is to be paid:

☐ Once a week ☐ Once every other week

☐ Once a month ☐ Twice a month on: __________ *Date* and __________ *Date* .

e. Child support payments begin on: __________ *Date* .

f. Obligor must also pay: _____ % of their ____________________ *Type of Additional Income* .

This must be paid as follows:____________________

Obligor must also give ☐ Obligee and/or ☐ the Clerk of the Court proof of their ____________________ *Type of Additional Income* within 7 days of receiving the income.

☐ 3. Other Support Orders: ____________________

____

____

B. Payment of Maintenance and Child Support:

☐ 1. An *Income Withholding for Support* may immediately be served on Obligor's employer. Until the *Income Withholding for Support* takes effect Obligor is required to pay directly to the State Disbursement Unit.

- Payments by Obligor or the employer must be made payable to: STATE DISBURSEMENT UNIT and sent to: P.O. Box 5400, Carol Stream, IL 60197-5400.
- Payments must include: 1) the case number, 2) the name of the county of the Court issuing this *Order for Support*, and 3) Obligor's name and social security number.
- A new court *Order* is not necessary to serve an *Income Withholding for Support* on any future employer of

☐ 2. Obligor will make payments:

☐ Directly to the State Disbursement Unit according to the schedule in Section A. Payments by Obligor must be made payable to the STATE DISBURSEMENT UNIT and sent to: P.O. Box 5400, Carol Stream, IL 60197-5400.

☐ Directly to Obligee as the parties have agreed according to the schedule in Section A. If Obligor falls behind in payments, an *Income Withholding for Support* may be prepared and served on Obligor's employer. Obligor will then have to make payments to the State Disbursement Unit as stated in Section B1.

☐ 3. Obligor must also pay a $36 per year child support collection fee. This fee is not maintenance or child support and cannot be subtracted from the support to be paid. This fee must be paid directly to the Circuit Clerk of the county issuing this *Order for Support.*

C. Payment of Maintenance Only:

☐ 1. Obligor will make payments

☐ Directly to Obligee

☐ Directly to the Circuit Clerk of this county

☐ 2. If payments are made to the Circuit Clerk, Obligor must also pay a $36.00 per year support collection fee. This is not maintenance and cannot be subtracted from the support to be paid. This fee must be paid directly to the Circuit Clerk of the county issuing this order.

D. Delinquency ***(maintenance or child support)*****:**

☐ 1. Delinquency Payments

If Obligor is delinquent in making a support payment after this *Order for Support* is entered, Obligor must

a. Continue to make current maintenance and child support payments, **AND**

b. Pay the sum of:

$______________ for child support per payment period ordered in Section A2d, **PLUS**

$______________ for maintenance per payment period ordered in Section A1d, until the delinquent amount is paid in full.

A maintenance or child support payment, or part of a payment, that is due and remains unpaid for 30 days or more will accrue interest at the rate of 9% each year.

E. Child Support Termination:

1. This child support order ends on: ________________ unless changed by a written order of the court.
Date

2. Unpaid Child Support at Termination
If Obligor owes an arrearage or delinquency on the termination date that is equal to at least one month's support payment, Obligor must continue to make payments. The payment amount must be the same as the amount Obligor was ordered to pay in Section A2a.

F. Health Insurance:

☐ 1. Decision Reserved

☐ 2. a. ☐ Obligor ☐ Obligee will provide health insurance for the children by:

☐ Enrolling them in health insurance coverage available through their employer.

☐ Providing other insurance ☐ dental ☐ orthodontic ☐ vision

☐ prescription medication ☐ other: ________________________________ .

☐ Giving a copy of the insurance policy and the insurance card to the other parent within 45 days of the date of this *Order*.

b. The cost of the insurance will be paid by:

☐ Obligor: ____________% ☐ Obligee: ____________%

NOTE: Health insurance premiums are added to the Basic Support Obligation and then divided pro rata. If Obligor's paying the premium, the amount that is Obligee's responsibility must be subtracted from Obligor's support obligation. If Obligee is paying the premium, Obligor's support obligation shall be increased by Obligor's share of the premium.

c. The cost of healthcare expenses not covered by insurance will be paid by:

☐ Obligor and Obligee equally

☐ Obligor: ____________% ☐ Obligee: ____________%

G. Child Care Expenses:

☐ 1. Decision Reserved

☐ 2. a. ☐ Child care expenses are reasonably necessary for ☐ Petitioner ☐ Respondent to be employed, attend educational or vocational training to improve employment opportunities, or to look for work.

b. ☐ The cost of child care expenses shall be paid by: ☐ Obligor ____________%

☐ Obligee __________%

c. ☐ Payment shall be made directly to: ☐ Obligee ☐ Child care provider

H. School and Extra-Curricular Expenses:

☐ 1. Decision Reserved

☐ 2. a. ☐ School and extra-curricular expenses covered by this *Order* ______________________________

____

b. ☐ The cost of extra-curricular expenses shall be paid ☐ Obligor __________%

Obligee ____________%

I. Other Orders:

The *Support Information Sheet* filed in this case shall be impounded by the Circuit Clerk in order to protect the confidential information contained in it.

1. Notice of Address Change

   Each party must tell the other of any change in address within 5 days of the change.

   This does not apply to the following parties ☐ Petitioner ☐ Respondent because the physical, mental or emotional health of that party and/or the minor children would be seriously endangered by disclosure of that party's address.

   Obligor must give written notice of any change in home address or mailing address within 7 days of the change to:

   - The Circuit Clerk of the county issuing this *Order for Support*, AND
   - The Illinois Department of Healthcare and Family Services, BUT ONLY if a party is receiving child and spouse services under Article X of the Illinois Public Aid Code.

2. Notice of Change to Other Information

   Obligor must give written notice of any change to personal contact information within 7 days of the change, including:

   - New telephone number; AND
   - If Obligor can get health insurance through the employer or other group coverage and if so list: the policy name, the policy number, and the names of persons covered under the policy.

   Obligor must give the written notice to:

   - The Circuit Clerk of the county issuing this *Order for Support*, AND
   - The Illinois Department of Healthcare and Family Services, BUT ONLY if a party is receiving child and spouse services under Article X of the Illinois Public Aid Code.

3. Notice of Change to Employment
Obligor must give written notice of any employment change within 7 days of the change, including:
   - If Obligor lost a job, OR
   - If Obligor got a new job, AND
   - The name, address and phone number of a new employer.

   Obligor must give the written notice to:
   - Obligee,
   - The Circuit Clerk of the county issuing this *Order for Support*, AND
   - The Illinois Department of Healthcare and Family Services, BUT ONLY if a party is receiving child and spouse services under Article X of the Illinois Public Aid Code.
4. Notice of Change to *Support Information Sheet*
Obligor and Obligee must give written notice of any change to the information on the *Support Information Sheet* filed with this case within 5 days of the change.
Obligor and Obligee must give the written notice to:
   - The Circuit Clerk of the county issuing this *Order for Support.*
5. Proof of Continuing Insurance Coverage
If Obligor has received an adjustment to their support obligation because of the payment of insurance premiums, Obligor must annually submit proof of continuing insurance coverage of the children to the Division of Child Support Enforcement of the Department of Human Services and to Obligee.

J. Additional Conditions or Findings:

☐ 1. The child support payment amount is different than the amount required by child support guidelines because:
- a. ☐ extraordinary medical expenditures necessary to preserve the life or health of a party or a child of either or both of the parties.
- b. ☐ additional expenses incurred for a child covered by this support order who has special medical, physical or developmental needs.
- c. ☐ the amount required by child support guidelines is: $_______________
- d. ☐ Other: _______________

☐ 2. ☐ Other: _______________

☐ 3. A child support calculation prepared by using the Illinois Department of Healthcare and Family Services estimator is attached: ☐ Yes ☐ No

☐ 4. The child support calculation was prepared by ☐ Petitioner ☐ Respondent ☐ Judge

K. Other: _______________

DO NOT complete this section. The judge will complete it.

ENTERED:

_______________ Judge _______________ Date

A JUDGE CAN FIND YOU IN CONTEMPT OF COURT IF YOU FAIL TO OBEY ANY PART OF THIS *ORDER.*

Print Form Save Form Reset Form

2. INCOME WITHHOLDING ORDER FOR SUPPORT

OMB 0970-0154
Expiration Date: 09/30/2023

INCOME WITHHOLDING FOR SUPPORT

I. Sender Information: (Completed by the Sender) **Date:** ______________

☐ **INCOME WITHHOLDING ORDER/NOTICE FOR SUPPORT (IWO)**
☐ **ONE-TIME ORDER/NOTICE FOR LUMP SUM PAYMENT**
☐ **AMENDED IWO OR ENFORCEMENT IWO**
☐ **TERMINATION OF IWO**

☐ Child Support Enforcement (CSE) Agency ☐ Court ☐ Attorney ☐ Private Individual/Entity (Check One)

NOTE: This IWO must be regular on its face. Under certain circumstances you must reject this IWO and return it to the sender (see IWO instructions www.acf.hhs.gov/css/resource/income-withholding-for-support-instructions). If you receive this document from someone other than a state or tribal CSE agency or a court, a copy of the underlying support order must be attached.

State/Tribe/Territory Illinois
City/County/Dist./Tribe ______________
Private Individual Entity ______________
Remittance ID (include w/payment) ______________
Order ID ______________
Case ID ______________

II. Employer and Case Information: (Completed by the Sender)

____
Employer/Income Withholder's Name
____
Employer/Income Withholder's Address
____
____

RE: ______________
Employee/Obligor's Name (Last, First, Middle)
____
Employee/Obligor's Social Security Number
____
Employee/Obligor's Date of Birth
____
Custodial Party/Obligee's Name (Last, First, Middle)

Employer/Income Withholder's FEIN ______________

Child(ren)'s Name(s) (Last, First, Middle) | Child(ren)'s Birth Date(s)

III. Order Information: (Completed by the Sender)

This document is based on the support order from ______________ (State/Tribe).
You are required by law to deduct these amounts from the employee/obligor's income until further notice.

$______ Per______ current child support
$______ Per______ past-due child support - Arrears greater than 12 weeks? ☐ Yes ☐ No
$______ Per______ current cash medical support
$______ Per______ past-due cash medical support
$______ Per______ current spousal support
$______ Per______ past-due spousal support

$______ Per______ other (must specify) ______________
for a **Total Amount to Withhold** of **$**______ per______.

IV. Amounts to Withhold: (Completed by the Sender)

You do not have to vary your pay cycle to be in compliance with the *Order Information*. If your pay cycle does not match the ordered payment cycle, withhold one of the following amounts:

$______ per weekly pay period
$______ per biweekly pay period (every two weeks)
$______ per semimonthly pay period (twice a month)
$______ per monthly pay period

Employer/Income Withholder's Name:__________________________ Employer/Income Withholder's FEIN: __________________

Employee/Obligor's Name: ____ SSN: _______________________

Case ID: ____________________________________ Order ID: ____

$ __________ **Lump Sum Payment:** Do not stop any existing IWO unless you receive a termination order.

PAPERWORK REDUCTION ACT OF 1995 (Pub. L. 104-13) STATEMENT OF PUBLIC BURDEN: The purpose of this information collection is to provide uniformity and standardization. Public reporting burden for this collection of information is estimated to average two to five minutes per response, including the time for reviewing instructions, gathering and maintaining the data needed, and reviewing the collection of information. This is a mandatory collection of information in accordance with 45 CFR 303.100 of the Child Support Enforcement Program. An agency may not conduct or sponsor, and a person is not required to respond to, a collection of information subject to the requirements of the Paperwork Reduction Act of 1995, unless it displays a currently valid OMB control number. If you have any comments on this collection of information, please contact the Employer Services Team by email at employerservices@acf.hhs.gov.

Document Tracking ID: ____

V. Remittance Information: (Completed by the Sender except for the "Return to Sender" check box.)

If the employee/obligor's principal place of employment is Illinois (State/Tribe), you must begin withholding no later than the first pay period that occurs 14 days after the date of mailing of the order/notice. Send payment within 7 business days of the pay date. If you cannot withhold the full amount of support for any or all orders for this employee/obligor, withhold 65 % of disposable income for all orders. If the employee/obligor's principal place of employment is not Illinois (State/Tribe), obtain withholding limitations, time requirements, the appropriate method to allocate among multiple child support cases/orders and any allowable employer fees from the jurisdiction of the employee/obligor's principal place of employment.

State-specific withholding limit information is available at www.acf.hhs.gov/css/resource/state-income-withholding-contacts-and-program-requirements. For tribe-specific contacts, payment addresses, and withholding limitations, please contact the tribe at www.acf.hhs.gov/sites/default/files/programs/css/tribal_agency_contacts_printable_pdf.pdf or www.bia.gov/tribalmap/DataDotGovSamples/tld_map.html.

You may not withhold more than the lesser of: 1) the amounts allowed by the Federal Consumer Credit Protection Act (CCPA) [15 USC §1673 (b)]; or 2) the amounts allowed by the law of the state of the employee/obligor's principal place of employment if the place of employment is in a state; or the tribal law of the employee/obligor's principal place of employment if the place of employment is under tribal jurisdiction. The CCPA is available at www.dol.gov/sites/dolgov/files/WHD/legacy/files/garn01.pdf. If the Order Information section does not indicate that the arrears are greater than 12 weeks, then the employer should calculate the CCPA limit using the lower percentage.

If there is more than one IWO against this employee/obligor and you are unable to fully honor all IWOs due to federal, state, or tribal withholding limits, you must honor all IWOs to the greatest extent possible, giving priority to current support before payment of any past-due support.

If the obligor is a nonemployee, obtain withholding limits from the **Supplemental Information** section in this IWO. This information is also available at www.acf.hhs.gov/css/resource/state-income-withholding-contacts-and-program-requirements.

Remit payment to____(SDU/Tribal Order Payee)
at____(SDU/Tribal Payee Address)

Include the Remittance ID with the payment and if necessary this locator code of the SDU/Tribal order payee_________ on the payment.

To set up electronic payments or to learn state requirements for checks, contact the State Disbursement Unit (SDU). Contacts and information are found at www.acf.hhs.gov/css/resource/sdu-eft-contacts-and-program-requirements.

☐ **Return to Sender (Completed by Employer/Income Withholder).** Payment must be directed to an SDU in accordance with sections 466(b)(5) and (6) of the Social Security Act or Tribal Payee (see Payments in Section VI). If payment is not directed to an SDU/Tribal Payee or this IWO is not regular on its face, you must check this box and return the IWO to the sender.

Employer/Income Withholder's Name:__________ Employer/Income Withholder's FEIN: __________

Employee/Obligor's Name: __________ SSN: __________

Case ID: __________ Order ID: __________

If Required by State or Tribal Law:
Signature of Judge/Issuing Official: __________
Print Name of Judge/Issuing Official: Illinois Does Not Require Judicial Approval
Title of Judge/Issuing Official: __________
Date of Signature: __________

If the employee/obligor works in a state or for a tribe that is different from the state or tribe that issued this order, a copy of this IWO must be provided to the employee/obligor.

☐ If checked, the employer/income withholder must provide a copy of this form to the employee/obligor.

VI. Additional Information for Employers/Income Withholders: (Completed by the Sender)

Priority: Withholding for support has priority over any other legal process under State law against the same income (section 466(b)(7) of the Social Security Act). If a federal tax levy is in effect, please notify the sender.

Payments: You must send child support payments payable by income withholding to the appropriate State Disbursement Unit or to a tribal CSE agency within 7 business days, or fewer if required by state law, after the date the income would have been paid to the employee/obligor and include the date you withheld the support from his or her income. You may combine withheld amounts from more than one employee/obligor's income in a single payment as long as you separately identify each employee/obligor's portion of the payment. Child support payments may not be made through the federal Office of Child Support Enforcement (OCSE) Child Support Portal.

Lump Sum Payments: You may be required to notify a state or tribal CSE agency of upcoming lump sum payments to this employee/obligor such as bonuses, commissions, or severance pay. Contact the sender to determine if you are required to report and/or withhold lump sum payments. Employers/income withholders may use OCSE's Child Support Portal (ocsp.acf.hhs.gov/csp/) to provide information about employees who are eligible to receive lump sum payments and to provide contacts, addresses, and other information about their companies. Child support payments may not be made through the federal OCSE Child Support Portal.

Liability: If you have any doubts about the validity of this IWO, contact the sender. If you fail to withhold income from the employee/obligor's income as the IWO directs, you are liable for both the accumulated amount you should have withheld and any penalties set by state or tribal law/procedure. __________

Anti-discrimination: You are subject to a fine determined under state or tribal law for discharging an employee/obligor from employment, refusing to employ, or taking disciplinary action against an employee/obligor because of this IWO.

Employer/Income Withholder's Name:________________ Employer/Income Withholder's FEIN: ________________

Employee/Obligor's Name: ________________ SSN: ________________

Case ID: ________________ Order ID: ________________

Supplemental Information: ________________

VII. Notification of Employment Termination or Income Status: (Completed by the Employer/Income Withholder)

If this employee/obligor never worked for you or you are no longer withholding income for this employee/obligor, you must promptly notify the CSE agency and/or the sender by returning this form to the address listed in the **Contact Information** section below or using OCSE's Child Support Portal (ocsp.acf.hhs.gov/csp/). Please report the new employer or income withholder, if known.

☐ This person has never worked for this employer nor received periodic income.

☐ This person no longer works for this employer nor receives periodic income.

Please provide the following information for the employee/obligor:

Termination date:________________ Last known telephone number: ________________

Last known address: ________________

Final payment date to SDU/Tribal Payee:________________ Final payment amount: ________________

New employer's or income withholder's name: ________________

New employer's or income withholder's address: ________________

VIII. Contact Information: (Completed by the Sender)

To Employer/Income Withholder: If you have questions, contact________________(sender name) by telephone:__________, by fax:__________, by email or website:________________.

Send termination/income status notice and other correspondence to: ________________ (sender address).

Employer/Income Withholder's Name:__________________________Employer/Income Withholder's FEIN: ____________________

Employee/Obligor's Name:____SSN:__________________________

Case ID: ____ Order ID: ____

To Employee/Obligor: If the employee/obligor has questions, contact______________________________ (sender name)

by telephone:________________, by fax:________________, by email or website:____

IMPORTANT: The person completing this form is advised that the information may be shared with the employee/obligor.

Encryption Requirements:
When communicating this form through electronic transmission, precautions must be taken to ensure the security of the data. Child support agencies are encouraged to use the electronic applications provided by the federal Office of Child Support Enforcement. Other electronic means, such as encrypted attachments to emails, may be used if the encryption method is compliant with Federal Information Processing Standard (FIPS) Publication 140-2 (FIPS PUB 140-2).

PRINT FORM SAVE FORM RESET FORM

HFS 3683, INCOME WITHHOLDING FOR SUPPORT

ILLINOIS SUPPLEMENT TO THE INCOME WITHHOLDING ORDER FOR SUPPORT (IWO), OMB 0970-0154
Duties of, and Fines and Penalties Applicable to, the Payor Under Illinois Law are contained in the Income Withholding for Support Act (750 ILCS 28/), including:

1) **The payor shall deduct the amount designated in the income withholding notice, as supplemented by any notice provided pursuant to section 45 (f) of the Income Withholding for Support Act, beginning no later than the next payment of income which is payable or creditable to the obligor that occurs 14 days following the date the income withholding notice was mailed, sent by facsimile or other electronic means, or placed for personal delivery to or service on the payor. The payor may combine all amounts withheld for the benefit of an obligee or public office into a single payment and transmit the payment with a listing of obligors from whom withholding has been effected. The payor must pay the amount withheld to the State Disbursement Unit within 7 business days after the date the amount would (but for the duty to withhold income) have been paid or credited to the obligor. If the payor knowingly fails to withhold the amount designated in the Income Withholding Notice or to pay the amount withheld to the State Disbursement Unit within 7 business days after the date the amount would have been paid or credited to the obligor, the payor shall pay a penalty of $100 for each day that the amount designated in the income withholding notice (whether or not withheld by the payor) is not paid to the State Disbursement Unit after the period of 7 business days has expired. The total penalty for a payor's failure, on one occasion, to withhold or pay to the State Disbursement Unit an amount designated in the income withholding notice may not exceed $10,000. This penalty may be collected in a civil action which may be brought against the payor in favor of the obligee or public office. An action to collect the penalty may not be brought more than one year after the date of the payor's alleged failure to withhold or pay income. For each withholding, the payor shall provide the State Disbursement Unit, at the time of transmittal, with the date the amount would (but for the duty to withhold income) have been paid or credited to the obligor. For withholding of income, the payor shall be entitled to receive a fee not to exceed $5 per month to be taken from the income to be paid to the obligor. Whenever the obligor is no longer receiving income from the payor, the payor shall return a copy of the income withholding notice to the obligee or public office and shall provide information for the purpose of enforcing the Income Withholding for Support Act. Withholding of income shall be made without regard to any prior or subsequent garnishments, attachments, wage assignments, or any other claims of creditors. The income withholding notice is binding upon the payor until service on the payor of an order of the court or notice from either the Department or Clerk of the Circuit Court to cease the withholding.**

2) If any unpaid arrearage or delinquency equal to at least one month's support obligation exists on the termination date stated in the order for support or, if there is no termination date stated in the order, on the date the child attains the age of majority or is otherwise emancipated, then the periodic amount required to be paid for current support of that child immediately prior to that date shall automatically continue to be an obligation, not as current support but as periodic payment toward satisfaction of the unpaid arrearage or delinquency. That periodic payment shall be in addition to any periodic payment previously required for satisfaction of the arrearage or delinquency. The total periodic amount to be paid toward satisfaction of the arrearage or delinquency may be enforced and collected by any method provided by law for the enforcement and collection of child support, including but not limited to income withholding under the Income Withholding for Support Act.

3) **Income available for withholding shall be applied first to the current support obligation, then to any premium required for employer, labor union, or trade union related health insurance coverage ordered under the order for support, and then to payments required on past-due support obligations. If there is insufficient available income remaining to pay the full amount of the required health insurance premium after withholding of income for the current support obligation, then the remaining available income shall be applied to payments required on past-due support obligations. If the payor has been served with more than one income withholding notice pertaining to the same obligor, the payor shall allocate income available for withholding on a proportionate share basis, giving priority to current support payments. No payor shall discharge, discipline, refuse to hire or otherwise penalize an obligor because of the duty to withhold income. Where a payor willfully fails to withhold or pay over income pursuant to a properly served income withholding notice, or willfully discharges, disciplines, refuses to hire or otherwise penalizes an obligor, or otherwise fails to comply with any duties imposed by the Income Withholding for Support Act, the obligee, public office or obligor, as appropriate, may file a complaint with the court against the payor. Upon a finding in favor of the complaining party, the court shall enter judgment and direct the enforcement thereof for the total amount that the payor willfully failed to withhold or pay over; and may order employment or reinstatement of or restitution to the obligor, or both, where the obligor has been discharged, disciplined, denied employment or otherwise penalized by the payor and may impose a fine upon the payor not to exceed $200.**

HFS 3683 (R-11-20)

HFS 3683, INCOME WITHHOLDING FOR SUPPORT

ILLINOIS SUPPLEMENT TO THE INCOME WITHHOLDING ORDER FOR SUPPORT (IWO), OMB 0970-0154

4) If an obligee who is receiving income withholding payments under the Income Withholding For Support Act does not receive a payment required under the income withholding notice, he or she must give written notice of the non-receipt to the payor. The notice must include the date on which the obligee believes the payment was to have been made and the amount of the payment. The obligee must send the notice to the payor by certified mail, return receipt requested. After receiving a written notice of non-receipt of payment under section 45 (j) of the Income Withholding for Support Act, a payor must, within 14 days thereafter, either (i) notify the obligee of the reason for the non-receipt of payment or (ii) make the required payment, together with interest at the rate of 9% calculated from the date on which the payment of income should have been made. A payor who fails to comply with section 45 (j) of the Income Withholding for Support Act is subject to the $100 per day penalty provided pursuant to subsection (a) of Section 35 of the Income Withholding for Support Act.

Rights, Remedies and Duties of the Obligor Under Illinois Law:

1) An employer cannot discharge, discipline, refuse to hire, or otherwise penalize the obligor because of the duty to withhold. If the employer does so, the employer may be ordered to reinstate or provide restitution to the obligor, or both, and may be fined up to $200, pursuant to a complaint filed by the obligor in the circuit court. The obligor is required by law to notify the Department/Clerk of the Circuit Court of any new address or employer within 7 days of the change. At any time after the initial service of the income withholding notice, the Department may serve any employer with the same income withholding notice without further notice to the obligor. New service of an income withholding notice is not required in order to resume withholding of income in the case of an obligor with respect to whom an income withholding notice was previously served on the payor if withholding of income was terminated because of an interruption in the obligor's employment of less than 180 days.

2) If any unpaid arrearage or delinquency equal to at least one month's support obligation exists on the termination date stated in the order for support or, if there is no termination date stated in the order, on the date the child attains the age of majority or is otherwise emancipated, then the periodic amount required to be paid for current support of that child immediately prior to that date shall automatically continue to be an obligation, not as current support but as periodic payment toward satisfaction of the unpaid arrearage or delinquency. That periodic payment shall be in addition to any periodic payment previously required for satisfaction of the arrearage or delinquency. The total periodic amount to be paid toward satisfaction of the arrearage or delinquency may be enforced and collected by any method provided by law for the enforcement and collection of child support, including but not limited to income withholding under the Income Withholding for Support Act.

3) The obligor may contest initiated income withholding under Section 30 of the Income Withholding for Support Act, or the obligor may contest income withholding after accrual of delinquency under Section 25 of the Act, by filing a petition to contest withholding with Clerk of the Circuit Court if the order was issued by the court, or petitioning the Department if the order for support was issued administratively by the Department. The obligor must file the petition within 20 days after service of a copy of the income withholding notice. However, as required by law, the grounds for the request to contest the initiated income withholding shall be limited to whether the parties' written agreement providing an alternative arrangement to immediate withholding continues to ensure payment of support, or misidentification of the obligor. As required by law, the grounds for the petition to contest withholding after accrual of delinquency shall be limited to a dispute concerning the existence or amount of the delinquency, or misidentification of the obligor. The obligor may, at any time, file with the Circuit Clerk or Department a petition to correct a term contained in an income withholding notice to conform to the terms stated in the underlying order for support for the amount of current support, the amount of the arrearage, the periodic amount for payment of the arrearage, or the periodic amount for payment of the delinquency, or to modify, suspend or terminate the income withholding notice because of a modification, suspension or termination of the underlying order for support; or, suspend the income withholding because of inability to deliver income withheld to the obligee due to the obligee's failure to provide a mailing address or other means of delivery. Any obligee, public office or obligor who willfully initiates a false proceeding under the Income Withholding for Support Act may be punished as in cases of contempt of court.

HFS 3683 (R-11-20)

Eight

Spousal Maintenance

Overview

When parties marry, they make long-range plans for their lives together. Perhaps one spouse works, deferring their education, while the other pursues an advanced degree. Perhaps they decide together that one spouse should stay home with their young children, at the cost of advancing in their career. When divorce terminates the marriage prematurely, one party may be left at a disadvantage. As you read, consider whether the spousal maintenance section in the IMDMA provides financial security to a spouse who had been counting on it.

Spousal Maintenance

Spousal maintenance payments, formerly known as "alimony," are payments from one spouse to another after a dissolution of marriage, legal separation, or declaration of invalidity of marriage. Although spousal maintenance laws have changed over time, as societal views about marriage have changed, under current law, the court may grant a maintenance award for either spouse "in amounts and for periods of time as the court deems just."[1]

The Award

An award of maintenance is a two-step process. First, the court must make a finding as to whether an award of maintenance is appropriate.[2]

Finding of Appropriateness

Relevant Factors

In making the finding that an award is appropriate in a specific case, the court considers all relevant factors, including:

> (1) The income and property of each party, including marital property apportioned and non-marital property assigned to the party seeking maintenance as well as all financial obligations imposed on the parties as a result of the dissolution of marriage;

(2) The needs of each party;

(3) The realistic present and future earning capacity of each party;

(4) Any impairment of the present and future earning capacity of the party seeking maintenance due to that party devoting time to domestic duties or having forgone or delayed education, training, employment, or career opportunities due to the marriage;

(5) Any impairment of the realistic present or future earning capacity of the party against whom maintenance is sought;

(6) The time necessary to enable the party seeking maintenance to acquire appropriate education, training, and employment, and whether that party is able to support himself or herself through appropriate employment;

(6.1) The effect of any parental responsibility arrangements and its effect on a party's ability to seek or maintain employment;

(7) The standard of living established during the marriage;

(8) The duration of the marriage;

(9) The age, health, station, occupation, amount and sources of income, vocational skills, employability, estate, liabilities, and the needs of each of the parties;

(10) All sources of public and private income including, without limitation, disability and retirement income;

(11) The tax consequences to each party;

(12) Contributions and services by the party seeking maintenance to the education, training, career or career potential, or license of the other spouse;

(13) Any valid agreement of the parties; and

(14) Any other factor that the court expressly finds to be just and equitable.[3]

EXAMPLE Wife resigned from a lucrative career in human resources to support Husband's career in the Foreign Service. The couple lived all over the globe for twenty years. When the couple divorced, Wife's education and work experience were out of date. The court will consider factors (4), (6), and (12) in her situation.

Marital Misconduct

Marital misconduct is not a factor, and therefore, will have no impact on the court's award of maintenance.[4]

EXAMPLE While never letting it interfere with her duties as homemaker and hostess, at each posting around the world Wife enjoyed an adulterous relationship with a member of the embassy staff. Wife's conduct will not be considered in the maintenance award.

The Calculation

If a court determines an award is appropriate, it proceeds to the second step, the calculation of support. The party paying support is the "payor," and the party receiving support is the "payee," or "recipient spouse." If the court determines an award is not appropriate, it will bar maintenance.

Calculation for Amount

Income

Spousal maintenance is based on the parties' net annual incomes.[5] As with child support, income from all sources is considered.

EXAMPLE Wife inherited 10,000 shares of Amazon stock, which pays a dividend of $1,000 per month. This income is included in her net income for the calculation of spousal maintenance.

Imputed Income

If a party is underemployed, or intentionally unemployed, income may be imputed, as it was with child support.

EXAMPLE Husband has retired from the Foreign Service and is employed by a private company as a consultant earning $175,000 per year. Wife is unemployed. The court can impute income from a job paying minimum wage, which has been $11/hour in Illinois since January 1, 2021.

Guideline Formula

The amount of maintenance is calculated by taking 33 and 1/3% of the payor's net annual income and subtracting 25% of the payee's net annual income.[6]

EXAMPLE Party A's annual gross income is $85,000. Party B's annual gross income is $28,000. The calculated amount of maintenance is $11,513.

The amount calculated as maintenance, however, when added to the net income of the payee, shall not result in the payee receiving an amount that is in excess of 40% of the combined net income of the parties.[7]

EXAMPLE Party A's annual gross income remains $85,000 per year. But now presume Party B's annual gross income increases to $50,000 per year. Their combined incomes equal $103,000. Maintenance plus the net income of Party B cannot exceed $41,261. The award is reduced to $1,541.

Calculation for Time

After calculating the amount of the maintenance payment, the court calculates how long it will be paid using the following formula:

> The duration of an award shall be calculated by multiplying the length of the marriage at the time the action was commenced by whichever of the following factors applies:
>
> - Less than 5 years (.20);
> - 5 years or more but less than 6 years (.24);
> - 6 years or more but less than 7 years (.28);
> - 7 years or more but less than 8 years (.32);
> - 8 years or more but less than 9 years (.36);
> - 9 years or more but less than 10 years (.40);
> - 10 years or more but less than 11 years (.44);
> - 11 years or more but less than 12 years (.48);
> - 12 years or more but less than 13 years (.52);
> - 13 years or more but less than 14 years (.56);
> - 14 years or more but less than 15 years (.60);
> - 15 years or more but less than 16 years (.64);
> - 16 years or more but less than 17 years (.68);
> - 17 years or more but less than 18 years (.72);

- 18 years or more but less than 19 years (.76);
- 19 years or more but less than 20 years (.80).[8]

EXAMPLE The parties were married for 10 years and four months, or 124 months. 124 x .44 = 55. Maintenance is payable for 55 months, or four years and seven months.

For a marriage of 20 or more years, the court, "in its discretion, shall order maintenance for a period equal to the length of the marriage or for an indefinite term."[9]

Guidelines

As with child support, the court shall order guideline support, unless guideline support is inappropriate.[10] The statute provides two instances when it is inappropriate.

Combined Net Income over $500,000

Guideline support does not apply if the parties' combined net income is over $500,000 per year.[11]

EXAMPLE Husband is an investment banker earning $450,000 per year. Wife is a nurse practitioner, earning $94,000 per year. Because their combined net income is over $500,000, guideline support is not applied.

Prior Support Orders

Guideline support doesn't apply if the payor has an existing spousal maintenance order from a prior relationship.[12]

EXAMPLE When Wife discovers Husband is having an affair with her best friend, Natalie, they divorce. Husband is ordered to pay Wife spousal maintenance of $500 per month. Husband and Natalie marry as soon as Husband's divorce is final. Some years later, Natalie discovers that Husband is having an affair with her best friend, Kayla. Should Husband be ordered to pay Natalie spousal maintenance, because he is still paying Wife spousal maintenance of $500 per month, guideline support would not apply.

Court's Discretion

Finally, as is the case with child support, the statute gives the court discretion not to follow guidelines. If the court finds it appropriate to deviate, the court will make findings as to why.[13]

EXAMPLE Hailey is the beneficiary of a family trust worth $500,000. Even modestly invested, the income it produces covers a significant portion of her needs. The court considers the trust income and can deviate from the guidelines.

Types of Maintenance

Three types of maintenance are available in Illinois: in gross, of definite term, and of indefinite term.

In Gross

An award of maintenance in gross is paid in one or two lump payments near the time of judgment.

EXAMPLE Guideline support from Husband to Wife is calculated at $1,500 per month for 10 years. Husband wants to get remarried and knows New Wife will resent his paying (now) Ex-Wife money she could be spending on herself. Husband agrees to give Wife an extra $150,000 from the sale of the marital residence. The $150,000 is an award of maintenance in gross.

Definite Term (Fixed Term)

Definite term maintenance is payable for a specific period of time. At the end of the period of time, maintenance may be barred, which means terminated with no possibility of future awards.

EXAMPLE Zachary is an engineer. Alexis is a nurse. Based on their twelve-year marriage, Zachary is ordered to pay spousal maintenance for six years and two months. At the end, the MSA states that the maintenance is barred.

Sometimes, however, the court wants to check back in and see if a payee has been able to become self-supporting. In that situation, maintenance is awarded for a definite term, subject to review. This type of maintenance, once known as "rehabilitative," is today known as "transitional."

> **EXAMPLE** Now, presume Zachary is an engineer and Alexis is a bookkeeper. When their children were born, Alexis stayed at home with them. During that time, computers were invented. After their twelve-year marriage, Alexis is granted spousal maintenance for a definite term of six years and two months. At the end of the term, Alexis is allowed to bring a petition to have the maintenance reviewed.

Standard for Review

If maintenance is for a definite term and reviewable, the court uses the following standard:

> In all such proceedings the court shall consider the applicable factors set forth in subsection (a) of Section 504 (the original factors used to determine if the award was appropriate) and the following factors:
>
> (1) Any change in the employment status of either party and whether the change has been made in good faith;
>
> (2) The efforts, if any, made by the party receiving maintenance to become self-supporting, and the reasonableness of the efforts where they are appropriate;
>
> (3) Any impairment of the present and future earning capacity of either party;
>
> (4) The tax consequences of the maintenance payments upon the respective economic circumstances of the parties;
>
> (5) The duration of the maintenance payments previously paid (and remaining to be paid) relative to the length of the marriage;
>
> (6) The property, including retirement benefits, awarded to each party under the judgment of dissolution of marriage, judgment of legal separation, or judgment of declaration of invalidity of marriage and the present status of the property;
>
> (7) The increase or decrease in each party's income since the prior judgment or order from which a review, modification, or termination is being sought;
>
> (8) The property acquired and currently owned by each party after the entry of the judgment of dissolution of marriage, judgment of legal separation, or judgment of declaration of invalidity of marriage; and
>
> (9) Any other factor that the court expressly finds to be just and equitable.[14]

> **EXAMPLE** Alexis was awarded spousal maintenance of $1,800 per month for five years. At the end of five years, Alexis brings a Motion to Review Spousal Maintenance. The court finds she has completed an Associate's Degree in Accounting at a community college and is employed as an entry-level bookkeeper. The court reduces the award to $1,000 per month and extends it for two more years, after which it is barred.

Indefinite Term

Indefinite term maintenance, the kind available for marriages of over 20 years, is awarded with no termination date. Although sometimes called "permanent," the term is inaccurate, because all kinds of maintenance are subject to terminating events.

Terminating Events

Maintenance will terminate if any of the following occur:

- Recipient marries;
- Recipient cohabits on a resident, continuing, conjugal basis;
- The payor dies; or
- The recipient dies. [15]

> **EXAMPLE** Based on their 35-year marriage, Husband is ordered to pay Wife spousal maintenance of $2,000 per month for an indefinite term. After the second year of receiving maintenance, Wife marries Boyfriend. Husband's obligation to pay maintenance ends. Should Wife move in with Boyfriend rather than marry him, Husband's obligation to pay maintenance would also end.

Because spousal maintenance terminates when the payor dies, good practice is to secure it with a life insurance policy on the payor's life.

Procedure

Initial Order

Petition

A party may request spousal maintenance in the petition for dissolution or by separate motion. It is possible a motion for temporary maintenance was filed early in the case and heard on an expedited basis. (See Chapter 5, Temporary Motions and the Financial Affidavit.)

Financial Basis

A temporary award is made on the basis of the financial affidavit. In cases where the matter goes to trial, additional information is likely required, such as the petitioner's work history and educational qualifications. Information about the property, including income-producing property will be required. (See Chapter 10, Discovery, Pretrial and Trial.)

Settle or Trial

After exchanging financial information, the parties either agree on a maintenance award, or the matter is set for trial. (See Chapter 10, Discovery, Pretrial and Trial.)

Ensuring Compliance

Income Withholding Order

An order for supposal maintenance and an income withholding order (IWO) may be served on the payor's employer. However while a combined deduction for child support and maintenance can be sent to the ILSDU for disbursement, a deduction for spousal maintenance alone cannot.[16] Instead, it is sent directly from the employer to the payee.

Enforcement

While an order for spousal maintenance can be litigated through a petition for rule to show cause, no additional statutory or administrative remedies exist for enforcement. (See Chapter 12, Post-Decree Litigation.)

Chapter Summary

Spousal maintenance payments, formerly known as "alimony," are payments made from one spouse to another after the marital relationship ends. The award of maintenance is a two-step process. First, the court makes a finding as to whether an award is appropriate, based on statutory factors, such as the income and property available to each spouse. If the court finds an award is appropriate, the amount and duration are calculated pursuant to a formula provided by statute. The formula provides guideline support; however, guideline support is not appropriate where the parties have high incomes or there are prior support orders. In addition, the court has discretion to deviate from guideline support.

A court can order maintenance in gross; for a period of time (called "definite term"), with the potential to review it at the end of the time; or for an indefinite term. Illinois uses the term "indefinite term" rather than "permanent" because all types of maintenance are subject to terminating events. To secure the payment of spousal maintenance, an income withholding order can be served upon the payor's employer; however, unless the deduction is for child support and maintenance, the funds are sent directly to the payee, not the ILSDU.

Key Terms

Spousal Maintenance ("Alimony")

In Gross

Definite Term (Fixed Term)

Indefinite Term

Reviewable

Discussion Questions

1. For many years, the IMDMA did not provide a formula for spousal maintenance. As a result, awards of spousal maintenance varied widely across the state. In 2015, the IMDMA was amended to provide a formula. Is consistency good? Does the statute give the court enough discretion to deviate from the formula?
2. Views on alimony have changed over the years. Does the IMDMA reflect the parties' roles within marriage in 2024? Is it appropriate in the post-pandemic economy in Illinois?
3. Protections exist for the enforcement of child support orders but not for spousal support orders. Why are they different? What public interests are involved?
4. Under current law, spousal maintenance is included in the income of the payor, meaning he pays income tax on it. And yet, spousal maintenance is included in the income of the payee for child support. Why are they different? Which approach makes more sense?
5. Consider a case in which a husband was allowed to pay less than guideline spousal maintenance because he took 79% of the marital debt. Should the court have recognized he could file for bankruptcy, thus eliminating the marital debt? *See In re Marriage of Underwood*, 314 Ill. App. 3d 325, 329, 731 N.E.2d 1003, 1007 (4th Dist. 2000).
6. Should a court consider a spouse's potential inheritance when awarding spousal maintenance? Perhaps the spouse does not have assets at the time of the divorce but expects to inherit a large sum of money on the death of a parent.

7. How heavily should the court weigh factor (7), the standard of living during marriage? Should a court award maintenance where Wife has a "substantial lifestyle deficit"? *See In re Marriage of Dunlap*, 294 Ill. App. 3d 768, 774, 690 N.E.2d 1023, 1027 (4th Dist. 1998). Or is maintenance intended only to prevent financial hardship?
8. When a U.S. citizen files an immigration petition for a foreign spouse, he signs an Affidavit of Support, which is a contract between the federal government and the U.S. citizen. If the foreign spouse receives federal benefits, the U.S. citizen agrees to pay the government back. The Affidavit of Support remains in effect even if the parties divorce, but it is not a guarantee of spousal maintenance. Should it be? Suppose a spouse could not speak English, had limited education, and no work experience. Is an application of the factors in the maintenance statute a sufficient guarantee of support?
9. Should an obligor be required to work past full retirement age to meet a spousal maintenance obligation? Or should he be allowed to retire at full retirement age, even if it means he will no longer be able to pay?
10. On the other hand, should he be allowed to take an early retirement, if it meant he could no longer afford spousal maintenance? *See In re Marriage of Smith* 77 Ill. App. 3d 858, 396 N.E.2d 859 (2d Dist. 1979).
11. Consider a case in which the evidence was uncontested that "during the nine years Harry was achieving his medical education, Helen was the primary breadwinner for the family." If the parties divorced when Harry graduated, the guideline maintenance award for Helen would have been 3.6 years. However, Harry would likely earn a physician's income his entire career, possibly 40 more years. Is this an equitable result? *See In re Marriage of Rubinstein*, 145 Ill. App. 3d 31, 38, 495 N.E.2d 659, 664 (2d Dist. 1986).

Endnotes

1. 750 ILCS 5/504(a) (West, Westlaw Classic through P.A. 103-21 of the 2023 Reg. Sess.).
2. *Id.*
3. *Id.* § 504(a)(1-14).
4. *Id.* § 504(a).
5. *Id.* § 504(b-1)(1)(A).
6. *Id.* § 504(b-1)(1)(A).
7. 750 ILCS 5/504(b-1)(1)(A).
8. *Id.* § 504(b-1)(1)(B).
9. *Id.*
10. *Id.* § 504(b-1).
11. *Id.* § 504(b-1)(1).
12. *Id.*

13. 750 ILCS 5/504(b-1).
14. *Id.* § 510(a-5)(1-9).
15. *Id.* § 510(c).
16. *Id.* § 507.1(a).

Nine

Property

Overview

In Chapter Two, we learned that marriage is the legal recognition of the union of two people. During the marriage, the parties accumulate property, such as a house, vehicles, and retirement assets. When the marriage dissolves, the IMDMA gives the court authority to allocate the property between the parties. However, it is not required to divide the property into halves. Instead, the court has the authority to allocate the property in "just proportions," or "fairly." In making the allocation, the court is guided by a number of factors.[1] Are there times when a 50/50 division is not fair?

Property

Marital Property

The court has the authority to allocate marital property, that is, property acquired by either spouse during the marriage.[2] It does not matter which spouse "earned" the money used to buy the property, and it does not matter whose name the property is in. What matters is when the property was acquired: was it before or after the marriage?

> **EXAMPLE** During the marriage, Husband begins a job that offers a 401(k). He contributes the maximum allowable each year. The 401(k) is marital property, subject to division by the court.

> **EXAMPLE** Similarly, during the parties' marriage, Wife buys a car. She puts the title in her name. She drives it exclusively. The payment is debited from her paycheck. The car is marital property.

Assets and Liabilities

"Marital property" means both the assets and the liabilities, or debts, the parties incurred during the marriage.[3]

Assets as Property

- Real property (the "marital residence," and any other real property)
- Personal property, such as furniture
- Checking and savings accounts, CDs, and investment accounts (outside of retirement)
- Pensions, IRAs, 401(k)s or other retirement accounts
- Vehicles such as cars, motorcycles, snowmobiles, boats, airplanes
- Intangible items, such as video game in-game currency, copyrights, frequent flyer miles, and vacation days
- Cryptocurrency (like Bitcoin)
- Awards from personal injury or worker's compensation claims
- Businesses started during the marriage ("Anderson's Plumbing")
- The cash value in whole life insurance policies.

Liabilities as Property

- Unsecured debt, such as student loans or credit card debt
- Secured debt, such as a loan for real property, in which the loan is secured by a mortgage, or a car loan, in which the lender holds the title of the car.

EXAMPLE As an example of unsecured debt, during the marriage, the parties had separate credit cards. Wife paid hers off in full each month; Husband did not. When the petition for dissolution is filed, the balance on Husband's credit card (for items such as groceries and car repairs) is $10,000. Wife is shocked to learn it is marital debt.

EXAMPLE As an example of secured debt, Grace drives a new BMW, with a loan greater than the fair market value of the car. The loan company holds the title to the car. The car loan is a marital debt (although the car is a marital asset).

Attorney's Fees

Attorney's fees and costs are considered marital debts, which can be allocated by the court. In the chapter on temporary motions, we saw that the court could order one party to contribute to the other party's attorney's fees, to enable both sides to participate in the dissolution process. Once the dissolution process is complete, the court can re-examine the issue.[4]

> **EXAMPLE** In Chapter 5 on Temporary Motions and the Financial Affidavit, the court ordered Husband to pay Wife's attorney $10,000 so she could participate in the divorce. At the time of judgment, the parties have incurred a total of $40,000 in attorney's fees. The court examines the settlement agreement and determines each party is capable of paying his or her own attorney's fees. The court has the authority to award Wife less property to make up for the $10,000 "advance" she has received.

Characterizing Property

Under Illinois law, all property acquired by either spouse after the marriage is presumed to be marital.[5] The statute provides limited exceptions to this rule. The only property acquired after marriage that is non-marital is as follows:

(1) Property acquired by gift, legacy or descent or property acquired in exchange for such property;

(2) Property acquired in exchange for property acquired before the marriage;

(3) Property acquired by a spouse after a judgment of legal separation;

(4) Property excluded by valid agreement of the parties, including a premarital agreement or a postnuptial agreement;

(5) Any judgment or property obtained by judgment awarded to a spouse from the other spouse except, however, when a spouse is required to sue the other spouse in order to obtain insurance coverage or otherwise recover from a third party and the recovery is directly related to amounts advanced by the marital estate, the judgment shall be considered marital property;

(6) Property acquired before the marriage, except as it relates to retirement plans that may have both marital and non-marital characteristics;

(6.5) All property acquired by a spouse by the sole use of non-marital property as collateral for a loan that then is used to acquire property during the marriage; to the extent that the marital estate repays any portion of the loan, it shall be considered a contribution from the marital estate to the non-marital estate subject to reimbursement;

(7) The increase in value of non-marital property, irrespective of whether the increase results from a contribution of marital property, non-marital property, the personal effort of a spouse, or otherwise, subject to the right of reimbursement provided in subsection (c) of this Section; and

(8) Income from property acquired by a method listed in paragraphs (1) through (7) of this subsection if the income is not attributable to the personal effort of a spouse.[6]

EXAMPLE One month after the parties marry, Jasmine's father dies. In his will, he leaves her a $10,000 CD. The CD is non-marital property. If the parties divorce, it is not subject to division. Factor (1) applies.

EXAMPLE Presume Jasmine cashes in the CD and puts the $10,000 cash into an investment account. Over the next 20 years, it increases to $21, 942. The total amount is non-marital. Factor (7) applies.

Commingled Property

Life is long. Sometimes property of one kind (or estate, as it is called in the IMDMA) gets combined, or commingled, with property of another kind. When that happens, property of one kind can transmute, or change, into the other kind.

The IMDMA contemplates three different situations in which commingling can occur: one estate contributes to another and retains its identity, one estate contributes to another and loses its identity, and finally, the two estates are combined into newly acquired property.

Retention of Identity

Sometimes marital and non-marital property are commingled by one estate being contributed into the other. When the contributed property retains its identity, it does not transmute, and remains the property of the contributing estate.[7]

> **EXAMPLE** Jasmine received a $10,000 inheritance, which she deposits into a newly opened savings account. During the marriage, the parties decide the savings account is a convenient place for their marital savings, and begin depositing $1,000 per year into the account. When the parties separate three years later, there is $13,000 in the account. It is possible to identify that $10,000 is non-marital and $3,000 is martial. Jasmine receives $10,000 (plus interest on it) and the marital estate subject to division by the court contains $3,000 (plus interest on it).

Loss of Identity

Sometimes marital property and non-marital property are commingled by one estate being contributed into the other. When the contributed property loses its identity, the contributed property transmutes to the estate receiving the property.[8]

> **EXAMPLE** Jasmine deposits the same inherited $10,000 into the marital checking account. For three years, the parties add their paychecks to the account and pay bills from it. Three years later, when the parties divorce, there is $12,000 in the account. It is all marital property. The non-marital dollars lost their identity and transmuted into marital property.

Contribution

In order to prevent unfairness when the contributing estate loses its identity, the IMDMA permits the contributing estate to petition for reimbursement.[9]

> **EXAMPLE** Jasmine can petition the court for reimbursement of the $10,000 she contributed to the marital account. If her petition is granted, the remaining $2,000 is marital. If not, all $12,000 is marital.

Newly Acquired Property

And finally, if marital property and non-marital property are commingled into newly acquired property resulting in a loss of identity of the contributing estate, the commingled property shall be deemed to have transmuted into marital property.[10] In this situation, too, the contributing estate may be reimbursed.

EXAMPLE Assume that Jasmine's $10,000 inheritance plus $15,000 from the marital savings account were combined to buy a Jet Ski. In this case, the entire Jet Ski is marital. However, as in the previous scenario, Jasmine has the right to petition for reimbursement of her non-marital $10,000.

Dispute over Characterization

If there is a dispute, in which one party claims the property is marital, and the other claims it is non-marital, the presumption is that the property is marital. The burden to overcome this presumption, by clear and convincing evidence, is on the party claiming the property is non-marital.[11]

EXAMPLE When Jasmine petitions for reimbursement, Husband alleges that Jasmine made a gift of the $10,000 to the marital estate. He testifies that they wanted to buy a Jet Ski for their teenage sons and their friends, but didn't have enough money in the marital savings account. Rather than disappoint their sons, Jasmine offered the $10,000. The burden is on Jasmine to show by clear and convincing evidence she had not intended to make a gift to the marital estate.

Factors Used in Allocation

The court allocates marital property between the parties in just proportions. When allocating property, the court considers all relevant factors, including:

(1) Each party's contribution to the acquisition, preservation, or increase or decrease in value of the marital or non-marital property, including (i) any decrease attributable to an advance from the parties' marital estate toward attorney's fees and (ii) the contribution of a spouse as a homemaker or to the family unit;

(2) The dissipation by each party of the marital property;

(3) The value of the property assigned to each spouse (including non-marital property);

(4) The duration of the marriage;

(5) The relevant economic circumstances of each spouse when the division of property is to become effective, including the desirability of awarding the family home, or the right to live therein for reasonable periods, to the spouse having the primary residence of the children;

(6) Any obligations and rights arising from a prior marriage of either party;

(7) Any prenuptial or postnuptial agreement of the parties;

(8) The age, health, station, occupation, amount and sources of income, vocational skills, employability, estate, liabilities, and needs of each of the parties;

(9) The custodial provisions for any children;

(10) Whether the apportionment is in lieu of or in addition to maintenance;

(11) The reasonable opportunity of each spouse for future acquisition of capital assets and income; and

(12) The tax consequences of the property division upon the respective economic circumstances of the parties.[12]

EXAMPLE Christine and Pat married right out of college when they were beginning their careers. Over the next few years, through working long hours and diligent thrift, they scrapped together $10,000 for a down payment on a starter home. The stress was too much, the relationship floundered, and Christine filed for divorce. During the marriage, Pat's father died, and she inherited $500,000. Under factor (5), the court can consider Pat's non-marital property as relevant to her economic circumstances and award Christine more than 50% of the $10,000 marital property.

Just as marital misconduct was not a factor the court considered in an award of spousal maintenance, it is not a factor in its allocation of property.[13]

Factor (2): Dissipation

Definition

A marriage acquires property through the efforts of both parties, with the understanding that the property will be used for marital purposes. Using marital property for a non-marital purpose is called "dissipation."

EXAMPLE Husband and Wife deposit their paychecks into their joint checking account. Wife uses the money to buy groceries for the family. Wife has used marital property for a marital purpose.

EXAMPLE In contrast, Wife uses the money from the joint checking account to buy her boyfriend a Rolex. Wife has used marital property for a non-marital purpose. Husband can make a claim of dissipation.

The Claim of Dissipation

A claim of dissipation is subject to the following conditions:

Timing

First, the dissipation must have occurred while the marriage was undergoing an irretrievable breakdown.[14] When the breakdown began can be subject to dispute.

EXAMPLE Husband alleges the breakdown occurred two years before he filed a petition for dissolution of marriage. However, Wife points to the fact that they were still occupying the same bedroom, entertaining friends, making joint investment decisions, and traveling together.

Notice

Second, a notice of intent to claim dissipation must include the date the breakdown occurred, a list of the property dissipated, and the period of time during which the dissipation occurred.[15] The notice of intent to claim dissipation is served on the opposing party and filed with the court along with a certificate of service.[16]

EXAMPLE Husband alleges every ATM withdrawal from their joint accounts was dissipation by Wife. He provides no supporting evidence to indicate what the funds were spent on, or even that Wife made the withdrawals. Husband has likely not adequately listed the property dissipated.

Hearing

If there is a dispute, the court determines whether dissipation occurred.

> **EXAMPLE** During the breakdown of the marriage, Husband invested $100,000 of marital funds in gold bullion, which turned out to be worthless. Husband asserts there was no way he could have known it was worthless, and it is a marital loss. Wife alleges Husband did not verify the reputation of the seller and has dissipated funds.

If the court finds a party dissipated marital assets, the other party is credited the same amount of property.

> **EXAMPLE** Husband prevails on his claim for dissipation against Wife. He is credited the amount of the Rolex from their joint checking account before it is allocated by the court.

Factor (7): The Premarital Agreement.

Definition

A premarital agreement, also known as a prenuptial agreement, is a contract between prospective spouses that provides how they will divide their property in the event of a marriage-terminating event. The entry of judgments for legal separation, dissolution of marriage, or declaration of marital invalidity are all marriage-terminating events. Premarital agreements in Illinois are controlled by The Illinois Uniform Premarital Agreement Act, which specifies what terms they can contain, what terms they can't contain, and when they can be enforced.[17]

The Content of a Premarital Agreement

What a Premarital Agreement Can Contain

Parties to a premarital agreement may contract with respect to:

(1) The rights and obligations of each of the parties in any of the property of either or both of them whenever and wherever acquired or located;

(2) The right to buy, sell, use, transfer, exchange, abandon, lease, consume, expend, assign, create a security interest in, mortgage, encumber, dispose of, or otherwise manage and control property;

(3) The disposition of property upon separation, marital dissolution, death, or the occurrence or nonoccurrence of any other event;

(4) The modification or elimination of spousal support;

(5) The making of a will, trust, or other arrangement to carry out the provisions of the agreement;

(6) The ownership rights in and disposition of the death benefit from a life insurance policy;

(7) The choice of law governing the construction of the agreement; and

(8) Any other matter, including their personal rights and obligations, not in violation of public policy or a statute imposing a criminal penalty.[18]

EXAMPLE William was a widower with two young adult children when he became engaged to Rachel. William owns a ski lodge in Aspen. He and Rachel agree that if their marriage ends, the ski lodge will remain his property. Pursuant to Factor (1), the ski lodge is acceptable content of a premarital agreement.

What a Premarital Agreement Cannot Contain

Parents cannot contract out of the duty to support a child financially.[19]

EXAMPLE William was 52 years old and Rachel was 35 years old when they become engaged. Rachel would like to have a baby, but William already has two teenagers from a first marriage and does not want additional responsibility. Their premarital agreement states that "in the event the marriage ends, William is not responsible for child support for any children born of the marriage." This is not acceptable content.

Enforceability

A premarital agreement comes before the court when one party does not want to be bound by it. When that happens, the statute puts the burden on the spouse that does not want to be bound to prove why it should not be enforced against him.[20]

EXAMPLE Ava and Elijah enter a premarital agreement. Five years later, the relationship breaks down, and Elijah files for divorce. Ava does not want to be bound by the terms of the agreement. The burden is on Ava to prove why it should not be enforced against her.

The statute provides the party who does not want to be bound by the agreement with two options: either the party did not enter the agreement voluntarily, or it was unconscionable and the party was unaware of the other's assets when they entered it.

Option One: Duress

For the premarital agreement to be enforceable, both sides must have entered it voluntarily. In other words, to avoid being bound, the spouse must prove they entered the agreement under coercion or duress.[21]

EXAMPLE Before they were married, Austin tells Joanna that unless she enters a premarital agreement, the wedding is off. Because Joanna has already announced her engagement on Facebook, she signs the agreement.

Courts have held that making a wedding conditional on the signing of a premarital agreement does not constitute coercion. Consequently, Joanna is still bound by it. However, option two is still available to her.

Option Two: Unconscionable and Inadequate Disclosure

For the premarital agreement to be enforceable under this option, the party must show two things. First, the party must show that the agreement was unconscionable when it was executed.[22] An unconscionable bargain is one "which no man in his senses, not under delusion, would make on one hand and no fair and honest man would accept on the other."[23]

A premarital agreement may be procedurally or substantively unconscionable. Procedural unconscionability is defined as some impropriety during the process of forming the contract that deprived a party of meaningful choice. Courts look at all of the circumstances surrounding the process, including when it was presented, and whether the parties had time for an attorney review.

EXAMPLE Austin gave Joanna the premarital agreement at the rehearsal dinner when she was distracted with the final details for the wedding. She glances at the first page, flips to the back page, and signs it without reading. She did not have time for an attorney review. This is likely procedurally unconscionable.

Alternately, premarital agreements may be substantively unconscionable, which means the terms are inordinately one-sided in one party's favor.

EXAMPLE In the premarital agreement, Joanna agrees that Austin will be awarded all of the assets the parties acquire during their marriage, and Joanna will be allocated all of the debts. This is likely substantively unconscionable.

If Joanna cannot prove the agreement was unconscionable, the analysis stops. If she can, she must also prove that she did not have knowledge of Austin's property.[24] To ensure the parties have knowledge of each other's property, most premarital agreements contain a disclosure of the assets and liabilities of each party.

In the unlikely event a premarital agreement does not contain a disclosure, a lack of knowledge can be demonstrated by the facts of the case.

EXAMPLE Joanna lives in rural Illinois, and Austin lives in New York City. When Austin visits Joanna in Illinois, he rents a subcompact car and stays at a Red Roof Inn. Joanna has never been to New York, where Austin drives a Ferrari and divides his time between his penthouse apartment in Manhattan and his oceanfront home in the Hamptons. After three exceptional weekend visits, the parties sign a premarital agreement and marry. The statute only requires "adequate" knowledge, or "fair and reasonable" disclosure, but even under this standard, Joanna likely does not have adequate knowledge of Austin's property.

Option Three: Unforeseeable Circumstances

At times, something happens during the marriage that the parties could not have reasonably foreseen when they entered the premarital agreement. Even then, they are likely still bound by it. The Act makes an exception only if the unforeseen circumstance causes a party who waived spousal maintenance undue hardship.[25] In that event, a court may order maintenance to the extent necessary to avoid such hardship.

EXAMPLE Because Wife is a successful periodontist, she waives spousal maintenance in a premarital agreement. During the marriage, she suffers a stroke. Permanently paralyzed on the left side of her body, she is unable to practice her profession. The stroke was not foreseeable at the time the agreement was executed, and Husband may be ordered to pay maintenance.

However, a real need must be demonstrated before the court will deviate from the terms of the agreement, not just a reduction in lifestyle. If Wife receives enough property, including income-generating property, to maintain her health and safety under the terms of the premarital agreement, the court will likely not modify the terms.

Chapter Summary

The court has the authority to allocate marital property, which is defined as the property acquired by either spouse during the marriage. It includes both the assets of the marriage and the liabilities. Non-marital property is defined as property owned by one party before the marriage, or acquired by gift or inheritance during the marriage. During the marriage, marital and non-marital property may become commingled. Where one type of property retains its identity after being combined with the other, it does not transmute, or change, into the other type. In contrast, where it loses its identity, it transmutes into the other type; however, to avoid unfairness, the court can reimburse the contributing estate. If the estates are combined into newly acquired property, the presumption is it is martial. In a dispute, property is presumed marital, and the presumption can only be overcome by clear and convincing evidence.

Allocation of marital property is made in "just proportions," which may not be 50/50. The General Assembly provides factors to guide the court in making the allocation. One of them, Factor (2), is any dissipation by one of the parties. Another, Factor (7), is the presence or absence of any premarital agreements, which are contracts executed by the parties before their marriage detailing the allocation of their property after a marriage-terminating event. Should a party not want to be bound by the premarital agreement, the Illinois Uniform Premarital Agreement Act provides three ways to avoid enforcement.

Key Terms

- Just Proportions
- Marital Property
- Non-Marital Property
- Transmute
- Commingle
- Contribution
- Dissipation
- Premarital (Prenuptial) Agreement
- Postmarital (Postnuptial) Agreement

Discussion Questions

1. Are assets accumulated after the parties separate part of the marital estate? If they are not, is Illinois condoning common law divorce? *See In re Marriage of Brooks*, 138 Ill. App. 3d 252, 486 N.E.2d 267 (1st Dist. 1985).
2. If a party acquired a professional degree during the marriage, should it be considered a marital asset? Or should it be a factor in the distribution of assets, such as "the future opportunity to acquire additional income?" *See In re Marriage of Weinstein*, 128 Ill. App. 3d 234, 245, 470 N.E.2d 551, 559 (1st Dist. 1984).
3. How should a court consider one party's investment of marital funds in cryptocurrency? As a gambling debt, which is dissipation, or as an unfortunate investment, which is a marital loss?
4. Prior law allowed the court to classify any property bought "in contemplation of marriage" as marital. Was that sufficient reason to turn a non-marital asset into a marital one? On the other hand, if a spouse is awarded the house he'd bought just before the marriage, should the marital estate be reimbursed for expenditures on taxes and upkeep? Is there a public policy behind ensuring a spouse is not left homeless?
5. How should a court define "contribution" from one estate to another? If a wife invested years of physical labor remodeling a house but didn't contribute non-marital funds, should she be reimbursed for her contribution? *See In re Marriage of Pittman*, 212 Ill. App. 3d 99, 569 N.E.2d 1278 (5th Dist. 1991).
6. At one time premarital agreements were disallowed because they were thought to encourage divorce. Have views toward marriage and divorce changed? If parties were secure in knowing how their property would be divided in the event of a divorce, could a premarital agreement encourage marriage? In what situations are parties likely to enter a premarital agreement?
7. The Fourth District Appellate Court would not enforce a term in a premarital agreement that required the parents to raise the children Lutheran. Why might that be? Religion is one of the significant decisions allocated between the parents. Would it make a difference if both parents were Lutheran? *See In re Marriage of Nuechterlein*, 225 Ill. App. 3d 1, 3, 587 N.E.2d 21, 22 (4th Dist. 1992).
8. Commercial contracts are considered "arm's length transactions," because the parties are in a financial, not emotional relationship. Should premarital agreements, which are made between parties in a deep emotional relationship, be viewed under the same legal standard as commercial contracts? If not, how should they be viewed?

9. At times, married couples enter a postnuptial agreement. Should they be examined under the same standard as a premarital agreement? Would parties be likely to feel more pressure to preserve a marriage than they had an engagement? Would the terms be more accurate, because they could see how things are going?
10. Nine states, including Wisconsin, are community property states, which divide marital property equally. Forty-one, including Illinois, are separate property states, which permit allocation in just proportions. Suppose a couple lives in a condominium in Chicago but spends occasional weekends at their home on Lake Geneva. Illinois law would apply to their divorce. Suppose they retire to Lake Geneva but keep the condominium for weekend trips to the city. In this case, Wisconsin law would apply. Should it matter which state is their primary residence? Should they be able to choose which law they want to apply to their divorce?

Endnotes

1. 750 ILCS 5/503(d) (West, Westlaw Classic through P.A. 103-21 of the 2023 Reg. Sess.).
2. *Id.* § 503(a).
3. *Id.* § 503(a)(1-8).
4. *Id.* § 503(j)(5).
5. *Id.* § 503(b)(1).
6. *Id.* § 503(a).
7. 750 ILCS 5/503(c)(1)(A)(ii). Consider a glass of Coca-Cola containing ice cubes. The Coca-Cola and the water (in the ice cubes) retain their identities.
8. *Id.* § 503(c)(1)(A)(i). The ice cubes melt. Now the Coca-Cola and water have lost their identities.
9. *Id.* § 503(c)(2)(A).
10. *Id.* § 503(c)(1)(B).
11. *Id.* § 503(b)(1).
12. *Id.* § 503(d)(1-12).
13. 750 ILCS 5/503(d).
14. *Id.* § 503(d)(2)(ii).
15. *Id.*
16. *Id.* § 503(d)(2)(iii).
17. 750 ILCS 10/1. (West, Westlaw Classic through P.A. 103-21 of the 2023 Reg. Sess.).
18. *Id.* § 4(a).
19. *Id.* § 4(b).
20. *Id.* § 7(a)(1).
21. *Id.* § 7(a)(1).
22. *Id.* § 7(a)(2).
23. In re Marriage of Carlson, 101 Ill. App. 3d 924, 428 N.E.2d 1005 (1st Dist. 1981).
24. 750 ILCS 10/7(a)(2)(i-iii).
25. *Id.* § 7(b).

Ten

Discovery, Pretrial, and Trial

Overview

Contested issues, such as whether an award of spousal maintenance is appropriate, or whether an award of joint allocation serves the child's best interest, are resolved based on the facts of the specific case. To obtain these facts, the litigants engage in "discovery," a pretrial process to obtain relevant information from the opposing party or a third party.

Based on the outcome of discovery, parties may settle the contested issues. If not, the information obtained may be introduced as evidence to the judge at trial. As you read, consider what evidence will support your client's position and which discovery method should be used to obtain it.

Discovery in Family Law

The discovery process in Illinois is governed by Article II of the Supreme Court Rules. These rules permit great latitude in discovery,[1] reflecting the policy that the more information the parties have, the better they will be able to evaluate the strengths and weaknesses of their case and arrive at a settlement.

Discovery Methods

The Supreme Court Rules provide a number of different discovery methods. Law offices can use all or some of the methods based on the information they need. In addition, they can use them in any order. Because discovery methods used in family law are the same as those used in other types of civil litigation, only an overview is provided in this text.

Method/Rule	Definition	On Whom	Time to Respond	Limits/ Requirements	Notes
Rule 213 Written Interrogatories	Written Questions	On Parties	Within 28 days; seasonably supplement	Not more than 30 total	213 (f) Identify Witnesses
Rule 214 Discovery of documents, objects, and tangible things	Commonly called "Requests to Produce"	On Parties	Within 28 days; seasonably supplement		"Documents" broadly construed; includes electronically stored information
Rule 215 Physical and Mental Examination		Party or Third Party			In Family Law, 750 ILCS 5/604.10 evaluations for custody purposes only.
Rule 216 Admission of Fact	Statements of Facts	On Parties	28 days; deny or deemed admitted	Maximum number 30	Warnings about failure to comply must be stated
Rules 202–209 Depositions	Oral examination under oath. May include Rider for Documents	Party or third party		Set seven days in advance. Limit three hours	Notice of Deposition on party, Subpoena on third party.
Rule 204 Subpoenas	Used to ensure deposition of third party	Third party		Pay witness fees and mileage	Can be served via certified mail
Rule 204 (a) (4) Subpoena duces tecum	Documents Only	Third party		May pay copy costs over $20.	Can be served via certified mail

Discovery of Child-Related Issues

Child-related issues are decided based on the best interest factors provided in Chapter 6. If the parties are unable to resolve these issues themselves or through the work of a mediator, these factors are investigated by a GAL. Very often, the parents accept the GAL's recommendations, because as court-appointed investigators, their reports carry significant weight at trial.

However, when the investigators disagree or one party rejects the GAL's report, the parties prepare for trial on child-related issues. They use discovery methods to obtain information to support their claims that the investigators were biased or did an incomplete investigation.

> **EXAMPLE** Mother and Father are locked in a dispute over who will have significant decision-making authority over their son Tyler, aged eight. When the GAL's report is strongly in favor of Mother, Father rejects the report. Father's attorney issues a subpoena for the deposition of Tyler's teacher, to discover whether Tyler has had breakfast and is clean and dressed appropriately for the weather each day.

At times, a parent may allege the other parent's mental health issues interfere with their ability to parent. To support their claim, the parent may seek to discover the other parent's therapist's or psychiatrist's records. Because of the deeply personal nature of mental health records, specific procedures must be followed before they can be subpoenaed. For example, no party may serve a subpoena unless it is accompanied by a written order issued by a judge. This process, as provided in the Illinois Mental Health and Developmental Disabilities Act,[2] must be carefully followed, because any person who knowingly and willfully violates any provision of the Act is guilty of a Class A misdemeanor.[3]

Discovery of Financial Issues

Financial Affidavit

The financial affidavit, which was discussed in Chapter 5, requires the parties to list their income and property. If the marital estate is small, and both parties are familiar with it, a financial affidavit may be sufficient.

> **EXAMPLE** Husband and Wife both work in the fast food industry earning minimum wage. They receive W2s and file taxes jointly. They have one checking account and rent an apartment. In a five-year marriage, a financial affidavit, plus supporting documentation, may be sufficient.

Additional Methods

More often, a financial affidavit is insufficient. In those cases, the attorneys do additional discovery to locate or value the property. Please note that parties must have completed their financial affidavits before they can issue discovery requests.

EXAMPLE Wife knows Husband has an account at Merrill Lynch. She has seen statements on his desk and overheard him talking to his broker. Yet on his financial affidavit, Husband does not list a Merrill Lynch account. Wife's attorney issues a subpoena on Merrill Lynch.

Managing Discovery

During the discovery phase of litigation, two things happen at once. Each party responds to discovery requests served on them, and at the same time, serves discovery requests on the other party. While attorneys supervise the discovery phase, in most law firms, paralegals are responsible for completing the discovery-related assignments.

Responding to Discovery Requests

Review

When a law firm receives a discovery request from the other side, the paralegal enters the response date into the firm management software. The attorney then reviews the request for any objectionable requests. An objection can be raised if the request seeks information protected by the attorney-client privilege or attorney work-product doctrine.[4] Additionally, objections can be raised if the request seeks information that is outside the scope of the litigation, is cumulative, is not relevant, or creates undue burden or expense.[5]

EXAMPLE Husband issues requests for production of Wife's bank statements for the past 10 years when they have only been married one year. Wife's attorney objects on the basis that the request is not relevant.

EXAMPLE In contrast, because he suspects dissipation, Husband issues requests for production of Wife's credit card statements for the year they were married. Wife's attorney would likely find this request appropriate.

Compliance

Having noted the requests objected to, paralegals forward the discovery request to the clients and work with them to collect the requested documents. In the example above, the paralegal would ensure she had received copies of all twelve statements from the credit card requested. The paralegal then forwards the documents to the attorney for review.

Once the attorney reviews the production, a copy is kept in the office file, and a copy is sent to the other side's attorney. In the past, discovery responses were produced as paper documents. Now, most firms send digital copies. They may send them on CDs or flash drives. More often, they send them as attachments to email or via drop boxes.

Proof of Compliance

Discovery is conducted between the parties.[6] Accordingly, the discovery responses are only sent to the other side. They are not filed with the court. To prove compliance with the discovery request, a certificate of production is filed with the court.

Issuing Discovery Requests

Assessment

When a law firm issues discovery requests, an attorney for the firm first determines the types of discovery that are needed and the order in which they should be issued. Many firms start with standard requests for the production of documents and marital interrogatories. Based on the response they receive to those requests, they may issue additional discovery as well.

> **EXAMPLE** During their marriage, the parties opened Anderson's Plumbing, Inc. After twenty years in business, it has established an excellent reputation in the community. The company owns three vans, fully equipped with plumbing tools, and generates a gross income of $500,000 per year. Husband alleges it is only worth $18,000, the fair market value of the three vans. Wife's attorney subpoenas the financial records of Anderson's Plumbing, which can be evaluated by an accountant.

Draft

Paralegals often complete the first draft of the discovery request. In addition, they ensure that discovery requests are complete. For example, a subpoena for a deposition must include a check for witness and mileage fees. A deposition must be scheduled in the county in which the case is filed, and a court reporter must be ordered. The discovery requests are given to the attorney for a final review and the required return dates are docketed.

Proof of Service

As with discovery responses, discovery requests are sent to the opposing party. Only a notice of service of the request is filed with the court.

Upon Receipt

When the responses to the request are received, the paralegal reviews them to ensure they are complete and passes them to the attorney.

Disputes about Discovery

As provided above, courts are not involved in the discovery process unless there is a dispute. Even then, the Illinois Supreme Court rules require the parties to engage in a personal conference to resolve the dispute before they can litigate.[7] Because this requirement is found in Illinois Supreme Court Rule 201(k), it is known as a "201(k) conference."

EXAMPLE Husband has not produced the requested documents by the due date. Wife's attorney issues a letter requesting a conference pursuant to Rule 201(k). During the telephone conference, Husband's attorney says he has the documents in his office, but the paralegal who managed discovery has been out of the office sick. Wife's attorney grants a one-week extension.

However, sometimes the 201(k) conference does not resolve the dispute.

EXAMPLE Wife's attorney issues a subpoena for the deposition of the attorney who represented Husband when the parties signed their premarital agreement.. Husband objects to the deposition under the attorney-client privilege. Wife argues that because the attorney discussed the premarital agreement with her at a real estate closing several years after the marriage, the attorney-client privilege no longer applies. The conference does not resolve the dispute.

Motion to Compel

In cases where the 201(k) conference does not resolve the dispute, the aggrieved party can file a motion to compel production. This motion is filed, scheduled, noticed, and served according to local rules. The matter is set for hearing.

If a party was late in responding to a discovery request, at the hearing the judge may issue an order compelling production by a specific date. If a party has objected to a discovery request, the judge either issues a protective order or an order compelling production.

Sanctions under Rule 219

The court can order sanctions against the party who did not comply with discovery requests, such as ordering them to pay the aggrieved party's legal fees and barring them from testifying.[8]

> **EXAMPLE** Respondent did not appear for his deposition (duly noticed). During the 201(k) conference, a second date for his deposition was set. He did not appear for that one either. Petitioner files a Motion for Discovery Sanctions, praying that the Respondent be barred from testifying on any disputed matters. Petitioner also prays that the Respondent pay the legal fees incurred because he failed to comply. The court could order sanctions against Respondent.

Outcome of Discovery

Based on the information obtained through discovery, parties can evaluate the strengths and weaknesses of their cases and make informed decisions about the possible outcomes.

Complete Agreement

If the parties resolve the disputed issues, they memorialize their agreement on financial issues in a marital settlement agreement (MSA) and their agreement on parenting issues in a parental allocation judgment (PAJ). The court will enter a PAJ if it finds it in the children's best interest and an MSA unless it finds it unconscionable.[9] They can now schedule their final court date, called the "prove-up." (More information on the prove-up is provided below.)

> **EXAMPLE** In their MSA, Wife is awarded the marital residence, and Husband is awarded his pension. Wife is interested in staying in the parties' home with the children until they graduate from high school. She is confident social security will provide a comfortable retirement. Husband's interest is in his pension. He has a high income and is not concerned about his ability to buy another home. Because the house and pension have roughly equal values, the agreement is not unconscionable and is entered by the judge.

Lack of Complete Agreement

If they do not agree or do not agree on all areas, the court will set a date for a pretrial conference with the judge.

The Pretrial Conference

The Pretrial Memorandum

To inform the court of the disputed issues, parties submit a pretrial memorandum to the judge (copying opposing counsel) prior to the conference. In a pretrial memorandum, the sides lay out the facts they would present if the matter went to trial and state their positions, as supported by caselaw. Pursuant to DuPage County local court rules, the pretrial memorandum must include the following:

- Attorneys' names, addresses, and phone numbers;
- Parties' names, ages, education levels, employment, and health;
- Children's names, ages, school information, and special needs;
- Assets, debts and liabilities, including values and characterization of marital vs. non-marital;
- Notice of Claim of Dissipation of Marital Assets, if any;
- Statement of areas of agreement;
- Statement of areas of disagreement; and
- Suggestions for settlement.[10]

The Pretrial Conference

Both attorneys (and for child-related issues, the GAL) will meet, often in the judge's chambers. Litigants must be advised of any pretrial conference date by their attorneys. Litigants need not appear but must be available for consultation with their attorneys by phone during the pretrial conference.[11]

At the end of the pretrial conference, judges make a recommendation as to how the parties should resolve their dispute, and a status date is set. Judges' recommendations are not binding; parties can accept or reject them. Pretrial conferences are most often not recorded and not made part of the court record.

On the status date, one of two things could happen. If the case has been resolved, a prove-up date is selected.

The Prove-Up

The parties return to court for the last time to prove-up the allegations in the petition for dissolution. The parties are sworn in and testify, and final documents are tendered to the court. The procedure for prove-up varies by county, so it is important to check local rules. For example, judges in Kendall County require copies of the final documents before they will set the prove-up date. In addition, some circuit courts are continuing to allow prove-ups by affidavit, a procedure that started during the pandemic.

Final Documents

At the prove-up, the petitioner's attorney tenders the following documents to the judge:

- The Judgment of Dissolution;
- The Marital Settlement Agreement (MSA);
- The Parental Allocation Judgment(PAJ);
- Certificate of Dissolution of Marriage (Illinois Department of Public Health); and
- Child Support Order and IWO (if not entered on a temporary basis).

Trial

If the parties have not settled the matter on the status date, the judge enters an order setting a trial date. At trial, the judge will decide, not recommend, and there is no further room for negotiation.

The Trial Order

Docket Dates

As soon as the attorney receives the trial order, the firm must docket the following dates:[12] the trial date, the trial status date (three days prior to the trial), and the discovery cut-off date (60 days prior to the trial). If additional discovery is needed, it must be issued prior to the discovery cut-off date.

Pretrial Tasks

Once the dates are docketed, the attorney draws up a list of pretrial tasks. Paralegals will be responsible for monitoring dates and ensuring the tasks are completed. While there may be additional tasks, given each client's specific circumstances, tasks common to all trials include:

- After the attorney has compiled the exhibits to be presented, prepare an exhibit book and three copies: one for the witness, one for the judge, and one for opposing counsel. Because some judges prefer electronic copies, be sure to ascertain the judge's preferences.
- After the attorney has determined the witnesses they will call:
  - Prepare a witness list for the court;
  - Serve trial subpoenas on non-parties; and
  - Serve 237 Notices to Appear and Produce on parties (production limited to documents previously requested under Rule 214).
- Monitor updates to previously issued discovery:
  - Supplement all responses to the discovery requests your client received, such as marital interrogatories under Rule 213 and notices to produce under Rule 214;
  - Confirm receipt of supplemental responses to the discovery requests your client issued on the opposing party;
  - Produce an updated financial affidavit and ensure receipt of the opposing party's financial affidavit; and
  - File certificates of service for all responses.
- Draft the trial memorandum.

The Trial Status Date

At the trial status date, the attorneys appear before the judge with the exhibit books, trial memorandum, and witness list. They may also present motions *in limine*, which are motions heard on the admissibility of evidence. For example, motions may be made to exclude evidence that is unfairly prejudicial or a witness who was not disclosed in 213(f) interrogatories.

In addition, if the parties have agreed on any facts, they may present a list of stipulated facts, or "stipulations." These facts can be introduced into evidence without the need to lay a foundation as required by the Illinois Rules of Evidence. Commonly stipulated facts include the grounds for the dissolution, the date of the marriage, and the age, address, and employment of the parties.

The Trial

The trial is conducted as any other civil trial, with both sides presenting evidence in support of their position. Family law trials are bench trials,[13] not jury trials, so in addition to deciding issues of law, the judge decides issues of fact. The judge may make his decision after closing arguments, or he may wait a few days or weeks to review his notes. After the judge makes his decision, he directs one of the attorneys to prepare the judgment of dissolution. The attorneys return to court one last time to enter the judgment.[14] At that time they will tender the child support order and IWO, if not entered on a temporary basis, and the Certificate of Dissolution.

Law Office Follow-Up

As soon as possible after the prove-up or trial, it is important to follow up on matters which could not be completed prior to entry of the judgment of dissolution, including:

- Order a copy of the trial transcript (required in some counties);
- Enter a Qualified Domestic Relations Order (QDRO), which is used to divide pensions and 401(k) plans. In Illinois, a Qualified Illinois Domestic Relations Order (QUILDRO) is used to divide retirement plans for state government employees;
- Draft a letter of direction to divide IRAs;
- Draft a quit claim deed if a party was awarded real property; and
- Advise a client on how to change beneficiary forms for life insurance and IRAs.

Unfortunately, it's not uncommon for a law firm's client to have outstanding legal bills. In that case, the IMDMA allows attorneys to file a motion for attorney's fees against their own clients.[15] Some counties require the attorney and client to arbitrate before filing, so it's important to check local rules.

Chapter Summary

Discovery is a pretrial process used to obtain information from the opposing party or a third party. Supreme Court Rules govern the types of discovery available, including interrogatories, notices to produce, depositions, and subpoenas. Attorneys can use some or all of the types and in any order. Paralegals generally manage discovery, issuing discovery requests on the other side and responding to discovery requests received from them.

Based on the information obtained in discovery, parties may resolve their disputed parenting and financial issues. If not, the matter proceeds to court for a pretrial conference, where the judge makes a recommendation as to how the parties should resolve their dispute. If the parties agree, the matter is set for prove-up. If the parties don't agree, the judge sets the matter for trial. In preparation for the trial, attorneys and paralegals complete tasks in compliance with the dates provided on the trial order. At the end of the trial, the judge makes a decision and the judgment of dissolution is entered. The marriage, entered into in Chapter 2, is now dissolved.

Key Terms

Discovery

Interrogatories

Request to Produce

Deposition

Subpoena

Subpoena duces tecum

201(k) conference

Pretrial Conference

Motion *in Limine*

Stipulations

Judgment of Dissolution

Marital Settlement Agreement

Certificate of Dissolution of Marriage

QDRO/QUILDRO

Discussion Questions

1. The Collaborative Process Act was enacted in 2018. *See* 750 ILCS 90. A collaborative divorce involves a series of meetings between the parties, their attorneys, and their collaborative team, which may include a financial neutral, a divorce coach, and a child specialist. Once the parties reach an agreement, the petition for dissolution is filed in court and the prove-up date is scheduled. How does this process compare to the process described in Chapters 4–10 of this text?
2. Before the digital age, discovery was printed and physically transported to the other attorney's office. Now, it is scanned and sent electronically. How safe are "drop boxes" and email systems? How can a firm guarantee its client's confidential information is not disclosed?
3. Parties may inadvertently post relevant information on social media, such as Facebook. *See* https://www.isba.org/ibj/2013/07/facebookwhatfamilylawyersshouldknow (last visited June 29, 2023). What kind of information would be relevant to a disputed custody case? To a disputed financial issue? How can a firm protect a client from posting relevant information?
4. If privileged information or work product is inadvertently produced in discovery, it cannot be used or disclosed. Instead, pursuant to Illinois Supreme Court Rule 201(p), it must be returned, sequestered, or destroyed. How

helpful do you think this rule is? Does the rule excuse a firm's failure to comply with an ethical duty to prevent disclosure of confidential information?

5. Alcohol and drug abuse or dependency records are confidential. A patient may consent to their disclosure, or the records may be obtained by court order upon a showing of good cause. *See* 20 ILCS 301/30-5(bb). What would constitute good cause?
6. Illinois Supreme Court Rule 219 provides the consequences of refusal to comply with rules or orders relating to discovery. These consequences include barring witnesses' testimony and dismissing an offending party's action with prejudice. Where the misconduct is willful, the court can impose a monetary penalty. Are these consequences appropriate?
7. The Code of Civil Procedure permits a party to vacate a judgment after 30 days for facts not known at the time of judgment if knowledge of the facts would have altered the results. *See* 735 ILCS 5/2-1401. Presume Wife accepted maintenance in gross because she was planning to remarry as soon as the judgment was entered. When she remarried six weeks after entry of the judgment of dissolution, Husband filed a motion to vacate the judgment of dissolution. What if information about her boyfriend was available, but Husband's attorney failed to issue sufficient discovery to obtain it, such as deposing the wife? The facts were not known, but they could have been. How should a court decide?
8. Trials are labor-intensive and expensive. Suppose one party rejects the court's recommendation at pretrial and then loses at trial. Should he be responsible for some of the other side's legal fees?
9. The IMDMA allows attorneys to sue their clients for unpaid legal fees, which makes the attorneys directly adverse to their clients. *See* 750 ILCS 5/508(c). How can this be reconciled with the ethical duty to avoid a conflict of interest?
10. Pursuant to Illinois Rules of Professional Conduct 1.5(d)(1), a lawyer cannot charge a fee for a domestic relations matter contingent upon the value of alimony or property awarded. Why is that? Would it create a potential conflict of interest?

Forms

1. Subpoena

   https://18thjudicial.org/18thJudicial/download/2224
2. Subpoena *Duces Tecum*

   https://18thjudicial.org/18thJudicial/download/2121

3. Pretrial Memorandum

   https://18thjudicial.org/18thJudicial/download/3180

4. Illinois Standardized Forms - Approved - Judgment of Dissolution of Marriage / Civil Union

   https://ilcourtsaudio.blob.core.windows.net/antilles-resources/resources/bb9ac862-175b-46df-a4da-09303cf4cc4f/DNC%20Divorce%20Judgment.pdf

5. State of Illinois Department of Public Health Bureau of Vital Records - Dissolution of Marriage Certificate (State Form VR700)

   https://ilcourtsaudio.blob.core.windows.net/antilles-resources/resources/6561a67a-2667-435e-b94a-5bac4f53c635/IDPH%20Dissolution%20of%20Marriage%20Civil%20Union.pdf

Endnotes

1. A party may obtain by discovery full disclosure regarding any matter relevant to the subject matter involved in the pending action. ILL. SUP. CT. R. 201(b)(1).
2. 740 ILCS 110 (West, Westlaw Classic through P.A. 103-21 of the 2023 Reg. Sess.).
3. *Id.* § 16.
4. ILL. SUP. CT. R. 201(b)(2).
5. ILL. SUP. CT. R. 201(a).
6. ILL. SUP. CT. R. 201(m).
7. ILL. SUP. CT. R. 201(k).
8. ILL. S. CT. R. 219.
9. 750 ILCS 5/502(b) (West, Westlaw Classic through P.A. 103-21 of the 2023 Reg. Sess.).
10. 18th Jud. Cir. Ct. R. 15.18(c)(1-8).
11. 18th Jud. Cir. Ct. R. 15.18(b).
12. ILL. S. CT. R. 218.
13. 750 ILCS 5/103.
14. *Id.* § 413(a).
15. *Id.* § 508(c).

1. SUBPOENA

SUBPOENA - FOR DEPOSITION 2127 (Rev. 12/20)

STATE OF ILLINOIS **UNITED STATES OF AMERICA** **IN THE CIRCUIT COURT OF THE EIGHTEENTH JUDICIAL CIRCUIT** **COUNTY OF DU PAGE**

____

vs

____

____
CASE NUMBER

SUBPOENA FOR DEPOSITION

File Stamp Here

TO: ______________________________

GREETINGS:

YOU ARE HEREBY COMMANDED to personally appear before a Notary Public at

______________________________ in ______________________________

Illinois on ______________ at ______________ then and there to submit to a deposition to be taken in a certain cause now pending before this Court, said deposition to be taken upon oral interrogatories propounded by the attorney or attorney listed.

YOU ARE FURTHER COMMANDED to bring the following documents or tangible things which constitute evidence relating to the said cause and which are listed below; and then and there to testify and the truth to speak concerning the . same. ______________________________

____

YOUR FAILURE TO COMPLY WITH THIS SUBPOENA MAY SUBJECT YOU TO PUNISHMENT FOR CONTEMPT OF COURT

Supreme Court Rule 204(c). The Discovery Deposition of nonparty physicians being deposed in their professional capacity may be taken only with the agreement of the parties and the subsequent consent of the deponent or under a subpoena issued upon order of court. A party shall pay a reasonable fee to a physician for the time he or she will spend testifying at any such deposition . Unless the physician was retained by a party for the purpose of rendering an opinion at trial, or unless otherwise ordered by the Court, the fee shall be paid by the party at whose instance the deposition is taken.

Supreme Court Rule 203. Unless otherwise agreed, depositions shall be taken in the county in which the deponent resides or is employed or transacts business in person, or, in the case of a plaintiff-deponent, in the county in which the action is pending. However, the court, in its discretion, may order a party or a person who is currently an officer, director, or employee of a party to appear at a designated place in this State or elsewhere for the purpose of having the deposition taken. The order designating the place of deposition may impose any terms and conditions that are just, including payment of reasonable expenses.

NOTICE TO WITNESS

The attorney who has requested this subpoena is listed herein. Any questions regarding your knowledge of the subject matter or testimony in the case should be directed to your attorney.

DO NOT CALL THE CIRCUIT COURT CLERK

Name: ______________________ ☐ Pro Se

DuPage Attorney Number: ______________________

Attorney for: ______________________

Address: ______________________

City/State/Zip: ______________________

Telephone Number: ______________________

Email: ______________________

WITNESS:

CANDICE ADAMS, Clerk of the Eighteenth Judicial Circuit Court, and the seal thereof, Wheaton, Illinois

____
Date

____
Clerk of the Eighteenth Judicial Circuit

CANDICE ADAMS, CLERK OF THE 18th JUDICIAL CIRCUIT COURT ©
WHEATON, ILLINOIS 60187-0707

SHERIFF'S FEES

Service and return .... $________________

Miles ______________ .... $________________

Total .... $________________

Sheriff of ______________________________ County

SHERIFF'S RETURN

I certify that I served this subpoena on defendant as follows:

☐ (a) (Individual - **personal**):
By leaving a copy and a copy of the subpoena with each individual as follows:

☐ (b) (Individual - **abode**):
By leaving a copy and a copy of the subpoena at the usual place of abode of each individual with a person of his family, of the age of 13 years or upwards, informing that person of the contents of the subpoena, and also by sending a copy of the subpoena and the interrogatories in a sealed envelope with postage fully prepaid, addressed to each individual at the usual place of abode, as follows:

☐ (c) (Corporation):
By leaving a copy and a copy of the subpoena with the registered agent, officer, or agent of each corporation as follows:

☐ (d) (Other service):

☐ (e) (Unable to Serve):
By ______________________________ , Deputy Badge Number: ____________

Name of Defendant ________________________	Name of Defendant ________________________
Name of Person summons given to ________________________	Name of Person summons given to ________________________
Sex ______ Race ______ Approx. age ______	Sex ______ Race ______ Approx. age ______
Place of service ________________________	Place of service ________________________
City , State ________________________	City , State ________________________
Date of service ____________ Time ____________	Date of service ____________ Time ____________
Date of Mailing ________________________	Date of Mailing ________________________
	Sheriff of ________________________ County
Special Process Server of ________________	County Illinois License # ________________
	By ________________________

I served this subpoena by delivering a copy to ____

and I paid the witness $ ________________ for witness and mileage fees.

____
Signature

Subscribed and Sworn before me ________________ ______________________________
Date Notary Public

AFTER SERVICE, THE ORIGINAL MUST BE FILED WITH THE CIRCUIT COURT CLERK ALONG WITH THE ENDORSEMENT OF SERVICE

2. SUBPOENA *DUCES TECUM*

SUBPOENA - DUCES TECUM 2121 (Rev. 1/23)

STATE OF ILLINOIS **UNITED STATES OF AMERICA** **COUNTY OF DU PAGE**
IN THE CIRCUIT COURT OF THE EIGHTEENTH JUDICIAL CIRCUIT

____

vs

____

____
CASE NUMBER

SUBPOENA
DUCES TECUM

File Stamp Here

TO: ____

____

YOU ARE HEREBY COMMANDED to personally appear before the Eighteenth Judicial Circuit Court of DuPage County at the

☐ DuPage Judicial Center, 505 North County Farm Road, Wheaton, Illinois

☐ ______________________________

before Judge ______________ in Room ________ on ______________ at __________

and produce at the time and place aforesaid the following documents or tangible things which constitute evidence relating to the said cause and which are listed below

and then and there testify, and the truth to speak concerning those things of which you may have knowledge, and the import of such documents or tangible things concerning the above captioned cause now pending and undetermined in the Eighteenth Judicial Circuit Court on the part of ______________________________.

YOUR FAILURE TO COMPLY WITH THIS SUBPOENA MAY SUBJECT YOU TO PUNISHMENT FOR CONTEMPT OF COURT.

In lieu of appearing in person, this subpoena may also be satisfied by mailing a copy of this subpoena along with the requested document(s) to:

____

____

____

NOTICE TO WITNESS
The attorney who has requested this subpoena is listed herein. Any questions regarding your knowledge of the subject matter or testimony in the case should be directed to your attorney.
DO NOT CALL THE CIRCUIT COURT CLERK.

WITNESS:

Name: ______________________ ☐ PRO SE
DuPage Attorney Number: ______________________
Attorney for: ______________________
Address: ______________________
City/State/Zip: ______________________
Telephone Number: ______________________
Email: ______________________

CANDICE ADAMS, Clerk of the Eighteenth Judicial Circuit Court, and the seal thereof, Wheaton, Illinois

____
Date

____
Clerk of the Eighteenth Judicial Circuit

CANDICE ADAMS, CLERK OF THE 18th JUDICIAL CIRCUIT COURT ©
WHEATON, ILLINOIS 60187-0707

SHERIFF'S FEES

Service and return .... $ ________________

Miles _______________ .... $ ________________

Total .... $________________

Sheriff of ________________________________ County

SHERIFF'S RETURN

I certify that I served this subpoena on defendant as follows:

☐ (a) (Individual - **personal**):
By leaving a copy and a copy of the subpoena with each individual as follows:

☐ (b) (Individual - **abode**):
By leaving a copy and a copy of the subpoena at the usual place of abode of each individual with a person of his family, of the age of 13 years or upwards, informing that person of the contents of the subpoena, and also by sending a copy of the subpoena and the interrogatories in a sealed envelope with postage fully prepaid, addressed to each individual at the usual place of abode, as follows:

☐ (c) (Corporation):
By leaving a copy and a copy of the subpoena with the registered agent, officer, or agent of each corporation as follows:

☐ (d) (Other service):

☐ (e) (Unable to Serve):
By _________________________________, Deputy Badge Number: ________________

Name of Defendant ____________________	Name of Defendant ____________________
Name of Person summons given to ____________________	Name of Person summons given to ____________________
Sex _______ Race _______ Aprox. age _______	Sex _______ Race _______ Aprox. age _______
Place of service ____________________	Place of service ____________________
City , State ____________________	City , State ____________________
Date of service ____________ Time _________	Date of service ____________ Time _________
Date of Mailing ____________________	Date of Mailing ____________________
	Sheriff of ____________________ County
Special Process Server of ______________	County Illinois License # ______________
	By ____________________

I served this subpoena by delivering a copy to ____

and I paid the witness $__________________ for witness and mileage fees.

____
Signature

Subscribed and Sworn before me __________________ ____________________________________
Date Notary Public

AFTER SERVICE, THE ORIGINAL MUST BE FILED WITH THE CIRCUIT COURT CLERK ALONG WITH THE ENDORSEMENT OF SERVICE

3. PRETRIAL MEMORANDUM

PRE TRIAL MEMORANDUM 3180 (Rev 12/20)

STATE OF ILLINOIS **UNITED STATES OF AMERICA**
IN THE CIRCUIT COURT OF THE EIGHTEENTH JUDICIAL CIRCUIT **COUNTY OF DU PAGE**

IN RE ☒ THE MARRIAGE ☐ CIVIL UNION OF

____
PETITIONER

VS

____
RESPONDENT

____
CASE NUMBER

File Stamp Here

This memorandum should be prepared by attorney for one of the parties or by the attorney for both parties in concert. It is helpful if the information is checked by the litigants prior to the pre-trial conference.

PRE-TRIAL MEMORANDUM

Residence:

Petitioner: ______________________________

Respondent: ______________________________

Length of Marriage/Civil Union: ______________ Date of Separation: ______________

Age of Parties: Petitioner: ______________ Respondent: ______________

Children:

Name	Age	Residing With

Employment: **(Occupation and net pay; general health; if unemployed, any special skills or talents?)**

Petitioner: ______________________________

Respondent: ______________________________

Assets: **(Include information on joint home, how owned, present value, amount of mortgage or liens and amount of monthly mortgage payments, also include information on other real estate, automobiles, stocks and bonds, claims, bank accounts and any other assets. If necessary, lists assets on separate sheet.)**

____

____

____

____

Debts: **(If relevant to pre-trial. Attach separate sheet, if necessary)**

____

____

____

Average monthly expenses: **(List on separate sheet only if relevant to issues to be discussed at pre-trial, i.e. amount of support or alimony, etc.)**

____

____

Do both parties agree that the marriage/civil union has ended? ____________________

Any special health (or other) problems with children?

____

____

Areas of agreement:

____

____

____

____

Areas of disagreement:

____

____

____

____

Use balance of sheet for any special problems or matters to be discussed at pre-trial:

This form prepared by: ____

(Note: this information NOT to be used on Trial of Cause)

4. JUDGMENT OF DISSOLUTION OF MARRIAGE

This form is approved by the Illinois Supreme Court and is required to be accepted in all Illinois Circuit Courts.

STATE OF ILLINOIS, CIRCUIT COURT ________ COUNTY	**JUDGMENT OF DISSOLUTION OF MARRIAGE / CIVIL UNION** (DIVORCE WITH CHILDREN)	*For Court Use Only*
Instructions ▾ Directly above, enter the county where you filed this case. Enter the full name of Petitioner, Respondent, and the case number as listed on the *Petition for Dissolution of Marriage/Civil Union (Divorce with Children).*	________ **Petitioner** *(First, middle, last name)* v. ________ **Respondent** *(First, middle, last name)*	________ **Case Number**

DO NOT complete this section.

A court date was held on the *Petition for Dissolution of Marriage/Civil Union (Divorce with Children)* filed by the Petitioner. The court heard the testimony of ☐ Petitioner ☐ Respondent and considered all of the evidence and relevant parts of the Illinois Marriage and Dissolution of Marriage Act (750 ILCS 5/101 *et seq*).

The Court makes the following findings of fact:

DO NOT complete **1a** and **1b**.

1. **Present in Court:**
   a. Petitioner present: ☐ Yes ☐ No
   ☐ represented by Lawyer: ________
   b. Respondent present: ☐ Yes ☐ No
   ☐ represented by Lawyer: ________

DO NOT complete **2a**, **2b**, or **2d**.

In **2c**, check the box that applies to the Respondent. If the Respondent is on active duty, you cannot get a divorce unless the Respondent files an appearance.

2. **Jurisdiction:**
   a. This court has jurisdiction of the subject matter and ☐ Petitioner ☐ Respondent
   b. Respondent is in default: ☐ Yes ☐ No
   c. Respondent is currently on active duty as a member of the Armed Forces of the United States of America: ☐ Yes ☐ No ☐ Unknown
   d. This Court has jurisdiction under the Uniform Child-Custody Jurisdiction and and Enforcement Act: ☐ Yes ☐ No

In **3a**, check the box that applies to you.

In **3b**, check the box that applies to the Respondent.

3. **Residency Requirement:**
   a. Petitioner has been living in Illinois at least 90 days immediately before the filing of the *Petition* or immediately before the time of this hearing:
   ☐ Yes ☐ No
   b. Respondent has been living in Illinois at least 90 days immediately before the filing of the *Petition* or immediately before the time of this hearing:
   ☐ Yes ☐ No

In **4**, check whether it is a marriage or civil union.

In **4a**, enter the date you were married/united.

In **4b**, enter the place the marriage/civil union took place.

4. **Information about the ☐ Marriage ☐ Civil Union:**
   a. Parties were married/united on: ________ *Date*
   b. Parties were married/united in: ________ *County* *State* *Country*

If this is an agreement, enter initials on each page.

Petitioner's initials: ____

Respondent's initials: ____

In **6a,** part one, check "Yes" if you are pregnant.

In **6a,** part two, check "Yes" if the child is Respondent's.

In **6b,** part one, check "Yes" if the Respondent is pregnant.

In **6b,** part two, check "Yes" if the child is yours.

In **6c**, check "None" if you have no children with the Respondent who are under the age of 18. Otherwise, list the names and birthdates of the children.

In **6d**, check "None" if you have no children with the Respondent who are 18 or older. Otherwise, list the names and birthdates of the children and select "Yes" or "No" for whether each child is disabled or enrolled in school.

In **6e**, check "None" if the only children you had during the marriage/civil union are listed in 7c and 7d. If you or the Respondent separately had or adopted other children during the marriage/civil union, list their names and birthdates here. **DO NOT** complete 7.

5. Grounds for Dissolution:

Irreconcilable differences have caused the irretrievable breakdown of the marriage or civil union and efforts at reconciliation have failed or future attempts at reconciliation would be impracticable and not in the best interests of the family.

6. Children of the Marriage/Civil Union:

a. Petitioner is pregnant:

☐ Yes ☐ No

The unborn child is Respondent's:

☐ Yes ☐ No ☐ Unknown

b. Respondent is pregnant:

☐ Yes ☐ No ☐ Unknown

The unborn child is Petitioner's:

☐ Yes ☐ No ☐ Unknown

c. The minor children *(under the age of 18)* born to or adopted together by the parties before or during the marriage/civil union are:

☐ None

	Name	Date of Birth
1.		
2.		
3.		
☐ I have listed additional minor children on the attached *Additional Minor Children* form.		

d. The adult children *(age 18 or older)* born to or adopted together by the parties before or during the marriage/civil union are:

☐ None

	Name	Age	Disabled	In School
1.			☐ Yes ☐ No	☐ Yes ☐ No
2.			☐ Yes ☐ No	☐ Yes ☐ No
3.			☐ Yes ☐ No	☐ Yes ☐ No
☐ I have listed additional adult children on the attached *Additional Adult Children* form.				

e. The **other** children born to or adopted by either Plaintiff or Respondent, but not both, this marriage/civil union are:

☐ None

	Name	Date of Birth	Born To or Adopted By	
1.			☐ Petitioner	☐ Respondent
2.			☐ Petitioner	☐ Respondent
3.			☐ Petitioner	☐ Respondent
☐ I have listed additional children on the attached *Additional Other Children* form.				

7. Allocation of Parental Responsibility:

a. ☐ No minor children.

b. ☐ It is in the best interests of the minor children that the *Parenting Plan* of

☐ Petitioner ☐ Respondent ☐ Both Parties *(agreement)*

be approved by the court.

c. ☐ It is in the best interests of the minor children that the court enter its own *Parenting Plan*.

Petitioner's initials: ________

Respondent's initials: ________

Complete sections **8a**, **8b** and **8c** if you and your spouse have an agreement, otherwise, **DO NOT** complete these sections.

In **8d**, check "Yes" if either of you owned real estate before you were married/united. Complete and attach the *Non-Marital Real Estate* form.

8. Real Estate:

a. Parties have an interest in real estate, which is an asset of the marriage/civil union:

☐ Yes ☐ No

b. The address of the real estate is:

____

Street, Apt # *City* *State* *ZIP*

c. A legal description of the real estate is attached to this *Judgment*:

☐ Yes ☐ No

d. Petitioner or Respondent has an interest in non-marital real estate: ☐ Yes ☐ No

☐ The non-marital real estate is listed on the attached *Non-Marital Real Estate* form.

Complete sections **9a, 9b, and 9c** if you and your spouse have an agreement, otherwise, **DO NOT** complete these sections.

9. Maintenance ***(also known as alimony)*****:**

a. These parties have waived the right to maintenance:

☐ Petitioner ☐ Respondent ☐ Neither party

b. This party is entitled to maintenance:

☐ Petitioner ☐ Respondent ☐ Neither party ☐ Other:

____

c. The amount awarded is $__________ ☐ based on guidelines; OR

☐ deviation from guidelines based upon these findings:

____

____

THEREFORE, IT IS ORDERED, ADJUDGED AND DECREED AS FOLLOWS:

A. The parties are awarded a *Judgment of Dissolution of Marriage/Civil Union* and the bonds of matrimony/civil union existing between Petitioner and Respondent are hereby dissolved.

If you and your spouse have an agreement, check the first box and the box for "Both Parties", otherwise, **DO NOT** complete **B**.

B. Allocation of Parental Responsibility:

1. ☐ That the *Parenting Plan* of the following party is approved and made a part of this court order:

   ☐ Petitioner ☐ Respondent ☐ Both Parties *(agreement)*

2. ☐ That the Court has entered its own *Parenting Plan*, which is made a part of this order.

3. ☐ Other orders: ____

   ____

If you have a Support Order in another case enter the information in **C2**.

C. Support for Minor Children:

1. ☐ An *Order for Support* shall be entered.

2. ☐ Support shall continue as ordered in court case: ______________________

   Court case number

   located in: ____

   County *State*

3. ☐ Child support is reserved *(no child support is ordered at this time)*.

If you and your spouse have an agreement, complete **D**, otherwise, **DO NOT** complete **D**.

D. Claiming Children as Dependants on State and Federal Tax Returns:

1. The right to claim children as dependants on state and federal tax returns belongs to:

   ☐ Petitioner ☐ Respondent for all tax years

   ☐ Petitioner ☐ Respondent for even-numbered tax years

   ☐ Petitioner ☐ Respondent for odd-numbered tax years

   ☐ Each party shall have the right to claim one-half of the children each tax year. If there is an odd-number of children, Petitioner shall claim the additional child in

Petitioner's initials: ______

Respondent's initials: ______

☐ even ☐ odd-numbered years and Respondent shall claim the additional child in ☐ even ☐ odd-numbered years.

2. This order does not address the right to claim the children as household residents for the purpose of applying for earned income credit.
3. If a party has a duty to pay child support for the minor children and is awarded the right to claim one or more of the minor children as dependents for tax purposes, that right may only be exercised if that party is current in their child support obligation by January 15 of the year following the relevant tax year.

If you and your spouse have an agreement, complete **E**, otherwise, **DO NOT** complete **E**.

E. Support for Adult Children ***(for education or disabled child)*:**

1. ☐ Support is ordered as follows:
   ☐ Petitioner ☐ Respondent
   will pay: ____________________
   ____
   ____
   ____
   ____
   ____
2. ☐ Support for adult children is reserved *(no support is ordered at this time).*

In **F1, DO** fill in the name of creditor and amount owed for debts after the date of marriage/civil union in the chart. If you and your spouse have an agreement, check who is to pay the debts, otherwise, **DO NOT** check who is to pay the debt.

F. Debts and Liabilities:

1. These debts shall be paid by parties as follows:

	Debt *(Name of Creditor)*	Amount Owed	To be paid by:		
			Petitioner	Respondent	Both Equally
1.		$	☐	☐	☐
2.		$	☐	☐	☐
3.		$	☐	☐	☐
4.		$	☐	☐	☐
5.		$	☐	☐	☐
6.		$	☐	☐	☐
7.		$	☐	☐	☐
☐ I have listed additional debts on the *Additional Debts and Liabilities* form.					

If you and your spouse have an agreement, complete **F2**, otherwise, **DO NOT** complete **F2**.

2. Debts not included in the chart above shall be paid by the parties as follows:
   ☐ Each party will be responsible for 50% of each joint debt.
   ☐ Each party will pay all of the debts in their own name.
3. Parties shall indemnify and hold the other party harmless for the debts they are assigned.

If you and your spouse have an agreement, complete **G**, otherwise, **DO NOT** complete **G**.

G. Pension and Retirement Accounts:

1. ☐ Each party is awarded the pension and retirement accounts in their own name.
2. ☐ Petitioner is awarded ____________% of the marital/civil union portion of Respondent's pension/retirement accounts.
3. ☐ Respondent is awarded ____________% of the marital/civil union portion of Petitioner's pension/retirement accounts.
4. ☐ ☐ Petitioner ☐ Respondent shall prepare a *Qualified Domestic Relations Order.*
5. ☐ Other orders: ____________________
   ____
   ____
   ____
   ____

Petitioner's initials: ______
Respondent's initials: ______

If you and your spouse have an agreement, complete **H,** otherwise, **DO NOT** complete **H**.

"Marital real estate" is an interest in real estate obtained during the marriage or civil union.

H. Real Estate:

1. ☐ ☐ Petitioner ☐ Respondent is awarded the marital real estate and shall pay the other party $ ______________ for their interest in the real estate.
2. ☐ The marital real estate shall be sold.
   The net proceeds of the sale *(sale price minus costs of sale)* shall be divided with Petitioner to receive ________ % Respondent to receive ________ %
3. ☐ Until the marital real estate is sold, mortgage payments will be paid by
   ☐ Petitioner ________ % ☐ Respondent ________ %
4. ☐ Until the marital real estate is sold, real estate taxes will be paid by
   ☐ Petitioner ________ % ☐ Respondent ________ %
5. ☐ Until the marital real estate is sold, insurance will be paid by ☐ Petitioner ________ % ☐ Respondent ________ %
6. ☐ Until the marital real estate is sold, cost of maintaining the property will be paid by
   ☐ Petitioner ________ % ☐ Respondent ________ %
7. ☐ ☐ Petitioner ☐ Respondent is entitled to claim mortgage payments for federal and state tax purposes.
8. ☐ ☐ Petitioner ☐ Respondent is entitled to claim property tax payments for federal and state tax purposes.
9. ☐ ☐ Petitioner ☐ Respondent will refinance the debt on the real estate to remove the other party from the obligation by: ______________
   Date
10. ☐ ☐ Petitioner ☐ Respondent will sign a quitclaim deed transferring their interest to the other party by: ______________
    Date
11. ☐ Other orders: ______________________________________

If you and your spouse have an agreement, complete **I,** otherwise, **DO NOT** complete **I**.

Chart: DO list the personal property obtained during the marriage/civil union in the chart. If you and your spouse have an agreement, check who gets the property, otherwise, **DO NOT** check who gets the property.

I. Personal Property and Bank Accounts:

1. ☐ Parties shall keep the property and bank accounts in their own name or possession.
2. ☐ Personal property of the marriage/civil union shall be divided as follows:

Personal Property and Bank Accounts *(Be specific in your description of each piece of property)*	Property goes to: Petitioner	Respondent
1.	☐	☐
2.	☐	☐
3.	☐	☐
4.	☐	☐
5.	☐	☐
6.	☐	☐
7.	☐	☐
8.	☐	☐
☐ I have attached an *Additional Personal Property & Bank Accounts* form.		

3. ☐ Any personal property exchange required by this order shall take place within 30 days of the date of this *Judgment*.
4. ☐ Other orders *(including pets)*: ______________________________________

Petitioner's initials: ______
Respondent's initials: ______

If you and your spouse have an agreement, complete **J**, otherwise, **DO NOT** complete **J**.

J. Maintenance:

1. ☐ Parties are forever barred from claiming maintenance from the other.
2. ☐ An *Order for Support* shall be entered.
4. ☐ Other orders: ______________________________

____

____

____

____

In **K**, if you or the Respondent want to go back to a former name, check the box and enter the former last name.

K. Former Name:

1. ☐ Petitioner is permitted to resume using the former last name of:

   ____
   Former Last Name

2. ☐ Respondent is permitted to resume using the former last name of:

   ____
   Former Last Name

If you and your spouse have an agreement, complete **L**, otherwise, **DO NOT** complete **L**.

L. Other Relief:

1. ☐ None
2. ☐ Relief as follows: ______________________________

____

____

____

____

M. This court reserves jurisdiction over the parties and the subject matter for purposes of enforcing this *Judgment*.

Petitioner's initials: ______

Respondent's initials: ______

DO NOT complete this section. The judge will sign and date here.

ENTERED:

______________________________ ______________________________
Judge *Date*

Print Form Save Form Reset Form

5. DISSOLUTION OF MARRIAGE CERTIFICATE

State of Illinois
Illinois Department of Public Health

ORIGINAL

STATE OF ILLINOIS

CERTIFICATE OF DISSOLUTION OF , INVALIDITY OR LEGAL SEPARATION

TYPE / PRINT IN PERMANENT BLACK INK

Name of County	Court File Number	State File Number

A ■ HUSBAND ■ WIFE ■ SPOUSE ■ PARTNER

1a. Name (*First, Middle, Last*)		1b. Last Name on Birth Certificate		2. Sex	3. Social Security Number	
4a. Residence — City, Town, Twp. or Road District Number	4b. County	4c. State	5a. Birthplace (*State or Foreign Country*)	5b. Date of Birth (*Mo., Day, Year*)		5c. Age Now

B ■ HUSBAND ■ WIFE ■ SPOUSE ■ PARTNER

6a. Name (*First, Middle, Last*)		6b. Last Name on Birth Certificate		7. Sex	8. Social Security Number	
9a. Residence — City, Town, Twp. or Road District Number	9b. County	9c. State	10a. Birthplace (*State or Foreign Country*)	10b. Date of Birth (*Mo., Day, Year*)		10c. Age Now

11a. Date of This Marriage/Civil Union (*Mo., Day, Year*)	11b. Place of This Marriage/Civil Union — City		11c. County	11d. State (*If Not in U.S., Name Country*)
12. Date Couple Last Resided in Same Household (*Mo., Day, Year*)	13a. Number of Children of This Marriage/Civil Union	13b. Children Under 18 in This Household (*Specify*)	14. Petitioner	

15a. Type of Decree (Specify: Dissolution, Invalidity or Legal Separation)	15b. Legal Grounds for Decree (*Specify*)
16. Number of Children Under 18 Whose Physical Custody Was Awarded to: ____ Husband/Wife/Spouse/Partner A ____ Husband/Wife/Spouse/Partner B ____ Joint ____ Other ____ No children	17. Legal Representative — Name and Address (*Street or R.F.D., City or Town, State, ZIP code*)

FOR COURT CLERK ONLY

18. Date of Recording Decree (*Mo., Day, Year*)	19. Signature of Court Clerk ▶

INFORMATION FOR STATISTICAL PURPOSES ONLY

	Race	Education (*Specify Highest Grade Completed*)		Number of this Marriage/Civil Union	If Previously Entered Into a Marriage/Civil Union — ***Last*** Marriage/Civil Union Ended by Death, Dissolution or Invalidity of Marriage/Civil Union			
	Specify (e.g., White, Black, American Indian)	*Elementary or Secondary (0-12)*	*College (1-4 or 5+)*	*First, Second, etc. (Specify)*	*Specify Type (Marriage or Civil Union)*	*Specify How*	*Specify When (Month, Day, Year)*	*Specify Where (County and State [abbreviated])*
HUSBAND/WIFE/ SPOUSE/PARTNER A	20.	21.		22a.	22b.	22c.	22d.	22e.
HUSBAND/WIFE/ SPOUSE/PARTNER B	23.	24.		25a.	25b.	25c.	25d.	25e.

26. Of Hispanic Origin? *Specify No or Yes — If Yes, Specify (e.g., Cuban, Mexican, Puerto Rican)*	HUSBAND/WIFE/ SPOUSE/PARTNER A	26a. ☐ No ☐ Yes Specify:	HUSBAND/WIFE/ SPOUSE/PARTNER B	26b. ☐ No ☐ Yes Specify:

VR-700 (REV. 12/17)
IOCI 18-303

ILLINOIS DEPARTMENT OF PUBLIC HEALTH — DIVISION OF VITAL RECORDS

Printed by Authority of the State of Illinois

State of Illinois
Illinois Department of Public Health

COUNTY CLERK'S COPY
COUNTY OF MARRIAGE

STATE OF ILLINOIS

CERTIFICATE OF DISSOLUTION OF , INVALIDITY OR LEGAL SEPARATION

TYPE / PRINT IN PERMANENT BLACK INK

	Name of County	Court File Number			State File Number	
A ■ HUSBAND ■ WIFE ■ SPOUSE ■ PARTNER	1a. Name (*First, Middle, Last*)		1b. Last Name on Birth Certificate		2. Sex	3. Social Security Number
	4a. Residence — City, Town, Twp. or Road District Number	4b. County	4c. State	5a. Birthplace (*State or Foreign Country)*	5b. Date of Birth (*Mo., Day, Year)*	5c. Age Now
B ■ HUSBAND ■ WIFE ■ SPOUSE ■ PARTNER	6a. Name (*First, Middle, Last*)		6b. Last Name on Birth Certificate		7. Sex	8. Social Security Number
	9a. Residence — City, Town, Twp. or Road District Number	9b. County	9c. State	10a. Birthplace (*State or Foreign Country)*	10b. Date of Birth (*Mo., Day, Year)*	10c. Age Now
	11a. Date of This Marriage/Civil Union (*Mo., Day, Year)*	11b. Place of This Marriage/Civil Union — City		11c. County	11d. State (*If Not in U.S., Name Country)*	
	12. Date Couple Last Resided in Same Household (*Mo., Day, Year)*	13a. Number of Children of This Marriage/Civil Union	13b. Children Under 18 in This Household (*Specify)*	14. Petitioner		
	15a. Type of Decree (Specify: Dissolution, Invalidity or Legal Separation)	15b. Legal Grounds for Decree (*Specify)*				
	16. Number of Children Under 18 Whose Physical Custody Was Awarded to: ____ Husband/Wife/Spouse/Partner A ____ Husband/Wife/Spouse/Partner B ____ Joint ____ Other ____ No children	17. Legal Representative — Name and Address (*Street or R.F.D., City or Town, State, ZIP code)*				
	FOR COURT CLERK ONLY					
	18. Date of Recording Decree (*Mo., Day, Year)*	19. Signature of Court Clerk ▶				

VR-700 (REV. 12/17)
IOCI 18-303

ILLINOIS DEPARTMENT OF PUBLIC HEALTH — DIVISION OF VITAL RECORDS
Printed by Authority of the State of Illinois

State of Illinois
Illinois Department of Public Health

COURT COPY

STATE OF ILLINOIS

CERTIFICATE OF DISSOLUTION OF , INVALIDITY OR LEGAL SEPARATION

TYPE / PRINT IN PERMANENT BLACK INK

	Name of County	Court File Number	State File Number

A — ■ HUSBAND ■ WIFE ■ SPOUSE ■ PARTNER

1a. Name (*First, Middle, Last*)		1b. Last Name on Birth Certificate		2. Sex	3. Social Security Number
4a. Residence — City, Town, Twp. or Road District Number	4b. County	4c. State	5a. Birthplace (*State or Foreign Country*)	5b. Date of Birth (*Mo., Day, Year*)	5c. Age Now

B — ■ HUSBAND ■ WIFE ■ SPOUSE ■ PARTNER

6a. Name (*First, Middle, Last*)		6b. Last Name on Birth Certificate		7. Sex	8. Social Security Number
9a. Residence — City, Town, Twp. or Road District Number	9b. County	9c. State	10a. Birthplace (*State or Foreign Country*)	10b. Date of Birth (*Mo., Day, Year*)	10c. Age Now

11a. Date of This Marriage/Civil Union (*Mo., Day, Year*)	11b. Place of This Marriage/Civil Union — City	11c. County	11d. State (*If Not in U.S., Name Country*)
12. Date Couple Last Resided in Same Household (*Mo., Day, Year*)	13a. Number of Children of This Marriage/Civil Union	13b. Children Under 18 in This Household (*Specify*)	14. Petitioner

15a. Type of Decree (Specify: Dissolution, Invalidity or Legal Separation)	15b. Legal Grounds for Decree (*Specify*)
16. Number of Children Under 18 Whose Physical Custody Was Awarded to: ____ Husband/Wife/Spouse/Partner A ____ Husband/Wife/Spouse/Partner B ____ Joint ____ Other ____ No children	17. Legal Representative — Name and Address (*Street or R.F.D., City or Town, State, ZIP code*)

FOR COURT CLERK ONLY

18. Date of Recording Decree (*Mo., Day, Year*)	19. Signature of Court Clerk ▶

VR-700 (REV. 12/17)
IOCI 18-303

ILLINOIS DEPARTMENT OF PUBLIC HEALTH — DIVISION OF VITAL RECORDS
Printed by Authority of the State of Illinois

State of Illinois
Illinois Department of Public Health

LEGAL REPRESENTATIVES COPY

STATE OF ILLINOIS

CERTIFICATE OF DISSOLUTION OF , INVALIDITY OR LEGAL SEPARATION

TYPE / PRINT IN PERMANENT BLACK INK

	Name of County	Court File Number		State File Number		
■ HUSBAND ■ WIFE ■ SPOUSE ■ PARTNER **A**	1a. Name (*First, Middle, Last*)		1b. Last Name on Birth Certificate	2. Sex	3. Social Security Number	
	4a. Residence — City, Town, Twp. or Road District Number	4b. County	4c. State	5a. Birthplace (*State or Foreign Country*)	5b. Date of Birth (*Mo., Day, Year*)	5c. Age Now
■ HUSBAND ■ WIFE ■ SPOUSE ■ PARTNER **B**	6a. Name (*First, Middle, Last*)		6b. Last Name on Birth Certificate	7. Sex	8. Social Security Number	
	9a. Residence — City, Town, Twp. or Road District Number	9b. County	9c. State	10a. Birthplace (*State or Foreign Country*)	10b. Date of Birth (*Mo., Day, Year*)	10c. Age Now
	11a. Date of This Marriage/Civil Union (*Mo., Day, Year*)	11b. Place of This Marriage/Civil Union — City		11c. County	11d. State (*If Not in U.S., Name Country*)	
	12. Date Couple Last Resided in Same Household (*Mo., Day, Year*)	13a. Number of Children of This Marriage/Civil Union	13b. Children Under 18 in This Household (*Specify*)	14. Petitioner		
	15a. Type of Decree (Specify: Dissolution, Invalidity or Legal Separation)	15b. Legal Grounds for Decree (*Specify*)				
	16. Number of Children Under 18 Whose Physical Custody Was Awarded to: ____ Husband/Wife/Spouse/Partner A ____ Husband/Wife/Spouse/Partner B ____ Joint ____ Other ____ No children	17. Legal Representative — Name and Address (*Street or R.F.D., City or Town, State, ZIP code*)				
	FOR COURT CLERK ONLY					
	18. Date of Recording Decree (*Mo., Day, Year*)	19. Signature of Court Clerk ▶				

VR-700 (REV. 12/17)
IOCI 18-303

ILLINOIS DEPARTMENT OF PUBLIC HEALTH — DIVISION OF VITAL RECORDS
Printed by Authority of the State of Illinois

Eleven

Parentage

Overview

In previous chapters, we discussed the law related to children born during a marriage; however, babies may be born to unmarried parents as well. In fact, over 40% of the babies born in Illinois in 2020 were born to unmarried parents.[1] While some parenting issues are the same, some, such as determining the father, are different. In addition, the time the unmarried parents lived together (if at all) and the roles they played in their children's lives may vary considerably.

The General Assembly provides law to resolve issues related to the children of unmarried parents in the Illinois Parentage Act of 2015.[2] As you read, consider whether the law addresses the specific parenting issues faced by unmarried parents.

The Illinois Parentage Act of 2015

The parent-child relationship, including support obligations, extends equally to every child and his or her parents, regardless of the legal relationship of the parents.[3]

Presumptions of Paternity

Married Mother

When a baby is born to a married woman, her husband is presumed to be the father.[4] However, this presumption can be challenged.

> **EXAMPLE** Wife and Boyfriend are engaged in an extra-marital relationship. Wife gives birth. Husband is presumed to be the father of the baby. However, either Husband or Boyfriend can challenge this presumption.

Unmarried Mother

In contrast, when a baby is born to an unmarried woman, no father is presumed. Accordingly, the first step in a parentage action is to determine the father-child relationship.

Determining the Father

Voluntarily

The father can voluntarily claim the child in one of two ways.

The Voluntary Acknowledgment of Paternity

First, he can sign a Voluntary Acknowledgment of Paternity (VAP).[5] The VAP is a form produced by the Illinois Department of Healthcare and Family Services (HFS). Once the VAP is signed, witnessed, and filed with the Department, a man becomes the legal father of the child.

Signing a VAP makes the father responsible for supporting the child financially, which may include paying child support, until the child is at least 18 years old. But it also gives him the right to ask for an allocation of parental responsibilities, including parenting time.

Once he signs a VAP, the father cannot ask for a DNA test.

EXAMPLE Father and Mother were both socially active when Mother conceived; Father does not sign the VAP.

EXAMPLE In contrast, Megan and Nicholas had been in a committed relationship for several years before their baby was born. Nicholas signs the VAP at the hospital. He has assumed the rights and responsibilities of a legal father.

Once it is signed, the VAP may be rescinded within 60 days by filing a Rescission of VAP with the HFS.[6]

EXAMPLE After they return from the hospital, Nicholas's mother remarks that the baby doesn't look anything like Nicholas did as a baby, and Megan confesses that while Nicholas was out-of-town on business, she engaged in a single act of intercourse with a man she met at a bar. Nicholas immediately files a Rescission of VAP.

After 60 days have passed the only way a father can challenge a VAP is to file a petition in court and prove fraud, duress, or material mistake of fact.[7] In other words, the father can only challenge the voluntariness of signing the VAP. He cannot challenge the presumption of paternity with a DNA test.[8] The challenging party bears the burden of proof, which is by clear and convincing evidence, a higher standard than a preponderance of the evidence.

To prove he was defrauded, the father must satisfy all five elements of fraud: "(1) [a] false statement of material fact (2) known or believed to be false by the party making it; (3) intent to induce the other party to act; (4) action by the other party in [justifiable] reliance on the truth of the statement; and (5) damage to the other party resulting from such reliance."[9]

EXAMPLE If Nicholas's mother had been on vacation when the baby was born and didn't see him until he was three months old, it would be too late for Nicholas to rescind the VAP. He would have to file a petition in court and prove fraud, duress, or material mistake of fact. Did Megan know the baby was not his and lie about it to induce him to sign the VAP? The burden is on Nicholas to convince the court she did.

While the case is pending, a court will not suspend the legal responsibilities of a person that signs a VAP, including his duty to pay child support.[10] Had Nicholas been ordered to pay child support, the obligation to pay would continue while his petition for rescission was pending.

Court Acknowledgment

If a father does not sign a VAP and the matter proceeds to court, he can either acknowledge the child in a pleading, such as a petition or answer, or file a court acknowledgment of paternity. Under either method, he is now an "acknowledged" father.

Although it is a common misconception, signing a birth certificate is not a legal acknowledgment of paternity.

EXAMPLE Father signs Child's birth certificate as the Father, thinking he has acknowledged paternity. However, should Unmarried Mother withhold Child from him, he has no rights to the Child.

Involuntarily

Genetic Testing

If a man does not voluntarily acknowledge the child, he is an "alleged" father, and a court can require him to submit to a DNA test.[11] If the results indicate there is a 99.9% probability of paternity, he is presumed to be the father.[12] If the results indicate he is not the father, the court will enter an exclusion order.[13]

> **EXAMPLE** Father refuses to sign the VAP. Mother files a petition for parentage. Father submits to genetic testing, which proves he is the father. The court enters an order of parentage.

The expense of the test is paid by the party requesting it, although the court can apportion the costs.[14]

> **EXAMPLE** Mother pays for the test. When Father is included in the test results, the court apportions the cost between the parties.

Consequence of Refusal

If a man refuses to comply with a court-ordered DNA test, the court can interpret the action against him.[15]

> **EXAMPLE** Father refuses to comply with the order for genetic testing. The court enters an order of parentage.

If as a result of a court action a man is included in the test results or adjudicated contrary to his position, he is an "adjudicated" father.

Procedure

An action to establish parentage can proceed under one of two methods: an administrative process or a court action.

Administrative

As we saw in Chapter 7, an initial child support order can be obtained through an administrative procedure. Title IV-D of the Social Security Act, a federal law, requires that all states offer and provide child support services to all families. In Illinois, child support services are administered by the Division of Child Support Services (DCSS) within the Illinois Department of Healthcare and Family Services. DCSS will help any parent ("non-assistance cases") but is automatically provided when the custodial parent receives public aid ("assistance cases.")

What Agency Can Do

Sometimes a parent (generally the mother) only wants to establish the identity of the father and secure child support. The Department of Child Support Services (DCSS) provides an administrative procedure to accomplish those goals. They will locate the father, administer genetic testing, establish a child support order, and tender an income withholding order on his employer.

This procedure is generally completed in 90 days. It is free to the parties and as no court involvement is required, it is completely private. Information about the process is available at https//www.illinois.gov/hfs/SiteCollectionDocuments/HFS1759.pdf.

EXAMPLE Mother and Father are 18 years old and live with their parents. During their casual dating relationship, Mother becomes pregnant. Father was not involved in the pregnancy and has only seen the baby a few times in the six months since birth. Mother contacts the DCSS, which establishes parentage and orders support.

What Agency Does Not Do

The administrative process does not resolve parenting issues, such as the allocation of parental responsibilities or parenting time. Should either party want to resolve those issues, the party must file a parentage action in the circuit court.

EXAMPLE During the pregnancy, Mother texts Father that she is moving to Florida with her fiancé and he will never see the baby. Father files a petition to establish parentage to establish his parental rights.

The Court Action under the Illinois Parentage Act

A court action begins when a party files a petition to adjudicate parentage.

Standing

Only certain persons have standing to bring such an action, as provided below:

(a) The child;

(b) The mother of the child;

(c) A pregnant woman;

(d) A man presumed or alleging himself to be the parent of the child;

(e) A woman presumed or alleging herself to be the parent of the child;

(f) The support-enforcement agency or other governmental agency authorized by other law;

(g) Any person or public agency that has physical possession of or has custody of or has been allocated parental responsibilities for, is providing financial support to, or has provided financial support to the child;

(h) The Department of Healthcare and Family Services if it is providing, or has provided, financial support to the child or if it is assisting with child support collections services;

(i) An authorized adoption agency or licensed child-placing agency.[16]

EXAMPLE Boyfriend was in a committed relationship with Girlfriend during the period nine months before she gave birth. Girlfriend does not wish to co-parent with Boyfriend and refuses him access to the baby. Boyfriend has standing to file a petition under (d) above.

EXAMPLE In contrast, Justin's girlfriend Sydney gives birth. Justin has no interest in the baby, but Justin's mother (Grandmother) is desperate to see her new grandchild. Grandmother does not have standing to petition for parentage. Should Justin and Sydney drop the baby off with Grandmother and move out of state, Grandmother likely has standing under (g) above.

The Petition

The petition must be verified and name the man alleged to be the parent of the child.[17] If more than one man is alleged to be the father, they receive separate petitions. A notice must be filed along with the petition.[18] The notice informs the alleged father that if he does not respond, he may lose his rights to the child.

> **EXAMPLE** Mother ended a relationship with Old Boyfriend and started another with New Boyfriend around the time she conceived. She can file two petitions, one naming Old Boyfriend and the other naming New Boyfriend as presumed fathers.

The petition can be filed before the birth of the child but may not be concluded until after the child's birth.[19]

> **EXAMPLE** As soon as she discovers she is pregnant, Mom files a petition for parentage naming Boyfriend as an alleged father. However, the action can only conclude after the baby is born and parentage can be determined.

Parentage Summons

As with other civil actions, a summons accompanies the petition. A parentage summons must include the return date (that is, the first date the matter is in court) and must contain the following information, in a prominent place and conspicuous language:[20]

> "If you do not appear as instructed in this summons, you may be required to support the child named in this petition until the child is at least 18 years old. You may also have to pay the pregnancy and delivery costs of the mother."

Service

The petition, summons, and notice are all served on the respondent as discussed in Chapter 4 (Jurisdiction, Service, and Initial Pleadings).

Return Date

On the return date, several things could happen. If the respondent does not appear, either by himself or through an attorney, an order of default may be entered. As a consequence of his default, he may be determined to be the father, pay child support, and lose any rights to the child. Alternatively, if he appears and wants to claim the child voluntarily but has not signed a VAP, he can admit to parentage in the court action. And finally, if he denies he is the father, the court can order paternity testing.

Child Support

Once paternity has been adjudicated, the parties will exchange financial affidavits (and additional discovery, as required) to determine an award of child support. In determining the amount of a child support award, the court shall use the guidelines and standards set forth in IMDMA.

The Judgment

At the end of the action, a parentage judgment is entered.

Must Contain

The Parentage Act requires the court to make an order adjudicating whether a person alleged or claiming to be the parent is the child's parent.[21] In addition, the judgment must contain or explicitly reserve provisions concerning any duty and amount of child support.[22]

Retroactive Expenses

Under the IMDMA, courts can only make financial awards for the time after the petition is filed. In contrast, in a parentage action, the court can make awards for the time before the petition is filed.

Pregnancy and Birth Expenses

If the action is filed before the child turns two years of age, the court can award the reasonable expenses incurred by either parent related to the mother's pregnancy and the delivery of the child.[23]

EXAMPLE Mother files a petition to establish parentage a few weeks after the baby is born. The court can order Father to pay for expenses incurred during her pregnancy and delivery.

EXAMPLE In contrast, after Mother and Father broke up, they remained friends and worked things out for five years, sharing financial responsibilities and parenting time. Should the relationship between Mother and Father break down, and Mother initiate a court action, she could not petition for expenses incurred during the pregnancy and delivery.

Child Support

In contrast, retroactive child support is not limited to the two-year look back.[24] In determining how far back payments can be ordered, the court considers the following factors:

(1) The factors for determining the amount of support specified in the IMDMA.

(2) The prior knowledge of the person obligated to pay support of the fact and circumstances of the child's birth.

(3) The father's prior willingness or refusal to help raise or support the child.

(4) The extent to which the mother or the public agency bringing the action previously informed the person obligated to pay support of the child's needs or attempted to seek or require the help of the person obligated to pay support in raising or supporting the child.

(5) The reasons the mother or the public agency did not file the action earlier.

(6) The extent to which the person obligated to pay support would be prejudiced by the delay in bringing the action. [25]

> **EXAMPLE** One year after their daughter Morgan was born, Parents' relationship broke down. Father moved out of state and changed his phone number. Mother cooperated with the Illinois Department of Child Support Services to locate Father; however, he worked for cash, registered his car in his girlfriend's name, and moved to a new apartment every year. When Morgan was ten, Father returned to Illinois for his brother's wedding and was served with a petition to establish parentage. Factors (2)–(5) apply.

May Contain

Allocation of Parental Responsibilities

The court judgment may contain issues related to parenting, such as the allocation of parental responsibilities and parenting time privileges with the child. If so, the court shall determine them in accordance with the relevant factors set forth in the IMDMA.[26]

In the absence of an explicit order or PAJ, sole allocation should be construed as being in the mother.[27]

EXAMPLE In the case of Mother who contacted DCFS to establish parentage and child support, presume father has not filed an action for parenting time. Mother is construed as having sole allocation. Should Father want to see his child, he does not have a parenting time award that can be enforced.

Name Change

Finally, as a result of a parentage action, parents may wish to change their baby's name. The Parentage Act allows parents to change the baby's name in the parentage action so they do not need to file a separate action to change the baby's name in chancery court.[28] Additionally, the court can order the issuance of a new birth certificate under the Vital Records Act.[29]

EXAMPLE Jessica Smith gives her baby Mark Doe's last name on the birth certificate. DNA testing indicates Ken Brown is the father. Jessica and Ken wish to change the baby's name to Brown. The parentage court orders the name change and issuance of the new birth certificate.

EXAMPLE Similarly, Jessica gave the baby her last name on the birth certificate. Once Ken is determined to be the father, he and Jessica decide to hyphenate the baby's last name to include both last names. The court changes the baby's name to Smith-Brown.

Chapter Summary

The parent-child relationship extends equally to every child and their parents, regardless of the relationship of the parents. The Illinois Parentage Act of 2015 provides law to resolve child-related issues of unmarried parents, such as determining parentage, awarding child support, and allocating parental responsibility.

While a married woman's husband is presumed to be the father of her baby, no father is presumed when an unmarried woman gives birth. A man can voluntarily claim a child by filing a VAP or acknowledging paternity in a pleading. Alternatively, a man may be adjudicated a father through DNA testing.

The law provides two ways to establish parentage: an administrative process provided by the Illinois Department of Health and Family Services (Department of Child Support Services) and a court action. While the administrative process is free to all parents, private, and relatively quick, it only establishes parentage and orders child support. If the parents want to allocate parental responsibilities, they must bring a court action. By statute, the court judgment must establish parentage and order child support. It may include an allocation of parental responsibilities. In contrast to awards made under the IMDMA, in a parentage action, financial support, including birth and pregnancy expenses, can be ordered for the period of time prior to filing the petition.

Once a child support order is entered by a court or established by DCSS, an IWO is served on the obligor's employer. The same enforcement mechanisms available to divorced parents are available to unmarried parents. (See Chapter 7, Child Support.)

Key Terms

Parentage Act

Voluntary Acknowledgment of Paternity

Acknowledged father

Alleged father

Adjudicated father

Retroactive Support

Discussion Questions

1. If a married woman gives birth, her husband is presumed to be the other parent. However, in many jurisdictions, if a woman in a same-sex marriage gives birth, her spouse is not presumed to be the other parent. If they divorce, the spouse has no legal relationship to the child. Some states allow the female spouse of a biological parent to be placed on a child's birth certificate. What is the law in Illinois? What should it be, and why?
2. If a man in a same-sex marriage adopts a child, his husband is not presumed to be the child's other parent and his name is not placed on the birth certificate. He has to adopt the child. Is this a violation of Equal Protection?
3. Are there times it is better not to reveal parentage? Consider the case of *In re Parentage of J.W.*, in which the court denied a biological father's petition for visitation because it would disrupt the relationship she had with her mother and the man she thought was her father. 2013 IL 114817, ¶ 57, 990 N.E.2d 698, 711.

4. How can an office protect the rights of a client who knows he is not the father but has raised a child for many years and wants to continue to have time with the child?
5. Consider a case from Brazil, in which identical twins were both ordered to pay child support after they failed to identify which of them was the baby's father. The court considered the brothers' history of impersonating each other to date as many women as possible. Does this seem like a good outcome? Should they each have paid half?
6. Petitions filed under the IMDMA are retroactive to the date of filing, while petitions filed under the Parentage Act are retroactive to a baby's birth. What do you suppose the policy is behind this difference?
7. In considering whether to award retroactive child support, should the burden be on the mother to show why she didn't pursue child support? Or should it be on a father to show why he failed to pay child support? Does the common law doctrine of laches apply?
8. What is the policy behind requiring mothers receiving public benefits to work with the DCSS child support enforcement division?
9. A paternity judgment must contain provisions for child support but not for the allocation of parental responsibilities. Given the state's interest in children having relationships with both parents, would it make sense to make allocation mandatory? Is this policy related to the fact parenting time will be protected but not enforced?
10. Pursuant to 750 ILCS 46/408, if an alleged father is unavailable, one of his relatives can be ordered to submit a specimen of DNA. Is it an invasion of the alleged father's Fourth Amendment rights to obtain his DNA without his consent? As we saw in Chapter 2, rights are not absolute. Is providing for children a compelling state interest? Would it make a difference if the alleged father had paid for genetic testing and his DNA was available to the public?

Forms

1. Voluntary Acknowledgment of Paternity
   https://www2.illinois.gov/hfs/SiteCollectionDocuments/hfs3416b.pdf
2. Rescission of Voluntary Acknowledgment of Paternity
   https://www2.illinois.gov/hfs/SiteCollectionDocuments/hfs3416e.pdf
3. Petition for Parentage
   https://18thjudicial.org/18thJudicial/download/2270
4. Parentage Summons
   https://18thjudicial.org/18thJudicial/download/226

Endnotes

1. https://dph.illinois.gov/data-statistics/vital-statistics/birth-statistics.html
2. 750 ILCS 46/101. (West, Westlaw Classic through P.A. 103-21 of the 2023 Reg. Sess.).
3. *Id.* § 102
4. *Id.* § 204(a)(1).
5. *Id.* § 301.
6. *Id.* § 307(a).
7. *Id.* § 309(a).
8. People ex rel. Jackson v. Mannie, 393 Ill. App. 3d 745, 749, 913 N.E.2d 1174, 1178 (1st Dist. 2009) (citing People ex rel. Department of Public Aid v. Smith, 212 Ill.2d 389, 405, 818 N.E.2d 1204, 1213 (2004).
9. Metro. Cap. Bank & Tr. v. Feiner, 2020 IL App (1st) 190895, ¶ 38, 179 N.E.3d 847, 854 (citing Merill Corp. v. Jack L. Hargrove Builders, Inc., 128 Ill. 2d 179, 193, 538 N.E.2d 530 (1989).
10. 750 ILCS 46/309(d).
11. *Id.* § 401.
12. *Id.* § 404(c).
13. *Id.* § 404(a).
14. *Id.* § 405.
15. *Id.* § 401.
16. 750 ILCS 46/602.
17. *Id.* § 602.
18. *Id.* § 605.
19. *Id.* § 612.
20. *Id.* § 606.
21. *Id.* § 802(a).
22. 750 ILCS 46/802(a).
23. *Id.* § 802(b).
24. *Id.* § 802(e).
25. *Id.* § 802(e)(1-6).
26. *Id.* § 803(a).
27. *Id.* § 802(c).
28. 750 ILCS 46/802(h).
29. *Id.* § 802(g).

1. VOLUNTARY ACKNOWLEDGMENT OF PATERNITY

File Date for ACU use only

Illinois Voluntary Acknowledgment of Paternity

PLEASE READ ALL PARTS OF THIS FORM INCLUDING YOUR RIGHTS AND RESPONSIBILITIES AND INSTRUCTIONS ON THE OTHER SIDE BEFORE COMPLETING THE FOLLOWING INFORMATION.

ALL ITEMS MUST BE ANSWERED (USE BLUE OR BLACK INK)

Child's Information as shown on or will be shown on Birth Certificate **Print all requested information**

Child's Name (First)	Middle (if any)	Last (same as on or will be on birth certificate) Suffix (Jr, II, III)	
Date of Birth (mm/dd/yyyy)	Gender ☐ M ☐ F	Name of Hospital or Place of Birth	City, County and State of Birth

Biological Father's Name (First)	Middle (if any)	Last	Suffix (Jr, II, III)
Current Address (street address and/or P.O. box)	City, State, and Zip	Daytime Phone (include area code)	
Place of Birth (city, state or foreign country address)	Date of Birth (mm/dd/yyyy)	SSN / TIN	

Biological Mother's Name (First)	Middle (if any)	Current Last Name	Maiden Name (before 1st marriage)
Current Address (street address and/or P.O. box)	City, State, and Zip	Daytime Phone (include area code)	
Place of Birth (city, state or foreign country address)	Date of Birth (mm/dd/yyyy)	SSN / TIN	

Were you married to or in a civil union with a person **other than** the above named father when this child was born or within 300 days before this child was born? ☐ Yes ☐ No
If yes, that person is presumed to be the father (presumed parent) of this child and you are required to provide the presumed parent's name (first/middle/last) ______________________ A Denial of Parentage must also be completed by the biological mother and presumed parent to place the biological father's name on this child's birth certificate.

By signing I acknowledge that I have read the rights and responsibilities and instructions on the other side of this form. I have been provided an oral explanation about the VAP and understand my rights and responsibilities created and waived by signing this form.

I UNDERSTAND THAT I CAN REQUEST A GENETIC TEST REGARDING THE CHILD'S PATERNITY. BY SIGNING THIS FORM I GIVE UP MY RIGHT TO A GENETIC TEST.

BIOLOGICAL FATHER and BIOLOGICAL MOTHER: Under the penalties of perjury provided by Section 1-109 of the Illinois Code of Civil Procedure, we certify that our statements in this document are true and correct. We acknowledge that we are the biological parents of this child, and voluntarily sign this acknowledgement to establish this child's paternity and give our permission to enter the biological father's name as the legal father on the birth certificate for this child. We understand that the acknowledgment is the same as a court order for parentage of this child and that a challenge to the acknowledgment is allowed only under limited circumstances and is generally not allowed after 2 years.

Biological Father's Signature ______________	Biological Mother's Signature ______________
E-mail Address ______________	E-mail Address ______________

Each parent must sign and date this form in the presence of a witness age 18 or older. The witness must not be a parent or child named on the VAP.

Witness Information	**Witness Information**
Printed Name ______________	**Printed Name** ______________
Signature ______________	Signature ______________
Address ______________	Address ______________
Phone Number ______________	Phone Number ______________
Date Parties Signed (mm/dd/yyyy) ______________	Date Parties Signed (mm/dd/yyyy) ______________

HFS 3416B (R-10-21)

For Official Use Only Case # Docket # CP RIN NCP RIN

Instructions for Completing the Illinois Voluntary Acknowledgment of Paternity

PURPOSE: The Voluntary Acknowledgment of Paternity (hereafter called VAP) legally establishes the biological father and child relationship (**when the biological father is not married to the child's biological mother**) and allows the biological father's name to be placed on the birth certificate. The biological father becomes the legal father of the child when the VAP is properly signed, witnessed and filed with the Illinois Department of Healthcare and Family Services (hereafter called HFS), creating certain legal rights and responsibilities for the child and the parents. The VAP may be completed before your child is born but is not valid until the child is born and the VAP is filed with HFS. A VAP (and Denial, if necessary) may be completed after you leave the hospital, and the VAP (and Denial, if necessary) may also be completed for a child born in another state. **Forms that contain errors will be rejected. As a result, paternity is not established and the biological father's name will not be placed on the birth certificate.**

If the biological mother is or was married to or in a civil union with a person who is not the biological father when the child was born or within 300 days before this child was born, a Denial of Parentage (hereafter called Denial) must be signed, witnessed and filed in conjunction with the completion of the VAP by the biological mother and biological father.

YOUR RIGHTS AND RESPONSIBILITIES

I understand that:

1. the VAP is a legal document, and when signed, witnessed and filed with HFS, is the same as a court order determining the legal relationship between a biological father and child.
2. if I am a minor, I have the right to sign and have this form witnessed without my guardian's permission.
3. it is my responsibility to provide financial support for the child that may include child support and medical support starting from the child's birth until the child is at least 18 years old.
4. this VAP does not give parental responsibility allocation or parenting time to the biological father; however, it gives him the right to ask for parental responsibility allocation and parenting time.
5. either the biological mother or biological father may rescind the action by signing a Rescission of VAP. The Rescission must be signed, witnessed and filed with HFS within 60 days from the effective date of the VAP or the date of a proceeding relating to the child, whichever occurs earlier.

INSTRUCTIONS – USE BLACK OR BLUE INK

1. The biological mother must indicate "yes" or "no" if she is or was married to or in a civil union with a person other than the biological father when this child was born or within 300 days before this child was born. If "yes", the biological mother must provide the name of that person (referred to as the presumed parent). The presumed parent and biological mother must sign the Denial and the biological mother and biological father must sign the VAP to establish legal paternity and place the biological father's name on the birth certificate. **If the presumed parent and the biological mother do not sign the Denial, the presumed parent is considered to be the parent of the child and that person's name, by law, must be placed on the birth certificate.**
2. Each person must sign and date all forms in front of a witness. A witness must be an adult age 18 or older but cannot be the parents or child named on the VAP.
3. If the VAP (and Denial, if necessary) is completed at the hospital when the child is born, hospital staff will add the biological father's name to the birth certificate and send the VAP to HFS for filing.
4. If the VAP (and Denial, if necessary) is not completed at the hospital, each person must sign and date the form(s) in front of a witness, age 18 or older but not the parents or child named on the VAP, and submit the original documents to HFS.
5. Send only the original document. Do not send a photocopy (must be original signatures)

Mail original document to: **(copies will be rejected)**	Administrative Coordination Unit (ACU) 110 West Lawrence Avenue Springfield, Illinois 62704

The Administrative Coordination Unit (ACU) will file the original VAP and send a copy of the completed VAP (and Denial, if necessary) to either the: 1. Illinois Department of Public Health, Division of Vital Records (for Illinois births); or 2. Vital Records Office in affected state (for out of state births)

To request a certified copy of the VAP go to www.childsupport.illinois.gov and complete and follow instructions on HFS 3416H, Request for a Certified copy of the Voluntary Acknowledgment of Paternity and/or Denial of Parentage.

This form is available in English and Spanish upon request and on the HFS website (www.childsupport.illinois.gov). The Spanish version may be used for translation purposes only. The **Spanish version is not acceptable as a legal document**. Only the English version of this document may be signed, witnessed and filed with HFS.

SI LAS PIDE, TENEMOS VERSIONES EN ESPAÑOL DISPONIBLES Y EN EL SITIO DEL DEPARTAMENTO EN EL INTERNET EN (WWW.CHILDSUPPORT.ILLINOIS.GOV), PERO SÓLO SE PUEDEN USAR PARA PROPÓSITOS DE TRADUCCIÓN. **LAS VERSIONES EN ESPAÑOL NO SON DOCUMENTOS LEGALES ACEPTABLES**. SÓLO LA VERSIÓN EN INGLES DEL DOCUMENTO SE PUEDE FIRMAR Y ATESTIGUAR.

If you have any questions relating to the child's birth certificate, contact the Department of Public Health's Division of Vital Records at www.idph.state.il.us/vitalrecords or 217-782-6554.

For a recorded explanation of your rights and responsibilities call 1-844-215-6576, or if you have any questions relating to completing this form call the customer service call center at 1-800-447-4278.

Printed by the Authority of the State of Illinois . IOCI23-0666

2. RESCISSION OF VOLUNTARY ACKNOWLEDGMENT OF PATERNITY

Rescission of Illinois Voluntary Acknowledgment of Paternity or Rescission of Denial of Parentage

File Date for ACU use only

Purpose: THIS IS A LEGAL DOCUMENT. This form cancels the legal father and child relationship created by the previously signed Voluntary Acknowledgment of Paternity and/or cancels the adjudication of the nonparentage of the presumed parent thereby making the presumed parent responsible for all rights and duties of a parent. **The form must be signed, witnessed and filed with the Department within 60 days from the effective date of either the Voluntary Acknowledgment of Paternity (VAP), and/or the Denial of Parentage (Denial), or the date of a proceeding relating to the child, whichever occurs earlier.**

Instructions: PRINT in **BLACK or BLUE** ink. Do not cross out words or make corrections or your form will be rejected. If you make a mistake, ask for a new form. See additional instructions on the reverse side of this form.

If using the Internet form, enter information and check for errors before printing. Forms with errors will be rejected.

Read carefully and complete all information before signing this form. Only one person must sign this form to withdraw the VAP and/or the Denial. The other party who signed the VAP and/or the Denial will be notified of your withdrawal of consent. In addition, the Department of Public Health's Division of Vital Records will be notified to remove the father's name from the child's birth certificate and/or add the presumed parent's name to the child's birth certificate. Call the Child Support Customer Service Call Center at 1-800-447-4278 if you have questions.

I would like to withdraw the (check one): ☐ **Voluntary Acknowledgment of Paternity** ☐ **Denial of Parentage**

Name		Date of Birth (mm/dd/yy)
Address	City/State/Zip	Social Security Number
Full Name of Child (as shown or will be shown on Birth Certificate)		Child's Date of Birth (mm/dd/yy)
Date VAP or Denial was Signed (mm/dd/yy)	Name of Other Person who Signed VAP or Denial (not the witness)	

I understand that the legal father and child relationship established by signing the VAP is canceled or the adjudication of the non-parentage of the presumed parent is canceled thereby making the presumed parent responsible for all rights and duties of a parent. Paternity may be established by other means.

Signature ______________________ Date of Signature ______________

Witness Information

Printed Name______________________

Address______________________ Signature______________________

Phone Number______________________ Date Signed______________________

Mail to HFS/ACU, 110 W Lawrence Avenue, Springfield, IL 62704.

HFS 3416E (R-4-17)

For Official Use Only ______________________

Case # Docket # CP RIN NCP RIN

Instructions for Rescission of Illinois Voluntary Acknowledgment of Paternity or Rescission of Denial of Parentage

PURPOSE: The Rescission of Illinois Voluntary Acknowledgment of Paternity or Rescission of Denial of Parentage (here after called the "Rescission") is completed when either the biological mother, biological father, or presumed parent wishes to withdraw the action of filing the HFS 3416B, Voluntary Acknowledgment of Paternity (here after called the "VAP") and/or the HFS 3416D, Illinois Denial of Parentage (here after called the "Denial"). **The Rescission must be signed, witnessed and filed with the Department within 60 days from the effective date of either the VAP and/or the Denial, or the date of a proceeding relating to the child, whichever occurs earlier. Forms that contain errors will be rejected. As a result, the VAP and/or Denial will not be withdrawn and the biological father's name will remain on the child's birth certificate.**

PLEASE READ AND COMPLETE ALL REQUESTED INFORMATION PRIOR TO SIGNING THIS FORM.

1. Only one person must sign this form to withdraw the VAP and/or Denial.

2. The other party(ies) who signed the VAP and/or Denial will be notified of your withdraw of consent. In addition, the Department of Public Health's Division of Vital Records will be notified to remove the father's name from the child's birth certificate and/or add the presumed parent's name to the child's birth certificate.

3. The person withdrawing the VAP and/or Denial must sign and date all forms in front of a witness. A witness must be an adult age eighteen or older but cannot be the biological mother, biological father, presumed parent or the child.

4. Mail the Rescission to the Department's:

   Administrative Coordination Unit (ACU)
   110 West Lawrence Avenue
   Springfield, Illinois 62704

For more information about the Rescission or other related forms, ask hospital staff for the HFS 3416A, "Two Parents...Give Your Child Hope" flyer. You may also obtain a copy from state and local registrars, county clerks, Department of Human Services offices, Child Support Services offices or by going to the Forms and Brochures section of the Child Support Services website.

This form is available in English and Spanish upon request and on the HFS website (www.childsupport.illinois.gov). The Spanish version may be used for translation purposes only. The **Spanish version is not acceptable as a legal document**. Only the English version of this document may be signed, witnessed and filed with HFS.

SI LAS PIDE, TENEMOS VERSIONES EN ESPAÑOL DISPONIBLES Y EN EL SITIO DEL DEPARTAMENTO EN EL INTERNET EN (WWW.CHILDSUPPORT.ILLINOIS.GOV), PERO SÓLO SE PUEDEN USAR PARA PROPÓSITOS DE TRADUCCIÓN. **LAS VERSIONES EN ESPAÑOL NO SON DOCUMENTOS LEGALES ACEPTABLES**. SÓLO LA VERSIÓN EN INGLES DEL DOCUMENTO SE PUEDE FIRMAR Y ATESTIGUAR. (translation from English paragraph above)

If you have any questions relating to the child's birth certificate, contact the Department of Public Health's Division of Vital Records at Birth, Death, Other Records | IDPH or 217-782-6554.

If you have any questions relating to completing this form, call the Child Support Customer Service Call Center at 1-800-447-4278.

3. PETITION FOR PARENTAGE

STATE OF ILLINOIS **UNITED STATES OF AMERICA**
IN THE CIRCUIT COURT OF THE EIGHTEENTH JUDICIAL CIRCUIT **COUNTY OF DU PAGE**

____

vs

____

____
CASE NUMBER

PETITION
DETERMINATION OF A
FATHER / CHILD RELATIONSHIP

File Stamp Here

Now comes the Petitioner _______________ and petitions this Court to determine the existence of a father / child relationship pursuant to Illinois Compiled Statutes, 750 ILCS 45/1 and in support thereof states as follows:

1. Name of the **Mother** _______________
   Address _______________
   Place of Birth _______________
   Date of Birth _______________

2. Name of the **Father** _______________
   Address _______________
   Place of Birth _______________
   Date of Birth _______________

3. Name of the **Child** _______________
   Address _______________
   Place of Birth _______________
   Date of Birth _______________

3a ☐ Check this box if a public agency is providing assistance to the child.
   Name of Agency _______________
   Address _______________

4. That the minor child of the parties _______________
   presently is in the custody of _______________

5. That one or more of the parties resides or can be found in DuPage County Illinois, or that probate proceedings of the father's estate have been or could be commenced in DuPage County, Illinois.

6. That it is in the best interest of the minor child that temporary and permanent care, custody control and education be awarded to _______________ who is a fit and proper person.

CASE NUMBER ____________________

7. That the ☐Mother ☐ Father lacks sufficient property or sufficient income to provide for the reasonable needs of the minor child of the parties, including education needs. That the ☐Mother ☐Father is gainfully employed earning substantial income and is well able to provide child support in accordance with the reasonable needs of the child.
8. That the ☐ Mother ☐ Father is without sufficient financial resources to pay their own attorney's fees and costs and that the ☐ Mother ☐ Father has sufficient resources to pay their own attorney's fees and costs.
9. That the mother is without sufficient resources to pay for the reasonable expenses of the pregnancy and delivery and that the father has sufficient financial resources to pay for these expenses.

WHEREFORE, the petitioner ____ prays for the following relief:

A. That a judgment be entered establishing the existence of a father and child relationship between the father and the minor child, according to 750 ILCS et seq.

B. That the ☐ Mother ☐ Father be awarded the temporary and permanent custody of the minor child of the parties, subject to reasonable visitation as ordered by the Court.

C. That the ☐ Mother ☐ Father be awarded the temporary and permanent custody.

D. That the Court order the ☐ Mother ☐ Father to pay such reasonable child support for the period from ____________________ to ____________________ which is prior to the commencement of this action.

OATH

I, ____ the undersigned, certify under penalties as provided by law pursuant to 735 ILCS 5/1-109 that the statements set forth in this instrument are true and correct.

____
Signature

Name: ____________________ ☐ Pro Se
DuPage Attorney Number: ____________________
Attorney for: ____________________
Address: ____________________
City/State/Zip: ____________________
Telephone Number: ____________________
Email: ____________________

Signed and sworn to before me

____
Date

____
Circuit Clerk or Notary Public

4. PARENTAGE SUMMONS

SUMMONS - PARENTAGE 2268 (Rev. 6/22)

STATE OF ILLINOIS **UNITED STATES OF AMERICA**
IN THE CIRCUIT COURT OF THE EIGHTEENTH JUDICIAL CIRCUIT **COUNTY OF DU PAGE**

PLAINTIFF

vs

DEFENDANT

CASE NUMBER

SUMMONS
PARENTAGE

File Stamp Here

To the defendant:
You are hereby Summoned and Required to Appear, either in person or remotely, before this Court at the DuPage County Judicial Center, 505 N. County Farm Road, Wheaton, Illinois on ______ Date Time Courtroom to answer the complaint of the plaintiff(s), a copy of which is hereto attached. You may be able to attend this court date by phone or video conference. It is preferred that you appear remotely via Zoom video or telephone conference. This is called a "Remote Appearance". Visit 18thjudicial.org to find the Zoom link and call-in information for your court appearance or call the Circuit Clerk at (630) 407-8700 or visit website www.dupageco.org/courts/ to find out how to do this.

If you fail to do so, a judgment by default may be taken against you for the relief asked in the complaint. If you do not appear as instructed in this summons you may be required to support the child named in this petition until the child is at least eighteen (18) years old. You may also have to pay the pregnancy and delivery costs of the mother.

To the Officer

This summons must be returned by the officer or other person to whom it was given for service, with endorsement of service and fees, if any, immediately after service and not less than twenty one (21) days before the date of appearance. If service cannot be made, this summons shall be returned so endorsed.

E-filing is now mandatory for documents in civil cases with limited exemptions. To e-file, you must first create an account with an e-filing service provider. Visit http://efile.illinoiscourts.gov/service-providers.htm to learn more and to select a service provider. If you need additional help or have trouble e-filing, visit http://www.illinoiscourts.gov/FAQ/gethelp.asp or talk to your circuit clerk's office.If you cannot e-file, you may be able to get an exemption that allows you to file in-person or by mail. Ask your local clerk for more information or visit www.illinoislegalaid.org.

DATE OF SERVICE

TO BE INSERTED BY OFFICER ON COPY LEFT WITH DEFENDANT OR OTHER PERSON

Name: ______ ☐ Pro Se

DuPage Attorney Number: ______

Attorney for: ______

Address: ______

City/State/Zip: ______

Telephone Number: ______

Email: ______

WITNESS:

CANDICE ADAMS, Clerk of the Eighteenth Judicial Circuit Court, and the seal thereof, Wheaton, Illinois

______
Date

______
Clerk of the Eighteenth Judicial Circuit

NOTICE TO PLAINTIFF or PLAINTIFF'S ATTORNEY:
When preparing the above summons, you insert a date not less than 21 days nor more than 40 days after date of issuance.

NOTE:
The filing of an appearance or answer with the Circuit Court Clerk requires a statutory filing fee, payable at the time of filing. If you are unable to pay your court fees, you can apply for a fee waiver. For information about defending yourself in a court case (including filing an appearance or fee waiver), or to apply for free legal help, go to www.illinoislegalaid.org. You can also ask your local circuit clerk's office for a free waiver application.

SHERIFF'S RETURN

I certify that I served this document on defendant(s) as follows:

☐ (a) Individual defendants - **personal**:
By leaving a copy and a copy of the complaint with each individual defendant personally

☐ (b) Individual defendants - **abode**:
By leaving a copy and a copy of the complaint at the usual place of abode of each individual defendant with a person of his/her family, of the age of 13 years or upwards, informing the person of the contents and also by sending a copy of the summons in a sealed envelope with postage fully prepaid, addressed to each individual defendant at his usual place of abode.

☐ (c) Corporation defendants:
By leaving a copy and a copy of the complaint with the registered agent, officer or agent of each defendant corporation.

☐ (d) Other services:
____

☐ (e) Unable to serve:
By ______________________ Badge No. ______________

Name of Defendant ______________	Name of Defendant ______________
Name of Person summons given to ______________	Name of Person summons given to ______________
Sex _____ Race _____ Approximate age _____	Sex _____ Race _____ Approximate. age _____
Place of service ______________	Place of service ______________
City , State ______________	City , State ______________
Date of service ________ Time ______	Date of service ________ Time ______
Date of Mailing ______________	Date of Mailing ______________
	Sheriff of ______________ County
Special Process Server of ______________	County Illinois License # ______________
	By ______________

Twelve

Post-Decree Litigation

Overview

At the end of a court action, with the entry of a final judgment, parties think they have resolved their legal issues once and for all. However, life is long, and circumstances change. For example, a parent may lose the job they held at the time of judgment, or a parent may remarry and move out of state. Moreover, new issues can arise as children mature and their needs change. As you read, consider whether the IMDMA provides the guidance needed to address the myriad changes parents experience during the years their children are growing up.

Change in Circumstances after Entry of Judgment

Financial Matters

Child Support

A child support order runs, like the meter in a taxi cab, until further order of the court. The order may be modified upon a showing of a substantial change in circumstances.[1]

> **EXAMPLE** When the judgment of dissolution is entered, Mother is the primary residential parent of the parties' two children. One year later, Son moves in with Father. This is a substantial change in circumstances.

In the alternative, child support can be modified without the necessity of showing a substantial change in circumstances, upon a showing of an inconsistency of at least 20%, but no less than $10 per month, between the amount of the existing order and the amount of child support that would result from the application of the child support guidelines.[2]

EXAMPLE A child support order is based on Husband's salary as an apprentice heavy equipment operator. When he completes the apprenticeship, his income increases from $24/hour to $40/hour. The difference between the existing order and an order based on his new income is over 20%.

Finally, a child support order can be modified to provide for the child's health care through health insurance or other means.[3]

EXAMPLE Father was ordered to provide health insurance for the minor children. Father loses his job, and, with it, his employer-sponsored health insurance. Mother enrolls the children on her policy, and their child support obligations are adjusted accordingly.

Spousal Maintenance

An order for maintenance, like an order for child support, may only be modified or terminated upon a showing of a substantial change in circumstances. In making the determination, the court considers both the factors used in setting the initial award and the following:

(1) Any change in the employment status of either party and whether the change has been made in good faith;

(2) The efforts, if any, made by the party receiving maintenance to become self-supporting, and the reasonableness of the efforts where they are appropriate;

(3) Any impairment of the present and future earning capacity of either party;

(4) The tax consequences of the maintenance payments upon the respective economic circumstances of the parties;

(5) The duration of the maintenance payments previously paid (and remaining to be paid) relative to the length of the marriage;

(6) The property, including retirement benefits, awarded to each party under the judgment of dissolution of marriage, judgment of legal separation, or judgment of declaration of invalidity of marriage and the present status of the property;

(7) The increase or decrease in each party's income since the prior judgment or order from which a review, modification, or termination is being sought;

(8) The property acquired and currently owned by each party after the entry of the judgment of dissolution of marriage, judgment of legal separation, or judgment of declaration of invalidity of marriage; and

(9) Any other factor that the court expressly finds to be just and equitable.[4]

> **EXAMPLE** Wife stays at home with the children when they are small. At the time the judgment for dissolution is entered, she is unemployed. She has not worked for ten years and her computer skills are out of date. She is awarded six years of maintenance. Over the next two years, wife obtains a certificate in paralegal studies and begins working at a litigation firm in the Loop. During that time, Husband's company has been acquired, and his job in the new firm is at a substantially lower salary. Wife is earning almost as much as Husband. Husband's petition for modification of maintenance will likely succeed, based on Factor (1).

Subsequent Only

"The provisions of any judgment respecting maintenance or support may be modified only as to installments accruing subsequent to due notice by the moving party of the filing of the motion for modification."[5]

> **EXAMPLE** Father is ordered to pay child support for five children. Over the next six years, three children emancipate. Only then does Father file a petition to modify child support. If granted, only the payments accruing after the petition is filed will be reduced.

Children-Related Issues

Allocation of Parental Responsibility: Decision-Making

In the interest of stability for the child who has been through the upheaval of a divorce, an allocation of decision-making cannot be modified for two years. The only exception is if the court finds, based on affidavits, that there is reason to believe the child's present environment may seriously endanger the child's mental, moral, or physical health or significantly impair the child's emotional development.[6]

EXAMPLE A PAJ is entered giving Mother sole allocation of parental responsibility for decision-making. One year later, Mother's boyfriend moves into the marital home and sets up a methamphetamine lab. Father files a petition to modify the allocation of parental decision-making responsibilities. A court would likely find this meets the serious endangerment standard.

After two years, a two-part standard must be satisfied before the court will modify the allocation of parental responsibilities: decision-making.[7]

First, a substantial change in circumstances must have occurred in the circumstances of the child or of either parent since the entry of the parenting plan or PAJ. Second, a modification must be necessary to serve the child's best interests.

EXAMPLE Three years after the PAJ is entered giving Mother sole decision-making authority, Mother enrolls in college. Having married right out of high school, Mother is fascinated by the world of new ideas she is experiencing. She begins using psychedelic drugs and random students "crash" on her couch. Child, now a young teen, is anxious and upset by the strangers living in his house. He resigns from his position as captain of the tennis team. Unable to concentrate in school, he fails two classes. He wants to move in with Father, who is a librarian. Father can allege the two-part standard of substantial change and necessity of modification to serve Child's best interest.

Allocation of Parental Responsibility: Parenting Time

The allocation of parenting time is not subject to the two-year bar. It may be modified upon a showing of changed circumstances that necessitate a modification to serve the child's best interests.[8]

EXAMPLE Mother and Father divorce when son is 10. Father is awarded parenting time on alternating weekends. At age 11, Son progresses from park district to travel hockey. Because of his out-of-town tournaments, he is away on Father's parenting time. Father's parenting time can be modified.

Finally, the court can modify an allocation of decision-making or parenting time without a showing of any change if the modification is in the child's best interest and any of the following apply:

> (1) The modification reflects the actual arrangement under which the child has been receiving care, without parental objection, for the six months preceding the filing of the petition for modification; or
>
> (2) The modification constitutes a minor modification in the parenting plan or allocation judgment; or
>
> (3) The modification is necessary to modify an agreed parenting plan or allocation judgment that the court would not have ordered or approved had the court been aware of the circumstances at the time of the order or approval; or
>
> (4) The parties agree to the modification.[9]

EXAMPLE Although their parenting time schedule provides for the children to be returned to Mother's house on Monday morning, the parents agree that it's easier for the children to be returned on Sunday night. The parents can modify without a change pursuant to Factor (4) above.

Sanctions

Because of the potential for a parent to use petitions to modify allocation of parental responsibilities in inappropriate contexts, the law provides that "attorney's fees and costs shall be assessed against a party seeking modification if the court finds that the modification action is vexatious or constitutes harassment. If the court finds that a parent has repeatedly filed frivolous motions for modification, the court may bar the parent from filing a motion for modification for a period of time."[10] Additionally, the court may require the offending party to seek leave of court before filing any further motions.

EXAMPLE Mother and Father enter a PAJ and work well together until Mother gets a Boyfriend. Father, representing himself, files one motion to modify after another, alleging that Boyfriend affects the child's best interest. Each time, Mother retains an attorney to contest the motions. The court can find the motions frivolous and bar Father from filing for two years.

Comparison between Modification of Decision-Making and Parenting Time

	Modify Decision-Making	Modify Parenting Time	Modify Either
Timing	Two-year bar with narrow exception: environment may seriously endanger child	No bar	No bar
Requires facts not known at entry?	Yes	No	No
Change required?	Substantial change	Change	No change required if modification is minor, parties agree, or reflects actual arrangement

Restriction at Any Time

If the court finds a parent engaged in any conduct that seriously endangered the child's mental, moral, or physical health or significantly impaired the child's emotional development, the court can enter orders to protect the child.[11] Please note: a motion to modify the allocation of parental responsibilities is allowed if a parent's conduct *might endanger* the child. A motion to restrict requires an allegation a parent *did endanger* the child.

> **EXAMPLE** Mother arrives at Father's house to pick up Child, age three, at the start of Mother's parenting time. Father, under the influence of opiates, is unconscious on the couch. Child, crying and confused, has been trying to wake him up. Mother's attorney files a motion to restrict parenting time.

When a court finds a parent met the standard, the statute provides a wide range of options to enable the court to craft an appropriate restriction. These options include:

> (1) A reduction, elimination, or other adjustment of the parent's decision-making responsibilities or parenting time, or both decision-making responsibilities and parenting time;

(2) Supervision, including ordering the Department of Children and Family Services to exercise continuing supervision under Section 5 of the Children and Family Services Act;

(3) Requiring the exchange of the child between the parents through an intermediary or in a protected setting;

(4) Restraining a parent's communication with or proximity to the other parent or the child;

(5) Requiring a parent to abstain from possessing or consuming alcohol or non-prescribed drugs while exercising parenting time with the child and within a specified period immediately preceding the exercise of parenting time;

(6) Restricting the presence of specific persons while a parent is exercising parenting time with the child;

(7) Requiring a parent to post a bond to secure the return of the child following the parent's exercise of parenting time or to secure other performance required by the court;

(8) Requiring a parent to complete a treatment program for perpetrators of abuse, for drug or alcohol abuse, or for other behavior that is the basis for restricting parental responsibilities under this Section; and

(9) Any other constraints or conditions that the court deems necessary to provide for the child's safety or welfare.[12]

EXAMPLE The court suspends Father's parenting time and requires him to be evaluated for drug abuse. Depending on the results of the drug tests, the court may permit supervised parenting time.

Parent's Relocation

Until 2016, the parent awarded majority parenting time could move anywhere within the state of Illinois without the other parent's agreement. A long-distance move significantly impacted the non-residential parent's ability to exercise parenting time.

In 2016, the law changed to protect the rights of the non-residential parent by restricting the distance the residential parent could move from the marital residence without the other party's agreement.[13] In Cook and the collar counties, the distance is 25 miles.[14] In other counties, it is 50 miles.[15] And finally, in all counties, the distance for an out-of-state move is 25 miles.

Notice Requirement

First, a parent intending relocation must provide written notice of the relocation to the other parent under the parenting plan or allocation judgment.[16] A copy of the notice is filed with the clerk of the circuit court. The notice must provide at least 60 days written notice before the relocation if possible.

If the non-relocating parent signs the notice, indicating his agreement to the relocation, the parent is free to relocate. As long as the relocation is in the child's best interests, the court will modify the parenting plan to reflect the modification.[17]

However, if the non-relocating parent does not sign the notice, the parent seeking relocation must file a petition seeking permission to relocate.[18]

EXAMPLE Parents live in Kendall County at the time of their dissolution. Kimberly, the mother, and the children remain in the marital residence. Three years after the date of dissolution, Kimberly becomes engaged to a City of Chicago police officer and wants to move the children to his home in Chicago, a distance of 53 miles. Kimberly files a Notice of Intended Relocation. The father, Jeremy, refuses to sign. Kimberly must file a Petition for Relocation.

Factors the Court Considers

The IMDMA gives the court authority to modify a parenting plan or allocation judgment in accordance with the child's best interests. In making the determination, the court considers the following factors:

(1) The circumstances and reasons for the intended relocation;

(2) The reasons, if any, why a parent is objecting to the intended relocation;

(3) The history and quality of each parent's relationship with the child and specifically whether a parent has substantially failed or refused to exercise the parental responsibilities allocated to him or her under the parenting plan or allocation judgment;

(4) The educational opportunities for the child at the existing location and at the proposed new location;

(5) The presence or absence of extended family at the existing location and at the proposed new location;

(6) The anticipated impact of the relocation on the child;

(7) Whether the court will be able to fashion a reasonable allocation of parental responsibilities between all parents if the relocation occurs;

(8) The wishes of the child, taking into account the child's maturity and ability to express reasoned and independent preferences as to relocation;

(9) Possible arrangements for the exercise of parental responsibilities appropriate to the parents' resources and circumstances and the developmental level of the child;

(10) Minimization of the impairment to a parent-child relationship caused by a parent's relocation; and

(11) Any other relevant factors bearing on the child's best interests.[19]

EXAMPLE Mother and the children live in an apartment in the Chicago suburbs, where she works minimum wage jobs. Three years after entry of the judgment of dissolution, Mother receives an offer of employment in Springfield, Illinois. As it is a government position, she will have job security and excellent benefits. Further, the cost of living is less than in the Chicago suburbs. She will be able to afford a house. The court will consider these factors.

Please note: a petition for relocation is always considered a substantial change in circumstances, as must be alleged before filing a petition to modify the allocation of parental responsibility: decision-making.[20]

EXAMPLE After Mother files a petition for relocation, Father files a motion to modify allocation of parental responsibilities. The court appoints a GAL to determine the best interests of the children under the dueling petitions: are they better served moving to Springfield with Mother or staying in the Chicago suburbs with Father?

Finally, in the case of subsequent moves, the distance from the newest home is compared to the original home.[21]

EXAMPLE Rather than file a petition for relocation and risk a potential motion to modify from Jeremy, Kimberly decides to stay in the marital residence in Kendall County. One year later, Kimberly moves from Oswego to Countryside, a distance of 31.6 miles by internet mapping service. She can do so without Jeremy's agreement. Kimberly then prepares to move from Countryside to the south side of Chicago, a distance of 22.5 miles. As the total distance from Oswego to the south side is over 50 miles, she can only move with Jeremy's agreement or the court's permission.

The Non-Minor Child

Although an obligation to pay child support ends when the child turns 18 (or graduates from high school, whichever is later), the IMDMA authorizes courts to impose financial obligations on divorced parents of non-minor children in two instances.

Educational Expenses for a Non-Minor Child

First, "the court may award sums of money out of the property and income of either or both parties or the estate of a deceased parent, as equity may require, for the educational expenses of any child of the parties."[22]

In making this award, a court considers the resources of the non-minor child as well as the parents.[23] Parents may have contributed to an account in a state tuition program under Section 529 of the Internal Revenue Code. Amounts contributed prior to the judgment of dissolution are considered a resource of the child. Courts may also consider scholarships to be part of the children's portion.[24]

> **EXAMPLE** Courtney plans to attend Joliet Community College which costs $10,000 per year. After examining Courtney's and her parents' incomes, the court allocates $4,0000 per year to Mother and $4,000 per year to Father. Courtney has received a $2,000 scholarship which the court considers her contribution.

Covered Expenses

Educational expenses may include, but are not limited to, the following: tuition, fees, books, housing expenses, medical expenses (including medical insurance), and dental expenses.[25] Additionally, the reasonable living expenses of the child during the academic year and periods of recess are included.[26]

Only In-State Tuition

The tuition, fees, and housing costs are capped at the in-state student costs at the University of Illinois, Urbana-Champaign.[27]

> **EXAMPLE** Child applies to and is accepted at Harvard, where tuition alone is $70,000 per year. Mother files a petition asking Father to pay. The court will only base an award on the cost of tuition at the University of Illinois, Urbana-Champaign, which is $17,572–$22,836 for the 2023-24 academic year. Father is ordered to pay $10,000. Mother can pay the difference if she wants to.

Other Conditions

The child must sign any consent necessary for the educational institution to provide a supporting party with access to the child's academic transcripts, records, and grade reports.[28]

In addition, support ends if the child attains the age of 23; receives a baccalaureate degree; or marries.[29] Finally, support ends if the child fails to maintain a cumulative "C" grade point average, except in the event of illness or other good cause shown.[30]

EXAMPLE Mother files a petition for post-secondary expenses. The court orders both parents to pay 33% of Student's tuition at the College of Lake County. After attending one year, Student develops clinical depression and is unable to attend school. By the time she is diagnosed, she is failing all her classes. As she failed to maintain a "C" average because of illness, she is likely excused.

EXAMPLE In contrast, after attending one year, Student forms a relationship with a classmate and skips class to socialize with him. At the end of the semester, Mother learns Student has gotten C's and D's in all of her classes. Her failure to maintain a "C" average is likely not excused.

Subsequent Only

An order for support can only be made for the time after the petition is filed.[31]

EXAMPLE Child enrolls in college in August. Mother files a petition in January. The court can order an obligation starting in January.

Factors the Court Considers

The IMDMA provides factors to guide the court in making an award for educational expenses for a non-minor child, including:

(1) The present and future financial resources of both parties to meet their needs, including, but not limited to, savings for retirement;

(2) The standard of living the child would have enjoyed had the marriage not been dissolved;

(3) The financial resources of the child; and

(4) The child's academic performance.[32]

EXAMPLE Mother files a petition for post-secondary educational expenses. Father, age 56, just started his first job that offers a 401(k) and has contributed $2,000 to it. Contributing to college would prevent him from saving for retirement. The court likely finds he does not have the present or future financial resources (per Factor (1)).

As opposed to an award of child support, which only considers the child's parent's income, in an award of post-secondary expenses, the court can consider the total financial resources available to the child's parent, including those provided by a new spouse.[33]

EXAMPLE In the example above, presume Father is married to a wealthy widow who receives over $750,000 each year in dividends. Given his total resources, his lack of retirement income is less important. The court may order him to contribute.

Support for a Non-Minor Child with a Disability

The second time a court may order support for a non-minor child is when the non-minor child is mentally or physically disabled and not otherwise emancipated.[34]

Definition

The IMDMA defines a "disabled" individual as one who has a physical or mental impairment that substantially limits a major life activity, has a record of such an impairment, or is regarded as having such an impairment.[35] Because the statute does not provide a specific list of impairments, a hearing is often required.

EXAMPLE Student was diagnosed with ADHD during high school, where she had an Individualized Education Program (IEP). Since graduating, she has developed extreme anxiety and is unable to work or attend college. Now aged 19, Student spends the day playing video games. Father thinks some "tough love" is needed; however, Mother has worked more closely with Student's doctors and teachers. Mother files a petition for support for a non-minor child with a disability, asking Father to contribute to food, housing, and therapy costs. A hearing may be required to determine if a disability exists.

Age of Disability

Even though the application for support may be made after the child has attained majority, "the disability that is the basis for the application for support must have arisen while the child was eligible for child support."[36]

EXAMPLE Kevin is diagnosed with autism at the age of two. He is non-verbal and can only be left alone for short periods. While he receives Social Security, it is not enough to compensate Mother, with whom he lives, for caregivers when she is at work. When Kevin turns 18, Mother can file a petition for support from Father.

EXAMPLE In contrast, Andrew suffers a closed head injury in a motorcycle accident at the age of 21. He will require live-in care for the rest of his life. Mother cannot petition for support from Father. Father is not prevented from offering, though.

Factors the Court Considers

The IMDMA provides factors to guide the court in making an award for a non-minor child with a disability, including:

> (1) The present and future financial resources of both parties to meet their needs, including, but not limited to, savings for retirement;
>
> (2) The standard of living the child would have enjoyed had the marriage not been dissolved;
>
> (3) The financial resources of the child; and
>
> (4) Any financial or other resource provided to or for the child including, but not limited to, any Supplemental Security Income, any home-based support provided pursuant to the Home-Based Support Services Law for Mentally Disabled Adults, and any other state, federal, or local benefit available to the non-minor disabled child.[37]

EXAMPLE During their marriage, Father worked in a factory and Mother drove a school bus. Their standard of living was modest. Father's current income and resources meet his needs, with very little left over. Factors (1) and (2) apply.

Non-Compliance with an Order

The post-decree motions for modification of financial support or allocation of parental responsibilities and the petitions for relocation, college costs, or support for a non-minor child with a disability are filed and served pursuant to standard motion practice. (See Chapter 5, Temporary Motions and the Financial Affidavit.)

However, the law provides a different pleading when one party fails to comply with a court order.[38] The pleading, called a petition for rule to show cause, requires the non-complying party to explain why they should not be found in contempt for failure to comply with a court order.

Financial Orders

Failures to comply most often occur with orders to pay spousal maintenance, child support, or child-related expenses.

EXAMPLE The parties are ordered to split extracurricular expenses on a 50/50 basis, payable within 14 days. Mother pays $12,000, the cost for Son to participate in one year of travel hockey, and sends proof of payment to Father. Father does not respond. Mother files a petition for rule to show cause for Father's non-compliance with the order.

Non-Financial Orders

A petition for rule to show cause can be brought if a party fails to comply with a non-financial order. For example, the MSA may require a party to obtain life insurance or refinance property. If a parent fails to comply with a provision of the PAJ, such as not speaking disparagingly about the other parent in front of the children, an action can be brought. But these actions are hard to prove and even harder to enforce.

Procedure

The Petition

When one party has not complied with an order, the other party files a petition for rule to show cause, identifying the order that was not complied with and specifying how the party failed to comply. If the petition is verified, the petitioner has established a *prima facie* case of civil contempt. This means the petitioner has "produced enough evidence to allow the fact-trier to infer the fact at issue and rule in the party's favor."[39]

> **EXAMPLE** Father does not pay his court-ordered child support. When he is $4,000 behind, Mother's attorney files a verified petition for rule to show cause with the court and serves Father by mail.

The Rule

On the date the petition is presented, the court can issue the rule, a document similar to a summons in that it compels the respondent to appear in court for a hearing. The rule indicates the amount the respondent is out of compliance. It is called the "purge amount" because it is the amount the respondent must pay to purge himself of the contempt.

> **EXAMPLE** At the first court date, the rule issues. The purge amount is set at $4,000 and the hearing date is scheduled 28 days ahead.

Service of the Rule

If the respondent does not appear for the hearing, he can be taken into custody and held in jail for contempt of court. Because of the possibility of confinement, the rule must be personally served on the respondent. If the respondent or his attorney is in court for the presentment of the petition for rule to show cause, as a matter of professional courtesy, they will accept service. If not, the sheriff must serve the respondent.

> **EXAMPLE** Father, representing himself, accepts the rule.

The Hearing

At the hearing, the burden shifts to the respondent to explain why they should not be held in contempt. Perhaps the respondent had complied (but the check got lost in the mail) or the failure to comply was not willful (because he had been injured at work).

If the respondent does not appear for the hearing, the court can issue a writ for body attachment for indirect civil contempt, which commands the Sheriff of the County and all Peace Officers in the State of Illinois to take custody of the respondent. If the respondent appears and is found in contempt, the judge can impose incarceration.

EXAMPLE At the hearing, Father explains he did not pay child support because he has a new girlfriend with expensive tastes. The judge imposes incarceration. Father is put in handcuffs by the deputies.

Incarceration for contempt is not for a fixed period of time; it is until the contempt is purged. In essence, the contemptor has the keys to the jail cell in his pocket.

EXAMPLE Later in the day, Father's new girlfriend pays the $4,000 purge amount, and Father is released from jail.

Attorney's Fees

In Illinois, parties pay their own attorney's fees unless permitted by statute or contract. The IMDMA provides "that in every proceeding for the enforcement of an order or judgment when the court finds that the failure to comply was without compelling cause or justification, the court shall order the party against whom the proceedings is brought to pay the costs and reasonable attorney's fees of the prevailing party."[40]

EXAMPLE Having learned at the hearing that Father's failure to pay child support was due to the trip to Las Vegas he took with his new girlfriend, Mother files a petition for attorney's fees. The court finds this failure was without compelling cause or justification and orders him to pay Mother's attorney's fees.

Chapter Summary

A judgment for dissolution, incorporating a marital settlement agreement and a parenting allocation judgment, resolves all issues as they existed at the time of judgment. However, changes may occur which necessitate post-decree action. A parent's income may change, through a promotion or job loss, necessitating a change in the award of spousal maintenance or child support. Or, a change may occur in the life of the parent or children such that modification of the allocation of parental responsibilities is necessary to serve the child's best interests.

While child support ends when a child reaches maturity, the court can impose financial obligations on parents of a non-minor child in two instances: to pay for post-secondary educational expenses and the care of a non-minor child with a disability.

Finally, a parent may not comply with an order or portion of the judgment for dissolution (or PAJ) entered by the court. The law provides a remedy called the petition for rule to show cause, which calls the non-complying parent into court to explain why he should not be held in contempt. If the court finds the non-compliance was without justification, the court can award attorney's fees to the petitioner.

Key Terms

Substantial Change in Circumstances

Accruing subsequent

Serious Endangerment

Sanctions

Relocation

Petition for Rule to Show Cause

Discussion Questions

1. Should a substantial financial change require both an increase in the parent's income and the children's needs? Or is an increase in the parent's income enough?
2. What is the purpose behind the two-year "freeze" on modifying an allocation of parental responsibilities: decision-making?
3. Why is there a freeze on an allocation of decision-making but not parenting time?

4. Why is a new spouse's income considered in a parent's contribution to post-secondary educational expenses but not in the calculation of child support?
5. Married parents can't be ordered to pay their children's college expenses. Should divorced parents? Is this a violation of Equal Protection?
6. Should an order to contribute to post-secondary education be limited to academic institutions? What if the non-minor child wants to pursue a non-academic vocation? What if the school is a for-profit institution or unaccredited?
7. The Family Educational Rights and Privacy Act (FERPA) is a federal law that protects the privacy of student educational records. To be awarded college expenses under the IMDMA, students have to waive these statutory privacy protections. Is it fair to require disclosure as a condition for financial support? If so, should they have to waive medical privacy protections to remain covered by their parent's medical insurance? How are they the same? How are they different?
8. The IMDMA allows support for a non-minor child with a disability. However, "disabled" is defined differently in the IMDMA than it is in the Probate Act. *See* 755 ILCS 5/11(a)(2). Should the definition be the same? Why or why not?
9. What is the policy behind requiring the disability to start during the period children are eligible for child support but not after?

Forms

1. Petition for Rule to Show Cause

   https://cic.countyofkane.org/eForms/P1-CS-006-E.pdf
2. The Rule

   https://cic.countyofkane.org/eForms/P2-MISC-007-E.pdf
3. The Mittimus

   https://cic.countyofkane.org/eForms/P2-D-007-E.pdf
4. Motion to Increase/Decrease/Terminate Support

   https://www.circuitclerkofwillcounty.com/Court-Forms/petition-to-reduce-increase-or-terminate-support-18e-part-4

Endnotes

1. 750 ILCS 5/510(a)(1) (West, Westlaw Classic through P.A. 103-21 of the 2023 Reg. Sess.).
2. *Id.* § 510(a)(2)(A).
3. *Id.* § 510(a)(2)(B).
4. *Id.* § 510(a-5)(1-9).
5. *Id.* § 510(a).
6. *Id.* § 610.5(a).
7. 750 ILCS 5/610.5(c).
8. *Id.* § 610.5(a).
9. *Id.* § 610.5(e)(1-4).
10. *Id.* § 610(f).
11. *Id.* § 603.10(a).
12. *Id.* § 603.10(a)(1-9).
13. 750 ILCS 5/609.2.
14. *Id.* § 600 (g)(1). Cook, DuPage, Kane, Lake, McHenry, or Will.
15. *Id.* § 600 (g)(2).
16. *Id.* § 609.2(c).
17. *Id.* § 609.2(e).
18. *Id.* § 609.2(f).
19. 750 ILCS 5/609.2(g)(1-11).
20. *Id.* § 609.2(a).
21. *Id.* § 609.2(h).
22. *Id.* § 513(a).
23. *Id.* § 513(j)(3).
24. In re Marriage of Gallagher, 2014 IL App (4th) 130481-U, ¶ 13. Not reported in N.E.2d. 2014 WL 3373450.
25. 750 ILCS 5/513(d).
26. *Id.* § 513(d)(4).
27. *Id.* § 513(d)(1-2).
28. *Id.* § 513(f).
29. *Id.* § 513(g).
30. *Id.*
31. 750 ILCS 5/513(k).
32. *Id.* § 513(j)(1-4).
33. *Id.* § 513(j)(1).
34. *Id.* § 513.5(a).
35. *Id.* § 513.5(c).
36. *Id.* § 513.5(a).
37. 750 ILCS 5/513.5(b)(1-4).
38. *Id.* § 511(a).
39. *Prima Facie Case*, BLACK'S LAW DICTIONARY (11th ed. 2019).
40. 750 ILCS 5/508(b).

PRINT

CLEAR

IN THE CIRCUIT COURT OF THE TWELFTH JUDICIAL CIRCUIT
WILL COUNTY, ILLINOIS

____
Petitioner
vs

______________________________ CASE NO: ______________________________
Respondent

PETITION FOR RULE TO SHOW CAUSE FOR INDIRECT CIVIL CONTEMPT

NOW COMES Petitioner/Respondent, (Circle one) ______________________________, petitions this Honorable Court, pursuant to Statute, to enter a Rule to Show Cause against Petitioner/Respondent, (Circle one) ______________________________, to be held in indirect civil contempt of this Court.

1. A Judgment of Dissolution of Marriage/Civil Union (or order) was entered on ______________________________, 20 _____, which awards the following:
____
____
______________________________.

2. That Petitioner/Respondent, (Circle one) ______________________________, violated the Judgment or Order as follows:
____
____
______________________________.

3. I have tried numerous times, without success to remedy the situation.

4. Petitioner/Respondent's (Circle one) actions are willful, contumacious and without just cause.

5. A copy of the Judgment (or court order) is attached.

WHEREFORE, the Petitioner/Respondent, (Circle one) ______________________________, respectfully requests that the Petition for Rule to Show Cause be entered against Petitioner/Respondent, (Circle one) ______________________________ seeking the following relief:

A. That Rule issues requiring Petitioner/Respondent, (Circle one) ______________________________, to appear and show cause if any as to why he/she should not be held in indirect civil contempt of this Court, that upon a finding of contempt, the Court enter such sanction and additional relief that it deems just.

____
(Signature)

ANDREA LYNN CHASTEEN, CLERK OF THE CIRCUIT COURT OF WILL COUNTY

CERTIFICATE

Under penalties of perjury as provided by law pursuant to Section 1-109 of the Code of Civil Procedure, the undersigned certifies the statements set forth in this instrument are true and correct, except as to matters therein stated to be on information and belief, and as to such matters, the undersigned certifies as aforesaid that he/she verily believe the same to be true.

____
(Signature)

Attorney or Party, if not represented by an Attorney
Name ______________________________
ARDC # ______________________________
Firm Name ______________________________
Attorney for ______________________________
Address ______________________________
City & Zip ______________________________
Telephone ______________________________

ANDREA LYNN CHASTEEN, CLERK OF THE CIRCUIT COURT OF WILL COUNTY

2. RULE TO SHOW CAUSE

IN THE CIRCUIT COURT OF THE SIXTEENTH JUDICIAL CIRCUIT
KANE COUNTY, ILLINOIS

Case No. ______________________

Plaintiff/Petitioner	Defendant/Respondent	File Stamp

RULE TO SHOW CAUSE

Rule to Show Cause Directed To:
☐ Defendant ☐ Third Party

Name:

Address:

City, State, Zip:

To Appear at: ☐ Kane County Judical Center, 37W777 Rt. 38, St. Charles IL ☐ Kane County Courthouse, 100 S. Third St., Geneva, IL

Date: ____________________ Time: ______________

Room No.: ________ Judge: ____________________

NOTICE
IF YOU FAIL TO APPEAR BEFORE THE COURT AT THE TIME AND PLACE SET FORTH ABOVE, YOU MAY BE TAKEN INTO CUSTODY AND HELD IN JAIL WITHOUT FURTHER NOTICE.

Name:

Atty. for:

Address:

City, State, Zip:

Phone:

RETURN

I Certify that on ____________________ I served this writ on the within named ____________________ by leaving a copy with him/her personally and informing him/her of its contents.

____
Sheriff

By ______________________________ Deputy

Fees - Service and Return.............	______________
Miles...	______________
Total..	______________

P2-MISC-007 (12/08)

THIS MATTER coming on before the Court:
☐ for hearing on Citation to Discover Assets
☐ on motion of Plaintiff

The Court finding that service and/or notice of these proceedings having been properly given, the Respondent appearing not, the Court being fully advised in the premises and having jurisdiction of parties and subject matter;

IT IS SO ORDERED that the party herein named shall appear at the time and place stated herein to show cause if any he/she may have, why he/she should not be held in Civil Contempt of Court:

☐ for his/her failure to appear before this Court on ______________ to answer and respond to a Citation to Discover Assets heretofore served upon him/her as provided by law.

☐ for his/her failure to obey an Order of this Court entered on ____________________ , requiring him/her to make installment payments of ______________ per __________ ,in satisfaction of this judgment.

☐ for his/her failure to obey the Order of Court entered on ____________________ .

IT IS FURTHER ORDERED that Respondent be personally served a certified copy of this order.

ENTER: ______________________________
(Judge)

3. MITTIMUS FOR CONTEMPT

ORDER - MITTIMUS FOR CONTEMPT - NON PAYMENT CHILD SUPPORT 3431 (Rev. 12/20)

STATE OF ILLINOIS **UNITED STATES OF AMERICA** **COUNTY OF DU PAGE**
IN THE CIRCUIT COURT OF THE EIGHTEENTH JUDICIAL CIRCUIT

IN RE THE MARRIAGE OF

____
PETITIONER

vs

____
RESPONDENT

____
CASE NUMBER

File Stamp Here

MITTIMUS FOR CONTEMPT

This cause having come on for hearing on the return of a Rule to Show Cause, heretofore entered on ______________ and the Respondent, ______________________ being present in open Court, and the Court having heard testimony and being fully advised in the premises FINDS:

1. That the Court has jurisdiction of the subject matter and the parties hereto.
2. That the Respondent was ordered to pay $______________ per ______________ Child Support commencing ______________ .

The Respondent was further ordered to pay $ ______________ per ______________ towards an arrearage of $ ______________ .

The Respondent has willfully refused to comply with this order, thereby causing an arrearage $ ______________ .

IT IS HEREBY ORDERED, ADJUDGED AND DECREED:

A. The Respondent, ______________________ is hereby held in Indirect Civil Contempt of Court for the willful failure to pay $ ______________ .

B. That a mittimus is issued directing that the said Respondent be taken into custody by the Sheriff of DuPage County and held until further order of Court, unless the Respondent shall purge himself/herself of the said contempt by paying to the Clerk of the Circuit Court the sum of $ ______________ * for the benefit of the petitioner. The Respondent is further obligated to remain current with all child support obligations. The drivers license suspension is hereby stayed.

*** No personal checks accepted**

☐ It is further ordered that the issuance of the Mittimus is stayed to ______________ at the hour of ______ at which time the Respondent, if he/she has not previously purged himself/herself, shall appear before the court in room __________ or the court will issue a body attachment forthwith without further order.

Name: ______________________ ☐ Pro Se

DuPage Attorney Number: ______________________

Attorney for: ______________________

Address: ______________________

City/State/Zip: ______________________

Telephone Number: ______________________

Email: ______________________

____
Judge

Date: ______________________

CANDICE ADAMS, CLERK OF THE 18th JUDICIAL CIRCUIT COURT ©
WHEATON, ILLINOIS 60187-0707

4. MOTION TO INCREASE / DECREASE / TERMINATE SUPPORT

PRINT

CLEAR

IN THE CIRCUIT COURT OF THE TWELFTH JUDICIAL CIRCUIT
WILL COUNTY, ILLINOIS

____
Plaintiff
vs

CASE NO: ______________________________

____
Defendant

PETITION

I hereby petition the Court as follows:

❑ Reduce ❑ Increase or ❑ Terminate:
Child support and/or maintenance order of ____________________, 20____, based on the following substantial changes:

____
____
____

❑ Enter a Rule to Show Cause to enforce the Court's order of ________________, 20___, for failure to:
❑ Pay:
❑ Support ❑ Maintenance ❑ Day Care ❑ Extracurricular Expenses
❑ Unreimbursed Medical Expenses ❑ Other (specify):______________________________

from ______________, 20____ to ______________, 20____ in the amount of $______________.

❑ Comply with visitation, specify dates and times: ______________________________
____
____

❑ Other: ____
____
____

❑ Change custody or visitation order of __________________, 20____ for the reasons stated below:
____
____

I hereby state, under the penalty of perjury as provided by the Code of Civil Procedure (735 ILCS 5/1-109) the foregoing to be true and correct, and I have given notice to the other party on ________________, 20____.

____
Petitioner

Name: ______________________________
Address: ______________________________
City/State/Zip: ______________________________
Telephone: ______________________________

ANDREA LYNN CHASTEEN, CLERK OF THE CIRCUIT COURT OF WILL COUNTY

Original– Court Copy – Plaintiff Copy – Defendant **Form 18 E (Part 4)** Revised (12/16)

Thirteen

Domestic Violence

Overview

Domestic violence (or intimate partner violence) is defined as a pattern of physical, sexual, emotional, economic, or psychological abuse committed by a partner with the intent of exerting power and control over the victim.[1] The Center for Disease Control estimates that 41% of women and 26% of men have been victims of domestic violence.[2] Besides being the leading cause of injury to women, domestic violence has a profound effect on the psychological and mental health of victims.

Lawmakers at the state and federal levels have provided a number of legal means to protect victims, especially the most vulnerable, the children. Although this chapter will focus on civil actions in a domestic relations court, as you read, consider the wide range of options available to victims of domestic violence so you are equipped to assist your clients in every way possible.

Legal Means to Protect Victims

State Laws

Criminal Statutes

- 720 ILCS 5/12C Harms to Children;
- 720 ILCS 5/12-3.2 Domestic Battery; and
- 725 ILCS 5/112A-15 Criminal Orders of Protection.

Civil Statutes

- 750 ILCS 60/101 Illinois Domestic Violence Act;
- 325 ILCS 5/101 Abused and Neglected Child Reporting Act; and
- 705 ILCS 405/101 Juvenile Court Act.

The legal options can be used in various combinations depending on the circumstances.

EXAMPLE Mother and Father are the parents of Child, aged eight months old. At the end of a soccer match they are attending with friends, Mother tries to take Child from Father, who resists. Mother slaps, kicks, and scratches Father. A bystander calls 911. The police arrest Mother and charge her with domestic battery. A criminal order of protection is entered, and a Department of Child and Family Services investigation is opened.

EXAMPLE Mother and Father are the parents of Child, aged six years. Father is awarded alternate weekend parenting time; however, he has become increasingly erratic and skips parenting time for several months in a row. Without warning, Father arrives at Mother's house demanding Child on a Wednesday. When Mother refuses to open the door, Father begins pounding on the doors in an attempt to break in. Mother calls 911. While the police make a report, they do not arrest Father; they tell him to go home and sober up. Mother can use the police report as the basis for an order of protection, or possibly an order restricting parenting time.

Federal Laws

Violence Against Women Act (VAWA)

The Violence Against Women Act of 1994 protects women at many levels.[3] In addition to making the violation of protective orders a federal crime, it provides funding to programs for domestic violence victims. Further, it permits the spouse of a United States citizen to self-petition for immigration status.[4]

EXAMPLE Husband, a United States citizen, is married to Wife, a citizen of Thailand. Although Husband can petition for permanent residency on her behalf, he refuses, using her unlawful status to control her. Without a social security number, she cannot work. She has no access to cash. Worst of all, if she is deported she will never see her children again. Wife can self-petition for permanent residency.

Immigration and Nationality Act (INA)

Further relief is provided by the Immigration and Nationality Act.[5] A petition for U visa status allows the victims of crimes, including domestic violence, to remain in the country to assist law enforcement in the prosecution of the crime.[6]

> **EXAMPLE** Rosa, who is undocumented, is the victim of abuse by her husband. Afraid of exposing her unlawful status, she does not go to the police for help. One night, a beating sends her to the hospital, and the police arrest her husband for the crime of domestic battery. If Rosa cooperates with the prosecution, she may be eligible for a U visa status.

The Illinois Domestic Violence Act

The General Assembly enacted the Illinois Domestic Violence Act[7] to support the efforts of victims of domestic violence to avoid further abuse by:

- Promptly entering and diligently enforcing court orders that prohibit abuse;
- Reducing the abuser's access to the victim; and
- Addressing any related issues of child custody and economic support.[8]

Through the support provided by the Act, victims are not trapped in abusive situations by fear of retaliation or the loss of a child, financial support, or accessible housing.

Family or Household Members

Protections in the Illinois Domestic Violence Act apply to family or household members. However, family and household members are broadly defined and include:

1. Spouses;
2. Former spouses;
3. Parents;
4. Children;
5. Stepchildren and other persons related by blood or by present or prior marriage;
6. Persons who share or formerly shared a common dwelling;
7. Persons who have or allegedly have a child in common;
8. Persons who share or allegedly share a blood relationship through a child; and
9. Persons who have or have had a dating or engagement relationship.[9]

EXAMPLE Boyfriend and Girlfriend leased an apartment together while attending the University of Illinois. Boyfriend began using drugs and stopped going to classes. When the lease ended, Boyfriend moved to his parent's basement. As someone who formerly shared a common dwelling, Boyfriend is a family or household member. Should Boyfriend become abusive, Girlfriend could file a petition for an order of protection.

The Definition of Abuse

In addition to expanding the definition of "household," the Act expands the definition of "abuse." The Act protects against non-physical abuse, such as harassment, intimidation of a dependent, interference with personal liberty, or willful deprivation.

EXAMPLE Husband follows Wife to her job as a cashier at Target. He spends the day approaching coworkers, attempting to show them pornographic pictures of Wife on his phone. After work, he follows Wife to the health club and then to a school board meeting. Husband's behavior likely meets the definition of harassment.

The Act also expands the definition of physical abuse, to include sexual abuse and any of the following:

(i) Knowing or reckless use of physical force, confinement, or restraint;

(ii) Knowing, repeated, and unnecessary sleep deprivation; or

(iii) Knowing or reckless conduct which creates an immediate risk of physical harm.[10]

EXAMPLE Because Wife wakes up at 4:30 a.m. to go to work, she goes to bed by 9:30 p.m. Husband intentionally wakes her up multiple times before going to bed himself at midnight. Wife is frantic, sleep deprived, and unable to concentrate at work.

Protections for High-Risk Adults

The Illinois Domestic Violence Act provides two additional protections for adults who are at high risk because of advanced age or disabilities.

Expanded Definition of "Family and Household Members"

First, it expands the definition of "family and household members" to include caregivers.[11]

Expanded Definition of "Abuse"

Second, it expands the definition of "abuse" to include exploitation and neglect.[12]

EXAMPLE Cassandra, age 94, has a live-in caregiver to assist her with the activities of daily living. Once the caregiver discovered Cassandra had a checking account with $100,000 in it, she began writing checks to herself and forcing Cassandra to sign them. One time, when Cassandra refused, the caregiver withheld her pain medication. Cassandra can petition for an order of protection against the caregiver.

Protective Orders for Non-Family or Household Member

Three types of order exist to protect victims from abuse by non-family members. The Firearm Restraining Order Act[13] provides the procedure to obtain orders prohibiting a named person from having in his or her custody or control any firearms. The Civil No Contact Order Act[14] provides the procedure to obtain civil no contact orders and is primarily used in the case of sexual assault. The Stalking No Contact Order Act[15] provides the procedure to obtain civil no contact orders and is primarily used in the case of stalking.

EXAMPLE Mia and Caleb shared an apartment after they graduated from college. Their next-door neighbor developed a fascination with Mia, waiting outside the door for her to leave, entreating her, and leaving gifts on the hood of her car. When Mia rejected him, Neighbor began making threats, following her, and looking through the apartment windows. Mia can request a stalking no contact order.

"Restraining Order" Distinguished from "Protective Order"

A "restraining order" is often used as a generic term for a protective order; however, the orders differ in two ways: duration and means of enforcement. Presume that Hunter who had been restrained from withdrawing funds from a joint bank account in Chapter 5 becomes so angry that he physically assaults Abigail. In addition to the restraining order, Abigail obtains a two-year order of protection.

Time

A restraining order prohibits a party from specific behavior during the pendency of an action.

> **EXAMPLE** Judgment for dissolution is entered one month after Hunter assaults Abigail, dividing the funds in the bank account equally between the parties. The restraining order is no longer in effect.

In contrast, protective orders are free-standing and remain in effect until they expire.

> **EXAMPLE** The judgment for dissolution does not affect the order of protection. It remains in effect the full two years.

Enforcement

The second difference concerns the enforcement of the orders. If a respondent violates a restraining order, the petitioner files a petition for rule to show cause in the civil court that entered the order.

> **EXAMPLE** Suppose that while the case was pending Hunter violated the restraining order by withdrawing the funds in the bank account. To enforce the order, Abigail would have filed a petition for rule to show cause in the divorce court.

In contrast, violating an order of protection is a crime enforced by the State's Attorney.

EXAMPLE Hunter has been ordered to stay 300 feet away from Abigail's place of work. When Abigail leaves at the end of the day, she sees Hunter standing next to her car. Abigail calls the police who arrest Hunter.

Difference between Types of Orders

Type of Order	Procedure to Obtain	Enforcement	Time
Restraining Order	Civil	Civil Contempt	Pendency of Action
OOP for family/household members	Civil	Criminal	Term
OOP for non-family/household members	Civil	Criminal	Term
Criminal OOP	Criminal	Criminal	Term

Procedure

The Petition

An action for an order of protection begins when a victim files a petition. Every petition is considered an independent action, even if it is filed while an action for dissolution is pending.[16]

Correct County

The petition must be filed in the correct county, which is where the petitioner resides, the respondent resides, the abuse occurred, or the petitioner fled because of the abuse.[17]

Online Petition

While it is possible to draft a paper petition and e-file it, most petitions are completed and submitted online.[18] In the petition, the petitioner identifies her relationship with the respondent and alleges the abuse received by the respondent. The petition must be verified or accompanied by an affidavit.[19]

The address of the petitioner (or the confidential address of a shelter for domestic violence victims) may be omitted from all documents filed with the court, if the disclosure would jeopardize the petitioner's safety.[20] Additionally, if the petitioner is seeking to have a child protected by the order of protection, the address of the child's school may be omitted from all documents filed with the court.[21]

No Fee

Pursuant to the Act, there is no fee for filing the petition or service by the sheriff.[22]

Initial Court Appearance

Once the petition has been submitted online, it will print out at the court clerk's office. Most often, a petition for an order of protection is heard on an emergency basis. The petitioner and her counsel pick up the petition from the clerk's office and take it to the courtroom for hearing. If the petitioner is a party to an underlying dissolution action, the judge assigned to the matter will hear the case. If the petition is free standing, it will go to the judge assigned to hear emergency matters that day.

When the matter is an emergency, the court will hear the petition *ex parte*, meaning with only one side present. The petitioner presents evidence of the abuse. Hearsay evidence can be admitted.[23]

Remedies Available

If the court grants an emergency order of protection, a number of remedies are available to protect the petitioner, including:

Prohibition of Abuse, Neglect, or Exploitation

This term prohibits the respondent's harassment, interference with the personal liberty, or intimidation of the petitioner. It also prohibits physical abuse, willful deprivation, neglect, or exploitation.[24]

Grant of Exclusive Possession of the Residence

This term prohibits the respondent from entering or remaining in any residence, including one owned or leased by the respondent if the petitioner has a right to occupancy there. The grant of exclusive possession does not change the ownership of the residence. In ordering this relief, the court is not limited to the standards required for Exclusive Possession of the Marital Residence.[25] (See Chapter 5, Temporary Motions and the Financial Affidavit.)

Stay Away Order and Additional Prohibitions

This term orders the respondent to stay away from the petitioner or any other person protected by the order of protection. Additionally, it prohibits the respondent from entering or remaining present at the petitioner's school, place of employment, or other specified places at times when the petitioner is present.[26]

Physical Care and Possession of the Minor Child

In order to protect a minor child from abuse, neglect, or unwarranted separation from the child's primary caretaker, or to otherwise protect the well-being of the minor child, the court may grant the petitioner physical care or possession of the minor child, or both.[27] Under an emergency order of protection, a change in the allocation of parental responsibilities or parenting time is made on a temporary basis.[28]

Service of the Order

To ensure the respondent has notice of the order, the respondent must be personally served. Even though orders of protection are issued by a civil court, they are enforced criminally. An order of protection entered in Illinois may be enforced in all 50 states and the District of Columbia.[29]

The respondent's name is entered into LEADS (Law Enforcement Automated Data System), so they can be tracked by law enforcement in other jurisdictions. The first violation of an order of protection is a Class A misdemeanor, punishable by fines and incarceration.[30] A second or subsequent violation is a Class 4 felony.

Hearing after Notice to Respondent

As an *ex parte* hearing is a violation of the respondent's due process right to notice, the emergency order of protection expires after 14–21 days.[31] At the end of that time, the matter is set for hearing. At that hearing, both sides present their cases. At the end of the hearing, the judge can enter an interim order, which lasts up to 30 days,[32] or a plenary order, which lasts up to two years.[33] These orders must be served by the sheriff as well.

Because personal service of the order of protection gave the court personal jurisdiction over the respondent, the court can grant additional remedies, such as monetary relief,[34] which it could not grant on an *ex parte* basis. (See Chapter 4, Jurisdiction, Service, and Initial Pleadings.)

EXAMPLE Under an emergency order of protection, Husband is ordered to stay away from Wife and Children. After Husband has appeared at the hearing, the court can enter a child support order as well.

Any order (emergency, interim, or plenary) can be extended one or more times as required. However, orders must be extended before they expire. If they expire, the petitioner has to file a new petition.

The Abuse and Neglect of Children

The Illinois General Assembly provides additional protections for children through the Abused and Neglected Child Reporting Act.[35] The Act authorizes the Illinois Department of Children and Family Services (DCFS), an administrative agency, to receive and investigate reports of child abuse and neglect and offer protective services.

The Initial Report

By statute, the Department must be capable of receiving reports of abuse 24 hours per day, seven days per week.[36] Hotline calls can be made anonymously, and there is no penalty for good-faith reporting. The number for the hotline is 800-25-ABUSE (800-252-2873).

The Act makes certain persons mandated reporters of suspected abuse, such as doctors, teachers, and mental health professionals;[37] however, paralegals and attorneys are not mandated reporters.

The Investigation

When the DCFS receives a report, they verify it and open an investigation. If the case is "unfounded," DCFS has determined there was not sufficient evidence to conclude a child had been abused or neglected. If the case is "indicated," DCFS has concluded there was credible evidence that a child had been abused or neglected. When a case is indicated, DCFS may file a petition in juvenile court to take the child into protective custody. The case has moved from an administrative matter to a judicial one.

In the Family Law Office

Firm's Client Reported

Parents who are the subject of a DCFS investigation face serious consequences, including the possibility their child will be taken into protective custody. Some family law firms have experience representing clients who have been accused of abuse or neglect. If your firm does not, to protect clients both civilly and criminally, it is critical to refer them to a firm that does.

False Reports

DCFS exists to protect children whose parents are unable to provide a safe environment for them. However, DCFS can be used as a weapon in a disputed custody case, where an allegation of abuse by one parent against another is a "nuclear bomb."

EXAMPLE Because Father provides a more stable home environment for the children, the GAL reports it is in the children's best interest he be awarded majority parenting time. Mother files a report through the DCFS hotline accusing Father of sexually abusing their six-year-old daughter, even though she has no proof. DCFS begins an investigation and notifies the State's Attorney's office.

To avoid such abuse of the system, making a false report is a Class 4 felony.[38]

EXAMPLE A DCFS investigation is returned "unfounded." The State's Attorney's office declines to press charges against Father. Mother is charged with making a false report. The GAL includes the DCFS investigation in her report to the court.

Chapter Summary

Recognizing the profound impact of domestic violence, state and federal laws protect victims in a number of ways. While crimes, such as domestic battery, require physical abuse, the Illinois Domestic Violence Act expands the definition of abuse to include non-physical actions, such as harassment and intimidation. Although the Illinois Domestic Violence is available only to family members, protective orders exist for non-family members. Not to be confused with restraining orders, protective orders can be enforced criminally and last until they expire.

A petition for an emergency order of protection can be filed free of charge with any court in Illinois and can be heard on an *ex parte* basis, that is, without notice to the respondent. If granted, the respondent is personally served with the order of protection by the sheriff. An emergency order of protection lasts 14–21 days. At the end of that time, the matter is set for hearing. With personal service over the respondent, monetary relief is available. The order can be extended for up to two years.

Finally, the Illinois DCFS is empowered to investigate reports of child abuse and neglect and, if necessary, take children into protective custody. To prevent the DCFS from being used as a weapon in a disputed custody case, filing a false report of abuse or neglect is a crime.

Key Terms

Family or Household Members

Harassment

Protective Orders

Restraining Orders

LEADS

Ex parte

Emergency

Interim

Plenary

Discussion Questions

1. Should a petitioner's false allegations on a petition for an order of protection be a criminal offense? Making a false report of child abuse and neglect is a criminal offense. Are they the same? If not, how are they different?
2. In some counties, there is a "no drop" policy for the crime of domestic battery, meaning that once the respondent has been charged, the victim cannot have the case dismissed. If victims change their minds about testifying, the prosecutor can subpoena them as a witness. How convincing might they be if forced to testify against their will?
3. How might a "no drop" policy impact a woman who fears retaliation? Are there ways to protect her from retaliation by the abuser?
4. Why do you think that the improper removal or concealment of a child falls under the Domestic Violence Act?
5. Should cyberstalking qualify as "harassment" under the Illinois Domestic Violence Act? Under current law, a person commits the crime of cyberstalking when he or she engages in a course of conduct (two or more acts) using electronic communication directed at a specific person, and he or she knows or should know that would cause a reasonable person to fear for his or her safety or the safety of a third person or suffer other emotional distress. This can include the threat of bodily harm, sexual assault, confinement or restraint to a person, or place the person or his or her family member in reasonable apprehension of harm, sexual assault, confinement or restraint. *See* 720 ILCS 5/12-7.5.
6. Currently, leaving a child under the age of 14 unattended is a crime and meets the definition of neglect. In March 2022, the House passed HB4305,

which lowers the age to 12. Is 12 a more appropriate age than 14? Should there even be a standard age, or should the maturity of the child be considered?

7. Children under the age of 14 cannot be left home alone, even for an hour after school before a parent comes home from work. Could this lead to hotline calls in disputed custody cases?
8. How should a paralegal respond if a client discloses he has abused his child? The duty of confidentiality prevents legal professionals from disclosing a client's *past actions*. However, an exception to the duty exists if a client discloses an intention to commit *future acts* that could result in death or serious bodily harm. Does a client have to indicate an intention in words? Or is past abuse sufficient to indicate an intention to commit future abuse?
9. The concept of the "cycle of abuse" originated in the 1970s. However, a newer model has been proposed. *See* https://www.thehotline.org/identify-abuse/power-and-control/ (last visited June 29, 2023). Does it reflect a more modern understanding of the dynamics of abuse?
10. Suppose a woman testifies that when she files for divorce, her husband will be so angry he will abuse her. Orders of protection are granted for past acts of abuse. Are there times they should be granted as preventive measures? If not, are there other ways to keep a petitioner safe?

Forms

1. Petition for Order of Protection

   https://ilcourtsaudio.blob.core.windows.net/antilles-resources/resources/2bc0a4a7-6235-49bd-8dd0-90272426d7d3/OOP%20Petition.pdf
2. Summons for OOP

   https://ilcourtsaudio.blob.core.windows.net/antilles-resources/resources/1306f206-8f63-4721-a102-f923dd9e9536/OOP%20Summons.pdf

Endnotes

1. https://icjia.illinois.gov/researchhub/articles/domestic-violence-trends-in-illinois-victimization-characteristics-help-seeking-and-service-utilization (last visited June 29, 2023).

2. https://www.cdc.gov/violenceprevention/intimatepartnerviolence/fastfact.html#:~:text=Data%20from%20CDC's%20National%20Intimate,related%20impact%20during%20their%20lifetime (last visited June 29, 2023).

3. Violence Against Women Act, Pub. L. No. 103-322, 108 Stat. 1902 (1994) (and as subsequently reauthorized).

4. 8 U.S.C.A. § 1154 (bb) (West). "During the marriage or relationship intended by the alien to be legally a marriage, the alien or a child of the alien has been battered or has been the subject of extreme cruelty perpetrated by the alien's spouse or intended spouse."

5. 8 U.S.C.A. § 1101 (West).

6. 8 U.S.C.A. § 1101 (West). "The alien has suffered substantial physical or mental abuse as a result of having been a victim of criminal activity…."

7. 750 ILCS 60/101 (West, Westlaw Classic through P.A. 103-21 of the 2023 Reg. Sess.).

8. *Id.* § 102(4).

9. *Id.* § 103(6).

10. *Id.* § 103(14).

11. *Id.* § 103(6).

12. *Id.* § 103 (5) and (11)(A)(i-iv).

13. 430 ILCS 67/1 (West, Westlaw Classic through P.A. 103-21 of the 2023 Reg. Sess.).

14. 740 ILCS 22/101 (West, Westlaw Classic through P.A. 103-21 of the 2023 Reg. Sess.).

15. 740 ILCS 21/1 (West, Westlaw Classic through P.A. 103-21 of the 2023 Reg. Sess.).

16. 750 ILCS 60/202(a).

17. *Id.* § 209(a).

18. https://www.illinoisprotectionorder.org/OOP/ (last visited June 29, 2023).

19. *Id.* § 203(a)

20. *Id.* § 203(b).

21. *Id.* § 203(c).

22. *Id.* § 202(b).

23. 750 ILCS 60/213.1.

24. *Id.* § 214(b)(1).

25. *Id.* § 214(b)(2).

26. *Id.* § 214(b)(3).

27. *Id.* § 214(b)(5).

28. *Id.* § 214(b)(6).

29. 750 ILCS 60/221(d).

30. *Id.* § 221(a)(1)(c).

31. *Id.* § 220(a)(1).

32. *Id.* § 220(a)(2).

33. *Id.* § 220(b)(0.05).

34. *Id.* § 210(d).

35. 325 ILCS 5/1 (West, Westlaw Classic through P.A. 103-21 of the 2023 Reg. Sess.).

36. *Id.* § 4.4(a).

37. *Id.* § 4.

38. *Id.* § 4. "Any person who knowingly transmits a false report to the Department commits the offense of disorderly conduct under (a)(7) of Section 26-1 of the Criminal Code of 2012."

1. PETITION FOR ORDER OF PROTECTION

This form is approved by the Illinois Supreme Court and is required to be accepted in all Illinois Circuit Courts.

STATE OF ILLINOIS, CIRCUIT COURT __________ COUNTY	PETITION FOR ORDER OF PROTECTION Civil Proceeding ☐ Criminal Proceeding ☐	

Instructions ▼		For Court Use Only
Directly above, enter the county where you filed this case.	**Petitioner:** ______________________ *(First, middle, last name)*	______________ **Case Number**
Enter your name as Petitioner.	v.	☐ Independent ☐ Juvenile ☐ Other Civil Proceeding ☐ Criminal
Enter name of the person you are seeking protection from as Respondent.	**Respondent:** ______________________ *(First, middle, last name)*	
Enter the Case Number given by the Circuit Clerk.	**People to be Protected by this *Order*** *(check all that apply)*: Petitioner refers to any protected person in this *Order.* ☐ Petitioner	
Check the boxes for **ALL** people you want to include in the *Order.*	☐ Petitioner's minor children with Respondent: ______________________ ______________________	
On the lines provided, enter the name for each person you are trying to protect. "Other household members" includes people living with you or working where you are staying.	☐ Petitioner's minor children not related to Respondent: ______________________ ______________________ ☐ Dependent adult: ______________ ☐ High-risk adult: ______________ ☐ Other household members: ______________ ______________________	

NOTE:	If you are completing this form for a minor child, dependent adult, or high-risk adult, insert information needed below as if you were that person. Do not use your information, except as directed at the bottom of page 10 where you will sign this form.

Check either or both boxes for the type of order you want. If you need protection today, check the first one.	**TYPE OF ORDER OF PROTECTION REQUESTED AGAINST RESPONDENT (check all that apply)** ☐ Emergency Order of Protection (civil case)/ Ex Parte Protective Order (criminal case) *(These short-term Orders of Protection can be granted on the same day you file your Petition without advance written notice to Respondent because advance notice would cause more abuse).* ☐ Plenary Order of Protection (civil case)/Final Protective Order (criminal case) *(These long-term Orders of Protection can only be granted at a court hearing after advance written notice to Respondent.)*
In background information **1**, enter the address and email (if you have one) where you want to receive Court notices. If you do not want Respondent to know where you live, enter a different address where you can get mail. If you do not want Respondent to know your email, enter a different email where you can get Court notices. If you do not have another email, leave this blank.	**BACKGROUND INFORMATION** 1. ☐ If Respondent should not know household address because it may cause more abuse, use this address for Court notices: ______________________ *Street Address, Apt. #* *City* *State* *ZIP* ______________________ *Email* OR ☐ Respondent knows household address and it is: ______________________ *Street Address, Apt. #* *City* *State* *ZIP* ______________________ *Email*

GETTING COURT DOCUMENTS BY EMAIL: You should use an email account that you do not share with anyone else and that you check every day. If you do not check your email every day, you may miss important information, notice of court dates, or documents from other parties.

Enter the Case Number given by the Circuit Clerk: ____________________

> In **2**, if you do not know Respondent's date of birth or Respondent's home or work address, write "do not know."

2. Respondent's Information

Respondent's date of birth: ____________

Respondent's home address: ______________________________

Street Address, Apt # City State ZIP

Respondent's work information:

____

Employer Street Address City State ZIP

> In **3**, check all the boxes that describe your relationship to Respondent. For example, if you are requesting an *Order of Protection* against your mother, you will check the box next to "Child" because you are the child of the Respondent.

3. Petitioner's Relationship to Respondent *(check all that apply)*

☐ Boyfriend / Girlfriend / Dating Relationship (including ex) (BG)	☐ Spouse (SE)	☐ Ex-Spouse (XS)
☐ Have Children with Respondent (never married to Respondent) (CC)	☐ Sharing or Shared Home (CS)	☐ Child (CH)
☐ Parent (PA)	☐ Brother / Sister / Sibling (SB)	☐ Other Family Member (OF)
☐ Other – Petitioner not Related to Respondent (OT)	☐ In-law (IL)	☐ Personal Caregiver to Disabled Petitioner (PC)
☐ Petitioner with Disability receives care from respondent (PD)	☐ Personal Assistant of Petitioner (PR)	☐ Grandchild (GC)
☐ Grandparent (GP)	☐ Step-Child (SC)	☐ Step-Brother / Step-Sister / Step-Sibling (SS)
☐ Prospective or Adoptive Child has Family or Household Relationship with Respondent	☐ Foster Child has Family or Household Relationship with Respondent	☐ Legally Appointed Guardian or Custodian of a Child who has a Family or Household Relationship with Respondent
☐ Step-Parent (SP)		

> Answer Sections **4** and **5** the best you can. If you check 'yes' but do not know some of the information asked for, then write "do not know."
>
> If you need more room, check the box, fill out the *Additional Case Information* form, and file it with this *Petition.*

4. Is there now, or has there ever been, another *Order of Protection* entered against Respondent involving Petitioner? ☐ Yes ☐ No ☐ Do not know

If yes, list information about the cases:

Names of People Involved	State & County	Year

☐ I have listed additional case information on the *Additional Case Information* form.

> In **5**, list all other types of court cases that you have been involved in with Respondent, such as divorce, custody, child support, parentage, parenting time, guardianship, adoption, and abuse and neglect cases.

5. Is there now, or has there ever been, another court case with Respondent involving Petitioner?

☐ Yes ☐ No ☐ Do not know If yes, list information about the cases:

Type of Case	State & County	Year

☐ I have listed additional case information on the *Additional Case Information* form.

> In **6**, check all boxes that are true.

6. This *Petition* may be filed in this county because *(check all that apply)*:

☐ Petitioner resides here.

☐ Respondent resides here.

☐ The abuse happened here.

☐ Petitioner fled here to avoid abuse.

Enter the Case Number given by the Circuit Clerk: ___________________________

In **7**, start with what happened most recently. Enter the date and time and describe what happened.

Be as specific about dates and times as you can. You can include any past abuse and any criminal convictions that resulted.

If you don't remember exact dates of things that happened long ago, just enter the month and year.

7. An *Order of Protection* is needed because Respondent did these things:

Date: ____________ Time: __________ What happened: ___________________________

Date: ____________ Time: __________ What happened: ___________________________

Date: ____________ Time: __________ What happened: ___________________________

Date: ____________ Time: __________ What happened: ___________________________

If you need more room, fill out the *Additional Incidents of Abuse* form or your own extra pages and file it with this *Petition*.

☐ I have attached the *Additional Incidents of Abuse* form or my own extra pages.

In **1**, check box 1 and each box below for the type of abuse you want to prevent. If you are unsure what the words after the boxes mean, you can look at definitions on the last page of this form.

PROTECTIONS REQUESTED BY PETITIONER

☐ **1. No Abuse**

Respondent be ordered not to threaten or commit the following acts of abuse towards Petitioner (*check all that apply*):

☐ Harassment	☐ Intimidation of a Dependent
☐ Physical Abuse	☐ Exploitation of a High-Risk Adult with Disabilities
☐ Stalking	☐ Neglect of a High-Risk Adult with Disabilities
☐ Willful Deprivation	☐ Interference with Personal Liberty

Check **2** if you want Respondent to stay away, at all times, from your home or provide you alternative housing.

Check **2a** if you want Respondent to stay away from your home. If you listed your address on page **1**, check the first box under **2a** and enter your address. If you did not list your address on page 1, check the second box under **2a**. Under BECAUSE, check the reason why Respondent should not be allowed to stay at the place you are living. Check **2b** if you want Respondent to provide you different housing.

In **3**, read the information in the box below and make sure that is what you want. If so, check box **3** and each box below that applies.

In **3a**, check if you want Respondent to stay away from places you need to go.

NOTE: Respondent will see these addresses. If you do not want Respondent to know where the children go to school, do not list it. Instead, check the box and fill out the *Confidential Name & Location of the School or Childcare Provider* form, and file it with the Circuit Clerk as "confidential."

Fill in **3b** only if Respondent attends the same school as Petitioner.

☐ **2. Possession of Residence** *(check a or b)*

These remedies do not affect who owns the property, only who gets to use or occupy it.

☐ a. Petitioner be granted exclusive possession of the residence and Respondent be ordered not to stay or be at the residence.

☐ Petitioner's residence is located at:

____
Street Address. Apt # *City* *State* *ZIP*

OR

☐ Petitioner's address is undisclosed.

BECAUSE *(check one)*:

☐ Petitioner has a right to occupy the residence and Respondent has no right; OR

☐ Petitioner and Respondent both have a right to occupy the residence but it would be harder on Petitioner to leave.

OR

☐ b. Respondent be ordered to provide, and stay away from, alternate housing for Petitioner to live in because the parties share a residence. *(available ONLY after actual notice to Respondent and/or a hearing with the judge).*

☐ **3. Stay Away from Petitioner and Certain Places** *(see box below)*

Respondent be ordered to *(check all that apply)*:

☐ Not have any communication with Petitioner.

☐ Stay away from Petitioner at all times.

IMPORTANT: If ordered to stay away from Petitioner, Respondent must not have ANY physical, non-physical, direct or indirect contact with Petitioner. If ordered to not communicate with Petitioner, communication includes oral communication, written communication, sign language, telephone and cell phone calls, faxes, texts, tweets, emails, posts, or communication by any other social media, and all other communication with Petitioner. This also includes contact or communication through others who may not know about the *Order of Protection*.

☐ a. Respondent be ordered not to be or stay at any of the following places while Petitioner is there:

☐ Places of employment of Petitioner, located at:

____
Name *Street Address* *City* *State* *ZIP*

____
Name *Street Address* *City* *State* *ZIP*

☐ Schools, kindergartens, or daycare centers of Petitioner, located at:

____
Name *Street Address* *City* *State* *ZIP*

____
Name *Street Address* *City* *State* *ZIP*

☐ I have given the name and location of the school or childcare provider on the *Confidential Name & Location of the School or Childcare Provider* form.

☐ Other locations:

____
Name *Street Address* *City* *State* *ZIP*

____
Name *Street Address* *City* *State* *ZIP*

☐ b. School Restrictions

______________________________ is an elementary, middle, or
School Name
high school attended by both Respondent and Petitioner for whom protection is sought.

Respondent be ordered *(check one)*:

☐ Not to attend Petitioner's school for as long as Petitioner is enrolled there;

☐ To accept a change of placement or program at Petitioner's school, as determined by the public school district or by a private or non-public school; OR

☐ Not to be present in these parts of Petitioner's school: ______________________

In **3c**, if Respondent is a minor, include the name of Respondent's Parent or Guardian, if you know it.

☐ c. Requirements for Parents and Guardians

Respondent is a minor. To ensure that Respondent follows this *Order*, Respondent's Parent or Guardian ______________________

Name of Parent or Guardian

be ordered to: ______________________

Check **4** if you want Respondent to get evaluation and treatment and all the boxes under it that apply to your case.

NOTE: A judge can only order counseling at a hearing where Respondent is present or has been given formal written notice.

☐ **4. Counseling** *(available **ONLY after** actual notice to Respondent and/or a hearing with the judge)*

☐ Respondent be ordered to participate in the following *(check all that apply)*:

☐ A Domestic Violence Partner Abuse program.

☐ An alcohol and substance abuse evaluation and to successfully complete all recommendations.

☐ A mental health evaluation and to successfully complete all recommendations.

☐ Other *(please specify)*: ______________________

Petitioner: **Fill out Section 5 only if you have children younger than 18 with Respondent.**

In **5a**, enter the names of all children under age 18 that you and Respondent have together.

Check the box after each child if you want to protect them from Respondent.

☐ **5. Care and Possession of Children**

☐ a. Respondent and Petitioner are both the parents of these minor children:

Child's Name *(first, middle, last)*	Age	State of Residence	Included as a Protected Person?
			☐ Yes ☐ No
			☐ Yes ☐ No
			☐ Yes ☐ No
			☐ Yes ☐ No

In **5b,** check the boxes that apply to your children with Respondent.

☐ b. Parentage of the Children

☐ The parties are NOT married and parentage HAS NOT been established.

OR

☐ Parentage HAS been established because *(check one)*:

☐ The children of the parties were born before or during the marriage of the parties, or within 300 days of termination of the marriage.

☐ The parties are NOT married but parentage HAS been established by one or more of the following:

1. Both parties have signed a Voluntary Acknowledgment of Paternity (VAP) *(if both parties' names are on the birth certificate, both parties signed the VAP)*
2. A court or administrative order
3. Other: ______________________

Check **5c** and check the box for the person who takes care of the children most of the time. If the primary caretaker of the children is someone other than you or Respondent, check the box for "Other person" and enter that person's name and address.

☐ c. The primary caretaker of the minor children is *(check one)*:

☐ Petitioner

Enter the Case Number given by the Circuit Clerk: ____________

> Check **5d** if you are protecting children you have with Respondent. Check the boxes that apply to your case and fill in the information.
>
> If you do not want Respondent to know where the children go to school, check the last box and fill out the *Confidential Name & Location of the School or Childcare Provider* form, and file it with the Circuit Clerk as "confidential."

☐ Respondent
☐ Other person: ____________
Name

____
Street Address, Apt # *City* *State* *ZIP*

☐ d. Care and Possession of Children
Petitioner requests the following *(check all that apply)*:
☐ Petitioner be granted physical care and possession of the minor children.
☐ Respondent be ordered to return the minor children to the physical care of Petitioner or another person, ____________ .
☐ Respondent be ordered to not remove the minor children from the physical care of Petitioner or from a school or childcare provider.
☐ I have given the name and location of the school or childcare provider on the *Confidential Name & Location of the School or Childcare Provider* form.

Petitioner:	Fill out Sections **6 - 7** only if you have children younger than 18 with Respondent.

> Check **6,** if you want significant decision-making responsibility (formerly custody).

☐ 6. **Temporary Significant Decision-Making Responsibility** *(formerly custody)*
*(available **ONLY after** actual notice to Respondent and/or a hearing with the judge)*
☐ Petitioner requests temporary significant decision-making responsibility for the minor children.

> In **7**, check box **a**, **b**, **c**, or **d** to let the court know if, how, and when Respondent should have parenting time.
>
> Check **7b** if you do not want parenting time decided now, then skip to **8**.
>
> If you checked **7c** or **7d**, check all reasons that apply.

☐ 7. **Respondent's Parenting Time** *(formerly visitation)* **with the Minor Children**
Petitioner requests that the court order parenting time as follows (*check a, b, c, or d*):
☐ a. GRANT parenting time for Respondent without restrictions *(if granting, fill out schedule below in part **7e**)*.
☐ b. RESERVE parenting time until a later hearing *(this means the Court will not make any decisions on parenting time right now)*. (*If you checked RESERVE, skip to Section **8**.)*
☐ c. DENY parenting time for Respondent *(no visits at all)*. *(If you checked DENY, **check your reasons below**, then skip to Section **8**).*
☐ d. RESTRICT parenting time for Respondent *(Visits with limits. **Check your reasons below**, then fill out the schedule below in **7e**.)*

If you chose DENY or RESTRICT, check your reasons below.
Respondent is likely to *(check all that apply)*:
☐ Abuse or endanger the children during parenting time.
☐ Use parenting time to abuse or harass Petitioner, Petitioner's family, or household members.
☐ Improperly hide or detain the children.
☐ Act in a way that is not in the best interest of the children.

> In 7, If you checked GRANT or RESTRICT and you want Respondent to have parenting time, complete **7e.** If you know what the schedule should be, either attach it and check **7e1** or pick your parenting time schedule in **7e2.** Enter when, where, and how you want parenting time to happen and fill in the blanks with specific times, days, and other information. Include a.m. or p.m.

If you chose GRANT or RESTRICT, request your parenting time schedule below:
☐ e. Respondent's parenting time should be *(check 1 or 2)*:
☐ 1. See attached parenting time schedule; OR
☐ 2. The following parenting time schedule *(check all that apply)*:
☐ Every ____________ from ________ to ________
Weekdays *Time* *Time*
☐ Each weekend OR ☐ Every other weekend as follows *(include am or pm)*:
☐ from Friday at ________ to Saturday at ________
☐ from Friday at ________ to Sunday at ________
☐ from Saturday at ________ to Saturday at ________
☐ from Saturday at ________ to Sunday at ________
☐ from Sunday at ________ to Sunday at ________

☐ Parenting time is to begin on: ____________
Date

Enter the Case Number given by the Circuit Clerk: ______________________

☐ Holidays: ____

____

______________________________ from: __________ to: __________
Time Time

Enter the name of the person who will be responsible for transportation during parenting time.

☐ The person responsible for transportation of the children for parenting time is:

____
Name

Enter the name or address of the place where pickup and return will take place.

☐ Pickup for parenting time to take place at:

____
Name of place (if any) *Street Address* *City* *State*

Enter the address of the place where the parenting time will take place.

☐ Return from parenting time to take place at:

____
Name of place (if any) *Street Address* *City* *State*

☐ Parenting time will take place at:

____
Name of place (if any) *Street Address* *City* *State*

If you want an individual to supervise parenting time, enter that person's name on the line. The *Affidavit of Parenting Time Supervisor* form must be completed and signed by the supervisor. This *Affidavit* is not required if an agency or center is supervising.

☐ Parenting time will be supervised by: ______________________
Name of Supervisor

who has filed or will file an *Affidavit of Parenting Time Supervisor* form with the court accepting responsibility and acknowledging accountability.

☐ Parenting time will be supervised at an official supervised visitation center *(if available)*.

☐ Respondent to return the children to Petitioner or the person designated by Petitioner Immediately at the end of parenting time.

In **8,** check if you are afraid Respondent will hide your children or take them out of state.

☐ **8. No Concealment or Removal of Children**
Respondent be ordered not to hide the children or remove them from Illinois.

In **9,** check if Respondent has your children and you want them to be with you.

☐ **9. Appear with Children** *(check all that apply)*
Respondent be ordered to appear in court with the children
☐ To prevent abuse, neglect, removal or concealment of the children.
☐ To return the children to Petitioner.
☐ To permit a court-ordered interview or examination of the children or Respondent.

Check **10a** if you want your things protected from Respondent. List things you want to keep with you.

Check **10b** if Respondent has some or all of the property you listed in **10a**. List the things you want back. Check all boxes below that apply to your case.

☐ **10. Possession of Personal Property** *(check all that apply)*
☐ a. Petitioner be awarded possession of this property: ______________________
____
____
____
____

☐ b. Respondent be ordered to give Petitioner this property: ______________________
____
____
____
____

BECAUSE *(check one)*:
☐ Petitioner, but not Respondent, owns the property.
☐ Petitioner and Respondent both own the property. Sharing it would put Petitioner

Instructions	Form
In **10c**, check if you have things that Respondent may need immediately. Then check the boxes that fit your case and list any other items.	at risk for abuse or is not practical. Not having the property would be harder on Petitioner. ☐ The parties are married and a divorce case ☐ has ☐ has not been filed. ☐ c. Respondent be awarded possession of: ☐ clothing, ☐ medicine, AND/OR ☐ other personal property *(list)*: ____________________
In **10d**, check if Respondent can enter the residence one time to get their things.	☐ d. Respondent be given the right to enter the residence <u>only one time</u> to retrieve their property, but only in the presence of law enforcement or another person named below.
Check **10e** if you checked **10b** or **10c.** Enter the address where you want the transfer to happen.	☐ e. Transfer of Personal Property Property to be transferred at: ____________________ *Street Address, Apt # City State ZIP*
In **10f**, check who you want to be there when it happens and enter that person's name. It may be safer if the transfer is in the presence of a law enforcement officer.	☐ f. Property to be transferred in the presence of *(check one)*: ☐ Law enforcement: ____________________ *Name of law enforcement agency* to be arranged with law enforcement. ☐ Another person: ____________________ *Name*
Enter the date and time you want to transfer these things.	Transfer Date: ____________ Time: ________
Check **11** if you want your things protected from Respondent and list what you want protected. Then, check all the boxes below the lines that apply to your case.	☐ **11. Restrictions on Property** ☐ Respondent be ordered not to take, damage, or otherwise dispose of this property: ____________________ BECAUSE *(check one)*: ☐ Petitioner, but not Respondent, owns the property. ☐ Petitioner and Respondent both own the property. Not having the property would be harder on Petitioner. ☐ The parties are married and a divorce case ☐ has ☐ has not been filed.
Check Restrictions on Resources to stop Respondent from using an elderly person's money or property for themselves.	☐ Restriction on Resources of an Elderly Petitioner Respondent be ordered not to use financial or other resources of an elderly Petitioner for the benefit of Respondent or any other person.
In **11.5,** check to protect your pets from Respondent.	☐ **11.5** Possession of Animals Petitioner be awarded possession of these animals: ____________________ *Name and description of each animal*
In **12**, check if you want Respondent to give you money to help you or children you have together. If you have it, bring proof of income to the next court date.	☐ **12. Temporary Support** *(available **ONLY after** actual notice to Respondent, and/or a hearing with the judge, check all that apply)* Respondent be ordered to pay support as follows: ☐ Respondent pay temporary child support ☐ Respondent pay temporary maintenance *(formerly called spousal support or alimony)*
In **13,** check all boxes that apply to your case. If you know, enter the amount of the cost in the blank. If you are not sure, you can estimate. Bring receipts, including proof of	☐ **13. Payment for Losses because of Abuse** *(available **ONLY after** actual notice to Respondent) and/or a hearing with the judge, check all that apply)* ☐ Respondent be ordered to pay Petitioner for losses caused by abuse, neglect, or exploitation, including: ☐ Medical expense.................... $ ________

Instructions	Petition
payment, and estimates of repairs to court if you have them.	☐ Lost earnings........ $ ____
	☐ Repair or replace property damaged or taken........ $ ____
	☐ Moving and other travel expenses........ $ ____
NOTE: A judge can only order economic remedies be awarded at a hearing where Respondent is present or has been given formal written notice.	☐ Reasonable expenses for housing other than a domestic violence shelter........ $ ____
	☐ Expenses for search and recovery of children........ $ ____
	☐ Reasonable attorney's fees........ $ ____
	☐ Other: ____________ $ ____

If you checked any box in Section **2** or one of the first two boxes in Section **3**, you cannot check box **14**.

☐ **14. No Entry or Presence Under Influence**

Respondent is allowed at the Petitioner's residence, but cannot be or stay there while under the influence of drugs or alcohol. This would be a threat to the safety or well-being of Petitioner or Petitioner's children.

In **14.5,** check if you want to ask for guns to be taken away and Respondent is a current intimate partner of Petitioner and represents a threat to the physical safety of Petitioner or Petitioner's child. Then check all boxes that fit your case.

NOTE: A judge can only order guns to be taken away at a hearing where Respondent is present or has been given formal written notice.

☐ **14.5 FIREARMS** *(available **ONLY after** actual notice to Respondent and/or a hearing with the judge)*

☐ Respondent is a current or former intimate partner of the Petitioner and represents a threat to the physical safety of Petitioner or Petitioner's child. Respondent should be ordered to turn over all firearms in their possession.

In addition, Respondent *(check all that apply)*:

☐ Has a history of violence.
☐ Has a history of possession or use of firearms.
☐ Carries a firearm on their person or in a vehicle.
Make and model of vehicle: ____________________
☐ May be a threat to the safety of the public or police officer.
☐ Is now, or has been, suicidal.

In **15,** check if you do not want Respondent to get your children's school records or other records. These records could provide Respondent with your protected address. Check all boxes that apply to your case.

☐ **15. Children's Records**

Respondent should not be allowed to access, inspect, or obtain school records, healthcare records, or any other records of the children BECAUSE *(check all that apply)*:

☐ Petitioner is requesting that Respondent not be allowed to have contact with the minor children.
☐ The actual address of Petitioner is not included in this *Petition* due to the risk of further abuse.
☐ It is necessary to prevent abuse or wrongful removal or concealment of the children.

In **16,** check if you want Respondent to pay the shelter. If you know, enter the amount of the cost in the blank. If you are not sure, you can estimate. Bring receipts to court if you have them.

☐ **16. Shelter Reimbursement** *(available **ONLY after** actual notice to Respondent and/or a hearing) with the judge)*

Respondent be ordered to reimburse a shelter providing temporary housing or counseling to Petitioner........ $ ____

Check **17** if there are other things you want Respondent to do or to stop doing. List those things on the lines. Explain the reasons on the lines after "Because."

☐ **17. Miscellaneous Remedies**

Respondent be ordered to:

____
____
____
____
____

Enter the Case Number given by the Circuit Clerk: _______________

BECAUSE: ___________________________________

____

____

____

____

In **18**, check if you are on Respondent's cell phone plan and you want to separate your account. Enter the provider name and telephone numbers.

☐ **18. Telephone Services**

A wireless telephone provider should transfer from Respondent to Petitioner the right to continue to use their own telephone numbers and be responsible for the cost of them. Petitioner, or a minor child in Petitioner's custody, uses the telephone numbers.

Provider: _______________

Name of Account Holder: _______________

Billing Phone #: _______________

Petitioner's Phone #s: _______________

Petitioner's Phone #s: _______________

Under the Code of Civil Procedure, 735 ILCS 5/1-109, making a statement on this form that you know to be false is perjury, a Class 3 Felony.

I certify that everything in the *Petition for Order of Protection* is true and correct. I understand that making a false statement on this form is perjury and has penalties provided by law under 735 ILCS 5/1-109.

If you are completing this form on a computer, sign your name by typing it. If you are completing it by hand, sign and print your name.

/s/ _______________

Petitioner Signature

____

Petitioner Name

If prepared by someone other than Petitioner, that person should enter their name, address, phone number, and email address.

Prepared by: _______________

Street Address: _______________

City, State, ZIP: _______________

Phone Number: _______________

Email: _______________

Attorney # (if any): _______________

Enter the Case Number given by the Circuit Clerk: ____________________________

DEFINITION OF TERMS USED IN THIS *PETITION*

These definitions are incorporated in and made a part of the *Petition* to which they are attached.

1. **Abuse:** "Abuse" means physical abuse, harassment, intimidation of a dependent, interference with personal liberty or willful deprivation but does not include reasonable direction of a minor child by a parent or person *in loco parentis*.
2. **Adult with Disabilities**: "Adult with Disabilities" means an elder adult with disabilities or a high-risk adult with disabilities. A person may be an adult with disabilities for purposes of this Act even though he or she has never been adjudicated an incompetent adult. However, no court proceeding may be initiated or continued on behalf of an adult with disabilities over that adult's objection, unless such proceeding is approved by his or her legal guardian, if any.
3. **Elder Adult with Disabilities**: "Elder adult with disabilities" means an adult prevented by advanced age from taking appropriate action to protect himself or herself from abuse by a family or household member.
4. **Exploitation:** "Exploitation" means the illegal, including tortious, use of a high-risk adult with disabilities or of the assets or resources of a high-risk adult with disabilities. Exploitation includes, but is not limited to, the misappropriation of assets or resources of a high-risk adult with disabilities by undue influence, by breach of a fiduciary relationship, by fraud, deception, or extortion, or the use of such assets or resources in a manner contrary to law.
5. **Family or Household Members:** Include spouses, former spouses, parents, children, stepchildren and other persons related by blood or by present or prior marriage, persons who share or formerly shared a common dwelling, persons who have or allegedly have a child in common, persons who share or allegedly share a blood relationship through a child, persons who have or have had a dating or engagement relationship, persons with disabilities and their personal assistants, and caregivers as defined in Section 12-4.4a of the Criminal Code of 2012. For purposes of this paragraph, neither a casual acquaintanceship nor ordinary fraternization between two individuals in business or social contexts shall be deemed to constitute a dating relationship. In the case of a high-risk adult with disabilities, "family or household members" includes any person who has the responsibility for a high-risk adult as a result of a family relationship or who has assumed responsibility for all or a portion of the care of a high-risk adult with disabilities voluntarily, or by express or implied contract, or by court order.
6. **Harassment:** "Harassment" means knowing conduct which is not necessary to accomplish a purpose that is reasonable under the circumstances, would cause a reasonable person emotional distress, and does cause emotional distress to Petitioner. Unless the presumption is rebutted by a preponderance of the evidence, the following types of conduct shall be presumed to cause emotional distress:
   a. creating a disturbance at Petitioner's place of employment or school; or
   b. repeatedly telephoning Petitioner's place of employment, home or residence; or
   c. repeatedly following Petitioner about in a public place or places; or
   d. repeatedly keeping Petitioner under surveillance by remaining present outside his or her home, school, place of employment, vehicle or other place occupied by Petitioner or by peering in Petitioner's windows; or
   e. improperly concealing a minor child from Petitioner, repeatedly threatening to improperly remove a minor child of Petitioner's from the jurisdiction or from the physical care of Petitioner, repeatedly threatening to conceal a minor child from Petitioner, or making a single such threat following an actual or attempted improper removal or concealment, unless Respondent was fleeing an incident or pattern of domestic violence; or
   f. threatening physical force, confinement or restraint on one or more occasions.
7. **High-risk Adult with Disabilities:** "High-risk adult with disabilities" means a person aged 18 or over whose physical or mental disability impairs his or her ability to seek or obtain protection from abuse, neglect, or exploitation.
8. **Interference with Personal Liberty:** "Interference with personal liberty" means committing or threatening physical abuse, harassment, intimidation or willful deprivation so as to compel another to engage in conduct from which she or he has a right to abstain or to refrain from conduct in which she or he has a right to engage.
9. **Intimidation of a Dependent:** "Intimidation of a dependent" means subjecting a person who is dependent because of age, health or disability to participation in or the witnessing of: physical force against another or physical confinement or restraint of another which constitutes physical abuse as defined in this Act, regardless of whether the abused person is a family or household member.
10. **Neglect:** "Neglect" means the failure to exercise that degree of care toward a high-risk adult with disabilities which a reasonable person would exercise under the circumstances and includes but is not limited to:
    a. the failure to take reasonable steps to protect a high-risk adult with disabilities from acts of abuse; or
    b. the repeated, careless imposition of unreasonable confinement; or
    c. the failure to provide food, shelter, clothing, and personal hygiene to a high-risk adult with disabilities who requires such assistance; or
    d. the failure to provide medical and rehabilitative care for the physical and mental health needs of a high-risk adult with disabilities; or
    e. the failure to protect a high-risk adult with disabilities from health and safety hazards.

    Nothing in this definition shall be construed to impose a requirement that assistance be provided to a high-risk adult with disabilities over his or her objection in the absence of a court order, nor to create any new affirmative duty to provide support to a high-risk adult with disabilities.
11. **Petitioner:** "Petitioner" may mean not only any named petitioner for the order of protection and any named victim of abuse on whose behalf the petition is brought, but also any other person protected by this Act.
12. **Physical Abuse:** "Physical abuse" includes sexual abuse and means any of the following:
    a. knowing or reckless use of physical force, confinement or restraint; or
    b. knowing, repeated and unnecessary sleep deprivation; or
    c. knowing or reckless conduct which creates an immediate risk of physical harm.
13. **Stalking:** "Stalking" means knowingly and without lawful justification, on at least two (2) separate occasions, following another person or placing the person under surveillance or any combination thereof and:
    a. at any time transmitting a threat of immediate or future bodily harm, sexual assault, confinement or restraint and the threat is directed towards that person or a family member of that person; or
    b. placing that person in reasonable apprehension of immediate or future bodily harm, sexual assault, confinement or restraint; or
    c. placing that person in reasonable apprehension that a family member will receive immediate or future bodily harm, sexual assault, confinement, or restraint.
14. **Willful Deprivation:** "Willful deprivation" means willfully denying a person who because of age, health or disability requires medication, medical care, shelter, food, therapeutic device, or other physical assistance, and thereby exposing that person to the risk of physical, mental or emotional harm, except with regard to medical care or treatment when the dependent person has expressed an intent to forego such medical care or treatment. This paragraph does not create any new affirmative duty to provide support to dependent persons.

Print Form | Save Form | Reset Form

2. SUMMONS FOR ORDER OF PROTECTION

This form is approved by the Illinois Supreme Court and must be accepted in all Illinois Courts.
Forms are free at ilcourts.info/forms.

STATE OF ILLINOIS, CIRCUIT COURT COUNTY	SUMMONS PROTECTIVE ORDERS	*For Court Use Only*

Instructions		
Enter above the county name where the case was filed.	Petitioner *(First, middle, last name)*	
Enter your name as Petitioner.		
Enter the name of the person you are suing as Respondent.	v.	
Enter the Case Number given by the Circuit Clerk.	Respondent *(First, middle, last name)* ☐ **Alias Summons** *(Check this box if this is not the 1st Summons issued for this Respondent.)*	Case Number

IMPORTANT: A case has been filed against you.

- Read all documents attached to this *Summons*.
- You MUST file an official document with the court within the time stated on this *Summons* called an *Appearance* and a document called an *Answer/Response*. If you do not file an *Appearance* and *Answer/Response* on time, the judge may decide the case without hearing from you. This is called "default." As a result, you could lose the case.
- All documents referred to in this Summons can be found at ilcourts.info/forms. Other documents may be available from your local Circuit Court Clerk's office or website.
- After you fill out the necessary documents, you need to electronically file (e-file) them with the court. To e-file, you must create an account with an e-filing service provider. For more information, go to ilcourts.info/efiling. If you cannot e-file, you can get an exemption that allows you to file in-person or by mail.
- You may be charged filing fees, but if you cannot pay them, you can file an Application for Waiver of Court Fees.
- It is possible that the court will allow you to attend the first court date in this case in-person or remotely by video or phone. Contact the Circuit Court Clerk's office or visit the Court's website to find out whether this is possible and, if so, how to do this.
- Need help? Call or text Illinois Court Help at 833-411-1121 or go to ilcourthelp.gov for information about going to court, including how to fill out and file documents. You can also get free legal information and legal referrals at illinoislegalaid.org.
- ¿Necesita ayuda? Llame o envíe un mensaje de texto a Illinois Court Help al 833-411-1121, o visite ilcourthelp.gov para obtener información sobre los casos de la corte y cómo completar y presentar formularios.

In **1**, enter the name of the person you are seeking protection from and their contact information.

1. Respondent's address and service information

a. Respondent's primary address/information for service:
Name *(First, Middle, Last)*: ______
Street Address, Unit #: ______
City, State, ZIP: ______
Telephone: ______ Email: ______

In **1b**, enter a second address for Respondent, if you have one.

b. If you have more than one address where Respondent might be found, list that here:
Name *(First, Middle, Last)*: ______
Street Address, Unit #: ______
City, State, ZIP:
Telephone: ______ Email: ______

Enter the Case Number given by the Circuit Clerk: ______________________

In **1c**, **c**heck how you are sending your documents to Respondent.

c. Method of service on Respondent:

☐ Sheriff ☐ Sheriff outside Illinois: ______________________ *County & State*

☐ Special process server ☐ Licensed private detective

In **2**, check the box that describes the type of case you started against the Respondent.

2. Petitioner has filed against you for the following

☐ Order of Protection ☐ Stalking No Contact Order

☐ Civil No Contact Order ☐ Other ______________________

Respondent:

- You are required to file an answer or otherwise appear within 7 days of service of this *Summons*.
- Appearance and Answer/Response forms can be found at: ilcourts.info/forms
- If you fail to appear on the hearing date or on any subsequent hearing date agreed to by the parties or set by the court, a plenary *(final)* order of protection may be entered by default for any of the remedies sought in the petition.

In **3**, fill in the date, time, and location of your next court date. Also fill in the clerk's phone number and website. All of this information is available from the Circuit Clerk. Find their phone number at ilcourts.info/CircuitClerks.

3. Instructions for person receiving this form *(Respondent)*

☐ Go to court on the date in the attached *Order*.

☐ Go to court on: __________ at: __________ ☐ a.m. ☐ p.m. in __________

Date *Time* *Courtroom*

____

Courthouse Address *City* *State* *ZIP*

You may be able to attend this court date by phone or video conference. This is called a "Remote Appearance."

Call the Circuit Clerk at: ______________________ or visit their website

Circuit Clerk's phone number

at: ______________________ to find out more about how to do this.

Website

In **4**, check the first box and enter your contact information. If you do not want the Respondent to know that information, check the second box and give a different address where you can receive legal documents.

4. Contact information for Petitioner

☐ This is Petitioner's information and address; OR

☐ The Petitioner's address is protected. The address below is a place where notices can be sent.

Name *(First, Middle, Last)*: ______________________

Street Address, Apt #: ______________________

City, State, ZIP: ______________________

Telephone and email: ______________________

STOP!
The Circuit Clerk will fill in this section.

Date Issued: ______________________

Seal of Court

Clerk of the Court: ______________________

STOP!
The officer or process server will fill in the Date of Service.

Date of Service: ______________________

(Date to be entered by an officer or process server on the copy of this Summons left with the Respondent or other person.)

Petitioner: To serve this *Summons*, ask the Sheriff to deliver it to Respondent. Ask the Circuit Clerk how to give the *Summons* to the Sheriff.

Enter the Case Number given by the Circuit Clerk: ______________________

<table>
<tr><td colspan="2">STATE OF ILLINOIS,
CIRCUIT COURT
______________ COUNTY</td><td>PROOF OF SERVICE
FOR PROTECTIVE ORDERS</td><td rowspan="2">For Court Use Only</td></tr>
<tr><td>Instructions</td><td colspan="2"></td></tr>
<tr><td>Enter above the county name where the case was filed.</td><td colspan="2">______________________________
Petitioner (First, middle, last name)</td><td></td></tr>
<tr><td>Enter your name as Petitioner.</td><td colspan="2"></td><td></td></tr>
<tr><td>Enter the name of the person you are suing as Respondent.</td><td colspan="2">v.
______________________________</td><td rowspan="2">______________________
Case Number</td></tr>
<tr><td>Enter the Case Number given by the Circuit Clerk.</td><td colspan="2">Respondent (First, middle, last name)
☐ Alias Summons (Check this box if this is not the 1st Summons issued for this Respondent.)</td></tr>
</table>

****Stop. Do not complete the form. The sheriff or special process server will fill in the form.****

My name is ______________________________ **and I state**
First, Middle, Last

☐ **that I served the *Summons, Petition,* and *Orders* issued in this case on the Respondent**
______________________________ **as follows:**
First, Middle, Last

☐ Personally on the Respondent:
☐ Male ☐ Female ☐ Non-Binary Approx. Age: ________ Race: __________
On this date: ____________ at this time: ________ ☐ a.m. ☐ p.m.
Address, Unit #: ______________________________
City, State, ZIP: ______________________________

☐ On someone else at the Respondent's home who is at least 13 years old and is a family member or lives there:
On this ____________ at this time: ________ ☐ a.m. ☐ p.m.
Address, Unit #: ______________________________
City, State, ZIP: ______________________________
And left it with: ______________________________
First, Middle, Last
☐ Male ☐ Female ☐ Non-Binary Approx. Age: ________ Race: __________
and by sending a copy to this Respondent in a postage-paid, sealed envelope to the above address on __________ , 20 _____ .

Enter the Case Number given by the Circuit Clerk: ______________________

☐ **I was not able to serve the *Summons, Petition*, or any *Order* on Respondent:**

____ .
First, Middle, Last

I made the following attempts to serve the *Summons, Petition,* and any *Order* issued in this case on the

1. On this date: ____________ at this time: ________ ☐ a.m. ☐ p.m.
   Address: ______________________
   City, State, ZIP: ______________________
   Other information about service attempt: ______________________

2. On this date: ____________ at this time: ________ ☐ a.m. ☐ p.m.
   Address: ______________________
   City, State, ZIP: ______________________
   Other information about service attempt: ______________________

3. On this date: ____________ at this time: ________ ☐ a.m. ☐ p.m.
   Address: ______________________
   City, State, ZIP: ______________________
   Other information about service attempt: ______________________

DO NOT complete this section. The sheriff or private process server will complete it.

If you are a special process server, sheriff outside Illinois, or licensed private detective, your signature certifies that everything on the *Proof of Service for Protective Orders* is true and correct to the best of your knowledge. You understand that making a false statement on this form could be perjury.

Under the Code of Civil Procedure, 735 ILCS 5/1-109, making a statement on this form that you know to be false is perjury, a Class 3 Felony.

By:

____

Signature by: ☐ Sheriff
☐ Sheriff outside Illinois:

____
County and State
☐ Special process server
☐ Licensed private detective

____
Print Name

If *Summons* is served by licensed private detective or private detective agency:
License Number: ______________________

Print Form Save Form Reset Form

Fourteen

Adoption, Guardianship, and Assisted Reproduction

Overview

In previous chapters, we discussed families formed through sexual relationships. In this chapter, we look at three ways the General Assembly has provided for unrelated parents and children to form families through the legal system: adoption, guardianship, and assisted reproduction. As you read, consider whether the laws enacted by the General Assembly protect the rights and interests of all those involved in the formation of these families.

Adoption

Adoption is a court process that creates a legal relationship between a parent and a child where no biological relationship existed. Adoption in Illinois is governed by the Adoption Act.[1] After completion of the adoption process, the legal rights and responsibilities of the newly formed family are the same as they are for a biological family.

Children

A child under legal age who is "available for adoption" may be adopted.[2] To be available, the parental rights of both birth parents must have been legally terminated. "Birth parents" may also be known as "biological parents."

Children with a Legal Father

A legal father is one who is married to the birth mother, has signed a VAP, or has been court-adjudicated a father, likely after a DNA test.[3] A birth mother and legal father are given the right to agree to the adoption (through consent or surrender). A consent or surrender signed 72 hours after the birth of a child is irrevocable.[4] A legal father is also allowed to deny paternity or waive his parental rights.[5]

> **EXAMPLE** Mother and Father are 16 years old and unmarried. Father signs a VAP in the hospital. Four days after the baby's birth, they both consent to the adoption. Even as minors, their consent to adopt is irrevocable.

Alternatively, a birth mother and legal father can be found by a court to be unfit and have their parental rights terminated.[6]

> **EXAMPLE** Mother and Father are married. Baby is born with cocaine in her system. Father abandons the infant at the hospital. Parents are found unfit. DCFS takes temporary custody and control, placing Baby in foster care until a permanent arrangement can be made.

Children without a Legal Father

Efforts are made to identify the birth father before placing his child for adoption. If the birth mother knows the name of the birth father, she signs an affidavit naming the birth father, called the "putative father." If more than one man may be the father, they are each named on the affidavit. These men will be notified and given the opportunity to claim their parental rights by filing a petition for parentage or, in the alternative, to waive, deny, or disclaim their parental rights.

If the birth mother cannot name the biological father, the child may be adopted without his consent. The adoptive parents can rely on the birth mother's statement that she cannot name the biological father.[7]

The Putative Father Registry

Illinois created the putative father registry (PFR) to protect men from having a child adopted without their consent.[8] If a man wants to be notified before any child he may have conceived is given up for adoption, he can register with the PFR. Adoption law requires him to be notified and given a chance to claim his parental rights before the child is adopted. Timing is critical: to ensure he is notified, he must register before the child is born or within 30 days of its birth.

> **EXAMPLE** Heather and Greg are in a volatile relationship. When Heather is eight months pregnant, she looks at Greg's cellular phone while he is in the shower and discovers he is in a relationship with another woman. After a violent exchange, Greg leaves for work. When he comes home that night, he discovers Heather is gone. Later that night, Heather sends him a text saying he'll never find

her or the baby. Afraid Heather will put the child up for adoption to spite him, Greg registers with the PFR immediately.

Adult Adoption

The law permits adults, as well as children, to be adopted. The process is similar: both of the birth parents, if living, must be notified and consent to the adoption.[9] An additional requirement is that the adults live with their adoptive parents for two years prior to the adoption.[10]

EXAMPLE Mother and Boyfriend lived together since Angela was an infant. Boyfriend raised Angela and walked her down the aisle at her wedding. When Angela is 52, Mother dies. Boyfriend, now age 80, adopts Angela, formalizing a relationship. Angela can take Boyfriend (now Father) to his doctor's appointments and assist him with end-of-life decisions.

Adoptive Parents

Any single adult (whether never married, divorced, or widowed) and any couple (married or unmarried, same-sex or opposite-sex) can adopt.[11] If married, the adopting parent's spouse must be a part of the adoption process.[12] The adopting parent must be over the age of 18, have lived in Illinois for six months, have a good reputation, and not be under a legal disability.[13]

Kinds of Adoptions in Illinois

Adoptions fall into one of three categories in Illinois: an agency adoption, a related adoption, and a private ("unrelated") adoption.

Agency Adoption

In an agency adoption, the parental rights of the birth parents are terminated and custody of the child is transferred to an agency. The agency then places the child with foster parents while adoptive parents are arranged. In Illinois, all agencies must be licensed with the State of Illinois Department of Child and Family Services.

EXAMPLE Mother and Father surrender Baby to DCFS. Baby is placed in foster care. Six months later, Baby is adopted by the foster parents.

Related Adoption

In a related adoption, the birth parents' parental rights are transferred directly to a relative.[14] As with an agency adoption, this process requires either consent, surrender, or a court finding of unfitness.

> **EXAMPLE** Mother and Husband divorce when Child is two. When Child is three, Mother marries Stepfather, who wants to adopt child. Husband is located and gives his consent to the adoption.

Private Adoption

In a private adoption, the birth parents' parental rights are transferred directly to unrelated parents without agency involvement.

> **EXAMPLE** Teenage Girl becomes pregnant. Her church connects her to Married Couple that cannot have children. After visiting their home and meeting Married Couple, they arrange the adoption. When Teenage Girl goes into labor, Married Couple, the adopting parents, come to the hospital for the birth.

The adopting parents are not allowed to pay the birth parents for their consent to the adoption; however, they are allowed to pay the birth mother's reasonable living expenses during the pregnancy.[15]

> **EXAMPLE** Married Couple petitions the court to pay Teenage Girl's expenses during her pregnancy, and the court grants the request. On the second day after birth, Teenage Girl decides to keep the baby. She cannot be forced to give up the baby even though her living expenses had been paid.

Procedure

The court procedure is similar in all three kinds of adoptions.

Petition and Service

First, the adoptive parents file a petition for adoption.[16] The petition must provide the name, place, and date of birth, if known, and the sex of the child.[17] The birth parents are not named as respondents if they have waived or disclaimed their parental rights, their parental rights have been terminated, or the child has been surrendered to an agency.[18]

Court Action

The court confirms that the parental rights of the birth parents were terminated, and a guardian *ad litem* is appointed to investigate the adoptive parents.[19] At this time, the court may issue an interim order of adoption. Finally, the court issues a judgment of adoption, creating a new family, and a new birth certificate is issued.[20]

Guardianships

A guardianship does not terminate parental rights. Instead, it transfers the legal custody and control of a child, called the ward, to another adult, called the guardian. Guardianship is governed by the Probate Act.[21]

Guardianships for Minors

Guardianships exist for children who do not have a living parent who is willing and able to make and carry out day-to-day decisions for them. The guardian assumes both the rights and responsibilities for the child's well-being.[22]

Designated in a Will

Parents can designate a guardian in the event they die before their children reach age 18. Most often, this designation is made in a will. A designation ensures a smooth transition for the children from the parents to the guardians.

EXAMPLE The parents of a young child execute a will, naming the mother's parents as guardians. When the parents die unexpectedly, a dispute is avoided between the mother's and father's parents for legal custody of the children.

Parents Unable to Care for Child

In contrast, a need for a guardian may arise when a child has a living parent who is unable to care for the child.

EXAMPLE Upon a finding of abuse and neglect, DCFS takes Child into protective custody. When Mother makes no progress toward her goals and is at risk of having her parental rights terminated, Grandmother agrees to act as guardian. As guardian, Grandmother can enroll Child in school and take Child to medical appointments.

Procedure for a Guardianship through Court

Guardianships come in three kinds: guardianship of the child, guardianship of the estate (or money) of the child, and guardianship of both the child and the estate, called a plenary guardianship.

The Petition

The petition must indicate which of the three kinds of guardianships it is seeking.[23] In addition, it must list the nearest relatives of the minor.

Service

Notice must be given to the persons listed on the petition and to the minor (if aged 14 or older) in person or by mail, at least seven days before court.[24]

Court Action

The court must first find that the minor does not have a parent willing and able to take care of him. It then determines the guardian has met the following requirements:[25]

- Has attained the age of 18 years;
- Is a resident of the United States;
- Is not of unsound mind;
- Is not an adjudged person with a disability; and
- Has not been convicted of a felony.

Finally, the court decides if the proposed guardian can provide an active and suitable program of guardianship for the minor. In making the decision, the court uses the best interest of the minor standard.

Once a guardian has been appointed, the court issues letters of office. If the guardianship is over the minor's estate, the guardian posts a bond. Each year, the guardian will appear before the court to document the ward's status. If the guardianship is over the estate, the guardian will provide an accounting as well.

Guardianships for Adults with Disabilities

Guardianships for adults with disabilities are provided in the Probate Act.[26] The process for forming the guardianship is the same as it is with minors, except that the respondent must be served.[27] In addition, a medical letter confirming the disability is required.[28]

EXAMPLE Kevin, from Chapter 12, has turned 18. Mother files a petition for guardianship to allow her to deposit his social security checks and pay his medical expenses. As the respondent, Kevin is served. At the court hearing, a letter from his doctor is submitted confirming his disability.

If an adult with a disability does not have a friend or family member willing or able to serve as guardian, the Office of the State Guardian will serve as guardian. *See* https://gac.illinois.gov/osg.html.

Short-Term Guardianships for Minors

The Probate Act provides a guardianship for minors that does not involve a court process, called a short-term guardianship.[29] A short-term guardianship is a standardized form. To be effective, it is signed and dated by the parent in the presence of two witnesses. While it is only valid for 365 days, the parent can choose when the 365 days start, either on the date of signing or upon the happening of an event.[30]

EXAMPLE Single Mother is living in Aurora without legal immigration status. Fearful that at any time she will be detained by Immigration Customs Enforcement, she names her mother as guardian of her daughter, effective the date she is detained.

Assisted Reproduction and Gestational Surrogacy

Illinois law provides two ways for children to be born through contractual arrangements with genetic donors. In gestational surrogacy, a woman carries and gives birth to a baby on behalf of intended parents who are unwilling or unable to undergo a pregnancy. The law governing gestational surrogacy is found in the Gestational Surrogacy Act.[31] In assisted reproduction, an intended parent receives a donation of genetic material. The law governing assisted reproduction is contained in the Illinois Parentage Act of 2015.[32]

Gestational Surrogacy

Genetic Contribution to the Child

With gestational surrogacy, at least one of the intended parents must have contributed a reproductive cell (also called a "gamete") to the baby.[33] However, neither the gestational surrogate nor her husband, if she is married, can have contributed a gamete.[34]

EXAMPLE An unmarried news announcer wants to become a father. His sperm is used to fertilize a donor egg. The resulting embryo is implanted into a woman, the gestational surrogate, who carries and gives birth to the baby.

Parental Rights and Responsibilities

Parental rights vest in the intended parent or parents immediately upon the baby's birth.[35] Neither the gestational surrogate nor the gamete donors have any parental rights to, or responsibilities for, the baby.

Contract Requirements

Requirements for a surrogacy contract are provided by the Gestational Surrogacy Act.[36] While courts can determine the parties' rights in the event of a breach, the statute provides that if a surrogate changes her mind before implantation, she cannot be court-ordered to comply.[37]

Assisted Reproduction

With assisted reproduction, one parent provides a gamete, and a donor provides the other. The law concerning assisted reproduction is contained in the Illinois Parentage Act. It does not apply to parents who use *in vitro* fertilization with their own gametes.

Artificial Insemination

A donor, other than the spouse, provides a gamete. The donor can be anonymous or known to the parent. The donation may be made privately or through a commercial sperm (or egg) bank.

EXAMPLE Destiny, a single woman, wants to have a baby. She chooses an anonymous donor from a book at a sperm bank and receives *in vitro* fertilization. She carries and gives birth to the baby.

Embryo Transfer

EXAMPLE A couple marries when they are in their late forties. They select a donor egg, which is fertilized with Husband's sperm. The embryo is transplanted into Wife's uterus.

Parental Rights and Responsibilities

With assisted reproduction, the donors of genetic material relinquish all rights to and responsibilities for the child.[38] All rights and responsibilities vest in the intended parent.[39]

Chapter Summary

The Illinois General Assembly provides three ways for unrelated parents and children to form families. The first is through adoption, which creates a legal relationship between the parents and a child where no biological relationship existed. In an agency adoption, parental rights are terminated and transferred first to an agency and then to the adoptive parents. In a related adoption, the parental rights are transferred to a relative, often a step-father. Lastly, with a private adoption, parental rights are transferred directly to an unrelated person without agency involvement.

In contrast to adoption, guardianship transfers legal custody and control of a child from the parent to another adult; however, it does not terminate the parent's rights. While establishing a guardianship requires a court proceeding, a short-term guardianship, lasting for less than one year, does not require court involvement.

Finally, Illinois law regulates gestational surrogacy, in which a woman, the surrogate, carries a baby on behalf of the intended parents, and assisted reproduction, in which an intended parent receives the donation of a gamete. Illinois law provides procedural safeguards to protect all parties involved: the surrogate, the donors, the intended parents, and most importantly, the child.

Key Terms

Adoption
Legal Father
Putative Father
Agency Adoption
Related Adoption
Private Adoption
Interim Order
Guardianship
Short-Term Guardianship
Gestational Surrogacy
Assisted Reproduction
Gamete

Discussion Questions

1. Consider the case of *Petition of Doe*, also known as the "Baby Richard case," in which a birth mother consented to the adoption of her baby and told the birth father the baby had died. 159 Ill. 2d 347, 638 N.E.2d 181 (1994). When the baby was 57 days old, the birth father learned he was alive and filed a petition to challenge the adoption. The appellate court upheld the adoption as being in the child's best interests. On the father's appeal, the Illinois Supreme Court found that since the father's parental interest had been improperly terminated (for failure to demonstrate a reasonable degree of interest in the child in the first 30 days of life), the child's best interests should not have been considered, and invalidated the adoption. By then, the child was almost four years old. Which court do you think used the right standard? Are procedural safeguards sufficient to prevent situations like this?
2. Pursuant to 750 ILCS 50/15, an effort must be made to place an adoptive child with parents of the same religion as the birth parents. Religion is one of the four significant decisions considered in the allocation of parental responsibilities. Should adoptive parents be allowed to make that decision? What policy is behind this section of the Act?
3. It is a criminal offense to compensate birth parents for adoption. *See* 720 ILCS 5/12C-70. What is the policy behind this act? What harm does it seek to prevent?
4. Federal law allows same-sex couples to marry, yet private agencies can refuse to place babies with same-sex couples. Is this equitable? What policy could justify this?
5. Safe Haven Laws allow babies to be left at a safe place, such as a hospital or fire station, if they are less than 30 days old and have not been abused. Are the birth father's rights protected? Does the infant's well-being outweigh the birth father's interest?
6. There is no requirement to notify a birth father, including a husband, before a birth mother aborts. Is this consistent with efforts made to notify a birth father of an adoption?
7. Consider a situation in which a judge awards sole allocation of parental responsibility to the mother because the father expresses no interest in their child's life. In her will, the mother designates her sister as the guardian of her minor children. When the mother dies, the father must be notified, and if he is willing and able, the probate court cannot proceed with the guardianship. Do his parental rights outweigh the decision of a mother with sole allocation?

8. While the process for a court-ordered guardianship is longer and more expensive than for a short-term guardianship, court-ordered guardianships do provide oversight of the child. Does the oversight of the child outweigh the inconvenience and expense? Or does the risk that a child without a parent will be taken into protective custody outweigh the lack of court oversight?
9. The Probate Act gives the guardian of the ward's person or estate authority to file a petition for dissolution of marriage on the ward's behalf, which the court will allow if it is in the ward's best interests. *See* 755 ILCS 5/11a-17(a-5). Is the decision to terminate a marriage one that can be delegated? Can you imagine a situation in which a divorce would be in the ward's best interests?
10. A boyfriend and girlfriend agreed to undergo *in vitro* fertilization. After the relationship ended, the girlfriend wanted to use the cryopreserved pre-embryos they had created, and the boyfriend filed an action to prevent her. How should the court determine whose interest is superior? *See Szafranski v. Dunston*, 2015 IL App (1st) 122975-B, 34 N.E.3d 1132.
11. Consider the adoption of frozen embryos, sometimes called "snowflake adoptions." Does the law concerning adoption or assisted reproduction apply? Or is new law needed to protect the rights of the parties involved?

Forms

Adoption

1. Petition for Adoption

   https://www.circuitclerkofwillcounty.com/Court-Forms/petition-for-adoption-4a
2. Surrender of Unborn Child for Purpose of Adoption

   https://www.circuitclerkofwillcounty.com/Court-Forms/surrender-of-unborn-child-for-purpose-of-adoption-3d
3. Consent to Adoption of Unborn Child

   https://www.circuitclerkofwillcounty.com/Court-Forms/consent-to-adoption-of-unborn-child-3c-1
4. Order Appointing Guardian *Ad Litem* - Adoption

   https://www.circuitclerkofwillcounty.com/Court-Forms/order-appointing-guardian-ad-litem-adoption-3b
5. Interim Order

   https://www.circuitclerkofwillcounty.com/Court-Forms/interim-order-3f

6. Decree of Adoption
   https://www.circuitclerkofwillcounty.com/Court-Forms/decree-of-adoption-3e
7. Certificate of Adoption Form from Illinois Vital Records
   https://www.circuitclerkofwillcounty.com/Court-Forms/certificate-of-adoption

Guardianship

1. Petition for Guardianship of a Minor
   https://18thjudicial.org/18thJudicial/download/3834
2. Physician's Report
   https://cic.countyofkane.org/eForms/P1-PR-027-E.pdf
3. Report of Guardian of the Person
   https://cic.countyofkane.org/eForms/P1-PR-041-E.pdf

Endnotes

1. 750 ILCS 50/1 (West, Westlaw Classic through P.A. 103-21 of the 2023 Reg. Sess.).
2. *Id.* § 3.
3. *Id.* § 1(X).
4. *Id.* § 9(A).
5. *Id.* § 11(a).
6. *Id.* § 1(D).
7. 750 ILCS 50/11(b).
8. *Id.* § 12.1.
9. *Id.* § 3.
10. *Id.*
11. *Id.* § 2(A)(a).
12. *Id.* § 2(A)(a).
13. 750 ILCS 50/2(A)(a).
14. "Related child" is defined at 750 ILCS 50/1(B).
15. "Reasonable living expenses" means those expenses related to activities of daily living and meeting basic needs, including, but not limited to, lodging, food, and clothing for the biological parents during the biological mother's pregnancy and for no more than 120 days prior to the biological mother's expected date of delivery and for no more than 60 days after the birth of the child. The term does not include expenses for lost wages, gifts, educational expenses, or other similar expenses of the biological parents. 720 ILCS 5/12C-70. (West, Westlaw Classic through P.A. 103-21 of the 2023 Reg. Sess.).
16. 750 ILCS 50/5B.
17. *Id.* § 5B.
18. *Id.* § 5B(f).
19. *Id.* § 6.
20. *Id.* § 19.

21. 755 ILCS 5/11 (West, Westlaw Classic through P.A. 103-21 of the 2023 Reg. Sess.)
22. *Id.* § 11-13.
23. *Id.* § 11-8(a).
24. *Id.* § 11-10.1(a).
25. *Id.* § 11-3(a).
26. *Id.* § 11(a).
27. 755 ILCS 5/11a -10(e).
28. *Id.* § 11a-9.
29. *Id.* § 11-5.4.
30. *Id.* § 11-5.4(c).
31. 750 ILCS 47/1 (West, Westlaw Classic through P.A. 103-21 of the 2023 Reg. Sess.).
32. 750 ILCS 46/701 (West, Westlaw Classic through P.A. 103-21 of the 2023 Reg. Sess.).
33. 750 ILCS 47/20(b)(1).
34. 750 ILCS 46/709(a)(1-2).
35. 750 ILCS 47/15(b)(4).
36. *Id.* § 25.
37. *Id.* § 50.
38. 750 ILCS 46/703.
39. *Id.* § 703.

1. PETITION FOR ADOPTION

STATE OF ILLINOIS)
)SS
COUNTY OF WILL)

PRINT

CLEAR

IN THE CIRCUIT COURT OF THE TWELFTH JUDICIAL CIRCUIT
WILL COUNTY, ILLINOIS

____

____

Petitioners

VS. CASE NO.________________

____

____

Repondents

PETITION FOR ADOPTION

Now come Petitioner(s) herein and allege as follows:

(a) The full name(s) of the Petitioner(s) and, if minor(s), their respective age(s) is/are as follows:

Name______________________________ Age________

Name______________________________ Age________

(b) The place of residence of Petitioner(s) and the length of residence in Illinois (for each) immediately preceding the filing of the within petition is as follows:

Place______________________________ Length__________

Place______________________________ Length__________

(c) The Petitioner(s) acquired/intend to acquire custody of said child from________________

________________________ whose address is________________________

________________________ on________________, 20___.

(d) The name, place and date of birth and sex of the child sought to be adopted is as follows:

____

(e) The relationship, if any, of the child to each petitioner is as follows:________________

____

(f) The names of the parents of the child, place of residence and whether minor or adult are as follows:

Father________________ Age______ Residence________________

Mother________________ Age______ Residence________________

Neither of the parents are under any legal disability except:________________

____

(1) The rights of the parents have been terminated by________________, a court of competent jurisdiction.

(2) The child has been surrendered to the following agency:________________

____

(3) The parent(s), namely____
have been served with the notice provided in Section 12a of this Act and____________________________________
____has filed_____________________________________

(g) The child has no living parent(s). The legal guardian of the child is____________________________
who was appointed by____

(h) The child has no living parent(s) and no legal guardian is known. The name of a near relative is_______________________________ Relationship_____________________
Address__________________________

(i) The name to be given the child (adult) is____

(j) (1) That____, being the person/agency having authority to do so, has/have consented/indicated a willingness to consent/to the adoption of the child by the Petitioner(s).

(2) That____, has authority to consent to the adoption of the child by Petitioner(s), is an/are unfit person(s) for the following reason(s):____

(k) Orders, judgments or decrees have been entered affecting:

(1) The adoption or custody of the child as follows:_____________________________________
____

(2) The adoptive, custodial or parental rights of either Petitioner as follows, including the prior denial of any petition for adoption pertaining to such child, or to the Petitioner(s), or either of them:_________________________________
____

(3) Additional allegation(s) required by the facts of this particular case:______________________
____

WHEREFORE Petitioner(s) therefore pray(s) that the above-named__________________________________
____
may be made Respondent(s) to this petition, and that a summons may issue for them and each of them, returnable according to law, and that they and each of them be required to answer this petition as is by statute provided.

Petitioner(s) further pray(s) that the court will, on the final hearing of this petition, ORDER, ADJUDGE and DECREE that ____________________shall, to all legal intents and purposes, be the child of your Petitioner(s), and that the name of said child shall thereafter be____.

That this Honorable Court will make such other and further orders in the premises as may be in accordance with law.

____
____
____
Petitioner(s)

STATE OF ILLINOIS)
) SS
COUNTY OF WILL)

____being first duly sworn upon oath depose(s) and say(s) that he/she/they signed the foregoing petition and that the contents thereof are true and correct.

NAME____
Attorney for____
ARDC#____
Address____
City____
Telephone____

Signed and sworn to before me this _____ of
_____________________________________, 20____

____
Notary Public

2. SURRENDER OF UNBORN CHILD FOR PURPOSE OF ADOPTION

STATE OF ILLINOIS)
)SS
COUNTY OF WILL)

PRINT
CLEAR

IN THE CIRCUIT COURT OF THE TWELFTH JUDICIAL CIRCUIT
WILL COUNTY, ILLINOIS

____

____
Petitioner

VS CASE NO.____________________

____

____
Defendant

SURRENDER OF UNBORN CHILD FOR PURPOSES OF ADOPTION

I,____, state:

That I am the father of a child expected to be born on or about __________________________________, 20__

to____.
(Name of Mother)

That I reside at____

County of____and State of________________________________

That I am the age of________________years.

That I hereby surrender and entrust the entire custody and control of such child to the_______________________

____,
(The Agency)

a ____ child welfare agency with its principal office in the City of
(Public) (Licensed)

___________________________________, County of___________________________ and State of ________________,
for the purpose of enabling it to care for and supervise the care of such child, to place such child for adoption and to consent to the legal adoption of such child, and that I have not previously executed a consent or surrender with respect to such child.

That I hereby grant to said Agency full power and authority to place such child with any person or persons it may in its sole discretion select to become the adopting parent or parents and to consent to the legal adoption of such child by such person or persons; and to take any and all measures which, in the judgement of said Agency, may be for the best interests of such child, including authorizing medical, surgical and dental care and treatment, including inoculation and anaesthesia for such child.

That I wish to and understand that by signing this consent I do irrevocably and permanently give up all custody and other parental rights I have to such child.

That I understand I cannot under any circumstances, after signing this surrender, change my mind and revoke or cancel this surrender or obtain or recover custody or any other rights over such child, except that I have the right to revoke this surrender by giving written notice of my revocation not later than 72 hours after the birth of such child.

That I have read and understand the above and I am signing it as my free and voluntary act.

Dated_______________________________, 20_____ ____
(Witness)

STATE OF ILLINOIS)
) SS
COUNTY OF WILL)

I,_________________________________, do hereby certify that____________________________
(Name and Official Title)
personally known to me to be the same person whose name is subscribed to the foregoing Surrender, appeared before me this day in person and acknowledged that he signed and delivered such Surrender as his free and voluntary act, for the specified purpose.

I have fully explained that by signing such consent he is irrevocably relinquishing all parental rights to such child or adult and he has stated that such is his intention and desire.

Witness,______________________________, 20____

____

STATE OF ILLINOIS)
) SS
COUNTY OF WILL)

I, a Notary Public, in and for the said County, in the State aforesaid, do hereby certify that ______________ ___________________________, personally known to me to be the same person whose name is subscribed to the foregoing certificate of acknowledgment, appeared before me in person and acknowledged that he signed such certificate as his free and voluntary act and that the statements made in said certificate are true.

Signed and sworn to before me

_____________________________________, 20____

____
(Notary Public)

3. CONSENT TO ADOPTION OF UNBORN CHILD

STATE OF ILLINOIS)
)SS
COUNTY OF WILL)

PRINT

CLEAR

IN THE CIRCUIT COURT OF THE TWELFTH JUDICIAL CIRCUIT
WILL COUNTY, ILLINOIS

____

____

Petitioner

VS. CASE NO.____________________

____

____

Defendant

CONSENT TO ADOPTION OF UNBORN CHILD

I,____, state:

That I am the father of a child expected to be born on or about____________________, 20___,

to____.
(Name of Mother)

That I reside at____

County of ______________________________, and State of____________________.

That I am the age of ___________years.

That I hereby enter my appearance in such adoption and waive service of summons on me.

That I do hereby consent and agree to the adoption of such child, and that I have not previously executed a consent or surrender with respect to such child.

That I wish to and do understand that by signing this consent I do irrevocably and permanently give up all custody and other parental rights I have to such child, except that I have the right to revoke this consent by giving written notice of my revocation not later than 72 hours after the birth of the child.

That I understand such child will be placed for adoption and that I cannot under any circumstances, after signing this document, change my mind and revoke or cancel this consent or obtain or recover custody or any other rights over such child.

That I have read and understand the above and I am signing it as my free and voluntary act.

Dated______________________, 20____

____

STATE OF ILLINOIS)
) SS
COUNTY OF WILL)

I,____, do hereby certify
(Name and Official Title)
that____
personally known to me to be the same person whose name is subscribed to the foregoing consent, appeared before me this day in person and acknowledged that he signed and delivered such consent as his free and voluntary act, for the specified purpose.

I have fully explained that by signing such consent he is irrevocably relinquishing all parental rights to such child or adult and he has stated that such is his intention and desire.

Witness,____________________________, 20____

____

STATE OF ILLINOIS)
) SS
COUNTY OF WILL)

I, a Notary Public, in and for the said County, in the State aforesaid, do hereby certify that ______________
___________________________, personally known to me to be the same person whose name is subscribed to the foregoing certificate of acknowledgment, appeared before me in person and acknowledged that he signed such certificate as his free and voluntary act and that the statements made in said certificate are true.

Signed and sworn to before me

___________________________________, 20____

(Official Seal)

____
(Notary Public)

4. ORDER APPOINTING GUARDIAN *AD LITEM*

STATE OF ILLINOIS

PRINT

CLEAR

IN THE CIRCUIT COURT OF THE TWELFTH JUDICIAL CIRCUIT
WILL COUNTY, ILLINOIS

____

____
Petitioner

VS. CASE NO.__________________

____

____
Defendant

ORDER APPOINTING GUARDIAN AD LITEM - ADOPTION

This cause now coming to be heard upon the above mentioned petition of____________________

and ___________________________, it appearing to the Court that the parents of the child sought to be adopted are dead and that the child has no guardian or near relative, or relatives, who can or will contribute to the support of the child or consent to its adoption, and no licensed child welfare agency is authorized to consent, and does consent, to the adoption of said child, and that

the defendant___________________________________ is a/are minor___, and it further appearing to the Court that said defendant___ has been duly served with summons.

IT IS THEREFORE ORDERED BY THE COURT, that__________________________,

a licensed attorney, is appointed Guardian ad Litem for the said minor defendant_____________
______________________________ to make answer unto said petition, to represent said minor__ in this proceedings, to be and appear upon the hearing of said petition in this Court, and defend the rights and interests of said minor__ in said cause. And the said Guardian ad Litem shall have the power and authority to consent to the adoption of said child should such Guardian ad Litem see fit to do so.

Dated______________________________, 20___

ENTER:_________________________________
(Judge)

STATE OF ILLINOIS

IN THE CIRCUIT COURT OF THE TWELFTH JUDICIAL CIRCUIT
WILL COUNTY, ILLINOIS

____

____
Petitioner

VS. CASE NO.__________________

____

____
Defendant

ANSWER OF GUARDIAN AD LITEM

And now came____, minor defendant__, by____, ___h__ Guardian ad Litem, and for answer unto said petition say ___that __he __is/are not advised of the matters and things in said petition contained, and neither admit nor deny them, and respectfully demand that said Petitioner__ be strictly required to prove the allegations in said petition contained.

Dated___________________________, 20____

____
(Guardian Ad Litem)

5. INTERIM ORDER OF ADOPTION

STATE OF ILLINOIS)
)SS
COUNTY OF WILL)

PRINT
CLEAR

IN THE CIRCUIT COURT OF THE TWELFTH JUDICIAL CIRCUIT
WILL COUNTY, ILLINOIS

____
____

Petitioners

VS. CASE NO.____________________

____
____
____

Defendants

INTERIM ORDER

The petition of____, having been filed herein on ____________________, 20____, for the adoption of__________________________, a minor child;

And it appearing to the court that the child sought to be adopted herein is a minor, and that the court should therefore appoint a guardian ad litem to represent the interests of said child in this proceeding;

IT IS THEREFORE ORDERED that ____, a duly licensed attorney under the laws of the State of Illinois and a member of this bar, be and he is hereby appointed as guardian ad litem to represent the interests in this proceeding of________________________, the minor child sought to be adopted herein.

And it further appearing to the court that all of the other defendants to this cause are of full legal age and under no legal disability, except ____
____,
who is/are____
____,
and that the court should therefore appoint a guardian ad litem to represent the interests in this proceeding of said defendants.

IT IS THEREFORE ORDERED that____, a duly licensed attorney under the laws of the State of Illinois, and a member of this bar, be and he is hereby appointed as guardian ad litem to represent the interests of this proceeding of said defendants,____________
____

And said petition now coming on for preliminary hearing as provided by Section 13 of the Illinois Adoption Act, and the court being now fully advised in the premises, **DOTH FIND**:

1. That written consents to the adoption of said child by petitioner__ have been executed and filed herein by the following-named persons, and/or agency:____________________________________

____

____

____

that all of said consents have been executed according to law, and are valid and binding.

2. (a) That____is/are willing to accept and assume temporary custodial care of the child sought to be adopted herein, pending a final determination of this cause; that such temporary custodial care is suitable and proper for the welfare of said child.

(b) That it is to the best interests of said child that the custodial rights of his/her parents be terminated, and that said child be temporarily committed to the care and custody of some competent person or agency pending a final determination of this cause; that______________________________________
is a suitable, proper and competent person/agency, and that it will be for the welfare of said child that he/she be temporarily committed to the care and custody of the said______________________________________,
pending a final determination of this cause.

IT IS THEREFORE ORDERED, ADJUDGED AND DECREED by the court as follows:

1. That the custodial rights of the parents of said child be and they are hereby terminated, and that said child be and he/she is hereby declared to be a ward of this court.

2. That said child be and he/she hereby committed to the temporary care and custody of

____,

pending a final determination of this cause.

3. ____

____

____

____

Dated______________________________,20___

ENTER:_________________________________
(Judge)

STATE OF ILLINOIS)
)SS
COUNTY OF WILL)

PRINT
CLEAR

IN THE CIRCUIT COURT OF THE TWELFTH JUDICIAL CIRCUIT
WILL COUNTY, ILLINOIS

____
____
Petitioners

VS. CASE NO.______________________

____
____
____
Defendants

DECREE OF ADOPTION

This cause coming on to be heard upon the verified petition of__________________________________
for the adoption of__________________________________, hereinafter sometimes referred to as the "child,
and____
and the court being fully advised in the premises finds as follows:

(1) Defendants are all the persons entitled to be notified of the within proceedings and have been so notified in the following manner:____
____
____
____
____
____

(2) Valid properly acknowledged consents to the adoption of said child and have been filed as required by an Act of the General Assembly of the State of Illinois entitled "An Act in relation to the adoption of persons and to repeal an act therein named", approved July 17, 1959 as follows:______________________
____
____
____

(2a) Consents to the adoption of said child have not been filed for the following reasons:________
____
____

(3) It appearing to the court that____
defendant ___ are in the military service of the United States, or that their military status is unknown, thereupon the court appointed____, attorney of record for such defendant__ or those who may be in the military service of the United States.

(4) The court heretofore appointed____
guardian ad litem of said child.

(5) On ____________________________, 20___, the court appointed____________________
to make the investigation required to be made under the provisions of said Act as to the allegations contained in said petition, the character, reputation and general standing in the community of the petitioners, the religious faith of the petitioners and, if ascertainable, of said child, whether petitioners are proper persons to adopt said child and whether said child is a proper subject of adoption. The said____
has mad a report of said investigation to the court which report the court approves.

(6) On ____________________________, 20___, which was at a time as soon as practicable after the filing of said petition, the court held a hearing for the purpose of complying with Section 13 of said Act and, as shown by the records kept by the Clerk of the Court, the hearing thereof and the order or orders entered by the court complied with said Section 13.

(7) Said child not being a related child, one of the orders referred to in Par. 6 hereof was an interim order entered _________________________, 20___, vesting temporary care, custody and control of the child in the petitioners.

(8) Upon this _________day of ____________________, 20___, petitioners have applied to this court for the entry of a decree of adoptions. Notice of said application was served by petitioners upon the following agency or person and at the following time and manner:____

____

____

____

(9) A hearing was held upon said application on _____________________, 20___, at which petitioner and the child appeared.

(9a) A hearing was held upon said application on _____________________, 20___, at which hearing____didnotappearbecausesuchappearancewas waived by the court for good cause shown which was as follows:_________________________

____

____

(10) The court is satisfied from the report referred to in Par. 5 hereof and from the evidence introduced at said hearing that the adoption is for the welfare of said child and that the consents for adoption referred to in Par. 2 hereof are valid and have been filed by all persons required to do so under the provisions of said Act in order for the court to enter this decree.

(10a) The court is satisfied from the report referred to in Par. 5 hereof and from the evidence introduced at said hearing that the adoption is the welfare of said child and that no consent for adoption is required as provided in Section 8 of said Act for the reasons given in Par. 2-a hereof.

(11) The evidence given at the aforesaid hearing sustained the allegations of said petition and said allegations are true.

(12) The said child was born on ________________________________, 20___, in the County of ________________________________, State of ________________________________. Petitioners reside in the County of ____________________, State of ________________________________. The parents of said child reside as follows: ____

____

Petitioners have satisfied all the requirements of said Act to entitle them to adopt said child and are subject to the jurisdiction of the court in this proceeding under the provisions of the Act. Said child is subject to the jurisdiction of this court in this proceeding under the provisions of said Act and is entitled to be adopted by petitioners.

(13) No consent or surrender for adoption was taken until the passage of seventy-two hours after the birth of the child.

(14) It will be for the welfare of the child to waive the waiting period of six months provided in Section 14 of the Act and grant a decree of adoption.

(15) ____

____

____

____

____

Now, therefore, it is ordered, adjudged and decreed as follows:

(A) The said ____
be and is hereby adopted by ____
and said ____
be and is hereby the child of ____.

(B) The name of said child be and is hereby changed to ________________________________.

(C) The natural parents of said child be and are hereby deprived of all legal rights as respect to said child and said child be freed from all obligations whatsoever to said natural parents.

Dated ________________________________, 20____

ENTER: ____

(Judge)

7. CERTIFICATE OF ADOPTION

State of Illinois
Illinois Department of Public Health

Division of Vital Records
925 E. Ridgely Ave.
Springfield, IL 62702-2737

CERTIFICATE OF ADOPTION

CHILD'S INFORMATION AT BIRTH

Name ______________________ Date of birth ______________ State file number______________

Place of birth
Hospital, city state and country ______________________

Mother/Co-Parent's name prior to first marriage/civil union ______________________

Father/Co-Parent's name prior to first marriage/civil union ______________________

❑ Male ❑ Female If foreign born, has Illinois previously created a birth record for this child? ❑ Yes ❑ No

Has any U.S. state previously created a birth record for this child? ❑ Yes ❑ No If yes, what state? ______________

CHILD'S NAME AFTER ADOPTION

First name(s) ______________ Middle name(s) ______________ Last name(s)______________

PARENT'S INFORMATION AFTER ADOPTION

❑ Co-parent ❑ Natural father ❑ Adoptive father ❑ Single father

Married? ❑ Yes ❑ No In a Civil Union? ❑ Yes ❑ No

Full name prior to first marriage/civil union ______________________

Date of birth ______________________

Place of birth ______________________

Current legal name______________________

Signature of this parent______________________

By signing this form, you are verifying that all information listed is true and correct.

❑ Co-parent ❑ Natural mother ❑ Adoptive mother ❑ Single mother

Married? ❑ Yes ❑ No In a Civil Union? ❑ Yes ❑ No

Full name prior to first marriage/civil union ______________________

Date of birth ______________________

Place of birth ______________________

Current legal name______________________

Signature of this parent______________________

By signing this form, you are verifying that all information listed is true and correct.

ADDRESSES

Adoptive parent(s)' address at the time of this child's birth. Street ______________________

City ______________ State ________ ZIP Code______________ County ______________

Attorney's name, current mailing address and telephone number______________________

Adoptive parent(s)' current mailing address and telephone number ______________________

Do you want a new birth certificate created? ❑ Yes ❑ No If yes, send the new birth certificate to ❑ Attorney ❑ Parents

CERTIFICATION

State of Illinois, County of ______________ Case Number ______________ Decree Date______________

I hereby certify that a decree of adoption was entered by the Circuit Court of this county on the above listed date which adjudged that the above mentioned child is deemed to be for legal intents and purposes the child of the adoptive parents identified above.

Date______________________

COURT SEAL

Signed ______________________

ILLINOIS DEPARTMENT OF PUBLIC HEALTH

Division Of Vital Records
925 E. Ridgely Ave.
Springfield, IL 62702-2737

CERTIFICATE OF ADOPTION

The certificate of adoption must be completed in its entirety. Failing to complete any portion of this form could result in the document being returned to you without the adoption information being placed on the birth record. The fee for completing the birth record of an Illinois born child is $15. This includes one certified copy of the new birth certificate. Additional copies ordered at the same time are $2 each. Make check or money order payable to Illinois Department of Public Health or IDPH.

If you are submitting a certificate of adoption regarding a foreign born child, you must submit one additional document as proof of the child's place and date of birth. Records of foreign birth are $5 each.

If the adopted child was born in a state other than Illinois, this certificate of adoption will be forwarded to the state of birth. No fee is required for the Illinois Department of Public Health to forward this document. If you are aware of the fee required by the state where the birth occurred it may be included and will be forwarded with the Certificate of Adoption to the birth state.

Please type or print all information clearly. If you have additional questions, call the Division of Vital Records at 217-782-6553. Office hours are 10 a.m. to 3 p.m., Monday through Friday.

Child's information at birth

Indicate the child's full name at birth; month, day and year of birth; hospital, city, state and country (if other than the United States) of birth. If the state file number of the birth record is known, indicate so. Provide the full names of the biological mother/co-parent and father/co-parent. Indicate the sex of the child. If you are submitting an adoption regarding a foreign born child, has the state issued a birth record for this child in connection with a prior adoption in Illinois? If you are submitting an adoption regarding a foreign born child, has any state in the United States previously established a birth record for this child? If so, in what state.

Child's name after adoption

Indicate in the appropriate space the child's first, middle and last name(s). Do not use white out or line through any part of the new name. If alterations are made to the name of the child after the adoption, a certified copy of the adoption decree will be required.

Parent's information after adoption

Indicate if each parent is a co-parent, natural father, natural mother, adoptive father or adoptive mother, or if this is a single parent adoption. Indicate if each parent is married or in a civil union. Give each parent's first, middle and last name prior to first marriage or civil union. Provide each month, day and year of birth; and the state or country (if other than the United States) of birth for each. Each parent must sign verifying his/her respective information. This information is what will appear on the new amended birth record. If the information provided is later determined to be incorrect the record will have to be amended by the IDPH correction unit at an additional cost.

Addresses

The address of the adoptive parent(s) at the time of the child's birth is required. Provide the complete address including any apartment number, city, state, ZIP code and county. If the biological mother/co-parent is also a parent after adoption, then her address from the original birth record will be placed on the new birth record. The attorney's name, complete address and telephone number are required. The current address and telephone number of the adoptive parent(s) are also required. Indicate if a new birth record is to be created and to whom it is to be sent.

Certification

This must be completed by the circuit clerk's office in the county where the adoption was completed. The circuit clerk must include his/her seal.

1. PETITION FOR GUARDIANSHIP OF A MINOR

PETITION FOR GUARDIANSHIP - MINOR 3834 (Rev 12/20)

STATE OF ILLINOIS **UNITED STATES OF AMERICA** **IN THE CIRCUIT COURT OF THE EIGHTEENTH JUDICIAL CIRCUIT** **COUNTY OF DU PAGE**

IN RE THE ESTATE OF

______________________ A MINOR

____

CASE NUMBER

PETITION FOR GUARDIANSHIP OF A MINOR

File Stamp Here

____ ,on oath states:

1. Each of the following named person(s) is a minor: **Name - Date of Birth - Residence Address - County** (if necessary, list on additional sheet)
____
____
2. ☐ No Order of Court has been entered in any jurisdiction concerning the Guardianship of the Minor.
☐ An Order of Court has been entered concerning the Guardianship of the Minor.
Case number ____________ Case Title ______________________
filed in ____________ and a copy of the Order awarding Guardianship is attached hereto.
☐ The following person(s) have been designated: ______________________ (attach copy of document)
____
____
3. The person having custody of the minor is ______________________
whose address is ______________________
4. The names and addresses of the nearest adult relatives of the minor(s): **Name - Relationship - Address** (list on additional sheet, if necessary)
____
____
5. Approximate value of the minor's personal estate $ ____________. Amount of the minor's anticipated gross annual income and other receipts $ ____________
6. It is necessary or convenient that a guardian of the ☐ person ☐ estate ☐ estate and person of the minor be appointed because ______________________
7. Petitioner asks that:
(a) ______________________ age ________
qualified and willing to act, appointed as guardian of the ______________________ of the minor.
(b) ______________________ age ________
qualified and willing to act, appointed as guardian of the person of the minor.

Printed Name

Name: ______________________

DuPage Attorney Number: ____________ ☐ Pro Se

Attorney for: ______________________

Address: ______________________

City/State/Zip: ______________________

Telephone Number: ______________________

Email: ______________________

____
Petitioner Signature

Signed and sworn to before me

____
Date

____
Circuit Clerk or Notary Public

2. PHYSICIAN'S REPORT

IN THE CIRCUIT COURT OF THE SIXTEENTH JUDICIAL CIRCUIT
KANE COUNTY, ILLINOIS

Case No. ____________________________

IN THE MATTER OF THE ESTATE OF (Alleged Disabled Person):

Name:_______________________________________

Address:_____________________________________

City, State, Zip: _________________________________

Date of Birth:___________________________________

File Stamp

PHYSICIAN'S REPORT

____, a physician licensed to practice medicine in all its branches in the State of Illinois, submits the following report on the above alleged disabled person.

1. Describe the nature and type of respondent's disability and an assessment of how the disability impacts on the ability of the respondent to make decisions or to function independently:

2. Describe the respondent's mental and physical condition and, where appropriate, describe educational condition, adaptive behavior, and social skills which have been performed within 3 months of the date of filing to this petition:

3. Your opinion as to whether guardianship is needed, the type and scope of the guardianship needed, and the reasons therefore:

4. Your recommendation as to the most suitable living arrangement and, where appropriate, treatment or habilitation plan for the respondent and the reasons therefore:

(PHYSICIAN'S REPORT continued) Case No.__________________________

Date:__________________ Physician's Name (please print):____________________________________

Signature of Physician:____

Address: ____

City, State, Zip:____

I, ____, hereby certify that:

1. I have personally examined., questioned, interviewed and/or evaluated the alleged disabled person named in the above Physician's affidavit.
2. As attested to below, the evaluation to which I have set me seal is in my opinion, true, correct and supported by fact.

Under penalties of perjury as provided by law pursuant to 735 ILCS 5/1-109, the undersigned certifies that the statements set forth in this instrument are true and correct, except as to matters stated to be on information and belief and as to such matters the undersigned certifies that he/she verily believes the same to be true.

____
Signature

____
Print Name

This report must contain the signatures of all person(s) who performed the evaluations upon which the report is based on, of whom must be a licensed physician, and a statement of the certification, license or other credentials that qualify the evaluators who prepared this report.

1. Name:____
   Signature:____
   Address, City, State, Zip:____
   Credentials:____
2. Name:____
   Signature:____
   Address, City, State, Zip:____
   Credentials:____
3. Name:____
   Signature:____
   Address, City, State, Zip:____
   Credentials:____

3. REPORT OF GUARDIAN OF THE PERSON

IN THE CIRCUIT COURT OF THE SIXTEENTH JUDICIAL CIRCUIT
KANE COUNTY, ILLINOIS

Case No. ____________________________

IN THE MATTER OF THE ESTATE OF
DISABLED PERSON OR MINOR:

Name: ______________________________________

Address: ____________________________________

City,State, Zip: _______________________________

Date of Birth: ________________________________

Name of Guardian: ____________________________

File Stamp

REPORT OF GUARDIAN OF THE PERSON

PERIOD OF TIME COVERED BY THIS REPORT: __________ to __________

CURRENT AGE OF DISABLED PERSON OR MINOR: _______

1. The current mental, physical and social condition for the disabled person or minor.

2. The present living arrangement of disabled person or minor. If the disable person or minor has moved, include brief description and address of the new residence.

3. A summary of medical, educational, vocational, and other professional services given to the disabled person or minor.

 Case No. ____________

4. Guardian's visits and activities on behalf of disabled person or minor.

5. Recommendation for continued Guardianship.

6. Any other information you believe would be helpful to the Court.

Date: ____________

Guardian's Signature: ____________________

Relationship to Ward: ____________________

Address: ____________________
Street/P.O. Box

____
(City, State, Zip Code)

☐ **Check here is you have moved**

Appendix

The Illinois Code of Paralegal Ethics*

Preamble

Ethics embody the principles of conduct expected to be followed in a professional activity. The Illinois Paralegal Association, hereinafter "Association," recognizes the importance of ethical standards to the paralegal profession. The Association's Board of Directors commissioned an *Ethics Task Force* to create a practical guide that would assist the paralegal in understanding ethical concepts and how to avoid ethical infractions.

The ethical characterizations of *The Illinois Code of Paralegal Ethics* are consistent with the Illinois Rules of Professional Conduct adopted by the Illinois Supreme Court for attorneys. The Illinois Code of Paralegal Ethics is intended to assist the paralegal to understand jurisdictional standards of ethical responsibility and to enhance the quality of the delivery of legal services.

Paralegal Ethics Task Force

The Ethics Task Force consisted of legal scholars and practitioners familiar with the enforcement of disciplinary rules, two authors of a textbook on paralegal ethics and paralegals\legal assistants with diverse legal backgrounds. The Task Force reviewed the Model Code of Ethics and Professional Responsibility, NFPA; The Code of Ethics and Professional Responsibility, NALA; The American Bar Association's Code of Professional Responsibility; and, the Illinois Supreme Court Rules of Professional Conduct, as guidelines to develop a unique jurisdictional authority governing ethical obligations and professional responsibility for paralegals.

The Illinois Code of Paralegal Ethics consists of rules set forth in lettered subsections with commentary. The rules are authoritative to the extent that they mirror the Illinois Supreme Court Rules of Professional Conduct. The Commentary is by explanation and example guidance with respect to the purpose and meaning of the rules. The Commentary is not intended as a statement of additional rules.

* Used by permission of the Illinois Paralegal Association.

The Illinois Code of Paralegal Ethics is not intended as an exhaustive guide for the conduct of paralegals. Paralegals must continue to pursue familiarity and knowledge regarding ethical obligations and professional conduct. "The attorney instructed me to do it" is no longer acceptable rationalism regarding ethical responsibility.

Rule One: Scope of Professional Duties

(a) The paralegal shall be familiar with and heed the directives found in the Illinois Rules of Professional Conduct or the Illinois Code of Paralegal Ethics. A paralegal shall not undertake any behavior which the Illinois Rules of Professional Conduct prohibit the supervising attorney from doing.

(b) A paralegal shall refrain from engaging in the unauthorized practice of law.

(1) The paralegal shall not work with a lawyer's client unless the paralegal's work is supervised by an attorney.

(2) The paralegal shall not draft pleadings or papers on behalf of a lawyer's client unless the paralegal's work is supervised by an attorney.

(3) The paralegal shall not sign pleadings or papers filed in a court or other judicial tribunal on behalf of a lawyer's client.

(4) The paralegal shall not appear as an advocate in a representative capacity in a court or other judicial tribunal on behalf of a lawyer's client.

(5) The paralegal shall not set legal fees.

(6) The paralegal shall not provide legal advice to a lawyer's client.

(c) A paralegal shall work under the direction of an attorney and shall abide by the decisions of the lawyer concerning the representation of a lawyer's client.

(1) The paralegal shall immediately consult the supervising attorney and defer to the decision of the attorney when questions regarding the scope of the client's representation arise.

(2) A paralegal who discovers that the client has, during the course of representation, perpetrated a fraud upon a person or tribunal, shall immediately report the fraud to the supervising attorney. A paralegal who discovers that a person other than the client has perpetrated a fraud upon a tribunal shall immediately report such fraud to the supervising attorney.

Commentary

The paralegal's supervising attorney has an obligation to supervise the paralegal so that the paralegal avoids engaging in action which violates the rules of ethics. IRPC Rule 5.3. Therefore, the scope of the paralegal's professional responsibilities is circumscribed by the rules of ethics found in this Code and the Illinois Rules of

Professional Conduct. This means that the paralegal may not undertake to provide any services which the lawyer is forbidden from undertaking. The scope of the paralegal's work is further limited by the rules defining the practice of law.

In Illinois, the practice of law has been defined to "embrace the preparation of pleadings, and other papers incident to actions and special proceedings, and the management of such actions and proceedings on behalf of clients before judges and courts." *People v. Alexander* (1964), 53 Ill. App. 2d 299, 202 N.E.2d 84, quoting *People ex rel. Illinois State Bar Association v. People's Stock Yards State Bank*, 344 Ill. 462, 476, 176 N.E. 901, 907. This does not include administrative agencies, where the paralegal would be bound by that agency's rules of procedure, because such agencies are not considered as a court of law. The interpretation of the limits of the practice of law is broader in Illinois than it is in many states, however. Unlike most other jurisdictions, Illinois allows nonlawyers to appear in court to present a routine motion. The nonlawyer cannot, however, participate in any activity which could be considered as "managing the litigation." *Alexander*, 53 Ill App. 2d at 303, 202 N.E. at 843.

Because the supervising attorney is presumed to be familiar with the rules of ethics marking the scope of the paralegal's duties, the paralegal is advised to turn to the supervising attorney when questions regarding the extent of the paralegal's role arise. For this reason, the rules direct the paralegal to defer to the advice of the attorney and not the client when seeking guidance regarding proper legal behavior.

Rule Two: Competence

(a) A paralegal shall achieve and maintain a high level of competence.

(1) A paralegal shall achieve competency through education, training, and work experience.

(2) A paralegal shall participate in continuing education to keep informed of current legal developments of the law and technical support areas.

(b) A paralegal shall not perform a task if the paralegal knows that he or she is not competent to handle the task and must seek help from one who is competent.

Commentary

To provide effective assistance to their clients, many attorneys delegate responsibilities to a paralegal. Work completed by the paralegal goes a long way toward achieving the goals of the lawyer's client. In fact, such delegation of responsibilities has been recognized by the United States Supreme Court as an important step in making the delivery of legal services less costly. See *Missouri v. Jenkins*, 491 U.S. 274, 109 S. Ct. 2463, 2471.

However, if the paralegal's work is not completed accurately or if the paralegal fails to keep abreast of trends in the law, the paralegal may actually contribute to increasing the cost of the services provided to the lawyer's client. For this reason, it is imperative that the paralegal attain and maintain high levels of competency through participation in continuing educational programs and paralegal associations. Competent performance requires legal knowledge, skill, thoroughness and preparation necessary for the responsibility.

Rule Three: Diligence

A paralegal shall act with reasonable diligence and promptness in assisting a lawyer in the representation of the lawyer's client.

Commentary

Diligence has been defined as "Vigilant activity, attentiveness or care, of which there are infinite shades..." Black's Law Dictionary, 5th ed., p. 411. "Paralegals are expected to work with reasonable diligence." What is reasonable may not always be clear to the paralegal. For guidance, the paralegal can look to the Comment to the Model Rules of Professional Conduct, which define a lawyer's duty to provide diligent representation:

> "A lawyer should act with commitment and dedication to the interests of the client and with zeal in advocacy upon the client's behalf..."

Likewise, the paralegal should be committed to the interests of the lawyer's client and should zealously assist the supervising lawyer in his or her representation of the client.

At a minimum, this rule requires paralegals to be conscious of such things as handling responsibilities promptly and keeping track of filing deadlines and statutes of limitation. The consequences of violating the ethical obligation to maintain reasonable diligence can be great. Often in a busy law practice, it is all too easy to put off unpleasant tasks and to concentrate on responsibilities that are more easily handled. A decision that allows a paralegal to procrastinate violates that paralegal's ethical responsibilities to the supervising lawyer and to the lawyer's client. A paralegal's failure to note that a statue of limitations is about to run could result in a client losing the right to pursue a cause of action and result in a lawsuit against the law firm for negligence.

The rule concerning diligent representation is also affected by the paralegal's responsibility to maintain competence. See Rule Two, Illinois Code of Paralegal Ethics. Failure to achieve competence can result in tasks taking longer than anticipated or in paralegals putting off work because they do not understand recent developments in the law. A paralegal's violation of the competency requirement could lead, therefore, to a failure to complete work with diligence.

Rule Four: Disclosure of Status

A paralegal shall disclose his or her status.

(1) A paralegal's status shall be disclosed in all business and professional communications to avoid misunderstandings and misconception about the paralegal's role and responsibilities.

(2) A paralegal's status shall be included if the paralegal's name appears on business cards, letterhead, brochure, directories, and advertisements.

(3) A paralegal shall promptly clarify any misunderstanding when there is a reasonable belief that the paralegal's status is misunderstood.

Commentary

To avoid misleading clients, opposing counsel, court personnel, and judges, paralegals must disclose their nonlawyer status. Disclosure designates communication of information reasonably sufficient to avoid misleading others.

As the rule makes clear, disclosure of nonlawyer status should be made in all written communications, such as in paralegal's business card, law firm letterhead that includes the names of paralegals, or other law firm advertisements. See e.g., ISBA opinion No. 449 (1974). The rule also states that paralegal status should be divulged upon a paralegal's face to face meeting with others during the course of the paralegal's employment. Inclusion of the latter rule was heavily debated by the Task Force, however. Some members of the Task Force drafting this rule believed that it was not necessary for paralegals to identify themselves as such when the subject of the communication was a routine matter and could not be confused as involving the practice of law. This matter was resolved by looking to the other codes in existence. For example, in Guideline 4 of the American Bar Association Guidelines for Legal Assistant Services, attorneys are directed as follows:

> "It is the lawyer's responsibility to take a reasonable measure to ensure that clients, courts, and other lawyers are aware that a legal assistant, whose services are utilized by the lawyer in performing legal services, is not licensed to practice law."

Many paralegal codes, likewise, direct that legal assistants should disclose their status as nonlawyers at the beginning of any communication. See e.g., *National Association of Legal Assistants Model Standards and Guidelines for Utilization of Legal*

Assistants Annotated, V; National Federation of Paralegal Associations Model Code of Ethics and Professional responsibility, Cannon 6.

In the view of the Task Force, then, the justification for this rule is to avoid confusion. A paralegal who does not identify himself or herself as a nonlawyer can create the appearance of engaging in the practice of law.

Rule Five: Conflicts of Interest (Duty of Loyalty)

(a) A paralegal shall not undertake to provide any services for a lawyer's client when the paralegal's personal or business interests may reasonably affect the interests of another client, unless the client has consented after full disclosure, and the supervising lawyer reasonably believes that the work will not adversely affect the paralegal's relationship with the other client.

(1) A paralegal shall avoid entering into business transactions with a lawyer's client unless full disclosure has been made to both the client and the supervising attorney;

(2) A paralegal shall not acquire literary, publication or media rights related to a client's representation during the course of the representation;

(3) A paralegal shall not advance or guarantee financial assistance to a lawyer's client;

(4) A paralegal shall not enter into an agreement with a lawyer's client purporting to limit the client's rights to file a complaint against the paralegal or the lawyer by whom the paralegal is supervised.

(5) A paralegal shall avoid conflicts of interest that arise from family relationships.

(b) The paralegal shall not undertake to provide services to a lawyer's client and thereafter undertake to provide services to another person in the same or a substantially related matter in which that person's interests are materially adverse to the interests of the former client, unless the former client consents after full disclosure.

(c) A paralegal shall create and maintain records to identify clients, parties and matters to determine whether a conflict exists or may arise.

(d) A paralegal shall not participate in any matter where a conflict of interest has been identified by the supervising attorney.

Commentary

Rules concerning conflicts of interest are designed to protect the client's interest. The foundation for conflicts of interest rules is the legal professional's responsibility to maintain client confidence and the legal professional's duty of loyalty to client interests.

While conflicts of interest can arise in a variety of settings, conflict of interest problems involving the paralegal most notably arise in the context of the former client. The consequences of a former client conflict involving the paralegal can prove devastating for both the client and the law firm. Most significantly, the law firm by which the paralegal is employed may be disqualified from representing the client.

The most highly publicized of such cases occurred in California and is documented in *In re Complex Asbestos Litigation* (1991), 232 Cal. App. 3d 572, 283 Cal. Rptr. 732. In this case, a solo practitioner was disqualified from representing several clients, plaintiffs in asbestos litigation, because the attorney had hired a paralegal previously employed by the firm representing the defendants in the same litigation. In reaching its holding, the court explained, "hiring a former employee of opposing counsel is not, in and of itself, sufficient to warrant disqualification of an attorney or law firm. However, when the former employee possesses confidential attorney-client information, materially related to pending litigation, the situation implicates ... considerations of ethics which run to the very integrity of our judicial process." *Complex Asbestos*, 232 Cal. App. 3d at 283 Cal. Rptr. at 744.

Therefore, because the consequences of a conflict can be so great, the paralegal must maintain a record-keeping system that tracks potential situations involving conflicts of interest. When a potential problem presents itself, the paralegal should advise the supervising attorney. Disqualification of the law firm may be avoided when proper procedures are in place that protect the confidentiality and loyalty owed to the client. See e.g., *Chicago Bar Association Committee on Professional Responsibility opinion* 93-5 (May 1994).

Other kinds of conflict of interest problems involving the paralegal's personal or business interests might also arise, but may be cured where, upon being notified of the potential conflict, the client consents and the supervising attorney reasonably believes that the work will not adversely affect the paralegal's relationship with the client. Therefore, the paralegal should do such things as entering into a business transaction with a client only with caution. Perhaps the best course of action to follow is to avoid the possibility of a future conflict altogether.

Conflict of interest rules are of special significance for the freelance paralegal. The freelance paralegal works for a number of attorneys, associated with different law firms, who represent different clients. Often, freelance paralegals find themselves doing a great deal of work in a particular area of law because they have developed a certain expertise. Therefore, the very nature of the freelance paralegal's work means that the prospect of a former client conflict arising is great. The freelance paralegal must take additional measures to avoid a conflict.

Rule Six: Confidentiality

(a) A paralegal shall not, during or after termination of the professional relationship with the client, use or reveal a confidence or secret of the client known to the paralegal, unless the client consents after the disclosure.

(1) A paralegal shall not use confidential information to the disadvantage of the client.

(2) A paralegal shall not use confidential information to the advantage of the paralegal, the supervising attorney or a third person.

(b) A paralegal may reveal confidential information only after full disclosure and with the client's written consent; or when required by law or a court order; or when necessary to prevent the client from committing an act which could result in death or serious bodily harm.

(c) A paralegal shall keep those individuals responsible for the legal representation of a client fully informed of any confidential information the paralegal may have pertaining to that client.

Commentary

One of the most important ethical responsibilities of the paralegal is maintaining the confidentiality of the client. The rule of confidentiality encompasses the attorney-client privilege and further secrets gained through the attorney-client relationship.

Consequently, the rule uses two terms that need to be defined. "Confidential information" denotes information relating to a client, whatever its source, which is neither public knowledge nor available to the public. "Secret" denotes information gained in the professional relationship that the client has requested be held sacred or the revelation of which would be embarrassing or detrimental to the client.

Although the paralegal is charged with the obligation to maintain confidentiality, the paralegal is allowed to reveal confidences with the client's consent. Further, the paralegal may be required to reveal client confidences when subjected to a court order. Failure to reveal confidences in such an instance can result in obstruction of justice charges. If a paralegal is ever faced with a court order requiring him or her to reveal confidences, the paralegal should first turn to the supervising attorney for guidance. The paralegal will also find instructive *In re Marriage of Decker*, 153 Ill 2d. 298, 606 N.E.2d 1094 (1992).

It is more likely, however, that client confidences will be revealed through inadvertent slips of the tongue. Conversation at cocktail parties or imprudent comments made to colleagues in elevators can result in damage to the client. The paralegal is well advised, then, to avoid speaking about the secrets of the client in settings outside of the law office or to third parties.

Rule Seven: Communications with Non-Clients

(a) In those instances in Rule One, when appearing in a professional capacity before a tribunal, a paralegal shall not:

(1) make a statement of material fact or law which the paralegal knows or reasonably should know is false;

(2) make statements or arguments that would constitute the practice of law;

(3) violate applicable rules of procedure;

(4) engage in conduct or use language that offends the dignity or decorum of the tribunal; or

(5) intentionally degrade a witness or other person by stating or alluding to personal matters concerning that person which are not relevant to the case.

(b) During the course of any adversarial proceeding, a paralegal shall not communicate, or cause another to communicate, as to the merits of the cause with a judge or an official before whom the proceeding is pending, except:

(1) in the course of official proceedings in the cause;

(2) in person or over the telephone, upon adequate notice to opposing counsel, or to the adverse party if such party is not represented by counsel; or

(3) as otherwise authorized by law.

(c) When appearing in a professional capacity other than before a tribunal, a paralegal shall not:

(1) make a statement of material fact or law to a third person which the paralegal knows or reasonably should know is false;

(2) fail to disclose a material fact to a third person when disclosure is necessary to avoid assisting a criminal or fraudulent act by a client, unless disclosure is prohibited as a privileged communication under the applicable rules of professional conduct for attorneys; or

(3) be rude, disrespectful or demeaning in communications with others.

(d) During the course of representing a client, a paralegal shall not communicate or cause another to communicate on the subject of the representation with a party the paralegal knows to be represented by a lawyer in that matter unless the paralegal has obtained the prior consent of the lawyer representing that party or as may otherwise be authorized by law.

(e) In dealing on behalf of a client with a person who is not represented by counsel, a paralegal shall not state or imply that the paralegal is disinterested. When the paralegal knows or reasonably should know that the unrepresented person misunderstands the lawyer's role in the matter, the paralegal shall make reasonable efforts to correct the misunderstanding.

(f) In assisting in representation of a client, a paralegal shall not engage in conduct for the purpose of embarrassing, delaying, or burdening a third person. A paralegal shall not engage in obtaining evidence that may violate the legal rights of such person.

Commentary

As paralegals enjoy ever-growing acceptance and use within the legal community, they face increasing opportunities to interact with individuals who are not considered to be the clients of the supervising attorneys.

For example, paralegals may interact in some capacity with opposing counsel, adverse parties, judges, court clerks, jury members, or other paralegals. Certainly, this list is not exhaustive.

Because paralegals do interact with so many others that are not clients of the supervising attorneys, paralegals need a rule to define the parameters of that interaction. This rule is intended to instruct paralegals to avoid misleading communications and communications designed to take advantage of the other party's position. The rules apply equally to paralegals who work in litigation settings or handle transactions that might properly be considered more of a transactional nature.

Therefore, Rule 7(b) sets forth limitations on a paralegal's communications with a judge during the course of adversarial proceedings. This rule is not confined to communications made only in courtroom settings or during hearings but extends to all communications with a judge or other official, from the moment an attorney accepts the representation of a client. The reason for such a rule should be apparent. When a judge is charged with making an informed decision about the outcome of a proceeding pending before him or her, allowing communications to that judge untested by opposing counsel's input and argument defies all notions of justice and prevents the judge from competently doing the job at hand.

Rule 7(c) defines the scope of paralegal communications when the paralegal is handling matters that do not involve adversarial proceedings. Paralegals may interact with others while acting in their professional capacity when they are doing such things as attending real estate closings, attending depositions with their supervising lawyer, or handling the intake interview of a client who seeks to have a will drafted or an estate administered. It is especially important to note that a paralegal who becomes aware of potential fraudulent or criminal conduct by a lawyer's client must disclose that information to the paralegal's supervising attorney.

Rule Eight: Personal and Professional Integrity

(a) A paralegal shall not:

(1) violate or attempt to violate these Rules;

(2) induce another to engage in conduct, or give assistance to another's conduct, when the paralegal knows that conduct will violate these Rules;

(3) engage in conduct involving dishonesty, fraud, deceit or misrepresentation;

(4) engage in conduct that is prejudicial to the administration of justice;

(5) state or imply an ability to influence improperly any tribunal, legislative body, government agency or official;

(6) avoid in bad faith the repayment of an education loan guaranteed by the Illinois Student Assistance Commission or other governmental entity. The lawful discharge of an education loan in a bankruptcy proceeding shall not constitute bad faith under this rule.

(7) violate a Federal, State or local statute or ordinance that prohibits discrimination based on race, sex, disability, religion, or national origin by conduct that reflects adversely on the paralegal's fitness as a paralegal.

(b) A paralegal possessing knowledge not otherwise protected as a confidence by these Rules or by law that a lawyer has committed a violation of Rule 8.4 (a)(3) or (a)(4) of the Rules of Professional Conduct shall report such knowledge to a tribunal or other authority empowered to investigate or act upon such violation.

(c) A paralegal possessing knowledge not otherwise protected as a confidence by these Rules or by law that a judge has committed a violation of the Code of Judicial Conduct which raises a question as to the judge's fitness for office shall inform the appropriate authority.

(d) Upon proper request of a tribunal or other authority empowered to investigate or act upon the conduct of lawyers or judges, a paralegal possessing information not otherwise protected as a confidence by these Rules or by law concerning another lawyer or a judge shall reveal fully such information.

(e) A paralegal who holds public office shall not:

(1) use that office to obtain, or attempt to obtain, a special advantage in a legislative matter for a client under circumstances where the paralegal knows or reasonably should know that such action is not in the public interest;

(2) use that office to influence, or attempt to influence, a tribunal to act in favor of a client;

(3) represent any client, including a municipal corporation or other public body, in the promotion or defeat of legislative or other proposals pending before the

public body of which such paralegal is a member or by which such paralegal is employed.

(f) A paralegal who holds public office may accept political campaign contributions as permitted by law.

Rule Nine: Safekeeping Property

(a) A paralegal may handle the property of clients or third persons that is in a lawyer's possession in connection with a representation only under the supervision and direction of the lawyer.

(b) A paralegal who handles the property of clients or third persons shall read and comply with the requirements of Rule 1.15 of the Rules of Professional Conduct, and shall not take such action or knowingly assist the lawyer in taking any action that would be considered a violation of the Rules of Professional Conduct or the lawyer's ethical duties.

Commentary

Safekeeping of client property is a significant responsibility of the attorney, and, as such, the attorney is given specific rules detailing the proper way to handle client money. See Rule 1.15 of the Illinois Rules of Professional Conduct. Case law is replete with examples of attorneys being found to have commingled and converted client property because they have failed to properly identify, segregate, and account for that property. See e.g., *In re Clayter*, 78 Ill.2d. 276, 399 N.E.2d 1318 (1980); etc.

As this rule makes clear, paralegals may properly assist the attorney in handling client property. Assistance provided by paralegals may help an attorney handling client property to safeguard the identity of that property as the client's. Therefore, paralegals may be made signatories on office accounts established as client trust fund accounts. Paralegals who find themselves assisting with management of client trust fund accounts would be wise to consult *Client Trust Account Handbook: A Guide to Creating and Maintaining Client Trust Accounts for Illinois Attorneys,* a publication of the Attorney Registration and Disciplinary Commission of the Supreme Court of Illinois. Paralegals should never forget, however, that their supervising attorney is ultimately responsible for monitoring their work with client trust accounts and, therefore, paralegals should not hesitate to turn to supervising attorneys for answers to problems that arise during the course of maintaining a client trust account. See *In Re Vrdolyak,* 137 Ill 2d. 407, 560 N.E.2d 840 (1990), for a discussion of an attorney's failure to properly monitor the work of nonlawyer staff handling client trust accounts.

Rule Ten: Billing and Fees

(a) A paralegal shall keep and submit to the client or law firm accurate and thorough time records whenever a client or law firm will be billed for the paralegal's time on an hourly basis.

(b) A paralegal shall bill only for work that was reasonable and necessary to complete the assignment undertaken.

(c) A paralegal shall not submit a bill or time records that will be used to prepare a bill for time the paralegal spent educating herself/himself without the prior consent of the client.

(d) A paralegal may not split legal fees with a lawyer, although a paralegal may receive a salary from a law firm and may bill a law firm for services provided on a contract basis.

(e) In addition to the above provisions, freelance paralegals should also abide by the following:

(1) A paralegal shall charge reasonable fees for services rendered.

(2) A paralegal shall not seek or keep compensation that has not been fully earned under a contract for employment or professional services, except to the extent that a paralegal receives an advance on fees the paralegal expects to earn, provided that the paralegal promptly refunds any unearned fees at the conclusion of the assignment.

Commentary

Generally, a paralegal will be generating fees for the law firm/attorney. All business matters related to fees should be left to the firm administrators or the attorneys. Paralegals should not be responsible for setting their own rate. The paralegal may be consulted when setting fees to ascertain the paralegal's experience level. The Illinois Paralegal Association publishes an annual Survey of Salaries and Benefits which provides information on billing rates by years of experience.

The paralegal is responsible for keeping track of the time spent on various matters. Accurate time keeping should be reported to the billing department on a regular basis. The paralegal should never determine to increase or reduce the amount of actual time spent on any matter. Any reduction or mark-up of a paralegal's time on a client's bill should be left to the firm administrator. Time spent in paragraph (c) of this rule should be properly identified so that the firm can account for the time and the client is not unfairly billed.

Freelance paralegals provide independent contractor services to attorneys and law firms. Freelance paralegals have the responsibility of running the day to day operations of their own business as well as providing services to attorneys or law firms.

Fees cannot be shared/split with an attorney or another party. When setting fees, the freelance paralegal should consider the years of experience, level of expertise and the specifics of the task at hand. The Illinois Paralegal Association provides guidelines for billing rates and billable hours in its annual Survey of Salaries and Benefits.

Rule Eleven: Advertising and Solicitation

(a) A paralegal may advertise the availability of his/her services to attorneys, but shall do so in such a way as to not be false or misleading.

(1) A paralegal who chooses to advertise may do so through the use of public media, such as telephone directories, legal directories, newspapers or other periodicals, billboards, radio or television, or through other forms of written communication.

(2) A paralegal shall not advertise services directly to a lawyer's clients.

(b) A paralegal may carry and distribute a business card which shall contain the following:

(1) the name of the paralegal;

(2) the designation "paralegal" or "legal assistant" or such other designation indicating the individual's status;

(3) the name of the employer; and

(4) not contain false or misleading information.

(c) A paralegal's name may be included on the letterhead of law firm stationery, if the paralegal's status is clearly indicated on the letterhead, so as to not be misleading.

(d) A paralegal shall not use the terms "certified, specialist, expert," or any other, similar terms to describe his/her qualifications unless the reference is truthful, verifiable and not misleading.

(e) A paralegal shall not solicit professional employment on behalf of an attorney where the significant motive for doing so is the lawyer and/or paralegal's pecuniary gain.

Commentary

The rules regarding advertising and solicitation apply equally to paralegals working in traditional employment settings and to those who are freelance paralegals. Both the traditional paralegal and the freelance paralegal provide legal services for attorneys. They do not provide services to clients while working independently of a supervising attorney. Consequently, paralegals are allowed to advertise their services to attorneys, with the caveat that such advertisement must not be false or misleading. A communication is false or misleading if it meets the criteria established in Rule 7.1 of the Illinois Rules of Professional Conduct.

Paralegals are allowed and encouraged to carry business cards and to have their names appear on law firm letterhead. This follows from the Supreme Court's decision in *Bates v. Arizona* (1977), 433 U.S. 350, 97 S.Ct. 2691, 53 L.Ed.2d 810, which held that a communication that is not misleading cannot be absolutely prohibited without violating free speech rights.

However, in order to avoid misleading clients as to the nonlawyer status of the paralegal, the paralegal must always include his or her title on any document designed to be seen by a present or potential client. Therefore, business cards and letterhead must clearly identify the nonlawyer as such. See, *In re Bachmann* (Bkrtcy. S.D. Fla 1990), 113 B.R. 769.

Paralegals are absolutely prohibited from engaging in the solicitation of potential clients. Solicitation is defined in Rule 7.3 of the Illinois Rules of Professional Conduct as "contact by a person other than a lawyer in person, by telephone or telegraph, by letter or other writing, or by other communication directed to a specific recipient." *In Ohralik v. Ohio State Bar* (1978), 436 U.S. 447, 98 S. Ct. 1912, 56 L.Ed.2d 444, the Court disallowed the solicitation of clients, holding that in-person solicitation presents certain dangers to the public. The Court reasoned that this includes solicitation by the lawyer's agents. Conceivably, this would include the lawyer's paralegal.

Rule Twelve: Organization as Client

(a) A paralegal employed by an organization or employed by an attorney retained by an organization, represents the organization, acting through its duly authorized constituents.

(b) A paralegal shall act in the best interest of the organization if and when the paralegal knows that an officer, employee, or other person associated with the organization is engaged in action, intends to act or refuses to act in a matter related to the representation that is a violation of a legal obligation to the organization, or a violation of law which reasonably might be imputed to the organization, and is likely to result in substantial injury to the organization. The seriousness of the above violations and their consequences is determined by:

(1) the scope and nature of the paralegal's job responsibilities;

(2) the responsibility of the paralegal in the organization;

(3) the apparent motivation of the person involved;

(4) the policies of the organization concerning such matters; and,

(5) any other relevant considerations.

(c) If a paralegal discovers such a serious violation, the paralegal shall immediately consult the supervising attorney. Together, they shall take measures designed to minimize disruption of the organization and the risk of breaching the confidentiality of others represented by the firm outside of the organization.

Examples of such measures, among others, are:

(1) asking reconsideration of the matter;

(2) encouraging that a separate legal advice on the matter be sought for representation to the appropriate authority in the organization; and referring the matter to higher authority in the organization, including, if warranted by the seriousness of the matter, referral to the highest authority that can act in behalf of the organization as determined by applicable law.

(d) If, despite the paralegal's efforts in accordance with paragraph (b), the highest authority that can act on behalf of the organization, insists upon action, or refusal to act, that is clearly a violation of the law and is likely to result in substantial detriment to the organization, the paralegal may resign his/her position within the organization, or if employed by a firm retained by the organization, may ask the supervising attorney to discontinue the paralegal's involvement with the organization.

(e) In dealing with an organization's directors, officers, employees, members, shareholders or other constituents, a paralegal shall explain the identity of the client constituents with whom the paralegal is dealing.

(f) A paralegal representing an organization may also work with the directors, officers, employees, members, shareholders or other constituents of an organization as long as:

(1) the matters are not adverse to one other.

(2) the confidentiality of both clients is maintained;

(3) full disclosure of such dual representation occurs; and,

(4) consent to the representation is obtained from both parties.

The consent of the organization shall be given by an appropriate official of the organization or by shareholders. In no event shall the individual who is to be represented grant the consent on behalf of the organization.

Table of Authorities

Glossary

Acknowledged father A man who has established a father-child relationship by signing a Voluntary Acknowledgment of Paternity (VAP) or acknowledging paternity in a court document.

Adjudicated father A man who has been adjudicated by a court of competent jurisdiction to be the father of a child.

Adopt The legal action to create a family from unrelated individuals. After judgment, the family has all the rights and responsibilities of a family composed of related individuals.

Adult adoption Adoption of an individual over 18 years of age. Requires the adult to have lived with the adoptive parent for at least two years prior to adoption.

Affinity Relatives connected through a relationship (such as adopted siblings).

Agency adoption Custody of a child available for adoption is transferred first to an agency and then to adoptive parents.

All Kids A program that provides comprehensive, affordable, health insurance for children, regardless of their immigration status or health condition. All Kids covers medical, dental, and optical needs.

Alleged father A man who alleges himself to be, or is alleged to be the biological father of a child, but whose paternity has not been established.

Allocation of parental responsibilities: decision-making The right to make significant decisions for the parties' children.

Allocation of parental responsibilities: parenting time Time during which a parent is responsible for exercising caretaking functions and non-significant decision-making responsibilities with respect to a child.

Answer The first pleading filed by the respondent, in which the respondent admits or denies the allegations of fact contained in the petition.

Assistance case DCFS automatically intervenes in a case to establish child support when the parent seeking child support receives financial assistance

Assisted reproduction A method of achieving a pregnancy through an artificial insemination or an embryo transfer and includes gamete and embryo donation. It does not include any pregnancy achieved through sexual intercourse.

Base child support obligation The percentage of combined net income that parents living in the same household ordinarily spend on their child, as put forth by the Illinois Department of Health and Family Services (DHFS).

Bench trial Trial in which a judge, not a jury, decides issues of fact.

Best interest of the child Standard used by the court in the allocation of parental responsibilities and other child-related decisions such as removal and modification of the parenting allocation judgment.

Bigamous marriage Marriage to more than one spouse at the same time.

Biological parent A person who is biologically or genetically related to the child as a parent. Also known as "birth parent" or "natural parent."

Caretaking functions Tasks that involve interaction with a child or those direct, arrange, and supervise the interaction with and care of a child provided by others.

Celebrant The individual who solemnizes a marriage. Also known as "officiant."

Certificate of Dissolution of Marriage Form required by the Illinois Department of Public Health at the entry of judgment of dissolution providing information about the parties and the dissolution.

Change in circumstances First of two-part standard required before a court will consider modifying a parenting plan or Parenting Allocation Judgment pursuant to 750 ILCS 5/610.5.

Child (for the purposes of child support) The term "child" shall include any child under 18 and any child age 19 or younger who is still attending high school.

Civil union The legal recognition of the union of two individuals at the state level; however, the union is not recognized at the federal level.

Collaborative process divorce Process that involves a series of meetings between the parties, their attorneys, and their collaborative team to arrive at a Parenting Plan and Marital Settlement Agreement without the use of litigation.

Commingled property The property that results when one type of property (or estate) is contributed to the other type. The contributed property may retain or lose its identity.

Common law marriage A marriage in which the parties hold themselves out to the public as married but have not complied with the formalities required.

Companion animal An animal jointly owned by the parties to an action under the IMDMA. Does not include a service animal.

Competency The legal knowledge, skill, thoroughness and preparation reasonably necessary for the representation of a client.

Conference, 201(k) Conference required by Illinois Supreme Court Rule before parties can litigate a discovery dispute.

Confidential information Information relating to the representation of a client, which must be safeguarded to prevent inadvertent or unauthorized disclosure.

Conflict of interest A legal professional must avoid a conflict of interest, which could result if the representation of one client were adverse to the representation of another client.

Consanguinity Relatives connected through a blood relationship (such as brothers and sisters).

Continuing jurisdiction Under the UCCJEA, once a child's home state has been determined, the home state continues to have jurisdiction over the matter.

Counter-petition for dissolution Pleading filed by a respondent which maintains a dissolution action should the petitioner withdraw their petition for dissolution.

Custody Solely for the purposes of all State and federal statutes that required a designation of custody, a parenting plan shall designate the parent who is allocated the majority of the parenting plan.

Declaration of marital invalidity Legal action to establish that no marriage existed because of a defect at the time it was entered. Also known as "annulment."

Default judgment Judgment entered if, after service, respondent did not appear, answer or otherwise become involved the case.

Definite term Spousal maintenance paid for a pre-determined period of time. At the end, it may be barred or reviewed. Also known as "fixed term."

Department of Child and Family Services (DCFS) Agency whose mission is to protect children who are reported to be abused or neglected, provide for the well-being of children in their care, and provide appropriate, permanent families for those children who cannot safely return home.

Discovery The process of acquiring information from the other party or third parties prior to trial.

Dissipate The use of marital property for a non-marital purpose.

Dissolution of marriage Legal action that dissolves the bonds of matrimony that joined the parties in a marriage. Also known as "divorce."

Division of Child Support Services (DCSS) Agency within the Illinois DHFS responsible for establishing and enforcing child support payments.

Domestic violence A pattern of physical, sexual, emotional, economic, or psychological abuse committed by a partner with the intent of exerting power and control over the victim.

Duty to support The obligation to provide for the reasonable and necessary physical, mental and emotional health needs of the child. A court may order either or both parents owing a duty of support to pay an amount reasonable and necessary for support.

Ethics The principles of conduct to be followed by professionals and paraprofessionals.

Exclusion order Order entered if the court finds that the conclusion of the experts as disclosed by the evidence based upon genetic testing is that the alleged father is not the parent of the child.

Exclusive possession of the marital residence The court may enter orders granting exclusive possession of the marital residence to either spouse during the pendency of the action. Also known as "marital eviction."

Family or household members Petitioners for an order of protection may be spouses, former spouses, parents, children, stepchildren and other persons related by blood or by present or prior marriage, persons who share or formerly shared a common dwelling, persons who have or allegedly have a child in common, persons who share or allegedly share a blood relationship through a child, persons who have or have had a dating or engagement relationship,

Financial affidavit Standardized form in which parties list their income, assets, and liabilities.

Gamete A reproductive cell, either a sperm or an egg.

Gamete donor An individual who participates in an assisted reproductive technology arrangement by providing gametes and relinquishes all rights and responsibilities to the gamete so that another individual may become the legal parent of any resulting child.

Gestational surrogacy The process by which a woman attempts to carry and give birth to a child through in vitro fertilization in which the gestational surrogate has made no genetic contribution to any resulting child.

Gestational surrogate A woman who is not an intended parent who agrees to engage in a gestational surrogacy arrangement under the Gestational Surrogacy Act.

Grant of exclusive possession Remedy available under Domestic Violence Act which prohibits respondent from entering or remaining in any residence, household, or premises of the petitioner, including one owned or leased by respondent, if petitioner has a right to occupancy thereof. It is not limited by the standard set forth for Marital Eviction/Exclusive Possession.

Gross income for child support The total income from all sources except benefits received by the parent from means-tested public assistance programs or benefits and income received by the parent for other children in the household. It includes spousal maintenance received pursuant to a court order.

Grounds Having a reason, or a basis, for a legal action.

Grounds for dissolution of marriage Irreconcilable differences have caused the irretrievable breakdown of the marriage and the court determines that efforts at reconciliation have failed or that future attempts at reconciliation would be impracticable and not in the best interest of the family.

Guardian *ad litem*. Illinois law provides three different types of attorneys for minor children. A guardian *ad litem* ("GAL") investigates facts and makes a recommendation to the court.

Guardianship Responsibility for a minor (called the ward) is transferred to another adult (called the guardian); however, parental rights remain intake.

Harass Knowing conduct which is not necessary to accomplish a purpose that is reasonable under the circumstances; would cause a reasonable person emotional distress; and does cause emotional distress to the petitioner.

Home state Pursuant to the UCCJEA, the state in which the child lived for the last six months. In the case of a child less than six months of age, the term means the state in which the child lived from birth.

Illinois State Disbursement Unit (ILSDU) The payment processing center for Illinois child support payments. The ILSDU receives the child support from the obligor or the obligor's employer and disburses the funds via check, direct deposit, or debit card to the receiving families.

***In personam* jurisdiction** Authority by the court over the respondent. Also known as "personal jurisdiction."

***In rem* jurisdiction** Authority by the court over a thing, such as a marriage.

Incestuous marriage Marriage to a close family member, as defined by statute.

Income shares model Calculation of child support based upon the parents' combined net income estimated to have been allocated for the support of the child if the parents and child were living in an intact household.

Income Withholding Order (IWO) A notice sent to the child support obligor's employer. By federal law, a standard IWO can be used in all states. The obligor's employer sends the child support payment to the Illinois State Disbursement Unit (ILSDU).

Indefinite term Spousal maintenance without a termination date. Although sometimes called "permanent," all maintenance is subject to terminating events.

Indicated A report of credible evidence of abuse or neglect at the conclusion of an investigation by the DCFS.

Intended parent A person who enters into an assisted reproductive technology arrangement under which he or she will be the legal parent of the resulting child.

Interim attorney's fee Order by court for one party to pay the other party's attorney's fees in order to permit both parties to participate equally in divorce.

Joint decision-making authority The allocation of parental responsibilities to both parents.

Law Enforcement Automated Data System (LEADS) An order of protection is entered into LEADS so the respondent can be tracked by law enforcement in other jurisdictions.

Legal father Pursuant to the Adoption Act, the husband of a woman who gives birth, a man who signs a VAP, or an adjudicated father.

Legal separation Action in which spouses living separate and apart can dissolve their financial union while maintaining the marriage itself.

Long-arm statute Statute in the Illinois Code of Civil Procedure which permits a court to reach beyond the state line to obtain jurisdiction over a non-resident respondent who committed certain acts within the state.

Mandated reporter Persons required to report suspected child abuse or neglect, as provided by the Abused and Neglected Child Reporting Act.

Marital property All property including debts and other obligations acquired by either spouse subsequent to the marriage, except for non-marital property.

Marital settlement agreement Document signed by parties setting forth how they have resolved the financial aspects of their dissolution.

Marriage The legal recognition of the union of two individuals.

Mediation A process conducted by a neutral third party to help parties resolve issues. The mediator has no authority over the parties.

Minimum child support order A child support order of $40/month/child will be entered for an obligor who has actual or imputed gross income at less than 75% of the most recent Federal Poverty Guidelines for a family of one person, with a maximum total child support obligation for that obligor of $120/month to be divided equally among all the obligors' children.

Minor A person who has not attained the age of 18 years.

Net income for child support Gross income minus federal income tax, state income tax, social security (or other mandatory retirement contributions) and Medicare.

No-fault grounds The basis for an action in which the petitioner does not have to prove the respondent was at fault in some way.

Non-marital property Property acquired by gift or inheritance after the marriage or property acquired before the marriage.

Obligee A parent who receives child support. Also known as "recipient parent."

Obligor A parent who pays child support.

Parentage action An action to determine the parent child-relationship.

Parenting allocation judgment A judgment allocating parental responsibilities including parenting time.

Parenting education requirement Pursuant to Illinois Supreme Court Rule 924, all parents shall be required to attend a parenting education program covering the subjects of parenting time and allocation of parental responsibility and their impact on children.

Parenting plan A written agreement that allocates significant decision-making responsibilities, parenting time, or both. Must be in writing, signed by both parents, and must comply with statutory minimums.

Parenting time schedule A schedule which designates in which parent's home the minor child will reside on given days, or a formula for determining such a schedule in sufficient detail to be enforced.

Payee Spouse who receives spousal maintenance. Also known as "recipient spouse."

Payor Spouse who pays spousal maintenance.

Petition The name of the first pleading filed under the IMDMA in which the petitioner makes allegations of fact.

Petition for rule to show cause Action brought by one party when the other party has failed to comply with a court order or judgment.

Petitioner The party who initiates an action by filing a petition under the IMDMA.

Post-decree Action occurring after a final judgment has been entered.

Postmarital agreement An agreement between spouses made after they are married which determines the disposition of property upon a marriage terminating event. Also known as a "postnuptial agreement."

Post-minority award Financial award for a child over the age of 18. Available for educational expenses or support for a non-minor child with a disability.

Premarital agreement An agreement between prospective spouses made in contemplation of marriage and to be effective upon marriage, which determines the disposition of property upon a marriage terminating event. Also known as a "prenuptial agreement."

Presumed parent An individual who is recognized as the parent of the child until that status can be rebutted or confirmed in a judicial or administrative proceeding.

Private adoption Adoption in which custody of the child is transferred from birth parents to adoptive parents directly.

Procedural law Law that controls the process of an action as it moves through the court system, contained in the Code of Civil Procedure and Illinois Supreme Court Rules.

Professional evaluation per 750 ILCS 5/604.10(b) The court may seek the advice of any professional to assist the court in determining the child's best interest. The professional's report must contain descriptions of procedures, reports of data, conclusions, and recommendations.

Prove-up Date at which final agreed upon settlement documents are provided to the judge and marriage is dissolved.

Purge amount The amount the respondent must pay to purge himself of a contempt finding.

Putative father registry Registry established by the Department. of Children and Family Services for the purposes of determining the identity and location of a putative father of a minor child who is, or is expected to be, the subject of an adoption proceeding, in order to provide notice of such proceeding to the putative father.

Putative father A man who may be a child's father, but who was not married to the child's mother on or before the date that the child was born and who has not established paternity of the child in a court proceeding before the filing of a petition for the adoption of the child.

Putative spouse A person who enters into a marriage with a person who is already married in the good faith belief they are single.

Qualified Domestic Relations Order (QDRO) An order used to divide a pension or retirement account such as a 401(k).

Qualified Illinois Domestic Relations Order (QUILDRO) An order used to divide a pension or retirement account for state of Illinois employees.

Rehabilitative maintenance Spousal maintenance awarded for a definite term after which it is reviewed. Also known as "transitional."

Related child A child subject to adoption where either or both of the adopting parents stands in any of the following relationship to the child by blood, marriage, adoption, or civil union parent, grandparent, great grandparent, brother, sister, step-parent, step-grandparent, step-brother, step-sister, uncle, aunt, great-uncle, great-ant, first cousin or second cousin.

Relocate A parent who has been allocated a majority of parenting time or either parent who has been allocated equal parenting time may seek to relocate with the minor child if the move is outside statutory limits.

Respondent The person who is sued in the legal action filed by the petitioner.

Right of first refusal If a party intends to leave the minor child/ren with a child care provider for a significant period of time, the party must first offer the other party an opportunity to personally care for the minor child/children.

Separation agreement A document signed by parties to an action for legal separation resolving issues between them.

Serious endangerment Standard required before modifying an order allocating parental decision-making responsibilities within two years of entry.

Service by publication In the event the respondent cannot be located for personal service, he may be deemed served by publishing notice of the action against him in a newspaper.

Service of process Delivery of the petition and summons to the respondent, to ensure he has notice of the action against him.

Shared physical care When each parent exercises 146 or more overnights per year with a child, the basic child support obligation is multiplied by 1.5.

Short-term guardianship A parent may appoint in writing, without court approval, a short-term guardian of an unmarried minor. The guardianship is effective for 365 days.

Significant decisions Those parenting decisions regarding education, health, religion, and extracurricular activities.

Simplified dissolution Procedure which permits parties to file a joint petition, available under limited circumstances.

Sole decision-making authority The allocation of parental responsibilities to one parent.

Solemnization Ceremony required for a valid marriage, performed by a judge, a retired judge, by a public official whose powers include solemnization of marriages, or in accordance with the prescriptions of any religious denomination.

Spousal maintenance Payments made from one spouse to another after a judgment of dissolution or legal separation (or declaration of invalidity if putative spouse). Also known as "alimony."

Stipulation Parties' agreement that certain facts be admitted into evidence without a foundation.

Substantial change in circumstances Standard required for modification of child support or spousal maintenance pursuant to 750 ILCS 5/510.

Substantive law The rights of action available within an area of law.

Temporary relief Relief available during the pendency of the action.

Temporary restraining order/ Preliminary injunction Orders restraining or requiring actions during the pendency of the action until they can be resolved at trial.

Terminating events Events which cause spousal support to terminate. The obligation to pay future maintenance is terminated upon the death of either party, the remarriage of the party receiving maintenance, or if the party receiving maintenance cohabits with another person on a resident, continuing conjugal basis.

Transmute Property from one estate may turn into property of another estate if after contribution it loses its identity.

Trust, 503(g) The court, if necessary to protect and promote the best interests of the children may set aside a portion of the estates of the parties in a separate fund or trust for the support, maintenance, education, physical and mental health of any minor, dependent, or incompetent child of the parties.

Unauthorized practice of law The practice of law by an individual who has not been licensed by the Illinois Attorney Registration and Disciplinary Commission (ARDC).

Unconscionable agreement An agreement that is totally one-sided or oppressive.

Unfounded A report of no credible evidence of abuse or neglect at the conclusion of an investigation by the DCFS.

Uniform Child-Custody and Jurisdiction Enforcement Act (UCCJEA) The UCCJEA determines which state has jurisdiction in interstate custody litigation. It has been adopted in all 50 states (except Massachusetts).

Violence Against Women Act (VAWA) Federal law that protects women at many levels, including making violation of an order of protection a federal crime and funding programs for victims of domestic violence.

Visitation In person time spent between a child and their grandparent, great-grandparent, sibling, step-parent, or a person designated by a member of the US Armed Forces to exercise substitute visitation on behalf of the deployed parent.

Void marriage The impediment to a valid marriage cannot be removed, such as incest.

Voidable marriage The impediment to a valid marriage can be removed, such as underaged spouse.

Voluntary Acknowledgment of Paternity (VAP) Form produced by the Illinois Department of Healthcare and Family Services (HFS). When it is signed, witnessed, and returned, a man becomes the legal father of a child.

Waiver of court fees Contained in the Code of Civil procedure, the process available to litigants to pursue or defend a claim at no or limited cost.

Zero child support order For parents who have no gross income, who receive only means-tested assistance, or who cannot work due to a medically proven disability, incarceration, or institutionalization, a zero dollar order shall be entered.

Index